D1220704

WISE AND FOOLISH KINGS
The First House of Valois
1328–1498

By Anne Denieul-Cormier

WISE AND FOOLISH KINGS
THE FRANCE OF THE RENAISSANCE
PARIS AT THE DAWN OF *LE GRAND SIÈCLE*
PRIX GOBERT DE L'ACADÉMIE FRANÇAISE

ANNE DENIEUL-CORMIER

Wise
and
Foolish
Kings

*The First House of Valois
1328–1498*

DOUBLEDAY & COMPANY, INC.
GARDEN CITY, NEW YORK 1980

DC
36.6
.D4613

Library of Congress Cataloging in Publication Data
Denieul-Cormier, Anne.
  Wise and foolish kings.
  Translation of Rois fous et sages de la première
maison de Valois.
  Includes index.
  1. France—Kings and rulers—Biography. 2. France—
History—House of Valois, 1328-1589. I. Title.
DC36.6.D4613   944′.025
ISBN: 0-385-04903-X
Library of Congress Catalog Card Number 77-175365

English Language translation Copyright © 1980 by
Doubleday & Company, Inc.
All Rights Reserved
Printed in the United States of America
First Edition

Contents

04700

To the Reader

This book belongs to no established genre. It falls within no fixed category, nor would I know how to place any sort of label on it. Not a history or a historical novel—an essay, rather, wherein through the lives of the princes of the first house of Valois I have tried to create a certain approach to the past. It is not the approach of established historians.

Within these pages I have set out in search of the Valois kings. It was no small undertaking: for Philip VI, nothing to go on, except for the marble features on his tomb. For John II, more evidence: four lines in Froissart's chronical and a portrait. As the century progresses, however, the darkness becomes proportionately less dense. I have tried to speak of these kings as one talks about people one knows—if one is interested in the human phenomenon—with perhaps a certain familiarity in tone and approach, perhaps a certain indiscretion. For my concern was to find out what made them tick, caring less about what they did than about what they were, but utilizing the former in order to arrive at the latter. Historical events were never an end to me but a means. And, for those with eyes to see and ears to hear, everything speaks. Thus I have hunted out the personalities of these kings everywhere I could find them: in the chronicles (the favored place), in political events (a revelation of the first magnitude where mon-

archs are concerned), in the iconographic documents, in their portraits, precious beyond reckoning.

I have attempted as well to place them in their context. Furnishing the setting is neither difficult nor contrary to historical
truth. We possess the basic components for the task, thanks to the
archaeologists and art historians, in our patrimony of monuments
and museums. It was sufficient to refer to these and to describe
them. As for the natural landscapes which will often appear in
these pages, they deserve to be here, for they are immutable; the
French soil has not changed for centuries, nor has the sky above
it. The fields of grain and the seasons still have the same color,
and the foliage of the great forests of Ile-de-France has the same
glory in the autumn sunlight.

And when none of that could help me, my knowledge of the
epoch yielded certain keys. For John the Good, the education of
the young baron; for Charles V, the rites of the coronation, of
prime importance for habits of thought at that time; for Charles
VI and VII and Louis XI, the new knowledge of the twentieth
century in the realm of psychopathology. Finally, for Charles VIII
and his great adventure beyond the mountains, where to find a
better Ariadne's thread than in the artistic treasures and the great
intuitions of the Italian Renaissance?

So it is a long book, for it bears upon nearly two centuries, as
full of variety as life itself, as these kings themselves, who vary, all
of them, from father to son. History with a certain license,
wherein rather little is said of politics, except for some disastrous
but astonishing battles, and still less of economics, which does not
interest me. But, filtered through a tight screen of evidence and established facts, it is a history of the adventure of these men who,
in a tragic context, had to try every day of their lives to be kings.

WISE AND FOOLISH KINGS
The First House of Valois
1328–1498

CHAPTER I

The House of Valois

The Valois were seven men, who from 1328 to 1498 succeeded one another, from father to son, on the throne of France. They are called the "Capetian Valois," for they replaced the descendants of Hugh Capet (to whom they were quite closely related) as rulers of the kingdom.

Their house was a most noble, powerful, and prolific line which, in less than two centuries, covered the entire map of Europe with its descendants. At the end of the Middle Ages the Valois were legion. There was not a single one of the great noble families, indeed the royal ones, of the world of that time that could not boast of carrying in the veins of its men or women some trace of the blood of Philip VI, the founder of the line. The island kingdoms of Albion and of Sicily, set like twin beacons—one misty-shored, the other bright-bayed—at the extremities of Europe; wealthy Flanders; scorched Aragon; Savoy, surrounded by its peaks; refined, dissolute Milan, a century ahead of its contemporaries, whom it would soon carry along in its wake; the wild German provinces . . . was there a single country whose princely abodes did not shelter a Valois whose alliance had been courted?

A good stock, an ancient race, for the most part, they traced their descent from Pierre de Courtenay, Emperor of Constantinople; from Henry II, the Plantagenet English king; from Bela IV and Andrew II, the kings of Hungary; from Alfonso VII of Castile

and Alfonso II of Aragon. There was nothing like a Valois to enhance the prestige of one's coat of arms. We thus find them everywhere, tied by alliance, blood, or marriage to all of Europe's powerful: Tudors, Lancasters, Viscontis, Wittelsbachs. The queens of
England and of Aragon were French princesses, born Valois on
the right bank of the Seine, in the Louvre or at St. Pol. The kings
of Naples and of Sicily were Valois, dukes of Anjou, the descendants of John the Good. The powerful house of Burgundy, which
was to dominate the Western world for the greater part of the
fifteenth century, was once again Valois. And how many daughters born under the fleurs-de-lis exchanged their names for those
of the great feudal lords of the realm: Bourbon, Brittany, Armagnac, Alençon, Harcourt?

The kings of France in the age of the Renaissance were also
Valois; in fact, the members of this second dynasty are the sole
bearers of the Valois name who are remembered today. But they
are not our subject here. This cadet branch of the Valois family,
descended from Louis of Orléans, the younger son of Charles V,
and as a result the second house of Valois is quite remote in the
order of kinship from the last Capetian Valois, Charles VIII.
Louis XII, who succeeded him, was but a cousin three times removed.

Furthermore, to study at one and the same time the Valois
kings of the first and those of the second dynasty would mean
jamming together two entirely dissimilar ages—the Hundred Years'
War and the Renaissance—not to mention the risks that combining
such disparate subjects might incur. What could be more different
from the France of the declining Middle Ages, set in its ways, than
the fertile years of the sixteenth century, when time suddenly
quickened its pace and the world started to change (or at least the
way people looked at it did)?

And so the first seven Valois kings of France will be enough for
us.

ROYALTY AS DESTINY

We shall study the Valois kings in succession, following both
their own chronology and that of history. And central to our story

will be the adventure lived by these men, who found themselves by chance of birth confronted with a king's destiny.

The first Valois had chosen it. When this great feudal lord saw the chance for himself and his line to wear the crown, he seized it without hesitation and—perhaps—without taking too much into account the consequences of such an act. The other Valois were born to their destiny among the brocades of the huge ceremonial cradles reserved for the first-born of France. They had no choice but to assume it. Such was the fate irrevocably imposed: kings were raised between heaven and earth by the rites of anointment, receiving the sacrament in both kinds, bread and wine, just as priests do, endowed with healing powers, and, whatever their feelings, bound to take in their charge, in addition to their own lives, those of a whole people, for which they would have, when the hour came, to give an account on the basis of which they would be judged.

Obligated by promises, hemmed in by difficulties, exposed to pressing needs, subjected to hard work and worry, ensnared by duty, predestined to set an example, to live in grandeur, to surpass themselves, weighed down with a burden that could not be set aside for an instant, they would have to discover that, for them, to attempt to live was first of all to attempt to be king, to reconcile their own needs with the obligations of the throne, and that their confrontation with power would remain a daily reality until their final breath was drawn.

How did they feel about such a life, through the constant movement of days, decisions, encounters—the most exalting of lives for someone whose soul is strong? How did these men, one after the other, from father to son, manage to cope with it? By what combats, what arms, what gifts laid in the balance? What marks, what burdens, what stigmata did they carry from childhood, mingled with their vital forces? Or did they pass through the time of innocence (which is that of the worst dangers) with their power to love still intact and their energies preserved? Did anxiety grip them—fruitfully or destructively? Did it work for their ruin or their glory? Where did they find their goals and their pleasures during the long years of reigning, which can be a joy or a burden depending on who is facing it? What did that verb—to be—wherein the soul takes its breath mean when their destinies as men and as kings were inextricably mixed, the most lofty expressions of the human adventure?

Events kept them on a tight rein, constantly off balance, breathless, tense, on the lookout. At each day's council, history furnished them their due: tangled skeins, bundles of rope and bundles of knots, which every day they had to unravel, explore, empty out, weigh, take inventory of, sift with their mistrust and their mother wit and, accordingly, augment to excess or place in expectation, and sometimes, new Penelopes, undo in darkness what they wove in daylight. An artist's task, if there ever was one, in which any false step would be punished. Events were thus the warp and woof of these lives, the raw materials for those master craftsmen of power called kings. They could suffer the events, be at their mercy, or take them in hand and lead them where they wanted to go. Events are thus important and cannot be passed over in silence. An Ariadne's thread through the labyrinths of time, they will lead us to these men about whom we know so little indeed.

Respectful of the king to the point of not daring to describe him, much less to judge him, the chronicles in the age of the early Valois kings content themselves for the most part with relating deeds. But for those who know how to look, the deed reveals the man, or at least allows you to approach him. It gives you his weight and measure. In our quest for a past half a millennium old, only events allow us to deduce what sort of man it was who molded them. These events will therefore figure in our work, the indispensable complement of the royal person whom they situate and illuminate, defining the reality with which he found himself confronted. What is more, they will prove a better guide than our kings, whose company will tend to be less unfamiliar than one might think, in our passage through the declining Middle Ages, whose violence and horror they will reveal to us.

It was a frightful epoch for France, the epoch of the Hundred Years' War. To call it that is a euphemism, a name already too promising in comparison to what the name conceals. The country found itself on the edge of the abyss. It is necessary to return to the High Middle Ages to find such a tragic juncture: a foreign invasion renewed from year to year, which it will take nearly a century and a half to bring to an end; the legitimacy of the dynasty contested; spectacular defeats, civil war, the kingdom put to fire and the sword; towns encircled by armed bands, the flatlands laid waste; a moral crisis, wherein a decline in morality is accompanied by a crisis of faith. Little by little the populace, decimated by roving mercenaries, epidemics, and famines, returns to stages of barbarism thought to have been left behind forever. Ancient pagan superstitions reappear. There is as much belief in the Devil as in God. The central problem remains survival. Such is the context in which the men we are dealing with found themselves face to face with history.

A FINE INHERITANCE

All the same it was a fine inheritance, the France bequeathed by the Capetian kings. Those fourteen kings who succeeded one another from 987 until 1328, with no break in the line, had plenty of time to amass their lands. They had started from scratch, or nearly. At the end of the tenth century the "kingdom" had been merely a collection of quasi-independent fiefdoms, a mosaic of small territorial units established by plucky adventurers, the descendants of Carolingian officials like Hugh the Great, the founder. Such lands as the Capetians had at that time were far from choice parcels: three counties, Orléans, Étampes, and Senlis; and three lesser territories, the fiefs of the castles of Poissy, Montreuil-sur-Mer, and Attigny. But they had something else: they were anointed kings, supported by the Church, and supported as well by feudal law which made the sovereign the keystone of the feudal system.

With this—plus time, patience, and a lot of hard work—they became "emperors in their own kingdom," rulers whose domains were roughly equal to two thirds of present-day France (or some 123,000 square miles), rich with the revenues of such vast lands, and powerful with the homage of so many vassals. Slowly they swallowed up the great feudal estates, till only four remained—Flanders, Guienne, Brittany, and Burgundy. These were border fiefs, far from the heart of the realm, or on the edge of the ocean, and the Capetians sought rather to conciliate than to eliminate them.

They were a closely knit family, who lived worthy, unspectacular lives. To their moderation they added a peasant cunning, a lawyerly common sense, qualities born of the obligation to live and endure. Essentially they were men of action, these Capetians, endowed with foresight, prudence, and tenacity. The family was devoid of grand designs—indeed, they were rather ill at ease with them. They harbored no excessive ambitions and chased no will-o'-the-wisps. They were in no hurry, took each day as it came, and held on for three centuries. They acquired thereby unchallenged prestige, thanks largely to their well-known strength, but also to their private virtues (which stood in such contrast to the moral disorder all around them), especially to those of that exemplary man of their line whom the Church canonized as St. Louis.

If they gathered land, they gathered men also. The nobles found a way to live, and to enrich themselves, in the service of their prince. From the time of St. Louis's successor, Philip III, they spent as much time as they could at the royal court, which had already achieved its place as the center of fashionable society. The Capetians, in turn, cherished their nobles. They stinted them in neither favors nor honors. They regarded them as their peers so that caste privileges might be preserved, and formed with them one great family of which the Capetians were the hereditary chiefs and protectors.

The burghers gave up their ties to the cities and chose to ally their interests with the king's. The clergy maintained strong ties with the throne, ties dating from the origin of the dynasty and never slackened. The University of Paris—where bishops and archbishops were trained and which guided the religious thinking of the kingdom—was in the hands of the Capetians. Finally they created, in Paris, a center toward which the vital forces of the West would henceforth converge. While France was not yet a finished creation, the greater part of the elements from which it would emerge were already in existence: territories had been amassed; a political regime had been established; the skeleton of an administrative apparatus had been set up; and a dynastic feeling had been created which linked commoners to the king and made them ready—as the formula goes—"to live and die for him."

Nor is that all. Under the Capetians the era came to flower. Coincidence, or the result of a policy which tended to assure the peace in those hazardous times? For a century and a half, starting in 1150, the Capetians presided over that astonishing flowering of the French Middle Ages which caused Pope Innocent IV to exclaim, in 1245, that their realm was "the crucible to which the gold comes to be melted down." This was the epoch when great works in the varied domains of art and thought appeared: the High Gothic cathedrals, the Royal Portal at Chartres, the Sainte Chapelle at Paris, the *Summa Theologica* of Thomas Aquinas, the lays of the troubadours, the legend of Tristan and Iseult, Reynard the Fox, and the Romance of the Rose. . . . The Western world had found itself. It built its temples, devised its rites, defined its values, and created its forms of expression. And perhaps, since we need places of refuge in the all too secularized world we inhabit, hemmed in by absurdity, it may be that we project onto that age, which was rough and hard, all of our nostalgia for what we do not find in our own, at the risk perhaps of altering reality. Sometimes it is good to dream. How can we help it, faced with a civilization whose center is God and whose axis is eternity? The man of that time was menaced in body but secure in soul, a creature in the hand of his Creator, united with Him. He had been told the essentials about the cycles of life and death, love and transcendence, and his undeclared, undeclarable dream took precisely the form of the myths wherein the heart grows calmer for being able to name its longing.

And then, all at once, he took it upon himself to forget the basic truths that had kept him going for two centuries. On orders from the grandson of St. Louis himself, Philip IV the Fair, he dared to lay his hands on the person of the Pope. Not long afterward, the same Philip attacked the Order of the Knights Templars, whose goods he coveted and whose power he feared. A trial was begun. The King himself did the interrogating. Bullied by the King, Pope Clement V decreed on April 3, 1312, the abolition of the order, whose wealth was confiscated for the benefit of the royal treasury. The Commander and the Grand Master of the Templars were led to the block. Legend has it that the Grand Master's dying words called on the Pope and the King of France to appear within a year before the throne of God for judgment. Can we lend credence to such a story? Events served to confirm it. Clement and Philip both met their Maker within the year foretold.

Even then they were not discharged of guilt. A terrible curse fell on the royal family. Within less than fifteen years the line of Hugh Capet was extinct.

A maniacal wind came up over France, an all-destroying and furious wind, a wind that signified the end of a dynasty, the end of a bloodline, the end of an era. Were these cataclysms a sort of payment due, the shadowy side of all that brilliance, the dark side of the world which evades us and undoes us, a suffering unwillingly undergone, yet redeeming, a cataclysmic seal placed on two centuries so fruitful for human progress that we still look back on them in wonder?

The people accompanied their rulers into the abyss and paid their share of destiny's penalty. Plagues descended on France: epidemics of the Black Plague, leprosy, and mass insanity. Blackened bodies, covered with buboes, piled up in the charnel houses, while hysterical mobs of country folk lay waste to the plains, only to end up drowned in the swamps of the Aiguesmortes. Hordes of lepers, fleeing relentless harassment, spread terror in the land, contaminating what was left of the exhausted water supply.

The end of the Capetian line. Not the end of the kingdom.

A THRONE TO BE TAKEN

And so it was that in the springtime of the year 1328, contrary to all that the master of the realm might have been able to foresee some twenty years earlier, with the death of Charles IV the Fair, the last Capetian, the throne of France was left vacant. Not entirely so, however. Charles's widow, Joan of Evreux, had hopes. If the child she was expecting was a son, all that was needed was to name a regent until such time as the young prince should be old enough to exercise his functions. But if it was a daughter, what course to adopt? The problem was a delicate one, which no law helped to solve. There was no legal precedent, since for three hundred years the Capetians had passed the succession from father to son without a miss.

Negative precedents there were, by which on two occasions in the course of the two preceding decades daughters had been kept out of power. In 1316, Louis X (called "the Stubborn"), who had succeeded his father, Philip the Fair, strictly in accordance with laws as an eldest son, died with no other progeny than a little princess, Joan. Immediately his younger brother, Philip, assumed the regency. That was the normal procedure. But Philip, having assembled a council of barons (whom he doubtless rallied to his cause by whatever means were necessary), arrogated the crown to himself and thereby deliberately deprived his young niece and her descendants of it. But he, too, died six years later, in 1322, leaving in his turn only female issue, Joan, Margaret, and Isabelle, whom his own younger brother, Charles, on the strength of Philip's example, eliminated without the slightest scruple, in order to install himself in the place which his own death six years later would leave vacant once again. And once again a regent was needed. Once again, peers and barons filled the palace and chose the closest blood relative of the deceased, Charles's first cousin, Philip of Valois. On April 1, Joan of Evreux gave birth to a daughter, Marie. On May 29, at Reims, Philip the Regent was crowned King of France with the assent of his peers. The law of males had prevailed.

A woman was nothing at the outset of the fourteenth century, nothing but an object, a face and a body, the image necessary for dreaming, inexorably thrust into a brutal reality, where she was never more than the first among the servants, destined for one pregnancy after another, an early death, Queen by virtue of her husband, Regent by her son's minority, by herself alone nothing . . . but a woman, and so no great thing, even when the woman in question was the King's daughter: "Lilies do not spin wool, and France is too noble a kingdom to be entrusted to a female," the barons had declared in deciding in favor of Philip.

But there was a woman who until that time had caused almost no talk, at least in France, a woman of royal blood and resolution, the daughter of Philip the Fair himself, Isabelle of France, the sister of the three deceased kings, and widow of Edward II, the King of England. There was no doubt that during the previous year she had successfully conspired to kill her husband and had thus secured the throne for her son, Edward III, who despite his great youth occupied it effectively. Even though princesses were denied the right to receive the crown from anyone but their husband, it was still conceivable that they might transmit to their sons the same rights they themselves were not permitted to exercise. Why should the male heirs of the feminine line not be just as qualified to inherit the throne as those of the masculine line?

On the strength of this principle, when the announcement of his uncle's death was still fresh, Edward III put himself forward as a candidate for the regency against Philip of Valois. To support his claim, he sent doctors of canon and of civil law to the nobles assembled for the purpose of naming the new king. The crown belonged to him, as a grandson of Philip the Fair, and not to this Regent Philip, a mere nephew, of whose claim so much had been made. . . . Yet the nobles dismissed Edward's claim. In all likelihood, at a time when the notion of patriotism would be an anachronism, some dim but already fervent national sentiment balked at establishing an English king in France.

Edward may well have seemed formidable to the barons. Their alarm was not unwarranted. He was still an adolescent, barely sixteen years old. He had just succeeded his father at the cost of a coup d'état, under the most somber circumstances. All the same, he was not without his attractive qualities. More of a Capetian than a Lancastrian, he had an appetite for power and a remarkable natural aptitude for bringing it within his grasp. It hardly seemed likely that he would renounce of his own free will the rights he considered his. Thus when the whole of France went to Reims to affirm its loyalty to the first representative of its newly chosen dynasty, there was someone missing at the celebration. . . . The unfortunate English pretender meant by his absence to contest the legitimacy of the barons' decision. His abstention was all the more serious since Edward III was the vassal of the Valois king, as Duke of Guienne, and in refusing to do homage to Philip for his duchy, the young Edward was contravening the fundamental laws of feudalism.

Let his cousin tremble, then. Despite his youth, Edward was no man to let his rights be encroached upon. Motivated by spite and ambition, he would continue to covet the kingdom, at whatever cost.

Thus the accession to the throne of the first house of Valois brought with it the seeds of a conflict. Who could have suspected, at the time, that the ensuing drama and war would be the warp and woof of the lives of those men who, for more than a century and a half, would have to expend their energies facing up to it?

THE SOIL AND THE NAME

Between the Oise, Aisne, and Ourcq rivers lies the county of Valois, an ancient tract situated in the heart of the Frankish territory. It takes its name from the *pagus Vadensis* of Caesar's legions, and from the chief Roman town there, Vadum, the modern Vez, in the region of the Oise River, today a tiny village. A human settlement since time immemorial, various tribes succeeded each other in establishing themselves there: Gallic peoples, the Meldes and Silvanectes, whom Caesar found on the spot when he arrived in Gaul, then the Gallo-Romans, and finally the Franks. The Merovingians were fond of it, and established domains there: Compiègne, Attigny, Verberie, where Charles Martel's son, the future Charlemagne, had himself recognized as king at the expense of his nephews. From that time forward this country had found its vocation: to be the seat of kings. Whether this was a coincidence or a token of destiny, it would never lose this calling. In that huge and fragile empire constructed by the genius of the great Carolingian, it was part of the province enclosed between Neustria, Burgundy, Austrasia, Saxony, and Friesland, known as France. It would retain this name throughout the long centuries of misery and confusion which followed upon the overthrow of Charlemagne's great edifice and accompanied the establishment of feudalism. And as such it belonged to Hugh Capet, who was "Duke of France" prior to his coronation, in 987, at the castle of Senlis.

Little by little, its territorial boundaries became fixed, and it was established as the county of Valois, an integral part of the royal domain and eventually attached directly to the Crown when the Countess Aliénor died childless in 1214. It was the preferred haunt of the great Capetians in their turn, of St. Louis above all, who, faithful to his father's dying wish to see his heirs found new monasteries, had the abbey of Royaumont built (on the model of the Cistercian abbey at Longmont) and oversaw the placing of its first stone in 1228. Later he ordered the rebuilding of Senlis cathedral, where he went to dispense the king's justice.

All of which is a way of saying that the Valois region was always appreciated by the kings of France. At the time which concerns us, it had a better claim than the region of the Loire to being called the "cradle of France." In 1293, Philip the Fair established it as the domain of his younger son, Charles. Thus it gave its name to the family on whom for two centuries the destiny of the kingdom would depend.

The soil is varied—fertile if you work it well, sometimes even opulent, owing to a combination of good luck and hard work; and hard, unrelenting labor was to be expected in that era when the land was first cleared. No concessions, no ease. Everything earned by the sweat of the brow.

The land holds its truth here, where a peaceful civilization tried to make a home for itself and where rootedness and hard work won out (but not without great difficulty) over chaos and barbarism and Christ over the ancestral cults of the old gods (peaceful woodland divinities) while not far eastward Odin still threatened with his bloody rituals. The truth of those dark, slow, difficult times is like the slow difficult progress of man over himself. Only what effort and perseverance obtain and reveal is lasting or worth while.

We can see the fruits of such an effort to this day. The art of stonecraft, masonry, vaulting, the art of extracting building stones from this soil which contains so many varieties of rock, some pale, some tinged with gold; the roofer's art, the carpenter's, who knew how to choose his wood, oak or chestnut destined to brave the centuries without the spider ever coming to install its webs, the weevil or the beetle its caverns, and who hewed from that wood those massive, indestructible beams and rafters which run from wall to wall and support the roofs of covered markets and granaries where the cereals are spread and the honeyed linden flower dries; the art of the master builder, who conceived of useful forms, whose beauty was an everyday affair, no less lovely for that, whose value endures, in Senlis, Royaumont, Chaâlis, Crépy, La Ferté-Milon, Pierrefonds, Villers-Cotterêts, Verrières, St.-Leu-d'Esserent, the bell tower of Raray, and so many other fabled places which encircle the countryside of Valois.

This land has its secret aspect as well, one which doesn't yield itself at first sight, which you must pursue, patiently explore, remaining and returning again and again. It is a land of admirable forests, such as Halatte, Chantilly, Compiègne, Pontarmé, and of ponds like Commelles and Mortefontaine. Woodland and water are made for man, for the hunt, for the rich game espied from afar. Tree trunks as tall as the naves of churches, smooth and gray, crackling in the seasonal winds. High in the blue sky the branches of trees spread their delicate boughs. Leaves flutter in the stillness of high places. Passivity of the plant life growing and withering, detaching itself, joining up again, in a long, slow fall, with the supple humus, muffled, thickened with the accumulation of so many autumns. The sky stretches out there between the treetops and the underwood. The eye seeks out a bird. Here and there in islets you find pine trees, with their sprays of green needles—round, pointed, thickset, hard, sweet-smelling. The tone grows warmer, the trunks grow darker, rougher, and the ground beneath your feet turns ocher, sandy yellow, while the azure overhead deepens. It is suddenly summer, a summer which will pass away.

The discrete charm of this land where it is rarely hot, a land of mosses, pale in their hues like the stone, the March skies, the flowers—lilies of the valley which abound in the woods, geometrical periwinkles, violets turning this way and that at ground level, lilac sprays, lilac trees growing above the walls of manses, and lilies, eglantines, acacias, elder blossoms, so light in their hues that they seem almost colorless, their white interrupted by pink or a touch of yellow, enhanced by a dot of purple. Those are all the colors.

In the springtime, stonecutters and master craftsmen pass through the woods in quest of the first new daylight. The winter has been long. At the sight of mother earth, at last reaching the end of her cycle of gestation and slumber, life grasps them once again, and they set out, striding down the paths in search of promises. They see the crooks of ferns, the budding oaks, the water lilies, flat and round, already at work upon the dormant ponds. Close to the Thève or the Aunette, they look for irises, their sword shapes pointing and all bindweed beneath, and for wake-robins. (Peasants in the Valois call the latter "arrowheads" as well, and take them as a sign of fertility which, since time began, has served for love potions and for antidotal draughts to ward off the evil eye.) Garlands of ivy drape the dead tree trunks and strawberry

vines cover the slopes. These are shapes they admire and remember when they pick up their chisels.

Sprouting, profusion, hubbub, wild follies—there you have May
and its festivals, brief passage before the dazzled eye. Then June,
reserved, reasonable, tempers the rising sap. It conceals its tenderness, hardens its down, darkens and glazes its leaves, tarnishes
the ephemeral mother-of-pearl of its orchards, covers the ground
with its tall grasses—a useful task. The restless forest bustles and
rustles. The sun is in its longest and highest course; from dawn to
dusk the days lengthen more and more, encroaching ceaselessly on
the night—the days seem reluctant to end, life cannot wait. We are
at the heart of the season, just the time we would believe it begins,
in cities, in the twentieth century, and elsewhere than in Valois.

In July all has been settled. And already it spreads its damp, its
wispy mists, over rivers and meadowlands, a sign that summer will
remain for its full span, as is fitting for it to endure if it deserves
its name. The sun is fiery, while the soil beneath it keeps its water,
its coolness, and bestows shadows. In this land there is measure,
reserve, a possibility of conciliation. The grain fields are decorated
with cornflowers and poppies, out of which children will fashion
scarlet dolls. Soon the stubble will cut like sharp flint, and the
haystacks will go to the heads of those who lie there careless of
the world. August is made of barns and orchards, and consumes
its delicious fruits. September is decked out in threatened splendors. The eye knows it will have no time to tire of the ineffable,
and so gives itself up fearlessly to its glories. The forests shimmer
and glow. The golds and purples of the trees which must die mask
with their vengeful brilliance the perennial green of those which
will survive the season. Deep within the glades the tree appears, its
golds extended toward the sky, a gold that is delicate, translucent,
revealing the whole of an architectural structure, starting with the
trunk, of branches and boughs and twigs, which are the bones and
veins of the tree and which the leaves, whose opacity has been reduced to such transparency, no longer hide: the beech is a smooth
gray, the chestnut is black, hardened by rough spots and nodules,
the plane tree is light, with a bark that peels off in thick scales,
rounded like the pieces of a puzzle, revealing the white, tender
wood beneath the bark.

What is the truth of this tree, if not its beauty of today? The people of that time must have covered any number of leagues in order to come to contemplate these final pledges of life in a world preparing to decline into cold and night, on Arbor Day when they showed themselves in their brilliant adornment, transfigured by light. The instant is congealed for eternity, inscribed in the Book. An illusion for the world of men, for their time, which is a cipher. All it takes is a cloud, a chillier night, a more biting wind, a sun slightly too warm, for the gold to lose its luster, tarnish, and die. Beneath the huge tree, lost in the sky, whose lowest branches touch the ground and still enclose a vast zone of shadows and secrets, nothing is left but a thin layer of leaves which crackle under your foot when it sinks into them, or in your hand. Already the heavy rains are setting to work, slaughtering and burying whatever is left of the year. The sky is lowering, the sun is veiled, the mist is palpable, the chill settles in. Valois has put on its alluring winter face, of frost, snow, and ice which turns of a sudden into rain and sleet. And this severe face is as real as the summer one, as true to the region's inner spirit.

In winter Valois is the land of Reynard the Fox in the medieval fables. Sitting upon the ice-covered pond, Isegrim, the starving Wolf, waits above the hole cut in the ice by the farmer to allow his animals to drink, waits the entire night for the fish to fill the bucket he has attached to his tail on the advice of Reynard, his treacherous nephew. The Fox himself, lying stretched out across the Crépy or Verrières road, stiffens his body, pretending to be dead, and keeping a watchful, half-closed eye on a cart of fish from the sea, foreseeing that his "corpse" will be tossed on the cart among the lemon soles and the flukes. Brichemer the Stag, Brown the Bear, and Beaulent the Wild Boar keep each other company as they search for food, their eyes downcast and their bellies hollow, by the woods of Coye or of Fleurines. Mouflart the Vulture follows them from afar, ready to contest with them for their prey with his powerful talons. Tilbert the Wildcat crouches in the hedges framing the vegetable and herb gardens. Near the stables of Master Constant the Squire, the Peasants, Roughneck and Bad Neighbor, chase off Primaut the Wolf, no less a menace to sheepfold and storehouse than his illustrious cousin Isegrim. Master Constant bellows, the dogs bark, the farm hands armed with clubs join the fray. . . .

Winter is a hard, long season for the beasts of prey, which are
numerous in this part of the country and against whom the inhabitants must defend themselves. Fortified farmhouses, untouchable
fishponds, guard dogs on the watch—mankind deploys a constant
vigilance against a nature which no longer nourishes her own.

At Royaumont the weather has turned to snow. The sky is low
with puffy clouds, the light a dirty beige, the cold unrelenting, the
air full of a humidity that turns water to ice. At half past three in
the afternoon the night begins to fall. Sadness. Within the thick
walls of the church, with its warming room and scriptorium for
monks long dead, the temperature is lukewarm. It is a place of
refuge, a place to wait out the wintry storm. Suddenly there is a
scarcely perceptible noise, sweet in its remoteness. The snow has
started falling. First the rain, a flurry; it barely grazes the surface
of the ground, and melts. Then the storm gathers force, and the
snow falls in earnest; thick, swift flakes, one upon another. The
wind has risen, from the east or the north, blowing the snowflakes
into dust, gusting them into dense spurts. It piles up without respite. For days on end. Until those rare moments when winter
achieves its own perfection.

The sun has come up in a ruddy sky, spreading its pinks, its
blues, its oranges, its lilacs over a transfigured earth. Spotless blue
sky. Spotless landscape. Strange wedding of the great elemental
forces of fire and water. Metamorphosis. The boundless play of
forms born of rain and cold, perfect as snow crystals. The be-
clouded transparency of icicles dangling from the trees, from the
corners of roofs; the soft shapes of snow blankets covering the architecture beneath them; the blackened, bare trees whose every
branch and bough is adorned with an equal amount of white, the
spruce trees bending under the accumulation, fan shapes and coral
reefs and sea depths; the earth smells of spray, of ocean stirred up
and lashed by waves. A white springtime with fragile, ephemeral
vegetation which shatters like glass, scatters at the slightest breath,
dissolves in the faintest ray of sunlight, fades like columbines
which bloom for a day. It will be brief. A few, irreplaceable hours.
Ice has covered the vast, rectangular ponds nearby, interconnected
by irrigation ditches and separated by screens of trees planted
along the dikes. Only yesterday each gust of wind, each cloud
would stir their gray surface. Today, opaque, blind, they offer

their unshimmering mirrors to the smooth sky. On the banks the ducks move about, looking hopelessly for some water to play in, then venturing forth on the ice, flipping, flopping, slipping, sliding, they give up the enterprise, pathetically, and dully soar off into the distance.

Two o'clock. The sun is higher, the air suddenly less chilly, less biting. A kind of letting up, or letting go: call it what you will. Nature—frozen inside her coat of brilliance, her dazzling death-matrix—has shuddered. Everything begins to crackle and groan. Already the whiteness has changed its hue; the sharp places have lost their edges, the snow its pristine appearance. The winds have come back.

Winter has its pageants in Valois.

CHAPTER II

Philip VI the Fortunate
1293–1350 (reigned 1328–50)

King Philip of Valois has sometimes been called, insultingly, *le roi trouvé* (the accidental king) by his detractors. With the passage of time, this was merely one step from thinking of him as the little tailor in the fairy tale who was summoned by destiny to govern a kingdom. Let us not take that step. This prince came from a most lofty line and a very noble house, the second in France during the preceding half century: powerful, prolific, and illustrious. Its founder was a grandson of St. Louis, known as Monseigneur Charles. It was largely thanks to what his father, Charles, had bequeathed him (luck had done a lot, to be sure, but Charles of Valois had improved that luck with his own two hands) that Philip managed to ascend the throne. Without Charles's legacy, it is unlikely that Philip could have benefited from the Salic law of male descent short of a lengthier and more heated struggle; nor is it certain that he would have won the crown had he not been the son of such a man.

In 1293, Philip had counted two grandfathers who were kings, one of France, the other of Sicily, and, among his ancestors, two saints, St. Louis of France and the lesser St. Louis of Anjou. His childhood passed amid the deafening cries of children which resounded under the Gothic arches of the Hôtel de Nesles and through the halls and warming rooms of his father's castles in

Valois, castles surrounded by woodlands for hunting and by meadows where he and his brother would ride about on Tristan's
palfrey, sometimes on elegant saddle blankets, but most often
bareback.

Two princesses kept an eye on young Philip's disordered household: first his mother, Margaret of Anjou, who died when the boy
was six; then Catherine of Courtenay, Charles's second wife. Both
of these ladies had been transplanted from the closed palaces,
white walls, and white skies of Sicily to the cold abodes and eternal grayness of the north.

Philip's youth was filled with mirages—of the Orient, of lands
across the sea, of power—and nourished on gray climes, on luxury,
on lack of money (a habit he would have to get used to) and also
on waiting for his famous father, who was busy running around
Europe making a name for himself and whose exploits bedazzled
the growing lad. Charles might have trained his older son for the
affairs of the world, since he himself made such a commotion in
them. But he probably never even dreamed of doing so, for he was
too absorbed by his own ambitions, dreaming of putting himself
on a throne rather than of being merely father to a king. Young
Philip thus lost something in stature, inhibited perhaps by his father's greatness. It has always proved difficult for the sons of great
men to make their own marks.

His young manhood as a prince of the blood was full of ease.
He married well: Joan of Burgundy, the daughter of a peer of
France who possessed rich lands and revenues. He was made a
present of the region of Maine in 1315, two years after the wedding, and of the seigniory of Courtenay, which had been part of
his wife's dowry. On the death of his father he would add Valois
and Anjou to his possessions.

He was already quite rich, if we may trust the visible evidence.
His residence at Gué de Mauny, near Le Mans, comprised a
household of two hundred and seventy persons, his wife's a mere
hundred and thirty-three. Which means that every day all these
people ate at his expense and received their wages as a result. It is
true that in 1315, for reasons we do not know but can guess, and
here his improvidence is already clearly displayed, he had to dismiss more than half of his personnel.

Looked on favorably by his peers at court, as well as by King

Charles IV, the young man had a sumptuous choice of residences
during his stays in Paris. At first he resided at the former mansion
of Enguerrand de Marigny, near Saint-Germain-l'Auxerrois, which
had been a gift from his cousin King Louis X (better known as
Louis the Stubborn); later on at the town house of his ancestor,
the King of Sicily, in the street which bears the latter's name today
and which he kept for five years before turning its ownership over
to his brother, the Count of Alençon. Philip was at this time a
calm, peaceful, loyal man, with no problems. Although over thirty
years old, he remained Monseigneur Charles's son. But it was
Philip who would wear the crown in less than five years.

He was then in the vigor of manhood, a large man of princely
bearing, long-limbed, long of face and nose as well. He wore the
dress of his time: robes of velvet and camaca, trimmed with fur
and embroidered with pearls and other precious stones, greatcoats
fastened at the shoulders by hand-worked clasps, hoods, rings. He
loved adornment. He also loved hunting, like the men around him,
and war, if wars there were; in them, he gave ample proof of his
courage. What he loved about war was its sociability, its pomps
and parades, the open camaraderie between noble lords. It was a
spectacle for him. The accouterments of battle enthralled him: the
helmets, the chiseled weapons, the basinets (he chose white
leather for his own), the strange variety of crests as in a shop display, the halberds and breastplates, the heavy two-handed swords
for cutting an opponent in two, the lances of inordinate length, the
chargers adorned with embroidered saddlecloths, with plumes of
many colors, the standards and banners, and the devices of the
noble houses of the realm everywhere on display like so many
affirmations of the self. He loved horseback riding, the human
warmth enfolding night watches, the manly pleasures of tourneys.
He was a true knight, smitten with the open air, the physical life,
the prowess. He believed in Lancelot, Galahad, Arthur, the solemnity of oaths, in the flower of chivalry. He dreamed of exalted
deeds and mighty sword blows. He took his seat among the gallant
knights of the Round Table and henceforth would never give it
up. He had a simple heart.

Not that, for all the emphasis on the life of the body, he was il-
literate, or anything near it. He read more than we might believe,
and thought himself rather fond of the books he assembled in his

library, the orders for which he personally oversaw. Out of such fondness came that manual of universal history, *Les Grandes Chroniques de France,* which has survived to our day, and which he had compiled by a monk of St. Denis.

He had no conspicuous vices, no hidden blemishes, no destructive passions. What he loved was legality, having the law on his side (and his conscience as well), keeping his relations with his fellow men and with heaven in order. Religion sustained him. So did his wife, who would see herself called "bad Queen Joan," for some clearly thought her wicked. Intelligent, schooled far beyond the education of women of her social class and time, she was no less perverse for that reason, hard on the people around her, haughty to the point of throwing tantrums, inclined toward intrigues against anyone she wished to dispose of, tenacious in her hatreds, and lastly, severe toward the lowly people of France. "Above all else she detested the villeins," comments the Norman chronicle, "and she would say that a commoner, be he merchant or burgher, should own nought but five sous and an ass, and wear only linen."

Once upon the throne, Joan would not look to sweeten her character, whose excesses bordered on neurosis. All the contemporary chronicles agree on that point: "The bad, deformed Queen was like a king, and she saw' to it that those who opposed her whims were destroyed or at any rate had them exiled, or confiscated what was theirs."

She was therefore held in unanimous dishonor, except by Philip, who was blind to her faults and whom she led by the nose. Except on occasions when, driven wild by her behavior, he would explode in Homeric rages. Then he would beat her, inflicting bruises which, all in all, she did not take too badly. Still, Philip was rarely brave enough to say no, above all to the "bad" Queen. These occasional temper tantrums betrayed his lack of self-control, his emotionality, his weakness.

Prince Philip's virtues were no great virtues of soul or of character, but the qualities of a private man who, abetted by luck, was able to avoid family catastrophes. We ought not to be too surprised that they proved insufficient for him on the throne of France.

FIRST AND FOREMOST: TO PLEASE

What an adventure for this newcomer, even if he was a great-grandson of St. Louis, who had spent the last years managing his estates in the west, to find himself raised in the prime of life to the first throne of Europe! Did he accept this already contested crown because such a gift is not refused, or did he carefully weave the snares which could lead him to the steps of the throne, watchful, on his guard, on the lookout, no longer sleeping, consumed with impatience, because he delighted in the exercise of power, in ruling? Did he have the taste for political life, for its games and its complexities, the concern of the commonweal? Did he dream of the good of his people? Was he able to take the consequences of such a choice in full awareness of his duties rather than his rights, his burdens rather than his pleasures? Had he any notion at the outset of the full weight that would fall on his shoulders? Or did he see only the vainglory, the funds at his disposal, the armed force at his command, the vast revenues, a people groveling at his feet? In short, was his soul realistic, foolish, chimerical, generous, or ignoble? His deeds would decide the matter.

Where it concerned his own possessions, Philip was indeed a realist. He knew that power was contained in a certain number of square feet of land which you did or did not possess, which you took or had taken from you, by fair means or foul. He acquired land like a peasant, a notary. On this level, he was at ease, an expert. He was able to add large provinces to the royal domain, Champagne and Brie, the county of Chartres, the Dauphiné, the seigniory of Montpellier and the port of Lattes. But his good sense was limited to matters of land.

Doubtless Philip faltered somewhat in facing the reality of his wholly new responsibility, but such faltering was excusable on condition that it did not last. Unhappily he prolonged it.

His first reaction, it seems, was fear. He was a man of scruples. Befuddled at the pretensions and braggadocio of his cousin Edward across the Channel, uneasy with the idea that they might find an echo on his side, might crystallize an opposition, he retained but one idea in his head: to rally hearts to himself. To become feared but above all respected and (who knows?) loved, less by the people, simple and submissive, than by the class that mattered in the nation, the one whose needs, tastes, and demands he knew well for having belonged to it: the nobility.

He thought of resorting to a sort of blackmail, which would consist of creating for the benefit of the nobles a stage production of royalty such as they had never seen, wherein he would show that a Valois could surpass in majesty and grandeur a Capetian who had had three hundred years to prove himself, and from whom, besides, he was descended. What mattered, thought Philip, was the image a king conveyed. This idea came from the mind of a great feudal lord, not of a monarch. None of his predecessors would have given it a moment's thought.

Philip had nurtured such an image during the time when he was only one lord among so many others. What he would do, then, was give his nobles the king of their dreams, the chivalric and magnificent hero who would serve as a model they might copy. And we have to admit the fact that, for Philip, to be king consisted above all else of appearing to be king.

Straightaway he set to work. And so we have the unheard-of pomp of the royal residence, the incredible number of attendants who made up that enormous household, that overabundant royal chamber spilling out retainers who were fed, lodged, dressed, and paid at the prince's expense.

Neither should we forget that the Queen and her son, the Duke of Normandy, each possessed a *hôtel*. Nor be astonished if the total cost of the operation for the year 1335 represented a third of the royal revenues. That's why it was called a royal retinue.

As for Philip's generosity, it knew no bounds. There were his offerings to the poor and to God. One example among many: that most burdensome custom, which consisted of giving the sick and the lepers of towns the court visited in its travels a share of the royal traveling funds. Thus these unfortunates might receive a tenth of the total expenditures for the lodgings of the King and his family, or sometimes only a tenth of the bread and wine, along with the vessels that had been used.

And also the ceaseless gifts which Philip felt obliged to offer to everyone and on every occasion, gifts of clothing for the most part, evince the importance he attached to spectacle, to show.

Perhaps it was necessary, this ostentation which seems so systematic. Perhaps it was indispensable to make an impression, to create an effect, to dazzle, when you didn't have a dead king for a father, and scoundrels taunted you to battle, brandishing standards depicting a rooster and rhymes such as these:

> The day that this painted cock will crow,
> The accidental king to our town will go.

So that Philip the "Fortunate," the "Lucky," as he was called, had no choice but to try to live up to his unheard-of destiny. And how better to prove to the crowds that he was a true king than by appearance? People judge by looks. What better excuse for being solicitous about one's appearance, for wearing martinskin cloaks, furred riding coats, robes lined with squirrel fur, and for sporting at his side a sword sheathed in a fine velvet of green and bright red. What a happy effect on the eye when the sovereign appeared in public surrounded by his family, similarly adorned!

And his entourage of haughty lords, men who were not kings, imitated him, out of their desire to please him, and to dazzle their peers as well, or indeed to dazzle the common people. They made great show and got caught up in the game, assiduously following that fashion in which elegance became extravagance, to such an extent that, abetted by the misfortune of the time, the public opinion Philip thought he was winning over began to condemn "the pride of their lordships, the lust for riches and the immodesty of dress, gowns so short that they came only to their haunches, breeches so tight that they needed help in dressing and disrobing, gowns grathered over their backs as if made for women, and hoods finely cut all around, hose of different cloth for each leg, headdresses and sleeves drooping toward the ground."

Thus a close study of the royal calendar for these ten years of folly leads to a clear conclusion: for Philip, royalty was at first a party. The facts speak for themselves. Five consecutive days of public rejoicing on the occasion of his coronation. Such a thing had never been seen.

Let a sovereign, say the King of Majorca or of Bohemia, visit him, and there would be feasting at the royal *hôtel*. Let the Patriarch of Jerusalem, Pierre de la Palu, pass through Paris, and there would be more feasting. Let there be a celebration of events in his family, the knighting of his son John, his son's marriage to Princess Bonne of Luxemburg, his daughter Marie's to the Duke of Limburg, and there would be feasting once again. This man was a reveler. Not that he was a womanizer, like his cousin, brother-in-law, and friend, Robert of Artois, Count of Beaumont-le-Roger and peer of France. On the contrary, Philip proved astonishingly well behaved. His morals were beyond reproach. His sensuality, his taste for possession, remained respectable, confining themselves to objects—innumerable objects, ceaselessly renewed, unflaggingly sought after.

Was there, at the origin of all this feasting, the same political necessity to dazzle? Was this a likely or normal mode of governing? Hardly. Its motivation must be sought elsewhere, in the fathomless depths of Philip's soul, his night. For this great lord, this man of pedigree, royalty was the great assemblage around his person, the shared games, the tourneys where, in a deployment of manly virtues, the best man won, a frenzy of ostentation, according to the rites of chivalry which he practiced like a second religion. It was these nobles in their adornment, giving an image of themselves carried to its greatest perfection, these sparkling gems, the shadow of halls sweetened with the features of ladies, this spectacle born of Philip's imagination, these nights prolonged at his will, his command, when he could make time stand still and reign over a magnified reality. A demiurge, as it were, a master of men and master of time, he would taste the illusion of a boundless power. Freed of the anguish which gripped him when he dreamed of life's passing, totally absorbed in his pleasure, he rooted himself in the moment in order to transcend it and abolish time itself.

Could a mortal man ask for more, experience a greater joy than those moments when the pride of his soul would mingle with a sanctioned delight of the senses? Even if he were fleeing a reality which was doubtless too heavy, too sudden, in which he lacked competence, which made him feel ill at ease, just as Monseigneur Charles, his father did, and from which the feasts delivered him, however vaguely he may have been aware of it.

A simplehearted fellow, Philip increased the number of his feasts and parties with a completely clear conscience, instinctively seeking his soul's comfort, heedless of the sums of money which these occasions consumed, sums furnished for him not only by the duchy of Anjou, the counties of Valois or of Maine alone, but now by all of France, and by the Pope to boot when the time came to discuss a crusade with him. Such considerations would have made a hardier man than Philip dizzy. What this accidental king needed was either a good head on his shoulders or less imagination. He had to see things with his own eyes, and his mental nearsightedness did not permit him to imagine an event until it was under his nose, even if the confrontation which resulted was brutal and disastrous. King Philip could never live in any time but the present, could never bear to imagine a future unless it was gilded, diverting. He never rode the back of any steed but Pegasus, whose hoofs never touched the ground; still he could never make his mount fly very high. By throwing those feasts Philip found himself. Politics had nothing to do with it.

In the glimmer of torchlight the revels exhausted themselves, the instant grew weary, and the night acquired a taste of ashes. Then, in the pale dawn, appeared the figure of Elsewhere, another country which looked kindly on vast designs, on far-off adventures. Feasting gave way to departures; the quest of the instant was carried into a future inhabited by chimeras.

Among the most frequent guests at the court of France was the King of Bohemia, John of Luxemburg. Together, he and Philip dreamed of crowns exchanged like gifts: "I make you Emperor, and you make me King of Arles." Arles was quite close by. Why not Italy? With its discords, it would make an easy prey. "I buy Lucca for my needy Bohemian colleague. I'm in correspondence with the towns of Lombardy, and I could mediate their disputes. His Holiness grants me the right to intervene in Parma, in Reggio, and in Modena. . . ."

Things already possessed lost their appeal. Other dreams issued forth from the Italian one: the Holy Land, lands beyond the sea, magic words for pious knights. Negotiations were undertaken in foreign lands: Venice, Cyprus, Armenia, Ethiopia. Plans for travel and attack were worked out, and the prince took the Cross. Departure was confounded with adventure. Wanderlust was also called conquest, murder posed as inherent justice, and war had become a crusade.

Philip won the first round. He rallied the nobles to his cause, like birds drawn toward turning mirrors. Muscles of steel and heads of straw, the flower of knighthood, caught up in these games, captivated by mirages, held fast to its Valois King. The credulous people admired Philip and paid. My kingdom is my feast, thought the King in the intoxication of his evening revels. And France herself was drunk on laughter and glory. She was dreaming.

But already the hour was approaching when reality could no longer masquerade as a dream, even for someone who still believed that combat meant entering the lists. The Pope in Avignon became alarmed and had someone inform the King of France that "if he took that journey beyond the sea which he had decided on, he would commit his kingdom to the most risky of ventures." But events were rushing forward, taking an irreversible course. Events which the King had neither foreseen nor understood, whose approach he had not even felt. Call it being tone-deaf; it's a grave deficiency in a statesman.

DISASTERS

On the first of November 1337 the Bishop of Lincoln, Henry Burghest, Lord High Treasurer of England, accompanied by the dukes of Salisbury, Northampton, and Suffolk, delivered to Philip of Valois in his Hôtel de Nesles in Paris a challenge conveyed by letters from his cousin Edward III, King of France and England, whose coat of arms had been quartering the fleur-de-lis since October 7. The event of the century had just taken place.

However, the Englishman let three years pass before attacking. He began with a master blow. On June 24, 1340, he destroyed a large part of the French fleet in the Battle of Sluys. He did not follow up his advantage immediately. While waiting for the opportune moment, he followed the French situation closely, supporting the opposition wherever it showed itself, provoking an incident every time he could. A war over the succession in Brittany furnished him with the chance he had dreamed about. Two pretenders were disputing each other's claim. One of them had been vested with the suzerainty of the duchy by the King of France; the other had taken up arms. Edward increased his aid to the latter, appeared in person before the people of the town of Vannes in Brittany, and welcomed fugitives while, on his orders, cavalry maneuvers were stepped up in his fief of Guienne. The Hundred Years' War was about to begin.

Then he decided to strike a great blow: On July 12, 1346, he landed at the port of St. Vaast-La-Hougue with twenty thousand men. Burning everything in his path, he marched through Valognes, Carentan, St. Lô, headed for Caen, which he captured. But to his great surprise the local populations everywhere offered him resistance he would have to reckon with. It was better not to linger in the isolated situation in which he found himself, and to get back to the north, where in an emergency he could more easily receive aid from his allies in Flanders. On July 16 he crossed the Seine at Roissy and by forced marches reached Picardy. He still had to cross the Somme, always a difficult operation. By whatever means were necessary he obtained from a prisoner the location of a ford which at low tide would lead him to the other bank. Once across, he learned that Philip, with all his mustered troops, was at his heels. Immediately, without losing his self-control, he looked for a strong position in which to entrench his own troops and wait. On August 25 he positioned them between Crécy and Wadicourt, above the Valley of the Clerks.

CRÉCY

"That evening," reports the chronicler Froissart, "the King of England gave a supper to the earls and barons of his army, made them of great cheer, then gave them leave to go and rest themselves. . . . That same night, as I have heard tell afterwards, when all of his men had gone and he remained with the knights who attended on his body and his chamber, he entered his oratory and knelt before his altar, devoutly praying God to grant that, if the next day he should engage in combat, he should come through the engagement with honor. After his prayers, around midnight, he went to bed. He rose fairly early the next day and heard mass with his son the Prince of Wales. They took communion, and most of their men similarly confessed, putting themselves in a state of grace.

"Then he caused his Constable and marshals to give orders to divide the army into three battalions. . . . When each earl, baron and knight knew what he had to do, the King mounted a small palfrey and, holding a white baton in his hand, rode slowly through all his ranks, escorted by his marshals, admonishing and asking his earls, barons and knights . . . to stand up for his honor and defend his right. So sweetly and smilingly did he speak these words, and with so fair a countenance, that the most disheartened would have taken comfort just to see and hear him. Afterwards he ordered all his men to eat at their ease, and have a drink as well. . . . Then they packed up the pots, kegs, and provisions in their carts, and went back to their battalions. They all sat down on the ground with their helmets and bows in front of them, in order to be fresh and well rested when their enemies arrived."

When this incident took place, Philip was in Abbeville, reveling and regaling all the princes of high estate who had joined him. Was this anxiety on the eve of a battle? He could not suppress the good feelings that rose to his lips. After supper he exhorted the princes to be friendly and courteous toward one another, to give up envy, hatred, and pride. And each of them promised him this.

The following day they set out, sure that their valor and their number would lead them to victory. The King's entourage was nonetheless better than one might have believed. There were among his council those who realized the disaster which could follow upon so much improvidence and who were not reticent about telling him of their misgivings. He was able to listen to them.

"Sire, it would be advisable to put your battalions in order, and to let all the foot soldiers go forward so that they are not trampled down by the horsemen. And you should send three or four of your knights ahead to reconnoiter the enemy's position."

Shortly afterward Philip received a report of what was going on in the English camp. He listened to his advisers and decided to stop where he was until the arrival of the rest of his troops, and to wait for the following day to mount an attack. By then the men would be well rested from a full night's sleep, and his battle plan would be laid out to conform with the reports he had received. He made up his mind and gave the necessary orders.

"The two marshals rode out, one forward and the other back, shouting to the standard-bearers: 'Halt banners on the King's orders, in the name of God and St. Denis!' Those who were in front halted, but those behind did not, . . . saying that they would not halt until they had caught up with the front ranks. And when the front saw the rear approaching, they too went on riding."

It was then that something unthinkable occurred: "Neither the King nor his marshals could control their men, for there were too many great lords among them, all determined to show their power. They rode on in this way, in no order or formation. Countless people from the local districts were there; they completely covered the roads between Abbeville and Cressy [Crécy]. When after a long time they came within three leagues of the enemy, they drew their swords and cried out: 'Kill! Kill!' And yet they had seen no sign of anybody. . . .

"The English, who were drawn up in three battalions and sitting most gently on the ground, got up with perfect discipline as soon as they saw the French approaching and undauntedly formed their ranks. The Prince of Wales's battalion was in front, with the archers in a sort of portcullis formation and the men-at-arms behind."

When King Philip saw the English "his blood boiled, for he hated them." "Send forward the Genoese and begin the attack," he said to his marshals. But the fifteen thousand Genoese crossbowmen, bone-weary and worn down by the six leagues they had just marched with all their gear, refused. The heavens intervened in the affair, a terrible storm broke out: it rained so hard and the drops were so big that it was a wonder to behold; there were thunderclaps and lightning bolts and great flocks of crows who made deafening noises as they set out in their heavy flight. An omen. For the English, then, the contest promised well.

"Then the sky began to clear and the sun to shine brightly. But the French had it straight in their eyes and the English behind their backs. When the Genoese had been marshaled into order and at long last to approach their enemies, they began to whoop so loudly that it was a marvel. They did this to frighten the English; but the English kept silent. The Genoese shouted the same way once again, and advanced a little farther, while the English maintained their silence and did not stir. Yet a third time the Genoese shouted, very loud and clear, moved forward, leveled their crossbows, and began to shoot. When the English archers saw this grouping, they took one pace forward and let their arrows fly so thickly and evenly that they fell like snow. And the Genoese, who had never met up with such archers as those of England before, were thrown into a state of discomfiture, for they felt those arrows piercing their arms, their heads, their faces. Quite a few cut their bowstrings and some threw their crossbows to the ground. They began to retreat.

"Between them and the main body of the French, there was a great hedge of men-at-arms . . . so well placed that when the Genoese thought they would fall back, they couldn't. The King of France, in great anger when he saw their pathetic array and how they were fleeing, gave the command: 'Quick now, kill all that rabble. There is no reason to let them get in our way.' At which point you would have seen men-at-arms begin to strike out at them on all sides. Many of the Genoese staggered and fell, never to rise again. And the English continued to shoot into the thickest part of the crowd, so skillfully that they wasted none of their arrows. They impaled and struck the bodies and limbs of horses and riders, who fell staggering toward the ground . . . and could not get up again, but for the aid of many men. . . .

"The gallant and noble King of Bohemia, John of Luxemburg" (our Philip's comrade of the nightlong feasts) ". . . heard from his people that the battle had begun. Although he was there, fully armed and equipped for combat, he could not see a speck, for he was blind. . . . He said a very brave thing to his knights: 'My lords, you are my men, my friends, and my comrades-at-arms. Today I have a special request to make of you. Take me far enough into the fray that I might strike a blow with my sword.' Those who were near him and loved his honor and their own preferment consented. . . . In order to acquit themselves well and not lose their King in the press, they tied their horses together by the bridles, and set the King their lord in front, so that he might accomplish his desire. In such a fashion they rode towards the enemy. . . .

"The good King of Bohemia . . . came so close to the enemy that he struck one sword blow, even three or four, and fought most bravely, as did all the knights who were his companions. They served him so well and threw themselves so much into the fray against the English that they all remained on the field that day.

They were found the next day in the same spot, lying around their lord, with their horses still fastened together."

The King of France was in despair to see a handful of Englishmen decimating his whole army. "What must I do?" he asked one of his companions, John of Hainaut. "Sire, withdraw," Sir John replied with all due respect.

"The King, shaking with anger and vexation, did not reply, but rode on a little farther. It seemed as if he wanted to head toward his brother the Count of Alençon, whose banners he made out at the top of a small rise. The Count was coming upon the English in good array and launching an attack on them, as was the Count of Flanders from another quarter. . . . These two lords and their forces moved along the flank of the archers and reached the Prince of Wales's battalion, which they engaged most gallantly for a long time. The King would gladly have joined them had he been able, but there was such a great hedge of archers and men-at-arms in front of him that he could not get through." The fighting went on till nightfall.

"Late in the evening, when the darkness was almost total, King Philip left the field in complete discouragement, accompanied by five barons only. . . . He rode lamenting and mourning for his men until he came to the castle of La Broye. When he came to the gate he found it shut, and the drawbridge raised, for it was now nighttime and pitch-dark. Then the King called for the lord of the castle . . . who came to the lookout turrets and shouted down: 'Who goes there, who is knocking at such an hour?' King Philip answered: 'Open up, open up, my lord castellan. It is the unfortunate King of France.'

"The lord of the castle lowered the drawbridge and opened the gate. Then the King entered with his whole troop. He had some refreshment, as did those who were with him. Then they left the castle and set out on horseback, taking with them some guides who knew the country, to show them the way to Amiens. . . . They rode so hard that by daybreak they entered that good town, where the King halted. He took lodgings in an abbey, saying he would go no farther as long as he had no true report on his men, so that he would know which had been left on the field, and which had escaped."

The news was cruel: eleven princes lay dead on the field, eighty banneret lords, twelve hundred bucklered knights, and about thirty thousand ordinary men. "The King mourned grievously for my Lord Charles, his brother, for the Count of Alençon, for his nephew the Count of Blois, for his dear friend the King of Bohemia, for the Count of Flanders, for the Duke of Lorraine, and for all the barons and lords, one after the other. . . . He arranged all the funeral rites for his kindred and close companions. Afterward he left Amiens, gave furloughs to men-at-arms of all stations, and returned to Paris."

CALAIS

Already Edward III was about to lay siege to Calais. Although he had achieved a great victory, he had not gained anything effective. He thus needed this town which for him represented "the most convenient access to the Kingdom of France." He blockaded Calais. The town, defended by a force under the command of Jean de Vienne, offered admirable resistance. But by the end of seven months provisions had run out. Reinforcements could no longer get through. Edward would allow no passage to the heroic defenders. "Let them all surrender to me, to live or die as I see fit."

"This would be too hard a thing for us," replied Jean de Vienne. "Inside here we are a little band of knights and squires who have served our lord the King of France loyally to the best of our ability, as you would serve yours in the same case, and we have undergone many hardships and sufferings as a result. But we would rather suffer more than anyone has yet endured than consent that the humblest groom or servingman in the town should suffer worse treatment than the greatest man among us. . . ."

King Edward had no intention of softening his heart. But so insistent was his entourage that he consented to yield. "Walter," he said to Sir Walter Manny, "you will go back to Calais and will tell its commander that this is the greatest clemency they will get from me: six of the principal burghers are to come out, with their heads and their feet bare, ropes around their necks, and the keys of the town and castle in their hands. I shall do as I like with the six of these, and have mercy on the rest." On August 3, 1347, six of the town's principal burghers, led by Master Eustache de St. Pierre, "barefooted and bareheaded, stripped to their linen undergarments, with halters round their necks," brought the keys of the town and the castle to the hands of King Edward.

"The King," reports Froissart, "was at this time in his chamber with a large company of earls, barons, and knights. He left the chamber, and went out to the open space before his lodgings, followed by all of his lords and by great numbers of others who were curious to see the men of Calais and what would happen to them. Even the Queen of England, who was pregnant, went out with her lord the King."

Sir Walter Manny went up to the King and said: "Sire, here is the deputation from the town of Calais, as you have ordered."

The king kept silent and looked very fiercely at the six burghers, for he hated the citizens of Calais, because of the great damage they had done him at sea in the past.

The six burghers went down on their knees before the King and, clasping their hands together, said: "Noble sire and King, here we are before you, long-established citizens of Calais and great merchants there. We bring you the keys of the town and the castle, surrendering them to you, to do with them as you please. We put ourselves as you see us, entirely in your power, in order to save the rest of the people of Calais, who have undergone great suffering. We pray you, in the name of that generosity for which you are renowned, have pity on us."

Surely there was no one present, no lord, no knight, none of the brave men all, who could refrain from weeping with pity. . . . The King glared at them with wrath, for his heart was so hardened and so bursting with anger that he could not speak. When he did speak, it was to command that their heads be struck off. But the barons and knights who were there, all of them in tears, begged the King to have mercy. . . .

"Ah, noble sire," exclaimed Sir Walter, "calm your heart. You have a reputation for clemency which befits a sovereign. . . ."

When he heard this the King gnashed his teeth and said: "Sir Walter, contain yourself, my mind is made up. Let the headsman be summoned here. The people of Calais have caused the deaths of so many of my men that it is proper they too should die."

Then the noble Queen of England, sorely advanced in pregnancy as she was, wept so tenderly that her legs could not support her. She threw herself on her knees before the King and said: "Ah, noble sire, since I crossed the sea at great danger to myself, as you know, I have not asked a thing of you. But now I beg you in all humility, in the name of the Son of the Blessed Mary and for love of me, to have mercy on these six men."

The King bided his time before speaking, looking at his gentle wife and lady as she wept on her knees before him. His heart was softened, for now he saw that, without wishing it, he was causing her such distress. "Ah, my lady," he said, "it would have been much more to my liking if you were elsewhere than here. Your appeal has touched me to the quick, so that I dare not refuse you. Although I do this most reluctantly, here, I give them to you. Take them, and do with them as you please."

That good lady said, "My lord, my heartfelt thanks." Then she rose and ordered the six burghers to their feet as well. The ropes were removed from their necks at her command, and she led them away to her own chambers. There they were given new clothes and a dinner in comfort. She made each of them a gift of six gold pieces and had them escorted safely out of the camp. They went on their way and found new places to live in several towns in Picardy. . . .

During this time the King called Sir Walter Manny and his two marshals and said to them: "My lords . . . go and take possession of the castle and the town of Calais. Take the knights who are there and make them prisoners or else put them on parole; they are gentlemen, and their word will vouch for them amply. All of the other soldiers, who have been serving there for pay, are simply to leave the place, and so are all the rest of the men, women, and children, for I mean to replace the population of Calais with pure-blooded English stock."

At the end of the month Edward made a solemn entry into the empty town of Calais. He gave splendid feasts at the castle and distributed all of the lodgings in the city to his entourage. Not long afterward the arrival of shiploads of burghers and artisans from England was announced. Edward had kept his word. Within a short time Calais had become completely English; and English it would remain for more than two centuries, up to the Treaty of Cateau-Cambrésis, signed in 1559.

In our own time a great deal less clemency would have been

shown. After the defeats at Sluys and Crécy, Philip would not have lasted for more than two days as head of a government. He would have been sent home to tend his fields in the county of Maine. Nothing of the sort in those distant times. The King was the Lord's anointed, his person remained inviolable, and his word was law. . . . And then, news did not travel very fast or very far in those days. . . . What did the people of Paris know of what happened in the plains of the north? Whatever reports there were circulated badly, and public opinion had no access to information. People knew what was going on in Brittany, on the Somme, in Guienne, places the armies had passed through and where there had been fighting. But these were fringe areas in relation to the center of France. For the moment the war was confined to limited areas. We must also add, in defense of the first Valois king, that if foreign armies were treading on French soil he had not yielded an inch of it to the invader, with the exceptions of Calais and its immediate surroundings and of some fortified towns in the southwest. On the other hand, we have seen that as a good landowner he had increased the royal domain with important and strategic acquisitions. Likewise on the administrative level his work was proving important. The royal institutions had continued to progress.

THE YEAR 1347

But what our King had just lived through would be nothing in comparison to what awaited him. Following on the heels of the English successes, a frightful catastrophe was waiting to sweep across Europe. It was one of those great calamities which all of a sudden swoop down upon humanity in mysteriously ordered cycles. Unmitigated evil. Death striking on the scale of a continent: the plague. The bubonic plague, the Black Death, had returned. It came out of Asia, ravaged Egypt and the plains of Lombardy, penetrated into France by way of the Alps and the ports of Provence, advanced through Avignon, Narbonne, Béziers, and Montpellier (where the death rate was five out of six inhabitants) all the way to the north. There it raged for a year and a half. Next it reached England and Flanders. In Paris it left fifty thousand dead, at the rate of eight hundred a day.

Nor was the royal family spared; the women were hit the hardest. The Queen of France, her eldest son's wife, and the widow of Charles IV, the last Capetian king, all succumbed. The King reacted with courage: he consulted the physicians of the University of Paris on means of combating the calamity and saw to it that measures were taken on their directives. That these measures were ineffective would soon be evident. At the King's request, Pope Clement VI instituted a mass to beseech heaven to put an end to the contagion. It was said immediately in every church in France. Moreover, to this day it is still celebrated in times of epidemic. As for the plague, there was nothing to do except flee it. Or else make use of medicines that were wholly without effect. Now the only medicines prescribed in that era to protect oneself from the plague were of the following sort, to be taken with myrrh and bitter aloes: "For the smell, take one lemon larded with cloves, an angelica root, some rue, some other strong herb, or a sponge soaked in vinegar compound; take only one of these safeguards at a time, and change the kind from week to week." Another remedy: "Flowers of sulphur, one ounce; trochisk of viper's serum, six drams; diacodium powder [an extract of poppy], one dram; diamargaritum frigidum powder [an extract of pearl], one dram; confection of hyacinth, one dram; confection of Alkermes [an insect], one dram. Make these into tablets with a pound of finely powdered sugar cooked with black salsify water or holy water with thistles in it, and cover the tablets with gold leaves. Take some of these three times a week, one dram in the morning, as a normal precaution; but if you are coming into contact with those infected with the plague, you must take two drams in the evening, put yourself in bed so that you perspire freely, and one hour afterward, take some broth."

We know that from such therapeutic measures France lost one third of its population.

Souls were driven to distraction. Blame was placed on the stars. The illness was due to the conjunction of Jupiter and Saturn in Aquarius, or to the comet which made its appearance in 1345. The guilty were hunted down. Surely the Jews had poisoned the springs and wells, and so the Jews were hounded and burned in

Narbonne, in Carcassonne. The survivors of these pogroms owed their lives only to the compassion of Pope Clement VI, who provided asylum for them in the papal county of Avignon.

The existing violence was compounded by outbursts of wild mysticism. People began to believe in collective sin. In the north of France, naked "flagellants," chanting and beating themselves with straps of hard knotted leather, spiked with little iron shafts, came through the towns and villages.

"They said that everything they were doing was based on the revelation of the Angel," reports the chronicle. "And they believed that the penance appointed for them was to be done for thirty-three and a half days, corresponding to the number of years which Christ had lived, and during that time they were to live purely, cleanly, discharged and absolved of all sins, as they had been after their baptism." They approached Paris and then turned aside toward Reims. The Pope and the King ordered them to head back whence they had come. So they turned toward Flanders. And terror reigned.

Others hoped to escape the illness by surprising means, which cannot help calling to mind the principles of Christian Science. Two friars from the abbey of St. Denis, who had set out upon a mission across the countryside on the order of their abbot, drew near a town. As they entered it, the sound of drums and bagpipes struck their ears. There was a feast going on, and people dancing. The entire population was there. Intrigued, the friars asked why. "We have seen our neighbors dead and dying," was the reply, "and we see more of them dropping off from day to day, but Death has not yet entered our town, and we hope it will not return here, we are joyful to be alive, and that's the reason we're dancing."

On their return the friars passed through the town again. They no longer found many people there, and sadness held sway in the streets. "Where are the men and women who led the feasting a short time ago?" they asked. "What, my fair lords!" a straggler replied. "The wrath of God has fallen on us, for so heavy and violent a hailstorm has blown over this town that some were killed, and others died of fright."

What else did these monks of St. Denis see, that they were unable to tell us, or that did not reach us? In the course of their long wanderings, undertaken at the order of their abbot in conformity with the spirit of obedience and contrition, they walked—a strip of linen over their mouths for protection—down roads which were nought but desolation, passing houses marked with a cross where people were dying with doors and windows boarded fast, and turning their eyes from those streets where corpses lay black and swollen. Fear gripped the bellies of these men; fear of the horror of what they were seeing, at the thought of what they might see at the next bend in the road. They no doubt beat their breasts, questioning themselves on the fault of the world. What was this plague but the ransom for sin, the unavoidable wages in suffering which must be paid, step by step, to cover the distance separating ourselves from God?

But for the King of France its first meaning was that his kingdom had been bled white, that seven million were dead, a matter of concern above all for the rural countryside, since at that time seven eighths of the population lived there. Which in turn meant property without a master and lands ripe for grabbing, with no other law than that of the survivor. Every kind of usurpation, every kind of impropriety, every kind of illegality, every kind of disorder: ruined nobles, fortunes accumulated in a day, agricultural workers waking up one fine morning landowners, a total upheaval of rural fortunes, and poverty, migrations, abandonment of the land. People died, people went elsewhere, there were no longer any hands available to work the earth, harvests withered on the stalk, flocks wandered aimlessly about, fields lay fallow, and hatred settled in the common folks' hearts for the nobleman, the strong man of yesterday. Defeated in battle, defeated by life, he no longer appeared capable of eluding the common upheaval. Why then pay him respect?

And there was no money. The King resorted to debasing the coinage, which in any case was an old habit of his. In the twenty-two years of his reign he had done it twenty-four times. Taxes were increased. Loans of money were obtained by violence. The Lombards were expelled. Offenses were once again attributed to the Jews, whose possessions went to fill the empty royal treasury. Circumstances were somber, and yet this was just a glimpse, with all the possible vicissitudes, of what the dynasty would have to face.

END GAME

Philip had come to the end of his road. He was fifty-six. Experience had been a rough school. Had he learned from it? Had he had the time? Could he prove it? He was an old man, encircled by death: his brother, his wife, his daughter-in-law, his cousins, his friends were dead, and his dearest friend, John of Bohemia, among them. . . . And those awful weeks of the epidemic, the flight from the royal residence, the abandoned rooms turned over to the medical mountebanks called "perfumers," and in each living man the fear: tomorrow perhaps it will be my turn. . . .

Death was familiar to him. Not that he could feel its approach in that body which bore him well, but by its obsessive work of the last years, those voids surrounding him. Well he knew the rites, the still bodies adorned and anointed with oils and perfumes, the tombs of stone and marble, the idealized figures awaiting the hour of judgment. Where were they now, those he had loved: his parents, Monseigneur Charles, his mother, Margaret, whom he had scarcely known, and all the others? Where had they gone? Where were they awaiting the hour when they would see God face to face? And when would that be? On Judgment Day doubtless, and not before. The beatific vision was reserved for souls in bliss alone. The masters of theology had assured him of this sixteen years ago, when he had assembled them in 1333 at Vincennes to have an authorized opinion on a problem which intrigued the minds of the age. "The blessed vision which the saints have at present," they had told him, "is and will last forever." On the strength of this declaration, he had had his subjects notified by letters sealed with his seal and copied over in triplicate in his chancellery.

The blessed vision, a promise soothing to the heart . . . a bit sooner, a bit later, at once for the blissful, afterward for the creatures who had worked in his earthly kingdom. He had not ceased to put his best efforts into it, increasing the number of charities, of donations, of pilgrimages, and assiduously practicing these himself.

No, he feared nothing. God and His angels would keep him in the other world.

And suddenly, by the mysterious play of alternation, the taste for the beauties of the moment returned to him. It was a violent taste, the more demanding the heavier had been his dread. Where might he flee a reality inhabited by Death, ceaselessly undermined by Death in the loss of dear ones and in old age itself? Where indeed, except in tasting the instant, just as he had done in former times. Nostalgia for his youth haunted King Philip, the yearning for those moments which he had probably known only in his first and far-off loves, perhaps with the "bad" Queen when she had not yet turned into the self-centered, bullying lady of his reign, the lady he loved no longer, who slept now under the flat stone. Did he know that he himself had but a few months left? Time passes, time presses, time destroys each and all, and King Philip, fascinated by the irreparable, would dare to be himself. Let tongues wag. This man of fifty-six let barely thirty days go by after the death of Queen Joan before marrying his own son's fiancée, a lass of eighteen springtimes, Blanche of Evreux-Navarre, whose great beauty is a legend.

Did he taste, at the end of his quest, the silence of a shared peace? A few fragile hours, before knowing those without number which awaited him in the realm of shadow, where words cease?

But who remembers King Philip today? Those early Valois kings are so badly known, people usually say. Thus history, with its whims, transmits to us only one ever so popular image of that aristocratic reign, the image of the burghers of Calais. Their sacrifices and selflessness have played a trick on death and time. Art has played its part too, some five centuries later, through the genius of a Rodin who rescued them from the banality of Epinal cartoons in order to install them in eternity.

The prince whose subjects they had been, the first sovereign of Europe, has been reposing, forgotten, since the end of August 1350, when his body was taken with splendid pomp to the royal tomb at St. Denis, to lie among his peers.

CHAPTER III

John II the Good
1319–64 (reigned 1350–64)

JOHN'S CHILDHOOD

The second King of France of the Valois line, known to posterity by the name of John the Good, was born on a Thursday—the twenty-sixth of April 1319—in the castle of Gué de Mauny. His father, Philip, was as yet nothing more than the Count of Maine; his grandfather, Charles, possessor of the Valois name, was still in this world.

It was a lovely feudal abode, the one in which the young prince uttered his first cries, a dark stone dwelling with thick walls, well situated at the gates of Le Mans, where two rivers flow together, a few leagues from the forests of Bercé, in the very center of the west country. Comfortable as such a dwelling could be at the beginning of the fourteenth century, it had been entrusted to the talent of an artist of renown, one Evrart d'Orléans, who had painted its ornate frescoes and thereby contributed to making it the preferred residence of the master of the house, who rejoiced on the day of his son's birth.

The air was bracing, the sky dappled: Eastertime. "Blessed is the hour of baptism." The meadows were just turning green, and only the chestnut trees had come into leaf when the procession gaily climbed the streets leading up to the Cathedral of St. Julian of Le Mans. Thick masts—the flying buttresses of the nave—houses piled pell-mell, the sudden forms of signboards hanging at eye level like puppets in a shadow play, round paving stones underfoot—people often stumbled. . . . The women went first, two by two, followed by the knights dressed in the new fashion, and, last, the infant carried by a matron.

Just a few hours earlier he had been sleeping in the paradise of his mother's womb. Reaching the ineluctable term, detached from his own flesh like ripe fruit from a branch, torn from his felicity, he lay helpless between the sheets. The air of the world burned his throat and chest. He cried. The cold, the noise, the kissing and the laughter, the servants' rough hands on his tender skin, the water bubbling on the hearth fire, the sudden infinite space around his arm, his leg stretching itself out as if by mistake, then the suffocating vise of the linen swaddling clothes; all the frights of the day, all the terrors of hell had in an instant replaced the inexpressible warmth of the darkness. And in order to procure the safety of another paradise, more lasting than the one he had just lost, this fragile infant already inhabited by the demon, tinged with the earth's sin, in accord with human destiny, had been routed from his sleep, dressed in a catechumen's robes, decked out in gold brocade, in the silk and ermine of princes, to be led to his Lord.

Walls and columns of white stone, vaults of intricate geometric design, thick uneven paving blocks over which footsteps rang haltingly, cold light pouring down from stained-glass windows . . . surrounded by strangers, the hours-old child blinked his eyes and shivered. The procession had halted. The priest questioned those who had accepted the spiritual guardianship of the new baby: "What do you ask for in the Church of God?" "Faith," the godfather and godmother replied in the child's name. "What does faith procure for you?" "Eternal life." Then, by incantations and signs, by word and gesture, the struggle was joined against the Fallen One who inhabited this frail body. Like every tiny baby in Le Mans, like every tiny baby in France for that matter to this day, John of Valois was baptized in the same Roman Catholic rite which has been kept almost unchanged to our time.

The priest went on to the first exorcism. Three times he blew on the baby. He made the sign of the Cross on his forehead and heart. He stretched out his hand over him to take possession of

him in the name of the Lord and entreated the Almighty to grant
his grace. There followed the laying on of salt, the laying on of
hands, signs of the Cross, prayers, exorcisms: "I entreat thee, im-
pure spirit, whoever you may be, in the name of God . . . leave
this creature of God, John. . . ." Then, as a symbol of the
strength he would need to triumph over the demon, the anointing
with holy oil. And the second anointing, with the oil and balm of
the holy chrism.

For these last ceremonies, the godfather and godmother did not
have to release the poor child from the wrappings of silk and linen
that bound him from head to foot like a mummy's bandages. . . .
The older custom had been to plunge the baby naked into the
font. Was he calm or fearful? Did he sleep, or did his inconsolable cries resound under the vault? The cries of a newborn
bothered by the salt on his tongue, the water on his forehead, the
unaccustomed grazing of hands over his ears, in his nostrils, on
his chest, and in his armpits, turning him over and over like a bun-
dle, in the name of the Lord? No chronicle tells us.

To the pealing of organs and bells, amid strewn leaves and
altars decked with forsythias and daffodils, with young boys in
white surplices shaking censers, while a thousand flames of hope
and faith flickered in adjacent chapels, John of Valois, in the
peace of a child of God and the glory of sons of princes, took possession of the place, among those of his blood, which destiny had
given him.

The child had been hoped and wished for, the first of the name
to survive after the Countess' two unhappy pregnancies. And he
was a son. He would be much loved and much fondled, especially
when we remember that the Count and Countess would have to
wait more than seventeen years before a brother would survive.
Accordingly John would have, in spite of a number of births anticipated by his parents, the childhood of an only son.

Like every other child of the nobility, in his early years John
was fed, bathed, wiped at the nose and bottom, punished,
spanked, beaten, consoled, and rocked among women. Wet,
smacking kisses, quick slaps, tears falling into his soup, fingers dip-
ping furtively and sweetly into jars of honey and preserves. Sometimes he had to lower his breeches, and then it hurt. Foolish
offenses and big childish hurts, face smeared with tears and snot,

glowing from fresh air and cold in the time of snow and brisk winds; or streaming with sweat, during evenings when the hay was harvested and the grapes gathered for the vintage; or overstuffed on St. Michael's Day at an age when he still tumbled like a melon when they picked him up by the armpits to toss him in the air, the only son of the house drifted off to sleep with his back to the hearth fire of the stone chimney, his nose buried in the lap of matrons with enormous aprons.

Then came the time for games. Whole days spent running, climbing, jumping, fighting, in the nearby forest, in the groves and thickets, the meadows of spearwort close at hand, with the other children who lodged in his father's house. He played with marbles, balls, bowls, rackets, and shuttlecocks. He would race along on stilts, build huts, and harness house or field mice snatched from the straw to tiny chariots. When the day was done he would be worn out, especially if Count Philip had taken him along on a great horse and the two of them had galloped. On such evenings, when he was seated at the table, it was all he could do to make the sign of the Cross when grace had been said. The next day he would pester all and sundry to be put on a horse, only to experience shivers up and down his spine. That was just a beginning. He soon got used to it, got his seat, straight in the saddle, learned to walk, to trot, to gallop, to tilt at stuffed dummies from the height of his steed. Already he was nearly a man.

Springtime passed and summer came. The grass was thick in the orchards and the shade of the trees was sweet. "In my father's gardens, how sweet it is to sleep." And not only to sleep, but to lean your back against a tree surrounded by friends and stuff yourself on the fruit you made fall from the branches with a hand that shook the tree as energetically as it gathered the fallen fruit. The lovely days were so short. The dark months were drawing nigh, the equinoxes and the storms from the west. The rains beat and dripped about the castle; the wind whistled through the empty forests; beams creaked and doors rattled everywhere. Nose pressed against the window, the bored child gazed out at gray days with long sheets of mist floating above his flooded lands, his dead meadows, and he thought, sometimes, that this season would last forever. Time seemed to have stopped on that gray afternoon, at that silence. The air smelled of damp wood, smoke, and hot chest-

nuts. It was nice, all the same, to be at home. To pass the time
there were always games of "tables" (our form of backgammon)
and of chess, just like the grownups, like the men among whom
he would now live.

His body accustomed to exercise, every muscle developed, having stirred about and played till he had had his fill, pampered and
fussed over, not having had to share his lady's love with a younger
sibling of his sex, John of Maine, a happy little boy, attained the
age of seven. It was then that he prepared to leave the world of
women and mothers for that of barons, of warriors, in order to receive from it that virile stamp which was indispensable to him.

Now he had to give up the sweetness, the tenderness, the decep-
tive illusions of childhood, in which he believed his mother, his
queen, his goddess, his sweet and perfect lady, completely his, for
no one but him, and face the fact that things were not the way he
might have wished them to be. He had to enter the reality of a
world where he was no longer allowed everything he wanted, as in
the other world, without rules, from which he had come, rich in
his new energy. Was his energy intact? Who can say? It is not
enough to have been able to frolic about freely, until the age of
seven, with no tutors or other pedagogues to ruin your mind and
heart with their inane restrictions, when your mother was the one
posterity would call "Bad Queen Joan." A child is virgin wax. Did
his fragile soul feel, alongside the tenderness which was always
lavished on him, what a lack of balance prevailed in that parental
couple, where the woman led the man about? A woman, moreover, remarkable for her culture, her learning, exceptional at that
time for someone of her sex, for she read Latin and had already
begun collecting manuscripts. Later on, at court, she would offer
her royal protection to scholars, her commissions to authors.
Works would be dedicated to her. But nonetheless she remained,
despite this taste for things of the mind, a disturbing woman, odd,
crotchety, later on displaying an insurmountable flair for hating,
an obligation to wreak vengeance which obsessed her, and which
she did not hesitate to pursue to the bitter end. Not at this time,
however, while she was still only the Countess of Maine; she was
too young. But with the passage of time she would reach the age
when people prefer power to love, and approach the omnipotence
her royal spouse would procure for her; then she would give free

rein to her occasionally deadly whims. "Whomever she brailed up in her hatred," Froissart would write of her, "died without pity." She carried all that inside her at the same time she carried John. As she watched him grow up she felt, after six years of marriage, an unalterable despair before the recognized nonentity of the man who made up her entire universe, a weak man, who would let her lead him by the nose when she had wished him to do the leading, herself to be led. Perhaps that was the source of the child's rages, for she often saw him throw a tantrum over nothing. He must have guessed that she was lying to him, have felt that she was luring him on, when she seemed to offer him the very face of happiness. And within him, without anyone's having wished it, in the most secret part of his being, a fault.

The world of women was quite a good one, but that was yesterday. The world of men awaited him. It fascinated him. It was a world of strength, swiftness, adroitness, efficiency, power. Over the nature which surrounded him, over the animal and plant kingdoms, over the forests, those mysterious and terrifying storehouses of life teeming with game whose flesh and fur must be taken—gray northern squirrels, sables, otters, foxes, wolves, stags and boars, bears sometimes—over them all man was master. And he, the offspring of man, would be master of it all tomorrow. He was able to catch his prey, and he did. For a warrior, does there exist a greater pleasure?

Hunting was the lord's pastime; also his store of wealth. Young John would therefore learn his craft: falconry and venery. He already had his hounds, his sparrow hawks, equipment proportioned to his size such as his scaled-down bows and arrows, and a hunting master. He would learn the rudiments quickly: letting the falcon fly, calling it, attaching it to the perch, belling its left foot, holding it, climbing into the saddle with it in his fist, feeding it. He wasn't allowed to forget that you hunt birds with decoys, with falcons, with bows and arrows, but you hunt hares and stags with greyhounds, and wild boars with spears. He was taken out into the field to recognize the game by its trace: were these, on this damp earth, this fine grass, the marks of the stag or the boar? Who had passed by here? And what were the names of the different species which haunted these woods? He was taught to hold the horn a cer-

tain way if he wanted to blow it full blast, and to hold his knife
another way to carve the beast well and give the entrails to the
hounds. Tomorrow's hunt would be with birds. The ladies would
be there, as usual, sitting on their hackneys, one hand covered
with a red leather glove, the perch where the falcon was set. The
child would come along.

It was September, with its brief, cool mornings, damp grass,
brisk light, the final glories of opulent foliage. The fruit rows and
the apple trees were heavy, the figs ripe, the poplars laden with
gold. At the hollow sound of hoofs in the clay, the forest grew
quiet; on the gray pool the crane and mallard hid among the
reeds, the heron took flight, the lapwings scattered into the air.
Too late. Already the falcons were flapping their wings, taking
flight, spotting their prey and pouncing on it, fixing it to the
ground, sinking their claws into its flesh, till their master came forward and took them off it, and they resumed their places on the
gloved fists. Woodcocks and teals, partridges and pheasants,
quails and thrushes were gathered up. There was talk of migrating
flocks of ringdoves during the next fortnight. They were heading
toward Spain and Africa. . . . The hunt had been good. They
would set off again shortly, with the hounds this time, and without
the ladies. What was needed, for the table and the winter, was
venison in abundance, which would be smoked and salted in the
cellars. John would spend two thirds of his time in the woods.
Winter left him with more leisure for arms, his traditional profession (noblemen were made for war), as well as for jousting. He
already knew pretty well how to ride, but not how to fight. He had
therefore to learn "skirmishing," as fencing was called, with the
sword, the lance, the truncheon. John applied himself to the art
and grew passionate about it. In turn he would be Roland, Eric or
Lancelot, Gawain and Percival, riding toward Camelot where
King Arthur held his court. By day he would break lances, gallop,
jump, and caracole; at night, in his sleep, he would do it all again,
his body tired but relaxed.

How much time could well be left for the tutor then engaged to
enrich the young Count's intellect? To tell the truth, the task was
hardly overwhelming. The first thing he taught the boy was to read
and write. Stylus in hand, John played at tracing his first letters on
wax tablets prior to trying his hand at pen on parchment. Soon he

would be able to read the bulky manuscripts in Gothic script in his parents' library by himself, following the exploits of his heroes among the illuminated capitals and the arabesques in the margins.

The course of study his mind was supposed to absorb over a period of eight years would not overwhelm it. His imagination found much to stimulate it there. The words bestowed on him in the course of his tutoring would, moreover, open doors for him. His soul prepared for departures, for journeys, for migrations constantly begun anew, within the reassuring limits of a closed cosmos. The universe was composed of sixteen concentric circles, taught the *Mirror of the World*. The earth constituted its center, and this earth was girded with the water of the oceans, capped everywhere with air and ether. Fire was concealed in the bowels of the earth. So much for the four elements. And on this flat, motionless earth, fixed in his place, stood man, in his dependency and frailty, and he, John, son of a potentate here below. Under his feet lay hell, into which he would fall if he were not watchful, but his eyes could make out heaven above him, toward which all the vague and poignant yearnings of his soul were turned. He would yearn for paradise and for the heavenly Jerusalem, the city with a thousand towers and twelve gates. When his hour had come, he would enter it by the gate of the Bull, among those of his sign. Far above, very far among the spaces from which he had perhaps come, radiant like the dawn, rustling with flights of angels, beyond the seven circles of stars which would influence him without, however, depriving him of free will, past the firmament and the ninth heaven, beyond the heaven of crystal, stood the abode of the Absolute: God sat enthroned in His empire, surrounded by angelic hierarchies. The child could name all nine of them in order— Angels, Archangels, Principalities, Powers, Cherubim, Virtues, Dominions, Thrones, Seraphim—reassuring and terrible images of peace and omnipotence, in the awful flight of eternity. Simply to evoke them, adorned with the gold nimbuses and the sparkling white wings, his heart would swoon with anguish and joy.

Thus the celestial empire hermetically sealed the universe within its spherical rampart. Resembling children's toys, the nesting eggs of the present day, the circles nested there, one inside another, from the smallest to the largest. What one played there was the game of Good and Evil, or of Life and Death, which came to

WISE AND FOOLISH KINGS

the same thing. As for this enormous globe, if you thought too much about it you might become afraid of seeing it collapse, both it and what it contained, like a gigantic kaleidoscope that someone had shaken too hard—but who or what? It was impossible to say whether the great globe reposed in the air, on the soft ground of an immense sward, or whether it lay afloat, borne on the dark and boundless waters of the ocean of the ages. To tell the truth, no one had yet dreamed of formulating such a question—a rather unsettling one, we have to admit.

The young Count proved less enthusiastic about learning a little Latin—a serviceable language, the knowledge of which was indispensable to him—and a little of history and romances. But navigators' guidebooks to the various ports, with their fish huge as islands, would set him to dreaming.

The curiosities in the universe enchanted him, and his tutor proved inexhaustible on the subject. Did he know that the men of Occiant Deserta wore leather harder than any iron, and went into battle without armor; that those of Albania were born with white hair; that those of Bocident lived on sweetmeats and pimentos, and bathed at regular intervals in the waters of youth, which kept them forever in their prime? The people of Bucion had horns in their foreheads; in Buriden, the people barked like dogs; the Macrobes of the Indies lived forever, were twelve cubits tall and spent their time fighting with griffons while the pygmies fought with cranes. You might meet horrible monsters there: one-legged men who broke all speed records as they hopped along on their single legs; poor headless creatures, who carried an eye upon each shoulder, and their noses and mouths on their chests. One set of monsters for another: the race of Gog and Magog in the Caspian foothills lived on human flesh.

As for the lands which never saw either sunlight or moonlight, there were many of these. Other lands, such as that of the pagan Charnuble, knew nothing of rain or dew; there the stones turned black, and no grain grew. The mares of Cappadocia were impregnated by the wind. The terrestrial paradise did not perish under the thunderbolts of divine displeasure, but still existed, a lost oasis in the sandy desert, situated between Europe and Africa.

Naked and standing on either side of the Tree of Knowledge around which the Seducer had coiled himself, Adam and Eve were waiting until their progeny had paid the price of the Fall. No one entered this enchanted spot, this tarnished Eden, protected by desert solitudes and also by walls of fire which reached the heavens. To the south of Africa, the ocean boiled and smoked like the cauldrons of hell. . . .

It never entered the mind of John of Valois to cast the slightest doubt on the reality of what he had just heard. In the company of his tutor, he continued his survey. From the countries they passed to the cities. In the Middle Ages they were three in number: Paris, which he knew already from having spent time there with his father, on visits with his cousins of the ruling house of France, or with his father's father at Villers-Cotterêts in the Aisne; Rome, the papal city; and above all Constantinople, the magnificent. And his master, who had heard the reports of travelers and poets, would comment: "In the palaces all the furnishings are of gold, and the walls are covered with paintings which depict all the beasts of the earth and the birds of the sky." Nor were the surroundings any less splendid: "Everywhere there are beautiful orchards, planted with pine and laurel; roses bloom there; twenty thousand knights are seated there, decked out in white silk and carrying falcons on their fists, with three thousand virgins of Constantinople adorned in gold-embroidered dresses, dazzling the land with their beauty."

On his return from his exercise, servants would plunge the boy, dusty and drenched with sweat, into a tub of hot water. Reclining, relaxed, his skin clean, nestled between two cushions in front of the hearth with its great chimneys, John would prepare himself for the journeys, from which every evening he would return with his fancy sated, toward the lands of the Orient, which resembled neither Le Mans nor the Sarthe—Bithynia, Cappadocia, strewn with gold and pearls, crossed by vast gray rivers, vaster by far than the Loire, the Tigris, the Euphrates, the Orontes, the rivers of paradise. . . .

THE HAPPY LIFE

Two years of this calm, orderly, well-occupied life went by, punctuated only by the rhythm of the seasons, broken only by holidays and minor events. The Count of Valois was away more

often, summoned to Paris by his prince. Charles IV had made him
his friend, sought his advice freely. As for the boy left behind,
John, he was counting the days, when suddenly the news broke
that his father was king. Between what had been and what had to
be there was no longer a common measure. Things changed rapidly. The charms of yesterday were forgotten, the pace of life
quickened, its dimensions changed. Le Mans was exchanged for
Paris, the forests of the Maine for those of Ile-de-France, Gué de
Mauny for the royal lodgings at Nesles, the Louvre, or Vincennes.
John had a palace of his own, with his own liveried servants, his
huntsmen, his falconers, his horses and hounds. The children of
the highest nobility in the kingdom made up his entourage, and he
directed them at his will. But most of all Count Philip had become
the first man in the kingdom, his sacred majesty, the Lord's
anointed. Like a priest, he took the sacrament in both kinds; over
his subjects he held the right of life and death.

In the eyes of a young son, a father seems to wield a kind of
omnipotence. But as soon as the mists of childhood clear, the adolescent realizes his mistake and imputes it to the one to whom he
owes his life, then judges him, sometimes pardoning him. But not
John. He knew nothing of these torments, these ordeals, salutary
for all that, through which a man's heart is ripened. He did not
have to blame his father for some imagined loss of power, for the
reality was that Philip had all power. Never had his father appeared greater, more majestic, to him than the day of the coronation, dressed in the attributes of his royal function, acclaimed by
the dozen peers of the realm, still haloed by the blessing of the
first prelate of France, the Archbishop of Reims: "Let him live in
eternity." An idea crossed John's mind fleetingly, burning, that a
day would come when he in his turn, dressed in the same tokens
of office, would come forward in the same nave, with the same
hurrahs. No sooner did he realize the price one paid for such a reality than he suddenly felt dreadfully guilty. Banishing this vision,
he gave himself over, body and soul, to the celebrations, which
had lasted for five days as we recall.

Oh, what a life he led for twelve years, what a childhood and
what a young manhood, until the year 1346, when everything was
spoiled. There were jousts and tourneys, hunts and merrymaking,
the most sparkling company, the most sumptuous raiment, illumi-

nated books, jewels, prized objects. Nothing was too beautiful for the heir to the throne, still the only one of his sex, whom his father cherished tenderly. The adolescent with his simple heart found a happiness in being.

John of France had just received his knighthood, a red-letter day. Another great event: on July 28, 1332, when he was only thirteen, he was married to the most charming princess of Luxemburg, Bonne, his elder by three years, who was descended like himself from the kings of Hungary—she through the Habsburgs, he through his grandmother, the Princess of Sicily. His father-in-law, John of Luxemburg, then King of Bohemia, spent most of his time at the court of France.

King Philip rejoiced at this marriage which united his only son with the daughter of his best friend. He created considerable domains for them by adding the duchy of Normandy to Maine and Anjou. He hoped that this union would be more fertile than his own had been. For the moment he was hardly concerned about whether or not the young Duchess was sterile, for she was barely of nubile age. Soon enough her spouse would do his duty with her, and we have got to believe that he loved her well, for in a dozen years of married life she was to bear him ten children, no less, and eight of them lived.

CLOUDS

At seventeen the Duke was on the point of death, and the future of the brand-new dynasty was in jeopardy. Was this the result of his conjugal precociousness? There is no way to tell. Stricken by erythematous swellings, his limbs covered with bumps that would appear and disappear daily, the young prince lay dry with fever. This had been going on for forty days. Despite attentive solicitations, despite the medical science of the best physicians of Paris, he lay with no strength left, every curtain drawn, in the silence and the half-darkness of his room. Footsteps slipping by on the flagstones and carpets, whispering voices, muffled noises, a window barely halfway open, the redolence of eucalyptus in the censers, rosaries told and retold, bead by bead, tapers lit before the triptychs. The Queen and the young Duchess did not stir from the bedside of the sick man. They lived in constant fear. The King came again and again for news. The fever was rising, the prince was delirious. He no longer recognized them. The rites were administered. The King had prayers said in every church in Paris. In his piety, he could not believe that the Most High would want to take from him what he held dearest. No, his son would not die. So the King took the road to the south—five hundred and sixty miles on horseback—he who never liked to leave the place he was installed in. Stopping at Avignon, he beseeched the highest ecclesiastical authority of this world, the Pope himself, to intercede in his place. Should that not be enough, he appealed to someone in a better position still, a saint of his family, St. Louis of Anjou, whose relics and tomb were in Marseille, where he went without stopping to rest. "Go, thy faith has saved thee." Heaven did not remain deaf. The fever broke and fell. Under the curtains of the canopied bed, the sick man raised himself, propped himself against the cushions which a light hand slid under him, a first, second, then a third one, of velvet or green serge. Day by day he recovered, sitting upright now, wetting his lips from the silver goblets in which he was offered whatever tempted him, milk sweetened with honey, broth, untoasted bread in his soup. He came back to life. His wife was there; she distracted him, kept him company, read him his favorite romances. Soon he was fit again for love, for tourneys, and for celebrations. The following year his first child was born, a son, Charles. Was it to honor Bonne's recovery from childbirth that the Duke appeared in a green fur-lined robe, hose of black Irish serge, under a cloak and doublet of various rich furs? He certainly made a fine impression.

All the same, despite the pomp and the brilliance, the euphoria of the outset of Philip's reign was fading fast. The King fiercely resented the difficulties of his burden. Seeking out the cause of his resentment, he found it in the fact that he had not been molded for it from childhood on. He reflected on how not to repeat in his son's situation and experience for which he was paying the price. And so he sent the young man into the field to learn the craft of kingship and to enter into contact with the realities of power. John did not prove awkward at the task.

By his obliging manner and his good grace he was able to influence the Dauphin of Viennois to bequeath Dauphiné to the

Crown. He quickly became popular in Languedoc, which he visited several times. But when he was sent to war, first in Hainaut
in 1340, then in Britanny the following year, despite his real valor
he gave no evidence of exceptional qualities. The siege of Aiguil-
lon, which he had to abandon pathetically in 1346, shows that he
was no great strategist. Crécy put him to the test as it did everyone, but the plague tried him more than anyone. It took from him
both his wife and his mother, within three months.

MOURNING

With Bonne's death the happy period of the prince's life came
to an end. He did not know this. What did he feel at the time, this
widower left with eight small children? We must believe that he
had appreciated the married state, since he felt incapable of doing
without a wife. Almost at once he got engaged to the very young
and pretty Blanche of Navarre whom his father (as we have seen)
hastened to take from him—without any kind of fuss, or so it appears. He soon remarried, a widow older than himself, Joan of
Boulogne; she had a son by her previous marriage, Philippe du
Rouvre. What was going on? Why such marriage arrangements,
why such haste? It was a matter of inheritance, for political reasons assuredly, since the duchy of Burgundy was involved. A marriage of reason, then, which was neither fertile nor, probably,
very happy.

The next year King Philip died, leaving his place to John, then
a man of thirty-one.

PORTRAIT

We happen to know the contours of the face of this second representative of the new dynasty, for his is one of the first portraits
to have come down to us. Western civilization would dare at last, in
the second half of the fourteenth century (the work dates from
1359), to represent man in his uniqueness. The face is that of
John of Valois, surging out of the night of the ages, just as in and
for himself, in his very imperfection, his inseparable mixture of

good and bad qualities, a poor sinner and creature of God, we
have come to recognize him. Whether this was a victory over
heaven or simply a promotion of his dynasty, a stage in that destiny which higher wills than his own had allotted him, here in this
portrait we see him who up to that point had been destined for destruction and the dust of the tomb judged worthy of braving death
and time, and figuring equally with the saints and angels, with
Melchizedek and Our Lord and Our Lady, as a subject for
painters and sculptors. Thus, he does not appear in the pomp and
gold of his royal person, but as if stripped bare, in accord with
the law of creatures, simple, even austere, he who was that so
rarely; almost humble, for this is but the portrait of a man.

Against a background of flaking wood, brown-haired, brown-
eyed, his beard brown as well, there is the King. What else do we
see? A slightly elongated jaw, in which somehow the instincts are
predominant, and large cheeks, which serve to confirm the
straightness of the frontal plane; real sensitivity in the fine, long
nose; one note gladdens this somewhat severe harmony: the white
spot on his fur collar, which brightens the entire face, underscor-
ing the blue of his gown. We are far from the gilded grace of the
figures we encounter in the illuminated manuscripts.

SIMILARITIES

What strikes us the most about our new King is the extreme resemblance he bears to the preceding one. Between father and son
there are nothing but similarities. First off, in bodily structure:
both men were tall, broad, all muscle and vigor; take back what
you will from them, they were both fine athletes. There is a similarity in their aptitudes (not too noteworthy, alas!) and in their
tastes, which were good. Finally, there is a similarity in their way
of life and their approach to the craft of ruling; and the same gen-
tility as well, the same love of show and luxury, the same coveting
of pleasure. These two men could not have been closer.

Given such identical natures and lives, how would the son be
able to assert himself with respect to the father whose replica he
was and with whom he could only identify, although circumstances obviously helped? Not by denying his father, for he loved

him; rather, in doing more and better. Once on the throne, King John would go even further. And we shall soon see what he was capable of.

Openhandedness and generosity, gifts in money and in kind, presents, ornaments, jewelry, mounts and weaponry, these rained on his following. His charitable works kept pace. The coronation festivities surpassed in splendor all that had been done previously; the tiniest events of everyday life were celebrated dazzlingly. Never had the court gleamed more brightly than it did in the time following the plague; nor was the treasury ever more depleted, as we may well imagine.

And yet it was not mere extravagance. The father had loved the arts; the son lent them his patronage, emphasizing this inherited taste, extending his bounty and sponsorship not only to goldsmiths but to clerics, the men of letters, as well. Great literary undertakings were planned for the realm. John, informed, encouraged them. He commissioned Pierre Bersuire, one of the most prolific writers of the century and a friend of Petrarch's, to translate Livy and asked Master Jean de Sy to produce a Bible in French, with commentaries—even if he had to get the Jews to pay for them. He tried to attract Petrarch to his court. He employed two exceptional manuscript illuminators, John of Montmartre and Jean Pucelle.

PROWESS: THE KEY WORD

As for King Arthur's legend, if the father had been enchanted by it, the son became its most fervent follower. He scrupulously practiced the ancient code of chivalry and made it his second Decalogue: the true knight was pious, loyal, generous, courteous, valiant. He himself would be known for his courtesy, his affability, the personal qualities which were useful in his calling, and for his loyalty, his indisputable courage, to which he would owe his epithet, "the Good," which meant the brave. All of these were qualities not given necessarily, but acquired, out of taste for excelling, for prowess, which was his key word.

RAGES

Let us not forget that John II was the son of Joan of Burgundy. People say that mothers are occasionally redoubtable for the males they engender. Here such a hypothesis is confirmed. John's portrait thus takes on meaning, his features sharpen. If he was good, courteous, agreeable to deal with, he also proved absolute, extreme, in affection as in wrath. "King John was of a hot and sudden temper," writes Froissart, "easily influenced but hard to budge once he had made up his mind about something." What this means in modern-day idiom is that he was violent, impulsive, credulous, and stubborn. In certain respects the King had remained an overgrown child, a state which is hard to reconcile with the burdens of ruling a kingdom. Indeed, the burdens weighed on him so heavily that he found himself a different man as a result.

The King's violence was no mere myth. It could plunge him to the depths of hysteria, yet he carried it through with a pitiless logic. If he felt punishment was called for, it would be punishment commensurate with his own rage, and none other than death; nor would death be swift, effective, discreet, but spectacular rather. If anger overwhelmed him, possessed him, drove him wild, deprived him of his free will, confronted him with his own impotence, then death would be long, bloody—a kind of celebration, which called for a ceremony and a public.

The King did not hold himself responsible for such deeds. Acts of justice were imposed on him; his hand had been forced; more— he had been attacked. If the fate of his kingdom, the good of his subjects, called for an act of authority, he would not shirk his duty, and his conscience would be clear.

He knew what anger was, for on rare occasions he had seen his father abandon himself to it. He learned what cruelty was when Philip, at the darkest moment in his reign, had recourse to it for political reasons. And he knew what fear was: not simple fear but panic, a disorder of the brain. He had been betrayed. The traitors were roaming loose; they were everywhere, the accomplices and allies of the invader, unless they were working for themselves alone. In the general interest he had to punish them, find guilty parties, make examples of them so that everyone would understand that they had to obey. His people called the results "the cruel acts of justice."

THE CRUEL ACTS OF JUSTICE

The first such act, as sudden as it was irremediable, occurred less than two months after the coronation, and inaugurated King John's reign. The High Constable of France, Raoul de Brienne, Count of Eu and of Guines, the King's personal friend, had recently returned from England, where he had spent four years in a gentlemen's prison. He was living at the King's palace as a friend and companion when the Provost of Paris presented himself at the Constable's apartment and, giving no other reason than the monarch's pleasure, arrested him and threw him in prison. This was on the twenty-sixth of November 1350. On the twenty-eighth Raoul de Brienne was beheaded. The noblest lords of the realm were assembled near the block: Pierre de Bourbon, the father-in-law of the Dauphin Charles; Count John I of Armagnac; Charles de la Cerda, the Count of Montfort, an uncle of the Queen; Lord John of Boulogne; Sir William Flotte, Lord of Revel, dead King Philip's chancellor; and some other knights. Against custom, the King had the corpse buried at the cemetery of the Augustins in Paris, out of respect for the friends of the condemned man.

The official chronicles give the reason for the execution in a terse comment: "very great and evil treason." The kind of treason would not be revealed, but the guilty man was said to have confessed his treasons to the Duke of Athens, Walter de Brienne, and to several other persons of his family. They kept their silence. At court, people were stupefied, but they kept quiet and waited. Questions arose with respect to the second Valois king, whose reputation had not yet been made. The man was courteous, as was well known, but what to think of such behavior? What omens for the future were there in it? When the courtiers did break silence, they did so prudently, whispering, and with reason: that sudden execution had all the earmarks of a settling of old scores. It probably was. Raoul de Brienne was said to have been the lover of Bonne, then Duchess of Normandy. The King had found some letters which his wife's rapid death had prevented her from destroying.

It is known that in the court of France the honor of princesses was taken seriously: a question of principle as well as of descent. It was all right for the King's bastards to be raised in their mothers' homes at their father's expense; but not the Queen's. The Lord's anointed had to be of the blood, or else a sacrilege had been committed. As soon as the story about Raoul de Brienne and the King's wife got out, it was forgotten. Silence was prudently maintained, and people could breathe again. No one felt affected by this affair any more because—for the moment—politics was not involved, but people discussed it in secret. They grew sad, remembered the High Constable, evoked his qualities—so noble a comrade, so courteous, engaging, and charming a man, a valiant knight, handsome above all. They remembered his seductive quality, his bearing, his manners; they argued, they reflected—the Duchess had never caused any gossip about herself; besides, she had always been pregnant. And even if she had stooped to such follies, the affair would have been over years ago, prior to the time the Constable was captured by the English at Caen in 1346, and the Duchess had died since, so that it was a matter of ancient history. . . . People grew uneasy. What were these letters no one had seen, these confessions no one had heard? The procedure seemed humiliating both for its victim and for those of his class. The King had not shown maturity in this misfortune. It would have been better to keep the matter quiet, at the risk of sending the guilty man back in disgrace to live in his own lands. At the risk of turning a false friend into an open enemy, a powerful traitor . . . Surely it was fear which had gripped the King.

And besides, John was no longer the same. He had changed. Was it those letters? Then a few lines had reduced fifteen years of mutual joys, of a brilliant shared life, to ashes. The happy moments of their youth, all the children she had given him—nothing counted any more. Death had undone her body, and some words traced on a page had sufficed to banish her image. The past no longer existed. A woman had deceived the King, the only woman whom he had been able to love without doubts, and through her all women. Women disappeared from his life. The maternal image held the field. Since his own mother was dead, he replaced her with a second spouse who mothered him. He probably asked nothing more of her, while waiting to seek out the company of aged widows or dowager queens, as he would later do in London. From then on friendship would take the place of love for him, or rather friendship with people of his own sex. The other sex was faulty.

And the King poured his favors on one of his remote cousins, Charles of Spain, the Infante de la Cerda, a great-grandson of St. Louis like John himself. The King made Charles Count of Angoulême and High Constable of France (the title was vacant), and arranged a most prominent and wealthy marriage for him with the daughter of a peer of France, the Duke of Brittany, Charles of Blois. The two men were together, always—jousting, banqueting, and hunting. For two years they were inseparable.

John II was extreme, as we know, both in his fury and in his friendship. Perhaps there is more here than meets the eye, but no hard evidence allows us to say anything of the kind. All the same, his friendship would prove fatal to the object of his attentions, as we shall see.

THE CHILDREN OF THE HOUSE OF NAVARRE

When he made a gift of the county of Angoulême to his favorite, Charles, the King had deprived the family of Navarre, to whom the land belonged. Now the house of Navarre was a powerful one, as much for its lands as for its prerogatives, and one to be reckoned with. With their possessions in Normandy—the counties of Mortain and Evreux, the latter a peerage, and Nonancourt and Longueville—with their strongholds in the Seine Valley overlooking Paris, and in the Eure Valley as well, the house of Navarre could constitute, if necessary, a formidable threat to the sovereign, particularly when rights to his crown were added to these powerful territorial bases. The Navarres were descended from St. Louis just like the Valois.

Joan, the dead Queen of Navarre, had been born into the royal house of France, for she was the daughter of Louis X and of Margaret of Burgundy. She had accepted the forfeiture of her claim to the throne for reasons of her sex, and also of a possible ambiguity associated with her descent. Her sons, however, had not accepted it. Still, the Valois had been careful with them up to then. They treated the sons with respect, offered them the most splendid gifts and made allies of them by marriage. Two dowager queens of France, Joan of Evreux and Blanche of Navarre, had been born Navarre and were living at court; the former was the widow of the last Capetian, Charles IV, and the latter the King's former fiancée, who had since become his mother-in-law. John II had installed Blanche's brothers, his cousins Charles, Philip, and Louis, in his palace, for they had been orphaned while quite young, and he treated them with rare generosity. He made the eldest, Charles, head of the family and entrusted him with important responsibilities, making him, despite his nineteen years, the King's deputy in Languedoc—a domain he held dear. He also gave Charles his own daughter in marriage, though it is true that she was only eight.

But the sovereign was unable to fathom the duplicity concealed beneath his protégé's affable exterior, or to see the limitless ambition and dissatisfaction that lay beneath. Frustrated in his hopes for the throne, which he considered ought to have been his, frustrated as well in his wife's dowry, the payment of which he had not succeeded in getting, and frustrated in the lands which he claimed, Charles of Navarre lived in perpetual discontent. Could he stand by idly while the very county which had been his mother's was taken back for the benefit of the King's favorite? One did not need to be a great scholar to foresee that such a measure was going to stir up a passionate reaction. Already the Infante had received a warning to "guard himself well against the children of the house of Navarre." On January 8, 1354, at daybreak, he was found assassinated in an inn in Laigle where he had spent the night. Philip of Navarre and some Norman lords, the Harcourts among them, had done the job. As the chronicle comments: "So distressingly, shamefully, and abominably did they serve him, that they made eighty wounds in his body." Charles himself awaited the outcome of the deed on the outskirts of the town, before laying claim to its authorship and publicly boasting of his fine deed in the cities, at the university, and in the councils of the King and the Pope. Such a justification strongly resembled a declaration of war.

The King could expect the worst from his young cousin. Charles was intelligent, bold, crafty, and totally unprincipled.

With a hand for politics and a gift of gab, a genius for intrigue and great powers of seduction—the polar opposite, one must say, of his royal relative—he was a dangerous man. Shocked as he was by the outrage, John seemed not yet to have realized what danger threatened him personally. He gave thought only to his grief. He remained, the chronicles tell us, four whole days without speaking a single word, then swore "a great oath that never would there be room for joy in his heart until he had avenged himself for this deed"—if he could. For ever since the assassination his handsome cousin had been leading him a dance, while waving before his eyes the bugbear of the English pretender, the fear of whom, he knew, constituted for the poor prince the beginning of prudence. Charles played on this fear and made marvelous use of it, obtaining, thanks to such a stratagem, the most astonishing concessions, monies, amnesty, lands, the many gifts which established his power.

For two whole years the King allowed himself to be manipulated. But he did not forget his desire for vengeance. It burst like thunder. We shall let Froissart tell the story.

VENGEANCE

"At that time [John's] eldest son Charles was residing in Normandy, of which he was Duke. He was residing in the castle of Rouen. He entertained the King of Navarre and the Count of Harcourt as often as possible, out of love and because they were neighbors. . . . One day he sent his knights to invite them to come dine with him at the castle of Rouen. The King of Navarre and the Count of Harcourt . . . accepted with good heart. . . . They came to Rouen and went by way of the fields into the castle, where they were received with great joy.

"King John, who was quite well informed of this fact and knew the very hour in which the King of Navarre and the Count of Harcourt would be in Rouen to dine with his son, on Saturday, set out on Friday with a small retinue. He rode the entire day and arrived on the evening before Palm Sunday. He entered the castle of Rouen while the lords were sitting at the table. He climbed the steps to the hall, with Lord Arnoult d'Audrehem ahead of him, who drew his sword and said: 'Let no man stir whatever he may see, if he does not wish to die by this sword.'

"You must know that the Duke of Normandy, the King of Navarre, the Count of Harcourt, and the rest of the group sitting around the table were quite amazed and dumfounded when they saw the King of France enter the hall in such a manner. Well would they have wished to be elsewhere. King John came up to the table where they were sitting. They all stood up before him with the idea of making their bows, but he had no desire to receive them. He moved forward toward the table, flung his arm on the King of Navarre, seized the edge of his cloak, and drew him fiercely against himself, saying: 'Come now, traitor, you are not worthy of sitting at my son's table. Upon my father's soul, I will never think of eating or drinking, so long as you are alive.'

"A squire named Colinet de Bléville was there, who sliced the King of Navarre's meat. Enraged to see his master mistreated like that, he drew his cutlass and brought it toward the King of France's chest, saying he would kill him. At this thrust, the King let the King of Navarre go and said to his sergeants: 'Seize this boy for me, and his master as well.'

"Mace-bearers and men-at-arms bounded forward, laid their hands on the King of Navarre and his squire, and said: 'You must leave this place when the King wishes.' The King of Navarre, deeply humiliated, said to the King of France: 'My lord, for God's pity, who has so ill informed you against me? As God is my help, I never did, save Your Grace, nor thought any treason against you or against my lord your son. For God's sake, please listen to reason. If there is any man in this world who wishes to accuse me, I shall purge myself of his charge by the order of your peers. . . . It is true that I had Charles of Spain killed—he was my adversary —but I have made my peace and done penance for it.'

" 'Go on, traitor, go on,' answered the King of France, 'by my lord St. Denis, first get out of my clutches, and then try your preaching and lying falsehoods!'

"Then they led the King of Navarre into another room, dragging him quite shamefully. . . . Whatever the Duke of Normandy could say, on his knees with his hands clasped before the King his father, the latter had no intention of changing his mind or calming himself. The Duke, who was only a boy at the time, said: 'Ah, my lord, for God's sake, you are dishonoring me: what will they say about me? I invited the King and his barons to dine with me and you treat them this way. People will say I've betrayed them. Yet I never saw in them anything but goodness and courtesy.'

"At these words, the King stepped forward, took a sergeant's mace, and went after the Count of Harcourt. He dealt him a great thump between his shoulders and said: 'Forward now, proud traitor, off you go to prison. . . . By my father's soul, you will know how to sing like a bird when you escape me, your rank offenses and treasons will soon be uncovered.'

"Excuses could neither be offered nor received, for the King was so incensed with wrath that he would hear nothing. On his orders Sir Jean de Guérarville and another knight called Sir Maubué were also seized and thrown most shamefully into prison.

"The Duke of Normandy and all the other men were sorely troubled by these things. . . . But none dared to step forward and say to the King: 'Sire, you have done ill to treat these brave men this way. . . .' And because the King wanted their deaths . . . but feared the population of Rouen, he called in the chief of his guards, and told him: 'Dispose of this one and that one for us.' The Count of Harcourt, Sir Jean de Guérarville, Sir Maubué, and Colinet de Bléville were dragged outside the castle of Rouen, led off to the fields, and beheaded, without the King allowing them to confess their sins, except for the squire . . . who had drawn his cutlass on him. The King of France said that traitors should have no confession. . . .

"The King of Navarre remained in prison and King John did not do everything he had planned. . . . Some members of his Council curtailed his wrath a little. But he certainly intended to keep Charles of Navarre in prison so long as he should live. . . .

"The King of Navarre was brought to Paris by a swarm of armed guards and sergeants, and put in the castle of the Louvre where he was subjected to fearsome threats: every day and every night, five or six times, he was given to understand that he would be put to death, that his head would be cut off, that he would be tossed in a bag into the Seine. He had to hear it all out and take it willingly, for he could not, in that place, play the master. He spoke so well and so sweetly to his guards, that those who so abused him on the order of the King of France, had great pity for him.

"At this time he was transferred, brought to Cambrésis, and put in the fortress of Crèvecoeur, under a heavy guard. . . . The King of France began to forget about him, but his brothers did not forget him. . . ."

POITIERS

In the month of July 1356 Edward, Prince of Wales, known as the Black Prince, left Bordeaux with a small troop of less than seven thousand men for a plundering expedition like the one he had led most profitably the summer before, in the valley of the Garonne. By way of Périgord, Limousin, Berry, and Touraine, he headed toward the Loire and was spending the night of September 7 in Amboise when some news reached him which caused him to retrace his steps in the greatest haste. The King of France was approaching at the head of a powerful army. It took the English prince two days and five different fords to cross the river; then, regrouping his troops, he descended toward the south, probably heading for Guienne. Fearing the worst but obliged to bar the way to John (or at least make the attempt to do so), he delayed as long as he could an encounter which the inequality of available soldiers would turn into a slaughter. Reluctantly he resigned himself to a meeting on the nineteenth and managed to establish himself in a very strong position a few miles to the southeast of Poitiers. He had no idea he would return to Bordeaux crowned with the victor's laurels.

The name of the second Valois king is linked with the disaster of Poitiers, as much for the fearlessness he showed in the action as for the total lack of military sense which characterized him. It must not be imagined that this spectacular defeat was the sad result of an act of betrayal or of inferiority in numbers. When an army of twenty thousand men gets torn to pieces on its own territory by an enemy force one third its size, on its way back from an expedition of plunder with its knees sagging under the weight of the loot, that implies a notorious deficiency on the part of its leader. All the same, one may conclude that John owed his nickname to the heroic conduct to which we shall refer, which came as the crowning achievement of an already well established reputation.

Should we be surprised to find physical courage in this violent, uneasy man? The fear of what might be, the anxieties of the heart, are as we know the worst ones. Take a gallant king in time of war and you have victory assured, think the simple-minded. But courage is a matter of honor, not of government, and the king's honor resides in his effectiveness, a notion with which John never overly concerned himself. He did not know either that fine and lovely sentiments are made for times of peace, for your confessor, your friends, or your lady, that the very physical courage which was his crowning glory would be worse for him than a fault—a disgrace—and would earn him dishonor, prison, albeit a gentlemen's prison. In John's mind, dishonor would have been to flee on his white charger as swiftly as possible from the plateau of Maupertuis, on a certain September morning, to turn around and show his backside to his fine cousin the Black Prince, as his son Charles had done, it is said, on his orders. To surrender to your conqueror, to recognize as a good sport the superiority of your adversary, such things do happen in the life of a knight. But not when you are King of France. John the Good had always confused being a great lord with being a monarch, had never drawn the essential distinction between the two estates. But things ripen in their own time, situations come to a resolution without the interested party's really having to make any decisions. For John, the choice was brought about without his knowing it, on its own, on the plateau of Maupertuis, when the two armies commanded by his eldest son and by his brother, the Duke of Orléans, were put to rout, while he, the King, at the head of the third and last army which he personally commanded, did not feel he had the right to flee (as his father, Philip VI, had done—and rightly so—at the Battle of Crécy). We are forced to conclude that under the circumstances loyalty to an outdated ideal played less of a role than the unavowed denial of a harsh reality.

On September 19, 1356, under a hot sun already high in an open sky, amid yellowing grasses, the tendrils and stems of vineyards, and clusters of grapes, with noon already past, more than three thousand men lay dying on the plateau of Maupertuis where the fighting had been going on since dawn. Barons, princes, and knights were abandoning the field, upright on their heavy mounts, imprisoned in their tall saddles as in the tops of towers: the French had gone to war decked out as if for love, confusing warfare with jousting, when ladies would sit in attendance at the challenge. The corpses were heavy with cloth of gold and with rings, and the dead grew stiff in their iron prisons under mother-of-pearl and plumes. The spoils lay about in heaps. The opened coffers spilled out their contents by armfuls: etched dining vessels, precious effects, jewels, weapons, and ornaments. Still the plundering and killing went on. Riderless horses wandered over the high fields, whinnying here and there. Light-footed English archers pursued some scattered groups of Frenchmen, daggermen finished off the wounded.

In a little clearing, surrounded by quarries and vineyards, the King of France and his last loyal men were cornered, fighting on, hand to hand. John still kept his hopes up. Toward him huge crowds of Englishmen and Gascons flowed endlessly, attracted by so fair a prize. He and his attendants fought on, five against one in a bitter fray, bristling with lances and pikes and hammers; the mass of arms was a wonder to behold. The knights could barely find room to brandish their outsized two-handed swords. The enemy was easier to cut down with a dagger planted in the chinks of his armor.

At the heart of this fiery furnace—prize and prey—stood the King, covered with sweat and blood, resisting, repulsing, attacking, and killing without respite. He was a formidable athlete whose strength increased tenfold in danger. He was unafraid. His son Philip, whom in due time he ordered to withdraw from the combat, came back despite his order and no longer left his side. "Father, look out on the right. Father, look out on the left." Philip was barely fourteen years old. The enemy foot soldiers were trying to recognize the King, the better to take him prisoner. They made out the lilies of his armor. A final wave of assailants confronted King John with certain death. A human tide, a wave of armor, men, and lances, converged on him. The King gave up the struggle. Resigned, he sought out a familiar face. "To whom shall I surrender? Where is my cousin, the Prince of Wales?"

"Sire, he is not here," replied a nearby voice. "But surrender to me, and I will take you to him." The man who spoke these words was powerful in stature. By strength of arms and body he had forced his way through to the King. "Who are you?" asked the latter. "Sire, I am Denis de Mortbecque, a knight from Artois, but I serve the King of England because I have been exiled from the kingdom of France."

"I surrender to you," said the King, while giving him his right glove. But the man could not take such a prisoner. Snatched at by a thousand hands, by a thousand longing looks, John and his youngest son were in much greater danger than when they had been at the heart of the battle. The crowd exploded, clamoring, "I took him! I took him!"

"Gentlemen, gentlemen," John protested, "take me in a courtly way, and my son with me, to my cousin the prince, and stop this brawling over my capture. I am a great enough lord to make each one of you rich." They could barely hear him. He was unlikely to have gone on breathing, but for two English barons who recognized him and, pushing their horses through the crowd, dispersed it. Then they sprang to the ground, bowed low before him, and escorted him to the Prince of Wales, who received him with honor.

The King's young sons, the Duke of Normandy, the Counts of Poitiers and Touraine, escorted by eight hundred lances, reached Chauvigny, weary in body and with their heads still full of screams and slaughter. They were quite frail to face what awaited them, which was no gentlemen's prison but the harsh wages of combat.

The English were still dumfounded by such a capture. A King of France as a prisoner was something unheard of, except for St. Louis, fallen for a pious reason into the hands of the Moors of Tunis in the course of the last crusade. Precedents were lacking to know what course of conduct to follow. How to behave toward his royal majesty in so pitiful a situation? With respect, for a king is a king; with courtesy, natural between honorable people; with prudence and vigilance above all, so that such a prize should not escape. For at that time and in countries like England and France, where courtesy prevailed—unlike Germany, which mistreated gentlemen fallen into enemy hands, brutalized them, clapped them in irons to obtain a larger ransom—a captive was honored but above all held for ransom. As for the money, King Edward could be trusted to demand what was suitable, a huge sum.

The Prince of Wales organized for the King of France a reception worthy of his rank. That evening, by the glimmering torchlight of the prince's tents, attendants offered wines and meat to the captive monarch. The prince served his guest himself, refusing to take his place at the King's table, and kneeling down before John to address these words to him: "Dear sire, do not make such a poor meal . . . for surely my royal father will show you all the honor and friendship in his power, and will reach so reasonable an understanding with you that you and he shall always remain good friends. . . . It is my view that you have good reason to be cheerful, although the struggle did not turn out as you willed it, for today you have won on the field the highest renown for prowess."

The very next day they all took the road toward Bordeaux. The pack animals staggered under the weight of their booty. Victors and vanquished walked along arm in arm, but with eyes on the lookout, watching every wall, every battlement, every turn in the road. Would no vassal take the risk of coming to the aid of his suzerain? No one did.

Bordeaux was waiting for the captive King. Winter there would be a festival, an escape more profound than the one he had refused on that fateful September day. The King may have been a captive, that was the hard reality; but, in another sense, he had regained his freedom. For he, who was weary with six years of reigning, had become a prisoner just in the nick of time, and his prison was well worth a kingdom. It would prove to be the best of escapes, for he wanted nothing more to do with power. How else could he have made this unmentionable and (to be sure) unmentioned desire a reality, had it not been for Poitiers? By means of what strikes us as the cruelest adversity which can befall a king, John II was restored to himself.

John of Valois, yielding his place under force and constraint, would disappear from the stage of France. His reign had lasted for only six years. Here was a country without a king, abandoned to lust, greed, hatred, and misery, destined for the worst, a ship of fools. At its helm was a very young man, lacking in both authority and power, delegated to rule by his sovereign, who sanctioned him before the masses.

For this boy, there would be abysses opening beneath his feet, unimaginable misfortunes to come. There would be no help from anywhere or anyone. His seaworthy ocean vessel was now nothing more than a miserable drifting rowboat, still afloat but bobbing and drifting like a cork, taking advantage of the slightest breeze, the slightest current to move closer to the mainstream while waiting for the strong, favorable, steady winds that would lead it back to port.

CHAPTER IV

Charles the Dauphin
(*1338–64*)

King John's first son was born when John was still Duke of Normandy, on January 21, 1338, St. Agnes' Day, at Vincennes Woods. They named him Charles in memory of his great-grandfather, the Count of Valois, as well as for his godfathers, Charles d'Alençon, his paternal great-uncle, and Charles of Bohemia, his maternal uncle, who together held the baby over the baptismal fonts in the Church of St. Peter at Montreuil.

The young prince was not "born old," as the historian Michelet once described him, but rather sickly and weak, for he was the child of extremely young parents. His father was only eighteen when Charles was conceived, and barely recovered from the nearly fatal illness we have touched on. He was thus less robust than his younger brothers would be, more susceptible to childhood fevers and diseases. He grew, this royal child, fondled by the peasant wet nurses and pampered among the brocaded infants whose number increased regularly year after year in the royal nursery, eventually attaining a total of ten.

To that circle of brothers and sisters were added the offspring of the highest nobility of the court, who shared his games and his days, except for those hours when his tutors, some churchmen of the royal household, attended to his education, which, contrary to what many have believed, was not particularly rigorous.

But the place where he lived was far more educational than the lessons of his schoolmasters. It was an enticing spectacle to grow up in the palace of the King, his grandfather; what he saw every day and on every occasion enchanted him. There were none in that company but heroes and demigods of great strength, clad in invulnerable armor and decked out in holiday clothes. What child could have dreamed of such pleasure, such ease for his heart? In such enchanted places who or what could he have had to fear? Nothing could happen to him. Until the day when this impregnable universe tottered. The news of the disaster at Crécy filled the palace with shame and mourning. Death touched the young prince quite closely, with the loss of his grandfather, the King of Luxemburg, and his godfather, Charles d'Alençon. The all-powerful master of the house, his grandfather, had been defeated. Thus, though the boy was only eight, he understood graphically a hard truth whose application he would not be spared henceforth: the destiny of princes is composed of vicissitudes, and none but the strong are equal to it. "Of those to whom God has given much, much will be demanded," his chaplain commented as he read his Hours to the boy; this may happen again and again, thought the child, overcome with sadness and fear.

THE JOURNEY TO DAUPHINÉ

Time passes, pain lessens, and life goes on, and with it, at that carefree age, the pleasure of existing. Especially when one is able to taste the pleasure of travel, of new places. Charles accompanied his father to Dauphiné to reap the fruits of the prolonged negotiations which Philip, his grandfather, and especially his father, as Duke of Normandy, had conducted in such a masterly way. The Dauphin of Viennois, Humbert II, had renounced the world and bequeathed all his rights in Dauphiné to the eldest grandson of the King of France, who from that time on would take the title of "Dauphin." Against the promise of plenty of ringing gold *écus,* naturally. This was Charles's first confrontation with the art of statecraft; his role was merely that of an extra but all the same he had to play it. It must not have been easy for a boy of eleven to sit still all those hours, listening attentively to endless speeches, or to attend banquets which lasted interminably and to behave as is expected of a figure on whom all eyes are converging.

The following month his father returned to Paris, and Charles remained behind as lord of the province. He toured his newly acquired lands, and from town to town he received the homage of his vassals. It was there that death touched him once again, but this time to the quick. On September 11 his mother died of the Black Plague in the abbey of Maubuisson. Three months later his maternal grandmother succumbed to the same disease.

A boy of nearly twelve is old enough to be fully aware of what death means, even if distance had spared him its physical proximity. He had not seen the livid masks, the closed eyes, the bodies stiff beneath their winding sheets, which only yesterday had seemed warm, protective, imperishable in their grown-up omnipotence. Death, then, was silence, absence, a sudden intrusion of the irretrievable, glimpsed at an age which has trouble conceiving of the word "nevermore." Soon death would convey to him an image of those empty apartments, abandoned intact, where he would no longer have the heart to go, those objects which others would usurp. Could he still believe that everything can always be worked out for the best when you are the son of the King?

On certain evenings he was overcome with terror and haunted by terrible visions of those corpses, lying perfumed and polished under the marble stone, abandoned to the mysterious forces of destruction in the cold and the darkness. A sleep of metamorphosis, the voice of the Church whispered to him: *Vita mutatur, non tollitur* (Life is changed, but not taken away). That voice gave him reassurance. Death is a part of life. He accepted it as an unavoidable reality which must be faced, with the help of his already lively faith. God and his guardian angel were watching over him. He was not afraid.

Absence allayed his grief, as did all the respectful bustling of which he was the center, and which he liked enormously. He was no longer completely a child when he celebrated Christmas in Grenoble, but an adolescent to whom the precocious experiences of power and of death had brought maturity.

Moreover, during that year 1350 events occurred in such rapid

succession for the royal family that even the worst became
blurred. On January 11 his grandfather, Philip, remarried; on
February 9 his father did the same. On April 8 it was his turn to
take a wife. He married his cousin, Joan of Bourbon, at Tain. He
was a few weeks older than his bride, and between them their ages
added up to twenty-four years. At the end of August the Dauphin
buried his grandfather, King Philip. On September 26, draped in a
cloak of gold, he officiated as seneschal at the coronation of his
father as King John II of France, and was knighted. Here he was
once again among the haunts of his childhood, a year after he had
left them. The world had changed, it seemed, or at least the way
he looked at it had. His childhood was assuredly dead and gone,
and he would have to live in the present. But for him it was a fabulous present.

FOLLIES OF YOUTH

The Dauphin's place in the palace was second only to that of
the King. He had a household of his own, comprising at the very
least some twenty-four persons—four chamberlains, eight gentlemen of the bedchamber, two butlers, a master of the wardrobe,
four secretaries, a treasurer, three royal chaplains, a physician in
attendance, not forgetting Mitton, his fool. He had a court of his
own, which meant that the princes of the royal family lived in his
"society," just as the great lords made up the entourage of the
King. They were in his "company," an expression which is quite
precise, from the standpoint of both etiquette and financial support. These princes were his companions, his compeers, and they
followed him everywhere: his young uncle, the Duke of Orléans,
scarcely two years older than he; his three younger brothers,
Louis, John, and Philip of France; his brother-in-law, Louis of
Bourbon; his father's stepson, Philippe du Rouvre, Duke of
Burgundy; and his Alençon cousin, the Count d'Étampes.

The King could refuse these young men nothing. He lavished
upon them, through the good offices of his silversmith, and to each
of them according to his rank, vessels of silver and gold, jewels,
and other valuable objects. Every year the members of Charles's
court were given new furniture, carpets, and tapestries for their

apartments. At regular intervals, on the great feast days—
Candlemas, Lent, and Easter, Ascension and Whitsunday, As-
sumption, Allhallow Day, St. Andrew's Day, and Christmas—as
well as on special days of royal festivities, which as we know
flourished under John the Good, robes and furs were distributed,
and naturally an assortment of hats and gloves and shoes to go
with them.

Charles's wife, the Dauphine, was for the moment in the
Queen's "company." She had a house of her own, important as
her husband's, and attended by the same number of servants.

The four years following the coronation and the royal weddings
were lived by the Dauphin with haste smacking of foreknowledge,
as if he perceived that never again in his life would such an opportunity arise. Suddenly eyes were open. Charles discovered the
world and its pleasures, the most refined and the least acceptable.
He took his fill.

He did not, however, show the same penchants toward sports,
arms, and hunting as his father, although he enjoyed them from
time to time. Nor did he share his father's aptitudes for such pastimes. Most often he preferred the conversation of the liveliest
minds at court, and John II had made a point of inviting the best
of his time to frequent it. The Dauphin, as is known, had a good
deal of curiosity, a taste for culture, and also a taste for beauty,
and for spending money. He was a Valois. He loved refinement
and luxury, tastes which had been cultivated in the ruling family
for four generations. He could never weary of poring over illuminated manuscripts, admiring paintings, gems, and golden jewelry;
and he would never count the cost when the jewelers and goldsmiths who knew his weakness for their craft brought him their latest creations. Nor did his father the King spare the expense when
he offered his son, on his fifteenth birthday, a present of "a golden
crown, studded with pink rubies, emeralds, pearls, and diamonds
round the rim, and on its points, Alexandrian rubies, pearls, and
emeralds."

And how the King paid! He paid for the Dauphin's pleasure
boat ("the little linseed" as it was affectionately called), which he
had built expressly for his son's use in cruising up the Seine,
sometimes all the way to Rouen, flying the quartered banners
of France and Dauphiné. As he paid for the damages caused by

the young man's pet bear, which roamed almost freely in his apartments and, one particular evening, employed its fine teeth and claws to tear up a tapestry within its reach, *The Heron's Flight*. As he paid for other, heavier damages, inflicted by the young men of the Dauphin's suite on the innkeeper at the Fleur de Lys, a hotel at Pierrefitte, when her house caught fire—no less! As a result of what violence, what orgy, we do not know. In any case Charles must have tolerated such performances, since it does not seem that the authors of the conflagration were in any way bothered about the matter. Unless he himself had a hand in it along with his little gang. At the same time he acquired a taste for women. He was enjoying himself. Or that was the story given out. And the father, who was so well behaved in his time, closed his eyes to these adventures, not without some envy, for all we know. Youthful follies, what do they matter? He'll get over them.

THE DIFFICULTY OF BEING

King John felt a great tenderness for this son of his. The Dauphin, however, did not return those feelings at this time. He grew distant, indifferent. This life no longer satisfied him. It seemed to him a vain thing, and empty. Other desires possessed him. Here he was already at the end of his quest, and the discovery he made is that every delight carries within it its own limit. The very essence of this journey on earth is nothing more than this void which he was suddenly aware of. Faced with such an abyss, the heart falters. His soul was overcome with a vast melancholy. How could he admit the cruel evidence of his senses? It was better to deny it. He had been happy, and he was no longer happy. Who was to blame?

To find the guilty party Charles must undergo the torments of the heart, shed his happy carelessness, live in bitter rancor as he had earlier lived in haste, discover the discomfort of self-reproach, and become conscious of the double life he was leading. Such are the human paths by which one becomes a man.

In ancient times the sons of the old chief would murder their father in order to get his wives. But in 1355 the Dauphin lacked not for wives—he had one of his own, without counting those of others

—but, rather, power. The year he had spent in Dauphiné receiving
the allegiance of his vassals returned to his memory; in his mind's
eye it took on a thousand charms. Ah! How annoying his father
was with his tourneys and his horses, his unshakable health, his
constant loyalty and high-mindedness. It was this hero, this valiant
knight, who was responsible for all his woes. What could he learn
from his father? Nothing, above all in matters of governing. What
did they have in common? Not very much. What was more, barely
nineteen years separated him from the man who gave him life. He
was in his prime. . . . Dark thoughts, which made it hard for the
Dauphin to breathe.

In fact, the young man was at an age when every clear-minded
person criticizes other people and the world in the name of his
own truth. An uncomfortable operation at best, requiring, as an
outlet for the anguish that wells up in the process, someone to pin
the blame on, generally the father. The latter, however, did not
like the role into which he had been cast and found the situation
intolerable. He was anxious. Ignorant of the twisting byways of
the heart, he could not see himself in this young man. He either
loved or hated. In the realm of the emotions, the notion of
nuances was foreign to him. But he understood (or someone advised him) that the boy simply wanted to try his own wings, that
power tempted him, that he, the King, had delayed too long in giving his son some responsibility, that the boy had always been precocious and was almost seventeen years old. . . . In that winter
of 1355, however, it was Normandy which worried the King. The
province was threatened on two sides, by an English invasion and
by Navarrese intrigue. What the Norman nerve center demanded
was a royal presence. What better idea than to calm the Dauphin's
impatience by sending him on a mission to Normandy, and adding
the county of Poitiers to his son's possessions?

What was said was done. In the last days of March 1355 the
Dauphin left for Rouen.

A TRAP

But the Dauphin's relations with his father were not improved
by this expedient. Once the young man had taken up residence in

the castle of Vaudreuil, he let himself be taken in by the seductive charms of Charles of Navarre and of Navarre's bad angel, Robert Le Coq, Bishop of Laon. They were constantly in one another's company, one another's sight, cloying one another with mutual affection and delight. Navarre took up residence in the castle. In the midst of that desert of misunderstanding where our ingenuous young prince imagined he was living he naïvely thought that he had found at last, in his guest, the one sure friend he had lacked. Navarre was for him the shining example, a mere six years older and already a king. In him, Charles discovered himself. They had the same aptitudes, the same tastes. He fell into the trap. Caught by the charm of fine phrases (which the Dauphin adored and himself knew how to manipulate when he needed to), Charles lost all critical sense and let himself be led into playing the enemy's game. Is there any greater pleasure, for a villain, than to ensnare the son of his worst enemy?

This father's prestige was just beginning to be re-established in the mind of his eldest son; now Navarre began to undermine it with veiled remarks, with muted objections, deploring and regretting.

Once he adduced that he had prepared the ground sufficiently, he went on to grievances, and then to open accusations of the most frightful sort. The Bishop of Laon, for his part, could no longer refrain from speaking the terrible truth: it was King John who was responsible for the death of Prince Charles's own mother.

Flabbergasted, Charles agreed to enter Navarre's conspiracy. The plan was simple. The young man would leave the kingdom secretly and go to Germany, where he would seek the aid and cooperation of his dead mother's brother, the Emperor Charles IV. The revelations he would make would win his agreement; the rest would follow as a matter of course.

One night's madness: from talking so much through the night behind locked doors the imagination gets overheated. It cooled down early next morning. The son, panicked by the commitments he had made, revealed the whole affair to the party concerned, who received them undramatically and closed his eyes, thankful for his son's effective—if belated—loyalty. He did more than that. He feasted his prodigal son, killed the fatted calf, and, in token of reconciliation, made him a gracious gift of the duchy of Normandy in exchange for his county of Poitiers, a much less important fiefdom. Knowing his son's extravagant tastes and requirements, he sent him as a new year's present some twenty-six thousand Parisian pounds for his household expenses, and four hundred fine silver marks for his table service.

On January 10, 1356, Charles became Duke of Normandy with all the traditional rites and, consistent with his character, devoted himself to taking his job seriously.

Nonetheless the intrigues went on. . . . The Norman barons were restless; some deputies refused to take their place among the States-General; rumors of conspiracies circulated once more. It was in this context that King John carried out his "cruel act of justice" on April 5, 1356—just plain justice, let us say, by which his handsome nephew, Navarre, found himself in the prison cell he had earned so well.

The sequel we all know: the Black Prince's ride, the battle of Poitiers, the captivity of the King. "His lordship the prince is so young," laments one of the chroniclers. . . .

The fate of a dynasty, and consequently of a whole kingdom, would then depend on this unfledged, inexperienced, easily influenced young man who was apparently intelligent and above all impatient to rule. He would face up to the task. King John, obsessed with his own old-fashioned ideals, did not know that the years which were going to follow would constitute the true test of his son's mettle, and would develop his prowess and ability to surpass himself far better than King Arthur.

BITTER AFTERMATH

The news of Poitiers filled the courts of Europe with consternation. The people of France wept and mourned for their King. His subjects in Languedoc constrained themselves "to wear no gold, or silver, or pearls, no squirrel's fur or badger's, no robes or tailored hoods or other appurtenances, until the King's ransom had been secured, nor to listen to minstrels or watch jugglers." The north, more reticent, was silent. The King's person was sacred, and no one dreamed of criticizing him in the least. His valor

in the battle had impressed everyone. But these were men who
believed that "too great a disaster conquers a noble heart." Bitterness which began in rumors and nagging suspicion soon found its
expression in broad daylight: the King had been conquered because those closest to him had betrayed him.

The nobles were traitors, "frightened rabbits, timid braggarts,
vile deserters." Let the young Dauphin remove his trust from them
and keep it for his peasants, suggested the complaint:

> Here's the best advice our Prince had yet:
> If Goodman Jack's the chum you get,
> Then none will run for their lives, I'll bet.

The Dauphin had just acquired the title of lieutenant general of
the realm. His tender age was a public concern, and he was completely isolated. The King of Navarre was still locked up, but his
party held the lower part of Normandy and the valley of the Seine.
The English were in possession of Calais; moreover, they were occupying almost the whole of Brittany and all of the southwest of
France, from Tours to Rodez and from Poitiers to the length of
the river Allier. And the city of Paris chose this moment to stir for
the first time. And what a moment to pick.

For the young prince the main problem over the next two years
would be survival.

To add to the Dauphin's troubles, in the aftermath of Poitiers
the royal coffers were even emptier than they had previously been.
Charles saw himself under obligation to tell the country of the disaster, and above all else to find some ready cash. The only way
open to him to get it was to take his case to the States-General,
and so he convoked them in Paris. On the morning of October 17
some eight hundred men gathered in the great chamber of Parlement. The representative of the nobility was the Duke of Orléans;
of the clergy, the Archbishop of Reims, Jean de Craon; of the
third estate, the Provost of the Paris merchants, Etienne Marcel. It
was noticed at the time that those elected from the cities made up
half the gathering.

The Chancellor, Pierre de la Foret, opened the session with the
story of the defeat at Poitiers and then went on to request advice
about ransoming the King, as well as the future conduct of the war

and the raising of public funds. Afterward the Dauphin addressed the assembly, "most wisely and most graciously."

On hearing the words of the Chancellor and their prince, the members of the States replied by declaring, in no uncertain tones, that they would prove themselves ready "to live and die" for their King. But they imposed certain conditions, beginning with their insistence on finding those guilty of treachery at Poitiers. The King had been ill served, and for a long time prior to the disaster. The appropriate response, then, was to remedy the situation by dismissing the malefactors and replacing them by functionaries chosen from among the three estates assembled there. It was equally appropriate to free the King of Navarre. The tenor of the reply was obvious: no reforms, no money.

THE BURGHERS WANT THEIR SAY

Such were the demands formulated by an opposition of burghers, who were active and powerful in the Paris of the mid-fourteenth century. They were capable and ambitious—and they showed it by the way they conducted their own affairs—were rich, and held an abundance of the funds which the monarchy so sorely lacked. No longer were they content with merely managing the town, even if they ruled as masters there. They claimed the right to oversee and to criticize royal policy, and they felt it was a grave injustice that they had not been consulted about it. The glaring abuses of the regime and the quite recent disasters made the scandal of such exclusion more striking still (and how aware they were of it). Now they could bear it no longer. Weary of the nobility and of royal absolutism, they claimed their rights in affairs of state. The moment was too propitious for them to allow it to slip by. For if the notion of democracy took its first steps in medieval Paris, the idea of the fatherland was still extremely weak and was confused with loyalty toward the reigning dynasty—which loyalty had been severely shaken of late.

The burghers of Paris were not lacking in either supporters or talents. Their spokesman in the States-General, as we know, was the Provost of the merchants, Etienne Marcel. Now Marcel, by virtue of his family, his associates, his friendships, as well as the

rise in his personal fortune and the roles he was called on to perform, together with the vast array of trades he oversaw, was the
master of the town. One word from Etienne Marcel, and the city
of Paris would stir, its people would take to the streets. And he
knew it. His merchants of Paris provided his army with a general
staff, among whose alderman officers were the following men:
Charles Toussac, Pierre Bourdon, Philippe Giffart, and his own
cousin, Gilles Marcel, the secretary of the Merchants' Guilds.
Joining their ranks was the personal enemy of the Valois dynasty,
Robert Le Coq, the King of Navarre's bad angel, whose sharp
tongue never ceased inveighing against the current state of affairs.

THE POWER IS IN THE STREETS

In the face of these pretensions, Duke Charles, isolated, without
funds and without experience, could do very little. His captive father's government served as a target for attacks, his entourage had
been vilified, and his authority had been found wanting. He, the
Dauphin, had to suffer the imposition of others' orders as well as
reforms and men not of his choosing. His decrees were blocked
and he was reduced to impotence—all with impunity.

All he could do for the nonce was to shift and turn, stall for
time, hand out wages, and yield ground out of necessity. For as
long as it was a matter of purging evil counselors, annulling ordinances, imposing reforms, even of letting Paris take up arms, so
he would let it be, although it was difficult for a chief of state to
allow a tribune like Marcel, fleetingly supported by the favor of
the mobs, to dictate his course of conduct. One of the chronicles
reports that "the Dauphin swallowed the remonstrances of the
States as a sick man swallows his pills." But when Etienne Marcel
boisterously proclaimed his sympathy for the Valois' sworn
enemy, the King of Navarre (whose escape Marcel had probably
aided), when he encouraged Navarre to defy the Duke, when he
imposed on his prince a reconciliation he himself knew to be a
sham, he went too far, even though his influence over the mob was
as powerful as we know it to have been. Things had developed to
such a point, the situation was so tenuous, that the slightest inci-

dent could cause an explosion. On January 24, 1358, just such an incident occurred.

THE PERRIN MARC AFFAIR

On that day, in Paris, on the Rue Neuve St. Merry, Jean Baillet, the Dauphin's treasurer, refused to pay a certain Perrin Marc, a money-changer's man, the price of a pair of horses. So enraged did this Marc become that he drew his sword and killed Baillet; whereupon he took refuge in the nearest available sanctuary, the Church of St. Merry. The Dauphin's response was to send Robert de Clermont, the Marshal of Normandy, to seize the murderer. The doors of the church were forced and the fugitive dragged out of the sanctuary. The following day, Perrin Marc's hand was cut off and he was hanged on the very place where he had killed Baillet.

At once the city was alarmed, denouncing tyranny, the violation of the right of asylum and of the common law. The Archbishop of Paris, who sided with Navarre, excommunicated the Marshal of Normandy. There were demands that the body of Perrin Marc be taken down from the gallows and brought back with honor to the Church of St. Merry. These things were done, and Perrin Marc was given a solemn funeral with Etienne Marcel and many other prominent burghers in the front pews. The little Dauphin had begun to go beyond limits they could tolerate. And so they were going to give him the lesson he deserved.

THE DAY OF FEBRUARY 22, 1358

Early in the morning of February 22, Marcel assembled some three thousand armed Parisian tradesmen at the priory of St. Eloi, within easy access of the royal palace. There the crowd had been waiting nervously, when one Regnaut d'Acy, a counselor in Parlement and a staunch supporter of the Valois, passed by. Kept in attendance on the Dauphin until a very late hour, he was on his way to his home, which was situated near the Church of St. Landry on the Quai de la Cité. Immediately the mob gave chase. A pastry shop happened to be open, and he dashed inside. The mob dragged him out and in less time than it takes to tell, he "received so many wounds, and such severe ones, that he died before he could utter a word."

The Provost, whose appetite had been whetted by this exploit, shouted, "On to the palace!" In a trice he was at the gates of the palace and directing the mob to force them. With his underlings at his heels, he passed through the courtyard, scaled the staircase, and burst into the chambers of the Duke of Normandy, who was lying on his bed, surrounded by a few loyal friends. "Sire," Marcel exclaimed, "do not be alarmed at the things you see, for they have been planned in advance."

The Duke barely had time to hear these words when before his eyes Marcel's men seized the Marshal of Champagne, Jean de Conflans, whose crime was to have deserted the party of the States-General after he had been elected one of its commissioners. Conflans fell across the prince's bed, his warm blood staining Charles's robe. Marshal Robert de Clermont attempted to escape the slaughter, but he was seized and suffered the same fate in an adjoining chamber. Screams and cries were resounding everywhere. The Dauphin's terrified servants fled from the palace without giving a moment's further thought to their master. Charles, alone now in his overrun living quarters, was abandoned to the seditious mob, unarmed and defenseless, among the disorders and risks of a revolution. He felt the hatred enveloping him, taking control of him, ready to burst around him, and was afraid. He feared for his life. His last trump was—oh, derision!—the individual standing so powerfully before him, impassive among the clamors, wearing a pied cap with the colors of the city. "Save me," cried the prince. "Sire," answered Marcel, "you are in no danger." And then, to prove this to him, he placed on his prince's head as a safeguard the cap which was his emblem, and took his prince's own—a cap of fine cloth, black with a golden fringe—in exchange. They remained that way the entire day, in pledge of their friendship.

The bloody bodies of the two marshals, already stiff, were kicked and dragged, under torrents of abuse, to the steps of the palace. They would be left there until evening, naked, exposed to view, as an example, while within the palace everyone shook with fright, including the Dauphin, who could ascertain by glancing from his window that no one took it upon himself to try to bury them, although they had been important men that very morning.

The Provost left the Duke alone with his thoughts, as well as with his impotence. But the Provost had problems of his own. It behooved him now to count his forces, revive the sympathy for his cause, and above all to find reasons which would justify such an act as the one whose consequences he was beginning to realize in those very minutes. Was what they had done for him what he had wanted? Had things gone beyond his control? It hardly mattered. He was already afraid of countermeasures, and dreading a shift in public opinion. How might he present the appearance of justice for those misdeeds committed at his command: the invasion of the royal palace, the killing of the Dauphin's attendants before his very eyes, and in his own quarters? He would have to move quickly, then.

From the windowed upper floor of the city hall in the Place de Grève, he harangued his armed tradesmen. They knew how to make speeches in Paris in the mid-fourteenth century. "Those who have been slain were evil men, false and perfidious," he explained. Let those gathered there stand up for him and support him, for he had done what he had for the good of the kingdom. Then with one voice the crowd shouted its agreement with its Provost and let the roofs of the city know that it was ready to "live and die" with him.

Without a moment's hesitation, Marcel returned to the palace, followed by the entire population. The courtyard was quickly filled. The corpses of the two marshals lay naked on the marble steps. Once again the Duke, "dumb-struck with much grieving," saw Marcel invade his quarters, proclaiming that his conscience was clear and, in the same breath, that to him pertained the rights of the stronger party. "What has happened," he told his prince, "was done by the will of the people, and justice was served, for those who died were evil men, false and treasonous." And so let's drop the subject, kiss and make up, and admit that I am right. In the name of the people, the Provost asked Monseigneur the Duke "to ratify the aforesaid deeds and to be one with them. And, if he judged that their actions required his royal pardon, then he should forgive them all." The Dauphin was only too happy to oblige him, and spoke with alacrity: let the people of Paris consent to be his good friends, and he would be theirs.

Then the Provost, in gratitude and as a token of friendship, gave the Dauphin two bolts of cloth, one of dark blue and the other of red, to make caps of. And Duke Charles immediately put them to this use, ordering everyone in his service to wear the colors of the city of Paris.

The following day Marcel had the bodies of the two slain men removed, for no one had dared to touch them. Two "lowly grooms" loaded them into a handcart and pulled them across the city until they reached the Church of St. Catherine, in the Vale of the Scholars. The only wages they got for their trouble was the cloak of one of the dead men. That might have marked the end of the affair, but it did not. The frightened monks hesitated to bury the corpses without the express order of Marcel. Marcel himself courteously referred them to the Duke, who did indeed authorize them to proceed with the burial—but enjoined them at the same time to do so with discretion, and without the usual pomp. The Archbishop of Paris got wind of the affair and intervened: Robert de Clermont, he reminded the monks, had been excommunicated just the month before for having driven Perrin Marc from his sanctuary in the Church of St. Merry, and he could not lie in consecrated ground.

In the meantime, the two bodies had been slowly decomposing in the open air of the garden of the convent, and the monks, with the backing of the Provost and the Dauphin, made up their minds to transgress the Archbishop's orders. In the end, they buried the bodies of the two marshals in secret, and with great haste.

That incident was the last twist of the knife for Charles. He had been humiliated; rage gnawed at his heart; he was penniless, he was personally unfree, and no one could vouch that his life was safe. He had been scoffed at by his former friend, the King of Navarre, and compelled by Marcel to take the title of Regent, so that the very name of the King was put out of Frenchmen's minds. The ways of peace had shown themselves to be futile, and he abandoned them. Leaving the Parisians to their folly, he left the city of Paris for the provinces on March 27, 1358. When he returned he would do so as a conqueror.

PARIS ISN'T THE WHOLE OF FRANCE

The Dauphin went from city to city, pleading his cause in person before the Estates-Provincial, which he had convened for that purpose. He went among his people, he saw to it that he was seen, and when he spoke to the people he spoke well, with a natural eloquence and a ring of truth which rallied support to his cause. The provinces waxed indignant against Paris, against the burghers' uprising, against Navarre's party. They showed the young prince the warmth they felt for him by furnishing him with subsidies, with men, and with weapons. His kingdom was loyal to him, and now he knew it. The weight of both opinion and numbers was on his side: Paris isn't the whole of France.

Charles grew calmer, regaining his confidence and his authority. Now he could speak as a king, could say openly that he meant to be the sole master in his own house, that he would see to it that order was restored, and that the first item on the agenda was to retake Paris. He therefore established his headquarters at Meaux and at Montereau, locations that would enable him to control the three great supply routes to the capital. With these supply routes cut off, the city faced the threat of famine, and suddenly the Parisians took alarm and begged him to return: "Dread lord, we assure you indeed that your people of Paris openly long for you and your government. . . . May it please you, most dread lord, to know that the good people of Paris are no villains, but your good and loyal subjects, just as you found them once and will find them in the future."

The Regent went on patiently gathering support and provincial troops. His response to a delegation from the University of Paris, sent to plead for his return, was a firm one: he was quite ready to pardon the Parisians and to restore them to his favor—but only on condition that they submit to him entirely and hand over to him ten or twelve of the ringleaders of the burghers' insurrection.

When he heard this news Marcel felt himself lost. Confusing the fate of the capital with his own, he could not envisage ceding the power he found so intoxicating. Justifying his attitude by the concern for the public good which had always been his chief aim, he chose to resist the Dauphin to the bitter end. And if fighting there had to be . . .

At his command, nearly three thousand workmen hastily undertook the construction of a defense system such as Paris had never known before. He raised funds and went about mustering troops, for each such armed man (whether his own, or English or Navarrese for that matter) would count in the struggle. He had coins struck. He hunted down the partisans of the Regent, and when he found them he confiscated their goods. Two men who were suspected of Valois sympathies were beheaded as traitors; their bodies were quartered, and the remains were hung on gibbets whose prominence helped usher in a reign of terror in the city of Paris.

THE BLOOD OF WRATH

But while the Dauphin was making his own preparations, toward the end of May 1358, some news reached him which the chronicles, unhyperbolic in this instance, describe as "most dolorous": to the Parisian insurrection there had now been added a peasant revolt by the Jacquerie. On the twenty-eighth of May some insignificant folk of the region of Beauvais, from the towns of St.-Leu-d'Esserent, Cramoisy, and thereabouts, had gathered for purposes that could lead to no good end. They came upon some noblemen who happened to be in the town of St. Leu and killed nine of them. In a matter of days the whole of the countryside between the Marne and the Somme, from Vitry in Champagne all the way to Montdidier, the regions of Beauvais, Soissons, Valois, and Senlis (some fourteen of the departments of present-day France) were up in arms.

These peasants were "the Jacks" (as the nobles derisively called them), good for being paid and for serving, good for hanging, the butt of the jokes of gentlemen of leisure, who would circulate jingles about them:

> *Treat a hick well,*
> *He'll kick you for a spell;*
> *But kick him back,*
> *And he's your Jack.*

The Jacks were washing off their poverty, purifying themselves of their long rancor in the regenerating blood of their noble victims. Terror reigned. History would give these days an eloquent name: the Days of Dread. Here is how Froissart describes them:

"Some of the men from the country towns gathered together in the region of Beauvais. They had no leaders and at first there were fewer than a hundred of them. They said that all the nobility of France, knights and squires, were betraying them, and that it would be a good thing to destroy them all. . . . Then they went off, with no more deliberation, unarmed except for pikes and knives, to the house of a knight who lived close by. They broke into the house, killed the knight, his lady, and his children, big and small, and set the house on fire. Next they went to another castle and did much worse, for they seized the knight and bound him hard and fast to a post; then several of them ravished his wife and daughter before his eyes. Then they killed the wife, who was pregnant, and the daughter and all the other children, and finally put the knight to death in great torment, and burned the castle to the ground.

"They did similar things in a number of castles and great houses, and their numbers grew until there were a good six thousand of them. . . . Knights, ladies, and squires, wives and children fled before them, leaving their houses open with all they had inside.

"These evil men, who formed a group without leaders or arms, pillaged and burned everything and killed like mad dogs. . . . I would never dare to write down the horrible and shameful things which they did to the ladies. But, among other acts of licentiousness and brutality, they killed a knight, put him on a spit, and turned him over the fire and roasted him before the lady and her children. After ten or twelve of them had violated the lady, they wanted to force her and the children to eat the knight's flesh. Then they put them to a cruel death."

The kingdom of France was afflicted at that time with hordes of men given over entirely to their rage. But the source of the Jacks's outrage was real enough: hunger, impotence, flouted dignity. Since the Battle of Poitiers, the flat plains had been overrun by rampaging mercenaries out to amuse themselves. They were called "brigands," after the thin coat of mail (*brigandine*) which they wore.

They attacked the weakest peasants they could find, and plundered them remorselessly, carrying off their working equipment, wagons, horses, even the very plowshares, so that your poor Jack was left with nothing. Nor were these "brigands" in name the only ones to commit depredations on the defenseless peasantry. There were rival armies, the English, the Navarrese, the Regent's own troops, abroad in the countryside, burning whatever presented itself to view, destroying crops, turning the level landscape into a wasteland, a desert space where only the briars could grow. In that dismal year of 1358 the vineyards went uncultivated, the fields went untilled and unsown, the livestock were no longer led to pasture, and churches and houses everywhere showed telltale marks of burning. . . .

As for the landed gentry, who had been defeated at Crécy and Poitiers, far from protecting their peasants, they extorted their last *sous* in order to pay their own ransoms, or even allied themselves with the roving brigands the better to put pressure on the peasantry. Completely discredited, then, both hated and hateful, the nobility no longer fulfilled its ancient obligation to protect the small and weak, but held onto all the privileges of its station, including disdain for the sufferings of its erstwhile wards.

Thus a wild clamor arose from the plains, and cries of hatred surrounded the towns and the castles. Banded together under a leader now—a king, as they called him—one Guillaume Carl, described by the chronicles as "a man of great presence and manner," the Jacquerie rallied to their cause every sort of small folk whose misery was too large to bear in peace any longer. Like a king, this Guillaume Carl issued decrees sealed with his own seal. The standards he raised carried the fleur-de-lis of France, and his war cry was that of the most loyal Frenchmen: *Montjoie*. For his following did not have it in for the King of France, but for the cursed noblemen. Into the ranks of that following there flowed tradesmen, butchers, coopers, wheelwrights, poulterers and egg merchants, as well as some royal men-at-arms and even a fairly large number of priests.

Etienne Marcel, who left no stone unturned, did not hesitate to call on these men to attack the landed estates near Paris, and afterward he brought them into the city itself. But his fellow Parisians had little taste for the crude manners of these new allies. The

Provost's reputation was damaged by this. He excused himself by belatedly condemning the excesses of the Jacks. The latter, rebuffed and driven out of Paris by Marcel, headed back toward Beauvais. Navarre and a thousand armed men were waiting for them on the road: for a massacre. After the battle came the bloodletting. The peasants were decimated like so many head of cattle. Between the tenth and twenty-fourth of June twenty thousand Jacks were burned alive, hanged, or run through with swords. The fines imposed on the survivors were staggering. Etienne Marcel, in character perhaps but stirred all the same by humane sentiments for which we cannot help praising him, expressed his outrage, in a letter he wrote to the communes of Flanders, at one of the greatest massacres of the age.

THE END OF THE DICTATE

On June 29 the Regent laid siege to Paris with his entire forces, which by now consisted of all the northern noblemen of France (who had been brought to those parts by the struggle against the Jacks), together with a great number of German barons—altogether nearly thirty thousand horsemen.

The city was in a state of panic. The Provost held the place with the King of Navarre. They searched on all sides for support, tried to negotiate. But without much success. The people, fickle and adaptable as always, began to grow weary of their idol of yesterday just as they had grown weary of the exactions of the English soldiery whom the Provost had brought inside the city walls with the intention of defending Paris against the siege; weary of the whole thoroughly unpleasant situation, which threatened to go on forever.

But now, guardedly, there sprang up a clandestine party inside Paris favorable to the Regent, which kept in constant contact with him. They had to move quickly. Charles of Navarre had made his peace with the English and was preparing to have himself crowned King of France with the complicity of the Provost of the merchants, who had already and in advance offered his backing for whatever executions should be politically necessary.

On July 31, 1358, Etienne Marcel was in the midst of giving

the order to the guards of the Porte St. Denis to hand the keys of that gate over to Josseran de Mâcon, the King of Navarre's treasurer, when two Parisian burghers, Jean Maillart and Pépin des Essarts, came up and hailed him noisily. A few hours later Etienne Marcel lay dead, felled by their ax-blows.

On the second of August, Charles of Valois entered Paris, to be welcomed by the people with a great celebration.

The Dauphin had won the Battle of Paris. There remained the two claimants to the throne of his kingdom: Edward of Lancaster and Charles of Navarre. There remained the true King, in his gilded English prison. There remained the country itself, to which great companies of armed men were laying waste.

THE FREE COMPANIES

I scarcely recognized this kingdom, once so opulent, now plunged into ruin. No houses have been left standing, except in towns that have been locked up. Where is that Paris which formerly had been so magnificent? Where are the swarms of scholars? Where is the wealth of the citizens? The tumult of the soldiery is no longer to be heard, yet there is no safety even behind the walls. Indeed, nowhere in the world is there so little security.

Petrarch

The enemy were everywhere, moving about, harassing, many-faced—"so numerous," a Norman chronicler pleasantly comments, "that it appeared they were playing a game of prisoner's base among themselves." In this year of 1358, France had become a gigantic game of slaughter.

The most dangerous of enemies was probably Navarre, who had encircled Paris and was blockading the Regent within the city and attempting to starve him into submission. On the fourth of August he entered Melun, thanks to the complicity of his sister Blanche, Philip VI's widow, the dowager Queen of France. Then he captured Mantes and Meulan, while one of his followers, Jean de Piquigny, seized Creil in his name. From above and below the Seine, and to the northeast of it, these four towns contain the capital. From there, Navarre's troops proceeded into Normandy, and then into the regions of the northeast, Beauvais and Picardy, a systematic takeover. The strategy was successful. And to assure this success, Navarre did not hesitate to ally himself with the English, with whom he signed a treaty of alliance as soon as he saw that he had failed to hold Paris.

Now, one consequence of the Truce of Bordeaux which followed on the English victory at Poitiers was that any number of captains, and common soldiers beyond number, found themselves at liberty on French soil, without a farthing in their pockets and never dreaming at such a time of leaving so green a pasture. There was plenty of work left, or so it seemed, in the kingdom of France. Nor were they selfish about their find: they contacted their younger friends and relations across the Channel about it, and those friends and relations hastened to join them. Navarre, therefore, had plenty of men to choose among. At the same time he was recruiting in Germany, in Hainaut, and in Brabant. Whether or not he had the wherewithal to pay these mercenaries, the land was large enough to sustain them and to make them all rich. With his cousin confined inside Paris, there was absolutely no one and nothing to prevent them from roaming about at will. From that time on the so-called "Free Companies" entered the stage of French history, with the complicity and at the instigation of Charles the Bad.

OH, WHAT A LOVELY WAR!

If you want to gain a foothold in a particular place, the tactic to employ is quite simple: you start by picking a lair, a base camp. Then you play the Big Bad Wolf, you frighten people, taking their livestock, starving them, burning their harvests, their homes, their barns. You rape a few women and kill some people here and there. The reaction is immediate. The natives are driven wild, seize their clothing and a few things, and head for the woods or some other spot thought to be inaccessible. So sudden was their flight that it no more suited the brigands than the Jacks they preyed on. It was left to the brigands, thanks to the natives, who were to furnish the brigands with provisions and hard cash, to find their own living (even a good one), to feather their own nests, and to set off again from their temporary quarters with ample stores for the future. In the swamps and mists the nights were cold, subsistence was hazardous, and the poor Jacks would therefore abandon their woodland retreats and do what was expected of them.

Nor were such extortions the whole story. We have to add the chance encounters, at the turn of the road, of these brigands with small, peaceful groups of merchants, returning to their towns and villages with horses laden with their trade goods. Nor were those towns exempt, to be sure, from sacking for the very rich booty they offered. This great and opulent land belonged to three different masters—that is to say, to no one. Thus everyone was working on his own account. "Oh, what a lovely war!" exclaimed one of the Navarrese brigands, Aimerigot Marcel by name. "Oh, what beautiful days! What beautiful memories these times will leave us. Alas that they can't last forever. There is no greater time, joy, or glory in this world for men-at-arms than waging war just as we've done it. How we rejoiced when we rode out to adventure, and met up on the fields with a rich abbot, a rich prior, a rich merchant, or a caravan of mules from Montpellier or Narbonne, . . . laden with cloth from Brussels or Moutiers-Villiers, or furs from the market at Landy, or spices from Bruges, or cloth of silk from Damascus or Alexandria. Everything we saw we either kept or ransomed as we chose. Each day would bring us new money, while the villeins of Auvergne and Limoges would supply us and bring us wheat, flour, loaves of bread, oats and straw for our horses, good wines, beef, sheep and fatted mutton, poultry and wild fowl. We were looked after and stuffed like kings, and when we rode out the whole countryside trembled before us. Everything was ours, going and coming. Surely we had found the good, sweet life."

Five hundred fortifications fell into the hands of the English and the Navarrese. It is enough to say that the King of Navarre held the north and the west of the kingdom; the English, Brittany and the southwest. In short, three quarters of France was in the hands of their armies.

An episode from the life of one of Lancaster's most celebrated officers, Sir Robert Knolles, will illustrate the unchecked brigandage of these companies. Knolles was descended from the petty gentry of Cheshire. His uncle, or cousin, Sir Hugh Calverley, a renowned soldier of fortune, taught Sir Robert his trade, which he plied for the first time in the War of the Breton Succession. Having tried his hand and lined his pockets there, Knolles had no intention of stopping. Once that dispute was over, or nearly over, and affairs there were at a standstill, he left Brittany to seek his fortune elsewhere. A braggart and a proud man, he declared at the top of his lungs that he was his own master and was worth plenty. His motto proclaimed, "Whoever takes Robert Canolle will gain 100,000 sheep." His road took him by chance toward the river Loire, which he ascended. Day followed day with new adventures and encounters, and he was the richer by 200,000 florins, the master of forty good castles and thirty thousand armed men. He halted at Orléans to burn the outlying districts, and at Châtillon-sur-Loing to take possession of the town. Already he was hankering after Auxerre, a rich and populous city at the center of a whole network of small fortresses protecting the access to Auxerre; he had these fortresses taken one after another by his men or his allies. Against him the Regent set another captain of great notoriety, Sir Arnaud de Cervoles, who apparently switched sides. On the tenth of March, Auxerre was in flames; among the considerable prisoners were a count's son and his wife, which meant consequential ransoms. After eight days of systematic methodical plunder, Knolles' booty (it was said) amounted to 500,000 gold florins, not counting ransom money. When there was nothing left to take, Sir Robert convened the principal townsmen. His intention, he told them, was to burn the city, unless it was redeemed on reasonable terms; he, Knolles, would keep all of the booty, except for the silver lamps from the cathedral, the ciboria and the monstrances, which were to be restored as soon as they had paid him. The bargain was concluded. From there, Knolles descended by way of the Berry Canal toward the province of the Auvergne. He probably intended to head for the Rhone Valley and Avignon, the papal city about which the Cervoles forces had told such glowing tales. By this time two famous heads of Free Companies, Jean Waldbouf, probably a German, and Jacques Wyn, known as the "suitor for love," whose quarters were in Burgundy, had joined forces with Knolles. But the Auvergne was up in arms, and a defense had been organized on the spot. Knolles, wisely, did not press the point, barely escaped an all-out battle which would

have been too risky for him, and by forced marches through the
Limoges region got back to his base in Brittany. On the way he
took prisoner an officer of the Regent's, whom Charles had just
singled out for his exceptional valor at the siege of Melun, one
Bertrand du Guesclin. He now had fourteen fruitful months at his
disposal to wait quietly for the right moment and to long for new
adventures in total security.

However, from the depths of his misfortune, the Regent began
to perceive a ray of light, a murmuring which was growing now
against the pillagers and the English who had made common
cause with them. A local self-defense was being mustered, over
which, whenever he was able to do so, Charles himself kept a
watchful eye. Inured by experience, Jack Goodman little by little
grew aware that once he had overcome his fear with the co-operation of his own people, his fellow villagers, men born on the same
soil and subjects of the same King—their only King, who was imprisoned in London, but whose son reigned in Paris—he could give
back as good as he got in the fighting. Little by little he had
learned to resist the invader by harassing him, not in murderous
battles, not in decisive engagements, but by crushing him and
wearing him out by stages.

It was in such a context that, some months later, there took
place the now famous episode of the "Great Farrier" who, at the
head of a peasant band from Longueuil-St. Marie, heroically defended his town against the English and forced them to quit the
field. In the words of the chronicler Cuvelier, these "poor men of
the fields thought it was better to die while defending themselves
hand to hand against their enemies than to be burned, men and
wives, in their lord's manor." Here we may properly see one of
the first signs of patriotism shown by the masses, which caused
Cuvelier to remark of the peasants: "Had you split them open like
a fattened pig, you'd have found in their heart a fleur-de-lis."

Charles now knew that his people were behind him and, so bol-
stered, he could oppose the disastrous Treaty of London which his
father had just agreed to, judging the freedom of his own person
well worth half of his kingdom and four million gold crowns. This
was unacceptable. On May 25, with the young man standing on
the steps of the royal palace, Chancellor Guillaume de Dormans
read the draft treaty aloud to the three orders of Estates of the

kingdom convened by his master expressly to hear it, and to the entire people of Paris as well, who had flocked there (where a passage had been cleared for them) to hear the Chancellor read. The proposed treaty they found immensely displeasing. After deliberation, they told their prince that "it was neither passable nor feasible." The war went on. . . .

But how to pay for it? With the meager resources which the Estates procured at that time. These would permit the Dauphin to try to settle accounts with the Navarrese once and for all. On June 18 he laid siege to Melun. Three queens were living there, two dowager queens of France and the reigning Queen of Navarre, herself a daughter of John the Good. Perhaps thanks to their presence, peace was concluded before the town even capitulated. Two months later the Dauphin received his former boon companion, Charles the Bad, at Pontoise. Was it possible for the two men to forget what they had just lived through? The Regent, who was trying to do just that because he had to, received the renegade at his table, regaled him, and kept him in his presence (profitably, or so it seemed) for several days. On August 21, Navarre declared publicly before the people whom he had invited into the great hall of the castle that he was ready to work with all his strength for the deliverance of the kingdom from the English invaders. In December a plot was uncovered in Paris, which he had fomented against his liege. . . .

MARCHES AND MISADVENTURES

The English still remained. In October of that same year old King Edward had debarked to press his claims. Furious at having seen the treaty he had obtained from one of his peers rejected by such a nonentity, Edward proceeded toward Reims, where the Archbishop, Jean de Craon (a relative of Edward's), would refuse him neither anointment nor a crown. He had made his arrangements well: every preparation for the expedition had been carefully allotted its place, for Edward believed that "to govern is to foresee." Quite well informed as to the state of the countryside on which he was counting to provide a living both for himself and for his men, and absolutely determined not to live skimpily (for he knew the text that an army lives on its stomach), Edward had foreseen that, lacking salt meats, they could nourish themselves on venison and on fish from the rivers and ponds. With such means of feeding his army in mind, he had thought to pack among his baggage (according to Froissart) "several skiffs and other small boats skillfully made from leather, each of which would take three men over the biggest lake or pond to fish whatever part of it they wished. In addition, the King had for his own use thirty mounted falconers and their loads of birds, sixty pairs of big hounds, and as many coursing-dogs, with which he went either hunting or wild-fowling every day, as he liked. A number of the nobles and wealthy men also had their hounds and birds like the King." Edward had also foreseen the lack of the most essential objects, given the lamentable condition of the kingdom he coveted so strongly. The nobles and men of wealth of his retinue took with them on their wagons tents, pavilions, mills for grinding, ovens for baking, forges for shoeing their horses, and all other necessities.

Thus provided, this whole company debarked at Calais on the twenty-eighth of October. But there were no Frenchmen to make war on or to destroy, for the hamlets and villages were deserted, the fortresses and walled cities fully manned, the drawbridges closed, the ramparts bristling with pikes, the people armed. By the Dauphin's order, the French were to avoid pitched battles, but if they had to undergo a siege they were to do so to the last man. The road to Reims became a long one beneath the downpours and squalls of an abnormally early autumn. Edward had to advance through flooded fields across a fallow countryside, over swollen rivers, through mist and mire. His falcons and his leather canoes must not have accomplished too many wonders. On the fourth of December he reached the walls of Reims without having done the least bit of fighting. A new disappointment awaited him there: the city showed him the same face as the countryside he had traversed. Where he had thought to find his partisans, more enemies awaited him. It was useless to continue in such weather; instead, always the practical man, he sought a comfortable retreat in which to wait out the bitter season. Upper Burgundy, whose reputation is well known, was nearby. Even Sir Robert Knolles had no complaints to make about this lovely country. Like the soldiers of fortune who had preceded him some months earlier, and with all too similar modes of behavior, King Edward III set up his winter quarters in this rich province.

When springtime and fair weather came he took to the road again, this time toward the capital, to give that whippersnapper of a Dauphin the lesson he deserved.

He reached Paris across a barren landscape, without a soul to be seen, in fact nothing. Edward wandered through the empty *faubourgs*—St. Marcel, St. Jacques, St. Germain. What he found in them was closed houses, streets devoid of life, no one at all to be seen. He set up his tents beneath the walls, then sent his heralds to challenge the Duke to battle. The latter refused to accommodate him. Edward waited one day, then two, then three. On the Regent's command, no one stirred. The siege lasted for eleven days; on the next, the twelfth of April, Edward marched pathetically away. He took the road to Chartres, consoling himself on the journey with sweet thoughts of further sojourns in France, springtime on the banks of the Loire, summer on the greensward of Brittany. Harvest time would do nicely for thinking of taking Paris. As he made his way, messengers arrived from the Dauphin, offering him peace terms. Other messengers came from England bringing most unwelcome tidings. The Dauphin (him again!) had concluded an alliance with Edward's Scottish enemies. A French raiding party had landed at Winchelsea and had broken in and pillaged the town. King Edward himself had few such sparkling results to boast of, and on this long road, through the mud and the rain which had not stopped for eight days, his mood grew more and more somber from hour to hour. His cousin the Duke of Lancaster, on whom he relied freely, at this point told him some unpleasant things which sorely displeased him: "My lord, this war is too costly for you. Your followers stand to gain by it, but you are wasting your time in it." The King would keep going forward, in quest of the fat lands. "My lord, my lord," Lancaster insisted, "if you take your own advice and pursue this warfare, you will wear your life out, and it's still not likely that you'll ever achieve your objective." But the King had a thick hide. He intended to remain King of France and to die with that title. "My lord, my lord," Lancaster permitted himself to insist, "here is my counsel. Leave while you can with your honor intact, take the offers you were given, for we stand to lose more in a day than we have conquered in twenty years."

To these words of wisdom were added omens from the heavens, which split open, thundering and cracking—a deluge, an Apocalypse, crisscrossed with lightning, belching thunder, and hail with stones so huge they killed men and horses—a sky like a last judgment broke over the King of England's army, which was by now within sight of Chartres. And then the King, terrified, convinced that he had seen a sign from the Almighty in such a cataclysm, turned his gaze toward the cathedral, and in the interval between two lightning bolts, amid ten signs of the Cross, made a vow to the Virgin and promised that he would make peace.

PALACE LIFE

All this time the King of France had been enjoying himself in London. Four years previously, he had made his entry there—on May 25, 1356, to be precise—appearing to the assembled multitudes along his way astride a white steed, attended with all the pomp worthy of his sacred majesty. At his side the Black Prince of Wales rode with self-effacing courtesy upon a small black hackney. Behind them followed John's companions in exile. It must have been hard to believe that such a display of splendor and honor was being accorded a prisoner. It had taken three hours for the procession to negotiate the few miles between London Bridge and the Palace of Westminster, where the English sovereigns were preparing a grand reception for their Valois cousin. That very evening they installed King John in the Savoy, the town house of the Duke of Lancaster, on the Strand.

John kept a real court there, surrounded by an entourage of devoted French courtiers, entertained and coddled and free to come and go as he pleased. He never thought of abusing this freedom by doing anything so dishonorable as attempting to escape—God save him from such disloyalty! Instead, he would turn it to good account, leading a life which he quickly came to enjoy. Completely devoted to the pleasures of the moment, like his father Philip before him, John forgot that his dynasty was threatened, his realm entrusted to a mere child, his burghers rebelling, his people up in arms, his countryside devastated, his nobles scorned, his land in ruins, and its conqueror intractable. Immured in that eternal present which he made into his refuge, John II daily watched the hard realities of the world become more and more remote, as its shape and content became a little more blurred with each passing hour. Letters came from France, but they affected him less and less. Paris seemed far away, and all he could feel in relation to affairs of state was an impotence which each day reinforced. His son Charles he hardly missed at all, so remote had the Dauphin kept himself from his father in recent years. As for his other children, they were still so young. The Louvre no longer concerned John.

London life was sweet. His fondest attachments had followed him there: his son Philip, who, unlike Charles, resembled him; his nephews the Counts of Artois; his friends; his loyal Count of Tancarville. He was living in beautiful and friendly surroundings, and his hosts made the most affable and courteous of companions. Both the language and the customs of the English courtiers remained totally French. And what a charming countryside! How lovely to go hunting or hawking where there was such an abundance of game! And how pleasant it was to find on his return the pleasant surroundings of the palace of Savoy, where he kept his paintings, his gold and silver and gems, his organs, chess sets, and his books, to say nothing of greyhounds and pointers in the kennel, falcons in the aviary, and chargers, palfreys, cobs, and hackneys filling the stables. What more did he need?

Whole days were spent in sports and ball games in which the English excel, in horseback riding, in boating expeditions on the Thames or pleasure outings to country estates. He visited London, with its churches and cloisters, to which he made charitable contributions, and he went down to the shipyards where workmen were building the King's great ship or amused himself visiting the lions of His Highness, John's cousin.

In the evenings, in a violet surcoat trimmed with sandal fur and a scarlet robe, he would sup at Westminster Palace or at the homes of great ladies of French origin, such as Joan, Countess of Warren, and Marie de St. Pol, dowager Countess of Pembroke, with whom he formed ties of friendship. He would also pay calls on dowager Queen Isabelle of France, the daughter of Philip the

Fair and mother of King Edward, on whose descent the English king based his claim to the throne of France. He took pleasure in Isabelle's company and made himself a frequent visitor at her country house in Hertfordshire, bringing down with him his two favorites, the Counts of Bourbon and Tancarville. Isabelle's life had not been a particularly tender one, and she reciprocated John's attentions with real affection.

He had no time to get bored. All of London held receptions in his honor, organized one revel after another, and competed to see which would be more ostentatious. The Lord Mayor of London, Henry Picard, an Englishman of French descent, arranged an evening affair in which John was the proud center of attention, and no less than four crowned heads sat at his table. Christmas of 1357 was a memorable one, for Edward III assembled the greatest names of England at Marlborough to pay court to Cousin John and his French companions and regaled them all. After which pleasures, the entire company left for Bristol to celebrate the new year. Was it already the custom to stay up until midnight on New Year's Eve? Edward III kept his waiting guests occupied with an evening tournament whose splendor had rarely been matched and was long talked about afterward. In February there was a dazzling display of fireworks to mark the session of Parliament. That entire year foreign visitors came to London in greater numbers than usual, drawn, most likely, by the presence of the illustrious French captives. For four years London glowed with a brilliance which it owed to the Valois.

All this could not have displeased John, and he played his part well. He had been cast as one of the great ones of this world afflicted by destiny with cruel reverses, which he bore with a serene brow, able throughout his ordeal to remain nature's nobleman, "a knight without fear and without reproach." He found the adventure exhilarating enough.

THE CHARMS AND RISKS OF EXILE

For his own part, John was satisfied with this peaceful existence as a prince without responsibilities. Exile for him meant quietude. For the moment destiny had freed him of a mission which was too

much for him and overwhelmed him. It is too heavy a thing to
have to answer before God and before one's fellow men for the
destiny of a whole people, when it has already proven difficult
enough to become yourself.

Unless you find it impossible to renounce yourself because you
can't admit—despite the anointment with oil and the authority that
goes with it—that once you are King you are no longer your own
man. To renounce himself to fulfill himself through history—a history which had been so ill disposed toward him at that—was asking
too much of a weak man, as we have seen, brought up in luxury,
ease, and refinement, whose entire life, to the very moment he put
on the crown, had been nothing but a perpetual search for pleasure
—the lawful sort, to be sure, what we might better call "courtly
pleasures" or, better still, entertainment. John perceived his royal
status as a burden, indeed as a form of self-abnegation, although
he had devoted his best efforts to it from the outset.

A contrary destiny had deprived him of the liberty to carry on
his duties. He was in no hurry to regain that liberty. All he could
do was undergo the moment which the courtesy of his English
peers made a livable, even a royal prospect for him, and to the
moment he submitted with good grace. What else could a captive
king do than let it happen, for want of a better possibility? It was
merely acting sensibly, even if time weighed heavy once in a while.
He would bear up quite elegantly, then, under the constraints
which the risks of politics had brought him.

But there were days when his nerves would crack and he would
lose his head, overcome by the thought of sailing ships in readiness
for his return, sniffing in his mind, so far from the Channel, the
smell of the spray, with a taste on his tongue of salt, of iodine,
which was really a taste for his lost France. At such moments the
gilded exile he lived in struck him as unbearable, and he was
prepared to give it up at any cost. It did not matter what they
asked him to sign over to them. And King Edward III was waiting
for just such a moment. "My good brother, sign," Edward must
have whispered. "It's so simple. In a short time you can pack your
bags, take your leave, and your stay here will be nothing more
than a dismal memory, a bad toss of the dice we all have to play
as kings." Nostalgia overwhelmed John, and he signed the Treaty

of London, in which he agreed to turn over half his kingdom to buy back his person.

But his son Charles was vigilant, for he had endured the Parisian revolt, the revolt of the Jacks, the ravages of the countryside by the mercenaries. He could take the risk of refusing Edward and his Treaty of London. He would do so. Edward, furious, resorted to reprisal measures. He restrained John's liberty of those early months, took away the commodious residence at the Savoy, and allowed his pique to get to the point where he had John locked up in the Tower of London. He then departed for France to put on the crown. We have seen the result of his expedition there.

After the apocalyptic downpour at Chartres, Edward proved more conciliatory. The Dauphin found himself in a position to sign at Brétigny a rather hobbling peace treaty, but the best obtainable under the circumstances, and a far cry from the disastrous one which John had been ready to agree to in London. Edward III solemnly renounced his claim to the throne of France, with the proviso that he would receive in exchange the ancient Plantagenet lands to the south of the Loire, and a sum of three million gold crowns as ransom for his prisoner, who returned—carefree—to his ravaged country amid general celebrations.

THE NOSTALGIAS OF HOMECOMING

Anyone but John, on kissing his regained native soil, would have shed tears at the sight of a kingdom bled white and would from that moment on have had but one care: to re-establish order and security, to restore its former wealth. Anyone. But not King John. Did he ever think of his good subjects who loved him and had agreed to bleed themselves dry on his behalf? From the moment of his return, or so it seems, his royal duties were to be limited to his relations with his cousin, King Edward, who had behaved so courteously and to whom, once free, he was duty bound to keep his word. John, therefore, reigned exactly as he had done in the past, as well such a king could reign, with no grand design. Nothing learned, nothing forgotten. He thought of nothing but collecting that huge ransom of three million crowns promised Edward for freeing him by taxes levied on a population whose resources had run out; and of helping raise that sum by offering his daughter ignobly in marriage ("selling his own flesh and blood" was the less charitable popular verdict) to a petty tyrant of Italy, Galeazzo Visconti, the son of a Lombard lord of Milan. The price he exacted unblushingly was 600,000 crowns. Nor did this prevent him from squandering the sums he had collected, which never reached their destination—the pockets of the King of England—to whom he remained indebted for the sum of one million crowns.

John's return did not provide the incentive one might have expected for the restoration of the kingdom. The menace of highwaymen grew in proportion to their increasing numbers, and they went so far as to take on a force of noblemen in open battle at Brignais and inflict a resounding defeat upon them. To their brigandage were added such calamities as bad harvests, epidemics, and a resumption of the Black Death. In a population weakened by endemic famine, the bodies of the dead could once again be counted in the thousands. The Reaper struck everywhere, including the royal family; one of his victims was Philippe du Rouvre, the King's son-in-law, heir to the rich duchy of Burgundy, which was given to Philip of France and would be the cause of many misfortunes. John traveled to Burgundy in the aftermath to set things in order there; thereafter, he pushed on into Avignon, to draw up a plan for a crusade with the Pope. His idea was to let a little sunlight, a little of the dream, into an existence which had become so gray that he was already unable to bear it any longer.

In fact, the King missed London. He thought of his English friends. Would he ever see them again? Had he left someone else across the Channel, someone whose absence weighed so sorely on him—this forty-five-year-old—that he took it upon himself to go back there, under the pretext, once again, of honor? His son Louis of Anjou had been released on parole in Calais and, once free, had fled to the side of his young wife, Marie, with whom he had been able to live for only a few months after their marriage. John declared that his perjured son had "quite sullied his honor," and the honor of his line. "When good faith is banished from the earth, it should still be found in the heart of kings," cried John. And loyal as ever, he set out again for London to make up for his son's breach of faith. Three months later he died there, on April 8,

1364, in the vigor of manhood, of causes which have never been determined.

This second member of the Valois dynasty had been able to consider the universe of monarchs as his own, to accept its hard reality, which consists in finding one's own happiness in the happiness of one's subjects. Self-denial on that order was hardly what John II had been cut out for. He has thus been accused (and rightly, to be sure) of having a frivolous soul. But John II, just as his father had done when he married John's own fiancée at the end of his life, and perhaps even more than his father, dared incur the risk of exposing himself to scandal in the eyes of posterity by taking it upon himself to act by the dictates of his own "good pleasure"—a motto that would go far in that family. John the Good had a taste for his own happiness, a simple happiness at that, consisting of the easy joys of everyday life, the private virtues: the pleasures of exercise, of friendship, of revelry, of reading, of admiring lovely subjects, of dreaming of chivalry. His ideal, in short, was that of the rich, great lord, of all those things which his coronation at Reims should have put into the background. By the time he had come to grips with the fact that it was lost, his nostalgia for his past was so great that it carried him off with it. But does a King of France have the right to yield to such things?

CHAPTER V

Charles V the Wise
(*1364–80*)

THE SACRAMENT OF KINGSHIP

> Sweet God . . . Who looked with pity upon Thy humble child
> Solomon, and who granted him a knowing heart and intelligence,
> wisdom, and knowledge, so that he might know how to choose be-
> tween good and evil and judge his people uprightly, I implore Thee,
> bestow Thy pardon on my sense, counsel, and understanding, that I
> might govern this people which it is given me to watch over in jus-
> tice and in order. . . .
>
> Jean Golein, *Prayers for the Coronation*

The first act of a prince called by the laws of heredity to take
his turn on the throne of his fathers was to make his way to Reims
for the coronation. That ceremony consisted of anointing his body
in nine distinct places with a holy oil supposed to be of miraculous
origin; after which he was invested with the tokens of his authority,
chief among which was the crown. At the end of the ceremony he
was invested with a supernatural character, endowed with the gift
of healing, and thus raised above our common lot. He became
(like a priest, again) an intermediary between God and men. He
was, by the grace of the Almighty, a monarch by divine right.

We are afloat in a sea of miracles. The supernatural character
with which the King's person was invested remained for whole

peoples and for thousands of years a necessary reality of which we moderns have lost all notion. Is this a fundamental truth, the very forgetting of which constitutes a regression for our world, or merely an outdated custom? Such a question is beyond the scope of our subject, but these beliefs occupied so central a place in the minds of that time that it is of importance to dwell on them.

The Frankish kings held their authority by the consent of their warriors. Chosen by the ranks, they asked no further consecration than to have themselves borne in triumph on the bucklers of their soldiers among the cheering crowds and, later, to let their hair grow long as a sign of their rank. The first Frankish kings, the Merovingians, were supplanted by a second dynasty, the Carolingians, by means of a coup d'état. The Carolingians, who wished to conceal their usurpation of the kingdom and to consolidate their new dynasty, turned to the supreme authority of that time, the Catholic Church. And they reverted to the ancient practice of anointment, of Hebrew origin and already revived by the Visigoths. The theologians of Gaul, steeped in the Holy Scriptures, could not help accepting such a rite, which they knew to have occupied a major place in Hebrew ritual. The ancient Jews were accustomed to having recourse to anointment whenever they wished to transfer a man or an object from the category of the profane to that of the sacred. Everyone had read in the Books of Samuel and Kings how God designated by means of His prophet the one whom He was calling to lead His people. That was how He had chosen David, the great king, as the detailed account in the Bible has it for anyone to read:

"The Lord said to Samuel, 'Fill your horn with oil, and go; I will send you to Jesse the Bethlehemite, for I have provided for myself a king among his sons.' . . . Samuel did what the Lord commanded, and came to Bethlehem. . . . And he consecrated Jesse and his sons, and invited them to the sacrifice. When they came, he looked on Eliab and thought, 'Surely the Lord's anointed is before him.' But the Lord said to Samuel, 'Do not look on his appearance or on the height of his stature, because I have rejected him; for the Lord sees not as man sees; man looks on the outward appearance, but the Lord looks on the heart.' . . . And Jesse made seven of his sons pass before Samuel. And Samuel said to Jesse, 'Are all your sons here?' And he said, 'There remains yet the youngest, but behold, he is keeping the sheep.' And Samuel said to Jesse, 'Send and fetch him; for we will not sit down till he comes here.' And he sent, and brought him in. . . . And the Lord said, 'Arise, anoint him; for this is he.' Then Samuel took the horn of oil, and anointed him in the midst of his brothers; and the Spirit of the Lord came mightily upon David from that day forward." (I Samuel 16.)

Hebraic tradition had it then that their kings were in direct communication with the Almighty, and, by virtue of that communication, mediators between heaven and earth. They were sacerdotal kings.

And naturally enough, when the Carolingians out of necessity were looking to consolidate their dynasty, they restored the link with the ancient conception of a sacerdotal royalty originating in the night of time, with the demigod kings, the Aesir and Woden of the Germans, with the kings who were shamans and warriors and rainmakers, the protectors of the harvests of Siberia and Polynesia, with the priest-kings of the Mediterranean civilizations of Assyria and Egypt. This ancient notion remained intact in Christianity, since Christ, priest and king on earth, in heaven, and in the intermediate world, incarnates the supreme priesthood and kingship. The old barbarian vein of the peoples of Gaul recognized and made its own this ageless principle which Christian revelation came to confirm in its full meaning. And so they quite naturally adopted a belief which held that the king was an ideal type of universal man, bound to God by mysterious ties. And they allowed strictly as a consequence that such a king was owed service and obedience, and that he could demand both the goods and the life's blood of his humble subjects.

It was in such a context that Pépin of Austrasia, Charles Martel's father, received the sacred unction. The anointing ceremony would be conferred thereafter on all of his successors.

And to this ceremony was soon added the placing of the crown, an object consecrated since His Holiness the Pope had crowned the Emperor Charlemagne. The crown symbolized the judicial aspect of the state, and the placing of the crown on the monarch's temples remained, like anointment but even more so, a decisive moment in the coronation. Still later the ceremonial became more burdensome. Additional magical objects took their place on the altar beside the crown, whose possession conferred the right to the throne—talismans into which the spirit of God had been able to penetrate, while from the time of Robert the Pious, Hugh Capet's son, the king was regarded as a miracle worker with curative powers gained as a result of his coronation.

Was this belief a mystification or a coincidence struck in the nick of time? It would appear that these powers confirmed the legitimacy of a new dynasty, the Capetian one, arising in its turn out of a much more recent violent overthrow. Given the primitive minds of the crowds of that time, it is easy to see how in their view the king cured illness because he had been designated by God to reign over the kingdom. The king, the Lord's anointed, like the saints and in the image of Christ, possessed a potential of energy enabling him to accomplish the kindest act of charity—healing the sick. This was the image, let us add, of the kings of the world's earliest ages, to whom their subjects attributed magical powers, as we learn from contemporary ethnology.

Thus humanity's most ancient myths were preserved well into the Middle Ages. And so we find them deeply rooted in men's souls in this far reach of Europe, and so lively still that they would remain the most solid foundation of monarchical loyalty.

In following years the powers of our kings to perform miracles were handed down and codified, although after the reign of Robert the Pious' grandson, Philip I, the king's curative powers were limited to the widespread illness known as scrofula ("the king's evil"). The proof was clear: God, once and for all, had extended His grace to the Capetian line, whose legitimate claim could no longer be doubted. Legends circulated at the right moment. The holy oil used to anoint the king was of miraculous origin. A dove had descended from heaven, holding the holy ampulla containing the oil in its beak. The fleurs-de-lis which the kings of France used in their coats of arms were there by the celestial will. Clovis, King of the Franks, on the eve of a decisive battle against a numerically superior enemy force, received a visit in his castle, Montjoie, from a saintly hermit of an Augustinian order, the Premonstrants. This hermit had come to Clovis after being vouchsafed a revelation by an angel, in the course of which the hermit saw that a shield of blue, adorned with golden fleurs-de-lis, would give Clovis victory the following day.

Finally, every prince carried in his flesh the sign that God had predestined him for the throne: a red or white spot (for the most part, red) in the form of a cross, impressed on his right shoulder. After the coronation, the spot would transform itself into a fleur-de-lis. Just as, in ancient times, the Seleucid kings had an anchor on the thigh, the kings of Georgia an eagle on the right shoulder. Did the prophet Isaiah not say: "For to us a son is given; and the government will be upon his shoulder . . . and of peace there will be no end, upon the throne of David, and over his kingdom"?

THE ROAD TO REIMS

Charles V, as he rode toward Reims in the company of his queen, his brothers, his cousins and near kinsmen, the great lords of the realm and the entire royal court, could not have helped thinking endlessly of the strength that the ceremony with which he was about to begin his reign would give to his dynasty, itself almost brand-new and still faltering under terrible ordeals. What of the future of his reign? Would it be a disaster, like the preceding one, a difficult reign, like his grandfather Philip's, or (for all anyone knew) a propitious and glorious one, like the reigns of those great Capetians who had made their line a holy one in the eyes of the populace?

And so Charles prayed as he rode on, as he would do presently in the cathedral, as he would do the whole night long. Already the towers of Reims were visible on the horizon.

Soon he would see the angel smiling, and all the kings who had preceded him and awaited him on the top of the tympanum of Reims cathedral. These were the first faces he would see, welcoming him from the height of the façade. Soon he would be kneeling upon the great flagstones of the cathedral, completely absorbed in the peace of the Almighty. The light of evening would be lovely sifting through the stained-glass windows, and so would the color of the stones, the lines of the arcade, the ascending pillars of the nave, the crook-shaped foliage of the capitals. This was the hour he had long hoped for in the darkest days of the Parisian revolt, of the "frightful" Jacks, of King Edward's ride across France, when all had seemed lost for the Valois! But God had protected him.

Was it His plan to protect Charles still and to guard the kingdom entrusted to him?

Reims was the coronation city par excellence, built around a cathedral erected to serve as a setting for those rites which, since 987, had consecrated the Capetian kings. If at Chartres, at Amiens, at Notre Dame de Paris the cathedrals mirrored the world, here at Reims, in the plains of Champagne, the cathedral mirrored the coronation. The sculptors of the third workshop, under the direction of their master, Bernard of Soissons, had inscribed in the stone they were carving commentaries on the liturgical rites over which the archbishop of the place would preside. The symbols of what constituted the cornerstone and very center of royalty—its sacerdotal character—greeted the worshiper from the upper parts of the façade and from the gable of the central portal. Once he had taken his eyes off the image of heaven, where God and His creatures awaited him on the tympanums and the piers of the portals, the sacrosanct character of the royal line which governed France obtruded on his awareness. The crowning of the Virgin, a depiction in celestial symbolism of the crowning of His prince, had been placed on the gable of the central door, whereas in Paris it was relegated to a side portal. Over the Gloria gallery a scene depicting the baptism of Clovis evoked the miracle of the holy ampulla. In the covings of the great rose window the story of David and Solomon, royal prefigurations of Christ, set forth in ten sculptural groups the ideal proposed for sovereigns of all ages. Finally, the fifty-six monarchs of the gallery of kings bore witness, in their hieratic severity, that the French monarchy was indeed "the eldest daughter of the Church."

Charles had scarcely arrived at the city gates when he observed an imposing procession making its way toward him. The churchmen of Reims, the canons, monks, and mendicant friars, had come out in procession to greet him. The King greeted them and kissed the cross and relics they carried, for he wished to show the deep desire of his heart to do homage to God for this kingdom, which he held by God's will and not only by the sword. Then he went to the apartments prepared for his use in the palace of the Archbishop.

VIGIL

In the silence of the night the King went to the cathedral. He prayed all night long if he so desired, like a knight about to receive his knightly orders, as his father, John, had done, till the matins were sung. Then he confessed himself. Charles would go to the altar absolved of all sin, yet fully aware of his human weakness. Then he returned to his rooms for the final preparations.

ON THE APPOINTED DAY

From six o'clock on the preparations were under way, beginning with the chanting of Prime by the coped canons in the stalls of the choir, and the arrival of the Archbishop of Reims at the head of a grand procession. At seven the ecclesiastical peers took their places in the choir on the summons of the Chancellor of France: the bishop peers of Laon, Beauvais, Langres, Châlons, and Noyon; then the lay peers—the Duke of Burgundy, the Count of Flanders, the Count of Alençon, the Duke of Bourbon, the Count of Étampes, the Duke of Brittany. The peers were twelve in number, a sacred dozen, like the twelve Apostles and the twelve signs of the zodiac. Little by little the cathedral was filled. The crowd surrounded the portals. Already the first major ceremony, the delivery of the holy ampulla, was being performed. Between Prime and Tierce, the monks of the monastery of St. Remi of Reims drew up to the parvis of the cathedral. The abbot of St. Remi, mounted on a hackney, rode under the shade of a silken canopy borne along by four of his monks. In his hands the abbot held the vessel containing the holy balm used for anointing. The Archbishop, Jean de Craon, waited for him at the church entrance: "My lord," said the abbot, bowing quite low, "into your hands I place this precious treasure sent by heaven to the great St. Remi for the anointing of Clovis and his successors. But before I do so, I implore you, in accord with the ancient custom, do you constrain yourself to return it to me once the anointing of our king has been accomplished." Jean de Craon swore the solemn oath to the abbot, and then, followed by his prelates, he carried the precious vessel to the high altar with great reverence.

It may well be that the oath was a carry-over from the period in the High Middle Ages when relics had been such frequent objects of plunder from one monastery to another. Be that as it may, four princes of the realm were named by the King as "hostages of the holy ampulla," and they would await the return of the reliquary at the monastery. In the meantime, the abbot took his place beside the Archbishop in the cathedral, at a vantage point from which he was able to keep his eyes on the vessel for as long as it remained on the altar.

Next it was time to summon the King. The Bishops of Laon and Beauvais, wearing holy relics around their necks, made their way at the head of a procession to his bedchamber in the archiepiscopal palace. There the King was waiting, stretched out on a splendid bed.

In later centuries the ceremonial would become still more elaborate. The King, who was supposed to be asleep, would be awakened by liturgical chanting. One of the canons would then knock on the closed door with his staff. The High Chamberlain, without opening, would ask: "Whom do you seek?" "The King," would answer the Bishop of Laon. The same sentences would be repeated twice more.

Thus the King, plunged into a slumber which signified metamorphosis rather than repose, could be roused from it only by the priests who came to fetch him. He died to his earlier being in order to be reborn as someone else, through the powers of the coronation which these priests were conveying to him. From the outset, then, we see that the ceremony was an initiation rite, imbued with rich symbolism.

BEHOLD, I HAVE SENT MY ANGEL . . .

The two bishops arrived at the side of the ceremonial bed. They greeted their King with this prayer: "All-powerful and eternal God, Who hast raised to the throne Thy servant, Charles, grant that he may secure the good of his subjects so long as he shall reign, and that he may never stray from the paths of justice and truth. In the name of our Lord, amen." Then they took him by the hand and led him in solemn procession to the threshold of the cathedral, while behind them could be heard the preceptors' antiphon: "Behold, I have sent my angel to go before you and to keep you always. Listen, and hear my voice; and I will become the enemy of your enemies, and I will chastise those who harm you. And my angel will go before you."

Once inside the church, the King slowly advanced across the nave to the chancel, where he awaited the Archbishop before the high altar. The two men prayed. Then Charles took his place on the chair which had been readied for him, facing that of Jean de Craon. The Archbishop brought the holy ampulla and immediately thereafter withdrew behind the high altar to a vestry which had been installed there for him, so that he could put on the sacerdotal garments in which he would say the mass. Only after revesting himself did he approach the King, to receive the oaths and promises requested of him and sworn for all the churches under Charles's sway.

"We ask of you," the high prelate began, "that you concede outright to each of us, and to the churches which are entrusted to us, the preservation of our canonical privileges, with the rights and the jurisdiction attendant on them, and that you make it your duty to defend us, as the King must defend every bishop and the Church which is entrusted to him."

"In the name of Christ," the King responded, "I do so promise the Christian people who have been entrusted to my care. I do promise that at all times I will preserve peace between the Christian people and the Church of God; that I will abandon neither the sovereignty nor the rights of the crown; that I will forbid every act of violence or iniquity, however important it may be or its perpetrator may be; and that I will uphold justice and mercy in all my judgments, so that God may show His clemency and His goodness to us all. Likewise I will see to it that any man declared a heretic by the Church will be driven out of my realm. Upon all that I have just spoken, I take my most binding oath."

As a token of his good faith, Charles laid his hand on the Holy Scriptures; and when he had sworn his oath, he kissed the Bible he had been touching. In response to their King, the congregation struck up the *Te Deum,* and the Bishops of Laon and Beauvais led him to the altar, where he fell to his knees and prayed until that hymn of thanksgiving came to an end.

SYMBOLS

The royal garments and ornaments had already been deposited upon the communion table. These consisted of sacred vestments and emblems which had been in the keeping of the monastery of St. Denis in France and had been personally delivered by the abbot of St. Denis to those who were to invest the King with them. Every single one of them had a symbolic import: what Jean Golein—a cleric who would write, at the command of Charles V, a treatise on the coronation—called a "mysterial meaning."

"The crown, with its closed circle," Golein's treatise tells us, "signifies true fidelity, since it is round in shape, and has no beginning or end. Such is royal nobility, unscathed and unshatterable. It is golden for charity, embellished with florets for kindness, and with precious stones for unassailable equity. It has to be worn on the head, to signify that it prevails over all in true dominion and encompassing of justice, without inclining toward one side or another in a dispute." In fact, the closed circle of the crown reflected the collective character of the coronation rite, which united the King with his people.

The sword was the attribute of the military might of the King. The grip, the hilt, and the top of the scabbard were of massive gold encrusted with gems, while the scabbard itself was of a violet velvet material mounted with pearls. The sword was at one and the same time an arm of death and an arm of justice; it was under the latter title that Jean de Craon blessed it and transformed it by his gesture into a spiritual sword. Tradition has it that the sword was the symbol of the world's axis, and that it put the King in touch with the forces of the cosmos.

The scepter, Golein tells us, signified "royal majesty in what must be probity through discretion." It was the emblem of authority and the symbol of the thunderbolt. Like the royal lily, it represented the male organ, the principle of the fertility and survival of man.

Charles V's goldsmiths had outdone themselves on this occa-

sion to create the admirable scepter which can be seen today at
the Louvre, of massive gold, overlaid with precious stones, diamonds, rubies, sapphires, and pearls, surmounted by a portrait of
the Emperor Charlemagne, whose face was especially dear to our
King, his namesake.

There were also some less familiar objects. The "hand of justice" was a wand of massive gold, one cubit high, mounted with
garnets, sapphires, and pearls and surmounted by a human hand
wrought of ivory. On the ring finger there was a gold ring with a
sapphire set in it. At the same time a symbol of judiciary power
and benediction, it was made of the same materials as Solomon's
throne, gold and ivory, the latter a sign of purity and of power,
signifying the alliance of spirit and matter.

There were spurs to help the prince who wore them rush across
his kingdom to the aid of the oppressed and the defense of the
faith. They were fashioned of gold, enameled in blue and strewn
with golden fleurs-de-lis and garnets.

Finally there was a ring, the symbol of a servitude freely consented to, which signified (like its image, the hollow crown) the
union of the sovereign and his nation.

The garments with which the King was to be invested—the
tunic, hose, and surcoat in the form of an unhooded cape—were of
blue silk embroidered with the fleurs-de-lis. "The color of blue,"
comments Jean Golein, "which is the color of the heavens, shows
that Heaven comes to the aid of good kings. The embroidery of
the lilies of France signifies humility, just as the peacock sees its
beauty in its tail, and in its feet, its decline."

MYSTERIES

Risen from his knees now and standing at the foot of the high
altar, Charles had removed his own outer garments. He was wearing only his silken undercoat and vermilion shirt, into which special slits had been opened on the chest and between the shoulders, laced with gold and silver thread. "And when the King has
stripped off his outer garments," says Golein, "the act signifies
that he is leaving his worldly state behind him, to take the religious state proper to a king. And if he understands this royal

religion, as he should, I hold him to be as clean of sin as one entering religious orders."

Then the abbot of St. Denis delivered the royal boots to the Lord High Chamberlain of France, for the Chamberlain to put them on his King's feet, and the royal spurs to the Duke of Burgundy, who put them over the boots and withdrew them directly. Next, the Archbishop of Reims picked up the sword and girded the King with it. Once the sword had been belted on, the Archbishop took it by the hilt, drew it from Charles's scabbard, and holding its naked blade aloft, he pointed into the air and said, "Take this sword, a gift of God eternal, and with it vanquish the enemies of my people." Then he blessed the sword and handed it back to Charles. Taking the sword humbly, Charles fell to his knees and presented it to the altar once again, where Jean de Craon received it and gave it immediately to the closest heir to the throne, the Duke of Anjou. It was Duke Louis's duty to bear the sword, unsheathed, wherever his brother the King betook himself, till evening fell.

The climax of the mysteries, the anointing and crowning of the King, was about to begin. The high prelate returned to the altar to prepare the holy oil. He took the paten from the chalice of St. Remi and put some of the holy chrism upon the paten, as much as he would have needed to consecrate a bishop. Then he dipped the point of the golden needle which hung from the holy ampulla in the holy oil and mixed the oil with the holy chrism.

While he performed these mysteries, the precentors and subcantors intoned antiphonies, the ecclesiastical peers and the choir chanted litanies, and Charles prostrated himself on the floor at the foot of the high altar, his face laid on a velvet cushion to the left of the equally prostrate Archbishop. Then the latter got up again. His miter upon his head, and holding his crook in his left hand, the Archbishop turned toward the sovereign, who still lay stretched out with his face toward the floor. Three times the Archbishop invoked heaven: "We pray Thee, bless Thy servant, Charles, present here, whom we shall crown as our King." Then he took his place once again to the right of the King for as long as the litanies went on.

Once they were finished, Jean de Craon would pronounce the loveliest of prayers, the ones which precede the anointing ceremony. At first he stood, his miter removed, near the prostrate King, and later he sat upon his throne, his miter once more on his head, while Charles got up and knelt before him. He raised his voice for the final orison:

"Lord God, omnipotent and eternal, ruler of heaven and creator of earth, King of Kings and Lord of Lords, who rules over the destiny of angels and of men . . . shed Thy abundant blessings on Thy servant, Charles . . . so that endowed with the constant faithfulness of Abraham, the gentleness of Moses, the strength of Joshua, the humility of David which uplifted him to the throne, and adorned with the wisdom of Solomon, he may please Thee in all things, and walk with a firm, sure footstep in the paths of wisdom, and provide for the needs of the churches of his realm, and by Thy power govern his Estates with all royal authority. Let him subdue all his enemies, visible and invisible; let him not disclaim his rights to the kingdoms of the Saxons, the Mercians, the Cimbrians, and the other northern peoples within his sway; let him inspire peaceful feelings in them all, and change their hearts . . . so that he may strengthen and establish a peaceful rule by Thy grace on the throne of his ancestors for a lengthy train of days. . . . Adorn him with all the virtues with which Thou hast adorned Thy faithful servants . . . honor him with Thy abundant blessings, set him up gloriously in the rule of his kingdom, and pour upon him the anointment of the grace of the Holy Spirit."

Now Jean de Craon, still seated, began the first of the nine anointments. The Archbishop took a small amount of holy balm with his right thumb and signed the King on the crown of his head in the form of a cross, saying: "I anoint you King with this oil, which has been sanctified in the name of the Father, the Son, and the Holy Spirit." "Amen," the congregation responded. The gesture was then repeated on the King's chest, between his two shoulders, then on each shoulder separately and in the small of his arms, punctuated each time by an "amen" from the throng. All the while the anthem was resounding, "Zadok the priest and Nathan the prophet anointed Solomon in Zion, and approaching him, told him joyfully, 'May the king live forever!' " The Archbishop, still sitting on his throne, prayed again: "O Christ, do Thou Thyself anoint this King that he may rule, as Thou hast anointed priests, kings, prophets, and martyrs, who by their faith have subjugated kingdoms, accomplished what justice required of them, and received what they were promised. Let this sacred balm flow upon his head, and let it penetrate to the depths of his heart and soul, that he may merit what he has been promised, as famous kings have been in their victories the fulfillment of promises made to them. In such a way let him reign happily in the present age, and be admitted to their company in the kingdom of heaven. . . . O God, Who hast been the strength of the elect . . . we beseech Thee to sanctify by the effect of this holy oil Thy servant present here. So do Thy work that he may share in the gentleness of the dove, and give peace to a whole people who have been entrusted to him in the simplicity of his heart. . . ."

Jean de Craon, with the help of two bishops, closed the slits in the royal shirt with the golden laces and raised the King, who was still upon his knees. The Lord High Chamberlain, assisted by a deacon and subdeacon, held out the tunic, the dalmatic, and the chasuble, which had been previously blessed, so the King could be clad in these sacerdotal garments. Then Charles knelt once more to receive the eighth and the ninth anointment on his palms, and to be gloved.

Charles V, now the Lord's anointed, was then invested with the emblems of his just authority: first the ring, which was slid upon his right ring finger, as a token of his marriage to his kingdom; then the scepter, which was placed in his right hand, and the hand of justice in his left. Then the Lord Chancellor of France ascended to the altar. Turning toward the King and the congregation, he summoned the twelve peers of the realm in a loud voice, according to their order and rank, beginning with the lay peers. The Archbishop rose at last from his throne and approached the altar in his turn. He took from its place on the communion table the great crown of Charlemagne, which the monks had brought to Reims from their abbey of St. Denis, and lowered it ever so slowly over the King. He did not allow the crown to rest on the King's head, but rather held it poised above, until each of the peers in his turn had time to approach and to hold up the crown, which the Archbishop was holding with his left hand, while blessing the King with his right. The gesture of the peers symbolized the gesture of the people who accepted their King and raised him to his full dignity. The prelate's blessing went as follows: "May God crown you with the crown of glory and justice, and arm you with strength and courage."

The Archbishop alone placed the crown on the King's head, saying: "Receive the crown of your kingdom . . . that you may be so zealous for justice, so open to compassion, and so equitable in your judgments, that you will merit receiving from Our Lord Jesus Christ the crown of the eternal kingdom in the company of the saints."

When he had crowned his King, the prelate invoked the benediction of the Lord: "May the Lord extend His blessing upon you. . . . May He grant you pardon for all your sins. . . . May He set his good angels about you, to protect you. . . . May He turn the hearts of your enemies toward peace and gentleness. . . . Bless, O Lord, the strength of our prince, and be at his side in all of his works, that with Thy blessing the land he holds in dominion may yield the fruits of the earth, the fruits of heaven, the dew of the valleys, the fruits of sunlight and moonlight, the fruits of the mountaintops and the eternal hills. . . . May the blessing of the One who appeared in the burning bush flow upon his head. May the Lord heap His blessings on his children. May he have the strength of the rhinoceros, and drive enemy nations before him like a whirlwind, to the uttermost ends of the earth."

The Archbishop then took the crowned monarch by the hand and led him to the throne prepared for him in the chancel.

MAY THE KING LIVE FOREVER!

"Remain there," the prelate told the King, "keep the place which has been transmitted to you by right of heritage, and by the authority of Almighty God, and which we hereby consign to you. . . ." Having seated the King in his throne, but not yet releasing his hand, the Archbishop once again invoked the Lord's benedictions on him. "May your hand be full of strength, and your right hand do dazzling things. May justice and equity be the grounding of your throne. Lord, hear my prayer, and let my cry come unto Thee. May the Lord be with you. . . ."

Then the Archbishop of Reims took off his miter. He bowed deeply to the King, kissed him, and exclaimed at the top of his voice, "May the King live forever!" Each of the dozen peers in turn approached Charles and cheered and embraced him, while the assembly repeated in each instance, "May the King live forever!" Then they all proceeded to the coronation of the Queen. Finally, mass was said. At the offertory the two sovereigns would each make an offering of a loaf of bread, a silver vase filled with wine, and thirty gold bezants. Charles V of France received the Body of Christ in both kinds for the first time in the communion that day.

The ceremony drew near to an end. The royal couple were escorted back to their apartments and divested. The gloves and the shirts which had covered the nine anointing spots were placed in the charge of the Lord Chaplain, who burned them to avoid the possibility of profanation. The King then changed his garments, in order to be suitably attired for the great hall of the Archbishop's palace, shaped like a tau cross, where a banquet prepared and served in accord with a quite ancient ritual awaited him. Outside the banqueting hall and the palace, the entire city gave itself over to a celebration, and hoped for the miracles the new King was to work on the following day.

MIRACLE

The afflicted had gathered in great numbers. The crowds were thick about the Archbishop's palace where they awaited the arrival of the one to whom belonged, by both his royal blood and the will of heaven, the recently acquired power to heal them of their illness. They were scrofulous, stricken for the most part with tubercular adenitis. The only cure the medicine of those times knew for their affliction was a miracle. Among them were people of every station and land, who had come from the most remote regions of France, from the farthest points of Europe: peasants and mendicants from Spain, Italy, the lands of the Holy Roman Empire, to say nothing of the region around Toulouse to the southwest and Armorica to the northwest. Such was the renown of the sovereign's healing gifts that they had not hesitated to undertake such long voyages.

After having prayed for some time, Charles V made his way

124

WISE AND FOOLISH KINGS

down into the all too wretched road. Reviving the old magical gesture of contact, which transmitted an invisible current of curative virtue to the afflicted part of the body, he laid his hand on the scrofula, then made the sign of the Cross over it. Afterward he pronounced the words Philip the Fair had passed on to his eldest son on his deathbed. Whatever the formula was, it has unhappily been lost to us; in the sixteenth century, Charles's descendants would avail themselves of the famous sentence, "The King touches you; God heals you."

After the laying on of the royal hand, the afflicted withdrew, having received a few coins each as a gift from the sovereign. But they were not yet ready to depart. First they would try to obtain some of the water in which the King had washed his hands after touching them. For nine days they were to drink of it, all the while fasting and praying. On the tenth day they would be cured, without the aid of any other medicine.

On the way back to Paris, Charles turned off the main road to go to Corbeny, where the relics of St. Marcoul were kept. St. Marcoul was famous for the wonders he had performed in curing the scrofulous, and Charles might well have thought to pray for the saint's intercession with the Almighty to strengthen the King's own healing powers. He was well aware that the success of such cures would be of great use to him in his dealings with the masses. The dynasty sorely needed them. For can we doubt the sincerity of the King's belief in the saint's intercessory role and in his own fervent prayers?

Charles returned to Paris on May 28, 1364. He was the fifth man so named to be crowned king of that kingdom, and followed three Carolingians, Charlemagne, Emperor of the West, Charles the Simple, and Charles the Bald, as well as the last Capetian, Charles IV the Fair. Now he had taken his place in the line which had ruled France through the ages. There was general joy as he passed through the bulwarked streets near the cathedral of Notre Dame and reached his palace. He had been transformed into another man, marked by God with His sign. Like King Saul and King David, like the Emperor Charles, he had been given the sacred anointment by the priests, had taken the communion of bread and wine, had received the healing powers. He was the King.

ORDEAL BY FIRE

> The only way one can conquer Fortune is by the eminent virtue of a steadfast soul.
>
> Petrarch

The man whom the Lord had just raised above his peers to preside over the destinies of the realm was now twenty-six years old. We are a long way from the young Dauphin of the aftermath of Poitiers: Charles had become a man. His passage through the ordeal of fire was like those rites of passage or ritual initiations by means of which shamans and other tribal authorities transform adolescents into adults. They wait for a privileged moment in the cosmic year, a propitious period, to achieve such transformations. Sometimes a single night will do, or at the most a few days. For Charles, that night had lasted for eight years, with neither a shaman nor a high priest to guide it to a happy conclusion. Eight years of tribulations.

Between his sixteenth and his twentieth years, he had been spared nothing: great reversals, troubles and sorrows, the disappearance of all those he held dearest in the world and, more recently, the loss of his two young daughters, victims of the plague. He had had to establish himself against an immature father. There had been betrayals, too: his friend Navarre, who had played on his ingenuousness and never ceased to work for his ruin, the years of terror, his own illnesses—nothing but tribulations during those years. Could he forget all that? For Charles, life would henceforth be reduced to a struggle: afflictions to be recovered from, an enemy to be vanquished, a cancerous occupying army of Englishmen gnawing away at his kingdom like the disease which was wasting his flesh. Life had been a battle, and a battle it would remain.

"Man must be slowly ground to pieces if he is to become better," said Loyola two centuries later. The symbolism of the Strait Gate. A Catholic verity. Salvation comes through the cross that each of us here below has to carry in his turn, and it was the

King's lot to carry the cross for all of his people. The soul takes on form and weight from its portion of suffering.

As a devout Christian, Charles accepted these Catholic ideas as given. Nor was the well-being of his soul the only thing at stake: on his submission to his lot depended the very survival of the realm. To put it differently, though life remained a battle, he was to conduct it not only for himself but for an entire community; the happiness of thousands of subjects depended on his royal pleasure, as well as on what he was and was not; the fate of millions of creatures depended on his own perfection. Since antiquity, there had been innumerable *Mirrors for Magistrates,* or what were called in the Middle Ages *Summas for Kings,* to teach sovereigns their rigorous duty. An early instance of such teaching was what the Emperor Theodosius said to his son Honorius: "The citizen may limit his terrestrial pilgrimage to the pursuit of his own destiny, whereas the Prince must vouch for the future of his subjects."

The tone of the French court had changed since the beginning of the Valois dynasty. We are far from those magnificent monarchs who really lived only amid the fanfares of tourneys and revelry, and who slept the pale dawns away in a state of bliss.

We see instead at the head of this kingdom a man in the full meaning of the term. He had no age any more, it seemed. His ordeal had fashioned him and changed him, into that self he would finally become. All of his life would be henceforth circumscribed by the functions and the costume with which he had been invested on the day of his coronation. Charles of Valois took on his royalty as other men take religious orders. He had put off the old man and silenced every contrary voice within himself. From this point on he would conduct himself as a monarch and find no other fulfillment. All of his energies would flow into the exemplary image of a prince dedicating his life to the good of the realm, and called on by God to govern it. A veritable metamorphosis had taken place within him through the alchemy of the coronation rite, for "the King must begin to rule over himself in every course of action he undertakes, and must provide his subjects with an exemplary figure for their own lives."

Modern readers are inclined to be skeptical about such declarations. They smack of the patriotic stereotypes of Epinal, of hagiography, of fourteenth-century propaganda, of Machiavellianism before Machiavelli. King Charles, we might think, was a sly devil, a fox. He had a chronicle of his reign written during his own lifetime by his own hirelings. Moreover, he corrected the manuscripts himself and did not confine such corrections, to be sure, to dotting *i*'s and crossing *t*'s, or pointing out lapses in his paid chroniclers' style. Yet the fact remains that contemporary accounts, and not merely those of the royal chroniclers, are in general agreement in the praise they bestow on Charles. We may discount Christine de Pisan (from whose biography of Charles we shall have occasion to quote at length), whose instincts were to oblige the power of her patron; but others, the Norman chronicler Pierre Cauchon, and the candid memorialist Olivier de la Marche, for example, confirm her views of Charles's reign. Even Charles's worst enemy, King Edward of England, paid homage to those merits which the balance sheet of Charles's reign only confirms. Were there no flaws then in his image? We are obliged to accept it as such, and, since we are unable to add any further nuances to the accounts that have come down in Charles's praise, we must join the chorus, sound the trumpets of renown in our turn, and salute the prince who became the greatest of the Valois kings.

WEAKNESS

All the same, Charles had not emerged unscathed from his eight-year ordeal. If his soul had benefited from it, his body bore the scars. Skeleton-thin, and remarkably wan in complexion, he had barely recovered from a grave illness, if we can truthfully say that he ever recovered at all. Rumor had it that he was poisoned by his cousin, the King of Navarre, who, unable to conquer him with arms, had prudently resorted to this sort of remedy to get rid of a recalcitrant opponent. The tribulations of the preceding years were also said to have weakened the young prince's health, as one might well imagine they would. The illness was serious and unusual, and it nearly killed the prince: "All of the King's hair fell out, as did his fingernails and toenails, and he became as dry as a stick." When the herbalists and doctors of Paris proved powerless to help him, his uncle, the Emperor Charles IV, hastily sent the

King his personal physician. Having diagnosed the poison in the King's body, "he drew out all or most of the venom that had been absorbed, caused his patient to regain his hair, nails, and general health, and restored his manly strength." However, the imperial physician had made a fistulous passage in his patient's left arm, to allow the malignant humors to drain out. On taking his leave, he gave strict instructions for the drainage to continue unobstructed. "As soon as this tiny fistula ceases to drain, and dries up," he told the King, "you will die without further hope of cure, and you will have at most fourteen days to consider and concern yourself with the state of your soul."

From that time on, Charles preserved on his left arm this open wound which never stopped suppurating. With the hindsight modern medical science affords us, we can advance hypotheses about Charles's ailments quite different from the fanciful notion of an attempt to poison him. In all likelihood he was suffering from some scrofulous condition or other, complicated by a slowly developing tuberculosis, or an osteoperiostitis of the left arm. As for the other symptoms of illness—the falling hair and nails—these could have been the result of the violent emotions which the Dauphin had felt so often since 1356.

Since the medical science of that time had failed utterly to relieve the King of his afflictions, he turned to heaven as a last resort. He went on pilgrimages, increased the offerings to the patron saints of the ill, Cosmos and Damian, and in despair of a cure ordered his tailor to make him gloves with silver cuffs, so that his left hand was always kept from view.

Despite these efforts, Charles never succeeded in regaining his equilibrium. From this point on he remained the sickly, pallid man whose image has come down to us in the chronicles and iconography of the time. He had paid for the aftermath of Poitiers with his health.

In his weakened condition, he succumbed all too soon to other illnesses. His hands were deformed by gout, so that in the end his right hand was paralyzed and swollen with a chronic edema which the doctors tried to reduce by means of regular incisions. To the gout and the swelling was added a painful chill, which no treatment could overcome. Finally Charles turned to his goldsmiths, who fashioned perfume burners, shaped like large apples, of copper or silver plated with gold, to warm his fingers. Nonetheless, he experienced difficulty in using his hands for anything requiring muscular exercise. He was deprived of the use of weapons; on the other hand, he took walks, rode on horseback, and went hunting—a sport of which Charles was particularly fond, and which furnished him with exercise up to the final years of his reign. (When in 1378, two years before his death, he found himself unable to ride any longer he had himself carried to the hunt in a litter.) He was fond of exercise and open air, and spent more time enjoying them than he is reputed to have done.

Such were the major handicaps of France's prince. We must add that he suffered from constant fatigue and chronic hypertension. The show of considerable activity on the King's part, with which we are acquainted, demanded of him that he muster all the energy he could summon from his frail body. What this meant, for someone who had to struggle against the tolls of fatigue, was an ever vigilant will, unflagging effort, the body's slow attrition. In this, too, he did not hold back.

What did he not try in order to regain his lost strength? Believing in the virtues of fresh air, he left his residence in the Louvre for other, better-ventilated lodgings, the Hôtel de St. Pol. Installing himself there, he furnished his new residence, decorated it, enlarged it, subdivided its grounds with lovely gardens so that he could breathe more easily, and diligently took a walk each day, searching always and in vain for the oxygen that would restore his health. With little success.

Further afflictions came to add to his torments: diseased kidneys, rotten teeth, chronic fevers, bad digestion. He was obliged, thanks to a stomach chill caused by his gout, to pay the strictest attention to his diet. A pious story of unknown origin made the rounds: "Sobriety is a divine virtue, which the King approved and practiced at his table." If he did indeed exercise such moderation, we can say that the poor fellow did so only because he was constrained inevitably by the weakness of his constitution.

And he tried, bravely, to the extent that he was able, to better the state of his health. Theriaca (a concoction containing opium and considered to be a panacea) was par excellence the remedy prescribed for gout in those times; he used it, taking the precious liquid in flacons which would make us dream today, and which tell us quite a bit about the tastes and refined habits of their possessor. What would we not give today to see those phials described in the royal inventories: a small cylinder made of gold or jasper; long or round flacons made of gems or chalcedony, white and bezeled with silver, which he hung on tiny chains of precious metal around his neck, so that he might have them always on his person.

Anxious to reduce the edema in his hand, he also resorted to mandrake. It was a wondrous plant, if we are to believe a classic of that time entitled *The Great Property of Things:* "Mandrake is an herb which bears on its leaves tiny apples which are of a sweet and delicate odor. Its roots have the form of a man or woman. You give the bark of this herb, with wine, to someone on whom you want to operate for stones, so that he will sleep through the operation and not feel pain."

According to the Hellenistic physician Dioscorides, "You must use it wisely, for whoever takes too much of it will die from the overdose. It has the virtue of chilling and mortifying, and as a result, the juice of this herb, placed on the temples with human milk, causes someone to sleep despite the fact that he may be suffering from an acute illness, just as Plateaires tells us. The mandrake has many other virtues, for it reduces all swelling." King Charles had a simple leather box made to preserve "a pair of mandrakes."

Stones also contained astonishing powers, or so Charles learned from the lapidaries of the royal library, and he got some of these. The bezoar was said to cure malignant fevers; he ordered a tiny purse "within which are hanging, each one upon a tiny chain of gold, two petrified bones, good against poison, namely, a tiny black snake's head called 'lapis albashar,' and another tiny square white bone." The stones found in large sponges constitute a sovereign remedy against gout, and so he owned one, bezeled with gold, engraved with Hebrew letters and a royal portrait. He had it placed inside a cypress chest, which never left his side, and to which he alone had the key.

Perhaps it is wise to see more than simple necessity in this constant preoccupation with taking care of his health. Behind it lay a great deal of anxiety. Feeling in his own flesh a menace which would never allow him rest, a real enough menace, but one which his nerves must have exacerbated, Charles sought outside help that was not solely in the physiological domain. Doctors and their remedies reassured him, and he tried every possible remedy so that his conscience would be at peace even if his body was not cured. The rest was up to God and His saints, the last and highest court of appeal.

It is impossible to keep count of the different reliquaries appointed for various saints whose curative powers related to Charles's ailments. St. Étienne, who had been stoned to death, was invoked by those with stones inside their organs. And so in the palace there were some quite beautiful objects which bore witness to the prince's special desire to win the favors of that holy martyr for himself. Itemized among these was "this golden gem, wherein there was a part of the head of St. Étienne surrounded by emeralds and Alexandrian rubies, standing on a silver pedestal, which said reliquary weighs two gold marks, and the pedestal (which is silver), two silver marks and two ounces." St. Lawrence and St. Ursula cured pains in the regions of the kidneys, regardless of their origins, whether muscular, like lumbago, or nephritic, like kidney stones. Each of these saints had his little gold reliquary in Charles's palace, St. Lawrence's bearing a gridiron in memory of his torture, shaped like a tiny pallet set in gold and dangling on a silken lace. St. Elizabeth of Hungary and St. Christopher, sovereign both of them against toothache, were each entitled to particular devotions. But they could not prevent the King from seeing, after 1374, that his condition was worsening, to the point that from that year on he made arrangements for a regency. He knew that his days were numbered.

THE MARK OF HIS MIND

Christine de Pisan, one of the first female writers in France, to whom we owe a biography of our prince, the *Book of the Deeds and Good Customs of King Charles V* (a book which smacks somewhat of hagiography), has left us a portrait of him. To tell the truth, she had never seen him, for she wrote this work after his death, basing what she said on testimony gathered from those who

132   WISE AND FOOLISH KINGS

had known him, among them her father, an Italian astrologer
whom Charles had brought to the Louvre.

The reality does not seem to match her description, which in all
probability was idealized. But what was this reality? The sole portrait of John the Good dates from 1359. But a few years later,
painters, sculptors, and illuminators worked wonders: the numerous miniatures in the royal manuscripts, among them a famous
one by the painter John of Bruges in the Bible given to Charles by
his adviser, Vaudetar; the statues of the Hospital of the Quinze-
Vingts, which represent St. Louis and Margaret of Provence beneath the reigning King and Queen; an altar cloth (called the
"Narbonne Altar Cloth"), of a remarkable design in grisaille on
white silk, in which Charles and his wife figure—all of these portraits are in accord. An expression, then, a profile, a certain thick-
ness of the lips suffice to re-establish contact with this man who
vanished half a millennium ago.

The prince seems frail, it is true, but with a face modeled by his
soul, a vivacity in his expression tempered by reflection. The man
does not appear overwhelmed or possessed by the world he experienced by way of his senses. He must have been able to place a
certain distance between himself and the world, that enabled him
to weigh, judge, discriminate, sort out the important from the sub-
sidiary, what endures from what passes. He must have taken the
measure of beings and of things, and made his choice among
them.

The nose is fine and sensitive; the mouth large and fleshy. This
is a man who knew life, but his instincts must have been mastered
and relegated to a secondary plane. Torments and uneasiness left
their mark in those eyes, their stamp on that cheek, their lines on
that forehead. An intense life of the mind still animates him. And
if Petrarch, who met Charles in 1362, wrote to his friend Pierre
Bersuire that he was struck by the "quite burning intelligence" of
this young man, his judgment hardly surprises us. The predomi-
nance of Charles's mind can be read upon his face, some six centuries later.

KINGSHIP HOLDS THE OBLIGATION OF VIRTUE

> The King must begin to rule over himself in every course of action
> he undertakes, and must provide his subjects with an exemplary
> figure for their own lives.
>
> Charles V

As the age understood virtue, the idea connoted marital fidelity
above all else. We know that, while still Dauphin, Charles's lot
had hardly been that of the faithful husband. Two bastards were
attributed to him: Oudart d'Attainville, the Bailiff of Rouen, and
Jean de Montaigu, the minister of Charles VI, who would later be
decapitated. A year before his accession, in 1363 to be precise,
Charles displayed the armorial bearings of a woman who was not
his wife: a letter "K" and a swan with extended wing—we can recognize the name of his Italian mistress Biette Cassinel, the mother
of Montaigu.

Such follies, however, were incompatible with the royal dignity,
and Charles would soon confine the favor of his attentions to his
wife, Queen Joan.

Joan of Bourbon was the daughter of Pierre I of Bourbon, who
had been killed on the battlefield of Poitiers, and of Isabelle of
Valois, Philip VI's half sister. She was therefore Charles's cousin
and a member of a very great noble family.

We might well wonder what it was that her young husband felt
for her at the outset of their married life, when she was the same
age as he, no more than twelve years old, and during their adolescent years when he so conspicuously deserted her. No doubt she
was a friend, a sister, someone to whom he would return one day.
She was a certainty in his life, if a slightly stifling one; a tranquil
reality as well. But not the Lady, the Dream, not yet the longed-
for Other. Each of them lived in separate lodgings; hers was a
modest life, watched over by attendants as befitted a future queen,
his a life of adolescent pranks. But in those somber hours when all
was tottering about him, she was there, never leaving his side, following him out of Paris. Two little girls were born to them, whom
they would lose to the plague. Their grief loosened the scarcely

formed ties between them. The Dauphin grew alarmed at the difficulty his wife had experienced in bringing her pregnancies to term. Did he already fear that he would die childless? Did he blame her? Once again he left her, and sought his fortune elsewhere. Joan wept for her dead children. She waited for her prodigal husband, who returned to take her to Reims for the coronation rites, in which, at last, she became his Lady.

We do not know much about this queen. We can imagine her, sweet, elegant, refined, entirely enclosed within the shadow of her royal husband. She represented fidelity, a steady anchorage in a storm, an unconditional welcome; and in so laborious a life, wholly given over to kingship, she was his tie to life, his peace, his permanence.

In the padded world where she reigned, with its repose for body and soul alike, its refuge, its pleasures for the eyes, "all," to quote Baudelaire, "is order and beauty, luxuriance, calm, and voluptuousness." In her presence the King regained his strength and life, as did Antaeus in contact with Mother Earth. In her company he led a settled, orderly existence, in an atmosphere befitting His Royal Majesty, and with all the splendor he desired.

THE ORDER OF THE DAYS

Here is the daily schedule which Christine de Pisan attributes to King Charles: "The King's levee took place regularly between six and seven o'clock in the morning. . . . After the sign of the Cross and a first prayer, he would exchange joyful, courteous words with his servants. . . . When he was ready, he would be brought his breviary, and a chaplain would help him recite his canonical hours. At eight o'clock, he would go to mass, which was celebrated gloriously every day with melodious, solemn chanting. . . .

"As he left the chapel, all manner of people, rich or poor, ladies young or old, widowed wives or others, who had business with him, could give him their requests, and he would stop most compliantly to listen to their supplications, and would make every effort to satisfy the reasonable and pitiful ones. The more doubtful ones he sent on to some administrator of requests. Then, if it was the day of the Council, he took himself there.

Philip VI and Joan of Burgundy. *(Bibliothèque Nationale)*

The naval disaster at l'Ecluse on June 24, 1340, began a series of defeats. The major part of the fleet was destroyed. *(Photographie Giraudon)*

The battle of Crécy. "The English bowmen moved forward . . . they fired in unison so that the arrows fell like snow on the kneeling mercenaries." *(Bibliothèque Nationale)*

John of France was a man who issued from the dark night of the times. *(Archives Photographiques*

The battle of Poitiers, 1356. *(Bibliothèque Nationale)*

John the Good and Joan of Boulogne. *(Bibliothèque Nationale)*

The townspeople of Jacques were massacred in the town of Meaux by the forces of the King of Navarre. *(Bibliothèque Nationale)*

Charles V is anointed by the Archbishop of Reims. "I bless you in the name of the Father, the Son, and the Holy Ghost." *(Bibliothèque Nationale)*

The christening of Prince Charles, eldest son of Charles V.
(Photographie Giraudon)

Charles V.
(Archives Photographiques)

Joan of Bourbon.
(Archives Photographiques)

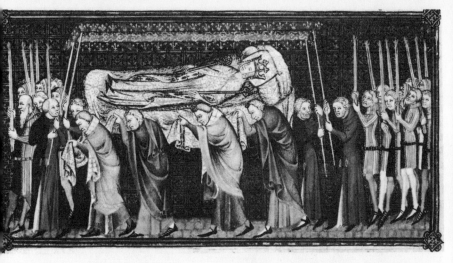

The funeral procession of Joan of Bourbon. The whole month of February 1378 was filled with mourning. *(Bibliothèque Nationale)*

An idealized image of the royal family. Charles V, Joan of Bourbon, and their children, Prince Charles, his brother, Louis, and their sisters, Marie and Isabelle. *(Bibliothèque Nationale)*

The murder of Louis d'Orléans. His young page, Jacob van Melkeren, tried to protect him by lying on top of him, but the assassins
killed him too. *(Bibliothèque Nationale)*

"Toward ten o'clock, if nothing interfered, he proceeded to the table. His repast was not long . . . and, following King David's example, he listened pleasurefully afterward to muted instruments, such as would make his spirits joyful, as softly and sweetly played as the art of music permits.

"When he left the table, all manner of foreigners or others could come toward him, to discuss their affairs with him. You would find there all manner of ambassadors and diverse lords, foreign princes, knights of diverse countries. And quite often there was such a press of knights and barons, as many foreigners as his countrymen, that you could scarcely turn around in his grand and magnificent chambers and halls. And this most prudent King received them all without fail, quite wisely and kindly.

"News of all manner of countries was reported to him there, or news of the fortunes and events of his wars, or of other battles, and thus of diverse things. He would give orders there as to what was to be done as the case demanded, or would entrust the decision to his Council, would argue a contrary position meetly, would bestow favors, would sign letters with his own hand, would give suitable gifts, and fill vacant offices, or grant legitimate requests. With these or similar occupations he would employ the space of nearly two hours, after which he would withdraw to take some rest, which would last about an hour.

"On his reawakening, he would spend a moment with his relations, and they would amuse themselves with agreeable things, and he would look after his jewels or other pretties. He would take this recreation so that the burden of his too numerous affairs would not harm his health. Then he would go to vespers. If it was summer, he would enter his gardens. If he was at the palace at St. Pol, the Queen would come to him and his children would be brought to him. There, he would speak to the women and make inquiries as to their state. On other occasions, he would be offered strange gifts from diverse places, artillery or some other trappings of war. Or else some merchants would come, bringing him velvet, cloth of gold, and all manner of lovely, strange things, or jewels, which he would let connoisseurs look at, for there were some in his family.

"In winter, he would often spend his time in hearing someone read beautiful stories from the Holy Scriptures, or from the *Deeds of the Romans,* or *Moralities of Philosophers,* and in other studies, until the supper hour. After supper, he would entertain himself with his knights and barons, then would withdraw and go to bed. And so, by continual order, the wise king would employ the course of his life."

In the conception which the King had formed of the obligations of his office, the Queen was to play an important role. She had to offer an exemplary image of herself, in which the dignity of life was allied with magnificence. Along with her account of the King's hours, Christine has described "the rule which King Charles kept with respect to the state of the Queen."

"Among the political matters and the rulings instituted by wise King Charles, in what triumph, what peace, what order was the court of that most noble lady, his wife, Queen Joan of Bourbon, governed, as much in the magnificence of its state, as in its honest manners of living. . . . In what dignity was this Queen crowned or adorned with great wealth of jewels, dressed with royal garments, large, long, and flowing, made of the most precious cloth of gold and silk, decorated and gleaming with rich gems and precious pearls, with sashes, buttonholes, and ties, garments which she changed several times over as the royal custom demanded. Such was her splendor that it was a marvel to see this noble Queen in the course of various solemnities, accompanied by two or three other queens, her predecessors or relatives, to whom she brought great honor as their right and due ordained it, her noble mother, and duchesses, wives of the King's noble brothers, countesses, baronesses, ladies married and unmarried in quite great numbers, all of lineage, virtuous, suited for virtue and well schooled in it. Otherwise they should not have been suffered in that place, and all of them were dressed in the proper garments, each according to her station, and as suited the solemnity of the celebration.

"The countenance of this lady, staid, praiseworthy and moderate in word, deportment, and look, assured with everyone, adorned with every beauty, surpassing other princesses, was something most agreeable to see and a sovereign pleasure. The decorations of her halls and chambers, of strange and rich embroideries, with large pearls on gold and silk diversely fashioned, the gold and silver plates, were a great marvel. . . .

"To the joy of his barons who took pleasure in their prince's presence, he would dine in a common room with them; similarly, he liked the Queen to be on her throne, among her princesses and ladies. . . . She was served by gentlemen entrusted to this purpose by the King, who were modest, loyal, good, and virtuous, and during her repast, in order to obviate vague and worthless words and thoughts, she had a wise man at the foot of the table, who never stopped speaking of the deeds of honorable customs of some good men, long deceased.

"In such manner the wise King governed his loyal spouse, whom he held in all peace and love and in continual pleasure, just as he sent her strange and lovely things, like jewels, and other gifts, if they were given him. If he thought that they might please her, he bought them for her. He was often in her company, and always with joyful face and pleasing words, and she, for her part, in bringing him the honor and reverence which pertained to his excellence, did similarly. And so the King in all respects kept her in sufficiency, love, unity and peace."

Such was the Queen wished by the King, fashioned to please him, essentially submissive, apparently happy, as she had to be. Was her serene face only a mask? What did Joan of Bourbon feel within her destiny as queen?

THE WORLD IS A CLOSED GARDEN

She was a princess of the highest lineage, of closed palaces and locked gardens, who since childhood had been given all the gold of the world, and gems and pearls as well, crowns and clasps, ruby rings, diamonds, emeralds. Incomparable ornaments, a pleasure for the eyes, and the security of knowing that her image had been brought to its highest perfection.

She was a princess brought up far from her own people. What mother dried her tears, what nurse, what lady of her entourage opened to her those loving arms in which the hurts of childhood vanish? She was brought up with no father to meet her every day, on whom she might have tried her powers of seduction in order to feel secure about herself. When young Joan gazed into her mirror, she saw reflected her frail complexion, her indecisive traits, a girl in search of herself, in search of the Other, which was a well-known face, a name endlessly pronounced, an exchange of promises and rings. For that one man only, one question only remained possible, one adventure only and one risk: would he like her? What man of the court would dare to raise his eyes upon the spouse of the King's eldest son? There was no surprise, nothing unforeseen, nothing to expect in this life. All had been said, traced out in advance, inscribed in the Dauphine's destiny, precise as a clock, slow and irremediable as time. The world was a closed garden. "There the rose and the lily of the valley bloom, and later still the hollyhock." The honeysuckles and the gillyflowers distilled their drowsy perfumes. On June nights they filled the air with their scents.

The Dauphine walked with submissive steps under the watchful eye of the Queen, in the company of her ladies, her chaplain, and her unseen good angel, down paths where the hyssop grew. "Where is the prince," the girl would think, "where is my handsome knight, my blameless spouse?"

Evening fell upon Paris. The air was soft, the light fine. "What more do I need?" sighed the Dauphine, adorned with silk and pearls, surrounded by servants in her palace. "What can it be that I miss so much?"

"Give thanks, Princess, for all that you've been given," whispered her confessor in his commanding voice, "and be careful, for sadness is a sin."

The Dauphine felt guilty. "Where is happiness?" she still dared to think. But who in this crowd could answer her? To whom could she admit what she suspected, indeed what she knew, though no one had had the heart to tell her? The Dauphine was proud, by birth as much as by marriage. And the Dauphine was waiting. The days went by, in banquets and celebrations. The Dauphine was still waiting. The Dauphine smiled, but nothing could distract her. The Dauphine, ill served in love, kept her silence.

With the misfortunes of the kingdom, the Dauphine saw this period of her life come to an end. Her young husband had sown his wild oats so that he might the better return to her; all that time had been nothing but a long betrothal. So everything turned out for the best. It was better for her to save her tears. For the anguish of waiting, which had undermined her yesterday, when she was still a girl, had turned, now that she was a woman, into the anguish of death: all those dangerous pregnancies that might have ended badly, all those children who did not survive, or who were born frail and grew up ill.

That man, who cared a good deal more for his kingdom than for his Queen, needed numerous descendants, whom Joan had to provide him with at all costs. This obligation carried a large risk for her, and she knew it. Would she fail in her duties as a queen, which were, first of all, to engender heirs?

All the same she was afraid, and her fear loomed larger from birth to birth, from mourning to mourning. This world was an Eden and a hell. She wanted to shout these feelings aloud, to tell someone, but who would understand her? Not her husband, taken up as he was with governing, and pursuing a much nobler concern than the terrors of a pampered wife. What he required of her every day was a silent, reassuring presence. Would she burden him with her own specters? Would he be able to find the words she needed to hear?

Finally the day came when she could no longer suppress her accumulated fears. The Queen was dying of this silence, this smiling. The Queen could no longer wear this mask of serenity. Then, for the first time, she abandoned her customary reserve. She refused and she evaded her duties as the wife of Charles V, by the only means available to her: illness, the last resource. Walled up within her anguish, the Queen, struck by psychosis, abandoned herself to forces stronger than she was.

The precise nature of her ailment is unknown, through a dearth of sufficient details. The chronicle tells us that she lost her memory entirely. What unbearable pain was she hoping to forget in this way? In order to live in a present unhaunted by her early fears, she had erased from her awareness every trace of her past existence.

Her amnesia lasted for only a few months, in the course of the year 1372, and allowed her time, for all we know, to catch her breath once again.

Five years later, on February 6, 1377, Joan of Bourbon died of a puerperal fever, while giving birth to a daughter, Catherine. The King remained inconsolable. His obligation of virtue had yielded its place to quite different feelings.

KINGSHIP HOLDS THE OBLIGATION OF KNOWLEDGE

A king without letters is a mariner without oars and a bird without feathers.

Evrart de Trémaugon

This prince was endowed with the greatest of gifts—one whose lack is irremediable and the only one which allows men to make up for certain character defects—intelligence. Today, after giving him the appropriate tests, psychologists would certainly give him a very high IQ. But what seems remarkable enough for us to emphasize it, and rare enough among people of his rank, was the fact that this intelligence (which can be qualified as exceptional) was accompanied by a quite lively taste for things of the mind. Our prince was an intellectual. Kings, their relations, their entourages generally have taste and open minds. They encourage arts and letters and culture, they are to a certain extent patrons, but they do not devote much of their time to study. Charles V, with his precarious health, was, we might well allege, for want of anything better, a man of the study. He accounted for the time he could not spend horseback riding or disporting by reading books, and little by little he acquired a taste for them. No doubt his physical handicap contributed to this taste, but that would hardly explain it.

Charles V possessed a genuinely intellectual temperament. He loved reading, and he loved learning. He was curious about everything that was being written and thought about, in his own age and earlier on. He loved the company of those who made a profession of the intellect, and he sought out their advice, followed and savored their subtle debates, judged them on their worth—which was no small thing. He understood what wealth they represented for the country and how to draw upon this wealth through good government. "We cannot honor the clerics too much," he was fond of saying, "because wisdom is in them. For as long as wisdom is honored in this kingdom, it will remain prosperous, but when wisdom is spurned, it will decline." And posterity did not err in attributing the epithet "the Wise" to Charles V, a word which means prudent but also erudite. "A true disciple of Wisdom, a true philosopher, a true searcher into the first principles of things," comments Christine de Pisan.

THE FALCONRY TOWER

One of Charles's first acts as king was to enlarge his private library. In 1367 he decided to transfer his books from the Palais de la Cité, where they had been kept, to the Louvre. He chose as a place to house his collection the Falconry Tower, which stood on the northwest side of the building, on the spot where the Clock Tower wing stands today, and he entrusted the task of accomplishing the move to the architect Raymond du Temple.

The affair was conducted swiftly. Master craftsmen, workers, and artists got busy, and the first floor was made an object of particular concern. The walls were covered over with panels of Irish wood, the arches with cypress. On the two upper floors, improvements were made, timberwork was checked, stone was scraped, and cleaning, painting, and decorating went on. Cloth drapes were hung on the walls; the various benches and desks and spindles for the books were looked over; lecterns were procured; the furnishings of the palace library (which were still usable) were restored like new; doors were added to protect against possible thefts; and iron-wire gratings were placed in the windows, "as a protection against birds and other animals." Chandeliers and candelabra were installed in the proper places. With the plugging and nailing and cleaning and gluing that went on, the air reeked of wax and fresh plaster. In eighteen months the work was completed.

The ancient store of books which the King had received from his Capetian and Valois predecessors was brought and put in place. The loveliest volumes came from Vincennes, where they had been carefully kept. These included the sumptuous liturgical manuscripts with gold backgrounds which the French monarchs had commissioned, over a century and a half, from the best artists of the time; the psalters of Ingeborg of Denmark (the first wife of Philippe-Auguste); a Bible, executed by Jean de Sy for John the Good. Other volumes, of lesser value, destined for readers of that time—popular works, works of moral edification, juridical treatises —made up the bulk of the collection from the Palais de la Cité.

Now they were all gathered in one place and entrusted to the care of Gilles Mallet, Charles V's manservant, who "read masterfully well and was skillful at punctuation." Mallet's new title was "Custodian of the Royal Library," but he was not to limit himself to preserving the collection that already existed. Rather, he was to carry on, under the personal direction of his royal master, a dynamic policy of acquisition and commissioning which would provide a considerable extension to the royal collection.

At the same time a team of copyists, illuminators, and bookbinders, of like tastes, was assembled, and henceforth they would work permanently in the King's library. No time was wasted in gathering together the stiff hides which cracked when touched, the quires of paper, the bundles of parchments, and the vellums on which Charles V's favorite scribes, men like Raoullet d'Orléans and Henri Trévou, would display their scholarly hands. Orders were transmitted for pressboards, for velvet patches, for decorated clasps. Provisions were laid up of writing kits of horn and silk, styluses and writing pens, rulers and erasers, leather bottles which contained inks of various colors, ochers and burnt siennas, powders of gold and lapis lazuli, and white and bright red waxes.

THE BOOK, THAT RESOURCE OF GOOD GOVERNMENT

The King had grand designs for his library. It was not to remain a closed, dead place, the repository of an esoteric learning reserved for his person only. Soon he would open it to his entourage, his advisers, and yet other readers, chosen from among those scholars of whom he was so fond. He conceived of his library as a center for studies, even a meeting place, a place for common reflection, for research and the exchange of scholarly views, all effected under his aegis. The book existed for recreation, to be sure, for delight, for the contemplation of amateur enthusiasts and scholarly bibliophiles, and had an extraliterary role to play in these times as well: the miniatures contained in old books often played the role easel paintings would play later on. But the major virtue of the book in Charles's eyes consisted in providing instruction of political significance. The book should be an aid to good government, and it was there to be consulted as a prelimi-

nary to any governmental action. The prince was keenly aware of
the shortcomings of his own upbringing. With respect to the craft
of kingship, he felt like a self-taught man, having had no other
master than himself.

The men of those times needed a father. The prevailing tone
was humility: you did not believe in your own individual virtues,
your own individual judgment. To support your pronouncements
and direct your footsteps, you had to have the security of a higher
authority than yourself, God perhaps, or the ancients, by whom
everything had already been said. Good government was regarded
as a science whose laws had been formulated in bygone ages by
uncontested masters, the authorities to whose thinking it was advisable that every monarch wishing to govern knowledgeably
should turn.

And it was here that Charles V was responsible for a great innovation. At the time of his reign, by some curious quirk of logic,
all that precious knowledge seemed reserved for members of a social order that had no direct influence over events—the clerics—
simply because the texts were in Latin. At the end of the fourteenth century, when the French language was becoming more and
more firmly established every day, the King and his entourage did
not know much Latin. Charles therefore decided to undertake a
policy of systematic translation, so that he himself, and those
charged with looking after the kingdom, might have available to
them the ancient texts necessary to sustain their reflections.

To carry through this project, the King recruited the best minds
of his time—among them, Raoul de Presles, Bishop of Lisieux;
Nicole Oresme; and Jean Golein, a Carmelite monk. Charles welcomed them into his service, turned to them for advice, and took
their counsel into account. Thanks to their conscientious labor,
there would be translated into French and so placed within reach
of a larger number of readers, the Bible—the book par excellence
for Christians, and one which the King read each year from end to
end—and Aristotle and St. Augustine, the masters of medieval
thought. Raoul de Presles would translate the sacred books and
Augustine's *City of God*, the latter work requested of him "for the
public use of the kingdom, and of all Christendom." Nicole
Oresme would transpose into the national language Aristotle's
Ethics, Politics, and *Economics,* while Jean Golein would do a

whole series of works, among them the *Treatise on the Coronation* of which we have spoken at length earlier in the chapter. Other translators would join them in this enterprise and extend what they had done. We can thus understand the political significance of these labors, performed methodically under the direct impetus of the monarch.

Nor was that all. Having sounded out the ancients, this King, who was nonetheless completely won over to the scholastic mode of thinking, found himself confronted with an unsettling discovery: the old masters had not said all there was to be said. Those reflections which the events of his time and his own experience had inspired in him had not been formulated by the old authorities. Yet it would be most useful for these new truths, growing out of the present moment, to be expressed and made known. For public opinion, he had learned to his cost, was a force with which power would have to reckon, and a new force at that. It was powerful, but changeable, malleable, for the people were fickle. If information was well understood it could ward off storms, nurture public loyalty, and enlighten minds as well, in the process of educating them. Charles could not conduct his reforms without popular support, and he knew this. It was necessary to let his people know the present situation, the dangers which had been incurred and which were still imminent, and what had been done by those who governed to protect them from those dangers. Thus, he ordered his historians to give an account of the reign of his father, and of his own reign, which would serve to continue the *Grand Chronicles of France*. By the same token, he had disseminated the positions of his government on the relations between the spiritual and the temporal powers, i.e., between popes and kings, in a treatise entitled *Le Songe du Vergier* (*The Prophet's Dream*). In this treatise, a scholar and a knight engage in a leisurely dialogue on this fundamental problem of medieval Christendom.

It was left up to the enlightened readers to adjust their opinions on the matter. For his part, the King had a tranquil conscience, for he had done all that he could to try to convince them.

It was, then, a veritable brain trust the King had gathered about himself. The role of these theoreticians was not confined to entrusting their ideas to books. We find their influence on Charles manifested in his legislative acts, which were significant, as well as in the various other domains of his action.

917 VOLUMES

Each day, in the late afternoon, Charles V, dressed in simple clerical attire, spent long hours in his library while someone read to him from Valerius Maximus or Aristotle. There he could contemplate with satisfaction some 917 volumes gathered in that place by his firm will, and now catalogued for him by his faithful Mallet. Certain of those volumes were on rolls of parchment, but the greater part of them were flat books, short and thick, either square or rather longish and closed with a key, sometimes written in two or three columns. The lettering was of an old, still appealing form, or of a newer, mongrel sort, or of the Bolognese fashion. The manuscripts were illuminated in gold, blue, and pink, with blue or gold fleurs-de-lis running the length of the columns. Their borders were embellished with gold and black or colored inks, and their edges were painted with the fleur-de-lis or gilded with bezant-shaped lozenges. Many of them were quite lovely volumes destined for booklovers. All of them were addressed to the man of learning. Works of theology, law, history, and literature found their place among the spindles of the Falconry Tower. But there were also treatises on the arts and sciences; encyclopedic compilations called "Images of the World" or "Book of the Properties of Things"; books about birds, beasts, and stones (which at that time were called "volucraries," "bestiaries," and "lapidaries"); sixty volumes of medicine and surgery, eight on the moral niceties of the game of chess ("chess moralized"), two treatises on music, not to mention an immense collection of books on astronomy and astrology. There was also an occult literature section, amounting to thirty volumes of geomancy, four volumes of chiromancy, and a volume of necromancy. What these thirty-odd volumes show is that our prince had always taken a lively interest in the occult sciences, and in astrology most of all. While he was still Dauphin, he had kept in his service an astrologer, Pèlerin of Prussia, several of whose treatises are extant. As we know, he brought into his court from Italy another astrologer, Thomas de

Pisan, Christine's father. For King Charles, whatever views about astrology Raoul de Presles or Nicole Oresme might have held (and Charles's reliance on them was extremely strong), "True astrology, free of superstition," was "the noblest science of this age," perhaps because it revealed the secret influences the stars were supposed to exert on men and on events. Like the whole of human knowledge, astrology was an aid to good government.

GOOD POLICY

> Our acts are attached to us as its glimmer is to phosphorus: they burn us, but make for our brilliance.
>
> André Gide

The King devoted the whole of his being to his royal functions. To them he offered his very life, his attachments, his tastes, his gifts, and his desires. Such was the homage he paid to the kingdom he regarded as an integral part of himself, his own flesh. He was accustomed to using the phrase, "We and our people." He drew no distinction between the two. There was no barter. It is an affecting and chastening thing to see him thus, stepping forward onto the stage of history, this frail man, stooped under so great a weight. "Power," he remarked, "was more of a burden to me than a glory."

But none of it had been given him in vain. In his hard labor, the man fulfilled himself.

A HEAD FOR POLITICS

Chance? A lucky accident? An event, in any case: for the first time in three generations, the reigning member of the Valois dynasty was suited for the exercise of power. Where did he come by this aptitude, up to that time in such short supply among the Valois? His tastes for luxury, pomp, lovely objects and books were family traits. His lively intelligence can be explained by the genes of some of his ancestors, who were fairly well endowed in that respect, such as Charles of Valois, his great-grandfather, Joan of

Burgundy, his redoubtable grandmother, not to mention the Luxemburg branch of the family. His lack of interest in jousting, the irritation he felt about physical prowess and high deeds of chivalry, were sufficiently justified by his state of health, and equally by his father's excessive addiction to these pastimes. His sincere piety recalls that of his grandfather, Philip. But so much political sense? We have to confess that he was surely the first of his line to have inherited it as his lot. Perhaps, for all we know, he owed it to his Capetian forebears.

He was a man well armed for the task of kingship: he possessed reflection, judgment, prudence, moderation, method, a lively and (as we know) well-rounded mind suited for learning, understanding, and speculating, a good deal of knowledge and a facility with words: all in all a strong mind, but—alas!—a weak body. That being the case, he would direct the country from the depths of his study. Such a thing had never been seen at that time: a king was supposed to appear on the field of battle at the head of his troops. Charles sent out war chiefs, judiciously chosen by himself. And admiring contemporaries would exclaim: "King Charles was extremely wise and virtuous, and so he appeared throughout his life; for while never leaving his chambers or giving up his private diversions, he regained the territory his predecessors had lost, with their helmets on their heads and their swords drawn, on the battlefields."

Let that pass as a chronicler's judgment. But when the King of England himself remarks: "Never has there been a king in France who took up arms less, and all the same never has there been a king who gave me so much trouble," the conclusion seems clear. Charles's bold innovation was altogether successful.

OTHER PEOPLE'S ADVICE

Nor was that all. At the risk of singing praises, let us pull out all the stops. To so many natural or acquired abilities, we must add that of discernment. This last gift conferred on our prince an unwavering knowledge of his fellow men. He was able, through long experience and pressing need, to fathom the very hearts of others, and to choose from among them those with firm backs and loyal breasts—true men who would serve him unconditionally, just as he himself served the country. Charles V had a knack both for finding great attendants and for holding their loyalty. Moreover, the choice of an entourage constitutes a method of governing. The King worked for his kingdom, but with the help of its best men. Nothing can be done alone, even if you are the King. Charles knew this, and he sought ceaselessly after subtle minds. He recruited wise men: clerics and laymen; dignitaries of the Church; members of the Parlement and of the Chamber of Accounts; knights and burghers. With the exception of his brothers, who were called "princes of the fleurs-de-lis"—Anjou, Berry, Burgundy, all of whom served at his side—he did not choose his counselors from the ranks of the upper nobility.

It was to these men, then, who had earned recognition for their exceptional competence, that the King each day submitted the questions which arose in the course of his governance. Each one was to speak as his convictions and his personal knowledge dictated—"to give counsel," a key phrase for this prince, who was endowed with a remarkable capacity for listening. The King would speak only after all the others had spoken. He always decided alone.

THE GREAT STEWARDS

In the first rank of the King's advisers was the royal Chamberlain, Bureau de la Rivière, of old gentry from Nevers. The Chamberlain was Charles's most intimate associate, as well as being the one whose counsel Charles heeded most. He was reputed to be "gentle, courteous, kindly, and forbearing toward the poor and humble." He followed his master about like a shadow, "for truly, if you pushed one of them, you knocked against the other." In all councils, missions, negotiations, he was Charles's personal agent; his friend, too.

Next in order of importance came two brothers of more modest origin, Jean and Guillaume de Dormans, the sons of an ordinary lawyer in the Parlement of Paris. One was a cleric, the other a layman; both had begun in the Parlement, and both were devoted body and soul to their prince, who put them at the head of the royal chancellery. Nor did his rights or his diplomacy, which he entrusted to their vigilance, suffer as a result. To Milon, Guillaume de Dormans's son, Charles gave some choice bishoprics, and later the presidency of one of the great political bodies of the state, the Chamber of Accounts.

Pierre d'Orgemont, of even more modest stock, was a man of clear, precise intelligence. It was said of him that he was "strong-minded, and so obstinate that it would have been easier to reverse a mill wheel than sway him from his course." He was a character, it seemed, and absolute in his love for his royal master, but he was extremely clever as well. Undaunted at the age of seventy, he succeeded Guillaume de Dormans in the chancellery. For the key positions, then, Charles found great stewards.

After the events of 1356, Paris had to be kept under control by skillful administration. The King required a forceful Provost, and found one in the person of a provincial bailiff, Hugues Aubriot by name. Charles had seen him in action in Burgundy, under difficult conditions, when he pitilessly scourged the brigands of the Free Companies. "I've got my man," thought the King, and he was not mistaken. Aubriot, too, was something of a character—active, hated and feared by instigators of civil disorder, loved by the artisans, he was a tireless worker, and took chances. So much for Paris.

And for the whole of his realm Charles found an unknown Breton of the petty gentry who had distinguished himself under identical circumstances at the siege of Melun for his unbelievable hardheadedness. His name was Bertrand du Guesclin. "Snub-nosed, swarthy, and petulant, the ugliest man there was from Rennes to Dinan," Du Guesclin was an unrepentant brawler whose physical strength was equal to any ordeal. He was a tenacious, aggressive man, loyal as only Bretons are loyal, and he was other things as well: a remarkable leader of men, crafty and sly when he had to be, and a battle-hardened officer, rather than a knight on horseback who turned out for reviews only. He was precisely the sort of good right arm that a sedentary king required, and Charles made him High Constable of France. To lead his navy, Charles chose Admiral Jean de Vienne, the only member of his circle of close advisers to come from the great nobility.

The King was extremely attached to these advisers. He met with

them every day, was well aware of the effort they made on his behalf, and rewarded them with gifts and favors. All of them in short
order amassed considerable fortunes. But perhaps the deepest
token of King Charles's recognition and affection was his wish that
two of the counselors who had served him so well, his Chamberlain and his Constable, were not to leave his side in death. Bureau de la Rivière and Bertrand du Guesclin were buried at his
feet, among the kings and queens who, all those long centuries,
had created the kingdom for which they, for their part, had
worked so well.

THE REFORMATION OF THE KINGDOM

In 1364, the year of Charles's coronation, the country looked
pitiful indeed. Less fortunate than his father and grandfather, the
third Valois king had inherited a huge liability. The governmental
apparatus was crumbling. The army, the treasury, and the system
of foreign alliances were practically non-existent. With his little
band of jurists, administrators, and captains working tirelessly,
within fourteen years the King would set France on its feet again.
To get the King of England out of France, and to neutralize the
King of Navarre for the future, he needed money and troops, on
both land and sea. And Charles, from the depths of his study in
the Louvre or from St. Pol, supported by his entire brain trust,
was able to improvise, to find a way, to give his solutions the force
of law, and to bring them to pass in the order of events. By means
of "fine and good ordinances," he undertook the "reformation of
the kingdom" for which public opinion had been yearning since
the time of St. Louis. The finances were revived, restructured, and
reconstituted, by the creation of a new tax structure, thus providing the backbone for war. Meanwhile, Du Guesclin achieved the
signal success of clearing the brigands out of France, by luring the
Free Companies all the way to Spain with the promise of more
fruitful booty there. At the same time, the army was reorganized
into a modern standing army, with a completely new branch, the
artillery. The fortresses of France were repaired under the supervision of royal inspectors and became one of the key elements in a
tactic initiated when Charles was Regent and unsuccessfully re-

vived by his Constable: to leave an empty terrain before the invading army, to refuse to join battle, and to let the enemy embark upon long and sterile marches, riding from Calais to Bordeaux, and from Calais to Brest, thus replacing fixed battles with skirmishes and attrition, wherein the Breton excelled.

To this new army was added a navy. France, after all, was a nation of coastlines, and its principal enemy was an island kingdom. A fleet of a hundred and twenty units was built, of which thirty-five were fully armed warships.

Allies too were needed, and these were procured through active diplomatic efforts in Castile, Portugal, Flanders, and the Holy Roman Empire.

Now all that was needed was to repudiate with some flimsy pretext the disastrous Treaty of Brétigny. Charles did so with his head held high and proclaimed to the rest of the world that "covenants and promises made to the detriment of public order, and especially when they have been extracted by coercion, need not be kept." We are reminded of Froissart's remark: "The King was not only a wise man, but a 'twister' "—by which Froissart meant that he was cunning.

And so war broke out once again between England and France. But this time the French wanted war, and had carefully thought it out so that in less than ten years they were able to recapture the territories they had abandoned to the invaders in 1360. It is true that in King Charles's reign the court of France knew the splendid feasting and celebration worthy of so great a country. But this time the merrymaking did not serve to conceal a void, as it had in the time of his father and grandfather; rather, it consecrated a solid reality. How not to sound the trumpets of renown in honor of a prince who started with so little, and who was able to reestablish himself as the King of a powerful France? He had managed to reduce his most dreaded enemy, the King of England, to occupying no more of his lands than Calais to the north, and in the southwest a slender fringe of territory stretching from Bordeaux to Bayonne. As for his other enemy, Bad King Charles of Navarre (whose epithet was appropriate), Charles of France charged him with treason at the end of Navarre's life and confiscated his Norman possessions, which had proved so dangerous for Paris.

Placing himself in the line of his Capetian predecessors, whose great administrative traditions he took up again, Charles furnished his kingdom with completely modern political structures that were docile and effective instruments in the hands of the near-absolute monarch Charles soon became. Finally he regained the high esteem French kings had once commanded in Europe. The visit of his maternal uncle, Charles IV, the Emperor of the Germanies, at the end of his reign, served to confirm King Charles's European reputation. So, in its own way, did the visit of a Saracen knight, who came all the way to Paris to extend an offer to Charles on behalf of his master, the "Sultan of Babylon." The Sultan had heard of the French king's renowned judgment and virtue and wanted Charles to come and stay with him in his country. There he would give Charles a kingdom three times greater and richer than the kingdom of France, while allowing him the liberty to profess whatever religion he pleased. The King's reputation for wisdom, then, had crossed over the seas.

Such was his work. It came out of the man's own flesh and substance and was the burden of a soul and was doubly strengthened by suffering.

On September 16, 1380, King Charles V died in his castle of Beauté, of a heart attack at the age of forty-two. His mortal remains have lain from that time forth in a crypt, all dust and ashes, the image of a king among other images. His work endures and consecrates his memory.

CHAPTER VI

Charles VI the Beloved
1368–1422 (reigned 1380–1422)

THE HEART HAS ITS TRANQUIL HOLIDAYS

Charles VI was born on December 5, 1368, under the sign of Sagittarius. His birth took place late enough in his father's reign for him to have known only its security, order, and magnificence. He was the first surviving son of a mother who, as we have noted, suffered in her pregnancies, and of a father who saw in his son the continuation of his own life.

Charles V did not wish to be a mythical personage, the perpetually absent great figure kept far from his family by the duties of his office. He saw to it that the Dauphin was brought to him each day, and he would relax for a while in the company of the boy and his mother. And so they would come together, in the afternoon most often, and, weather permitting, in the gardens of their residences: St. Pol, the Louvre, or the castle of Beauté. The child knew that he was the joy and relaxation of that man who worked so hard and did not allow himself any other moments of rest in his long day. He also knew that his father cared about him. He had overheard his father making inquiries of the nursemaids about his son's health, exploits, boyish deeds, and words—about him, Charles.

The boy could see in the manuscripts of his father's library some enchanting pictures, those wonderful miniatures on a gold background which Charles V prized so highly. The one he loved the best adorned the title page of the Book of Holy Offices, a work by Guillaume Durand: under twin arcades, his parents sat with crowns on their heads, and the translator of Durand's book, the monk Jean Golein, sat at their feet. To his father's right there he was, in person, although a little boy, dressed in the same robe of blue velvet, embroidered with golden lilies and lined with ermine. With him were his brother Louis, two years his junior, and at his mother's side his sisters, Marie and Isabelle. He thought happily of how this painting, as he had heard it explained, had been executed on his father's orders, so that everyone in the kingdom might know how united the royal family was.

These daily gatherings, these harmonious visions marked his early childhood, and the Dauphin felt accepted and recognized. He was comforted by many signs of love, while the two tutelary images of authority and tenderness took root within him. Thanks to them, he would be able to grow, to love, and to become that solid, loving, and affable little boy fond of fresh air and a physical life, the image of his grandfather, King John, and his great-grandfather, Philip.

But this was not enough to make a good ruler in the mind of King Charles V, who judged his son's education of great importance and planned to turn him over, as soon as the lad was old enough, to Philippe de Mézières, one of the best minds of the age. It would be De Mézières's task to make a sovereign of the Dauphin. For the moment, however, the boy was put in the hands of Guichard, Dauphin of Auvergne, an illustrious knight.

He was certainly a nice boy, gentle and engaging, but he showed little or no aptitude for study. His only enthusiasm was for weapons. His tutor, gravely concerned, informed the King of the situation, but Charles tried not to draw definitive conclusions too quickly. The lad was young.

The King recalled his own love for jewelry, which dated from an early age. Searching for a resemblance which might be a foretaste of resemblances to come, he showed the lad his collection of precious objects. The gold and gems sparkled in the little boy's eyes.

"Choose the one you like best, my son," the King proposed. The boy was silent, indifferent to so fabulous a display. He saw nothing and was aware of nothing in that hall, except for a sword hanging in a corner of the wardrobe; he could not take his eyes off that sword. And since King Charles was taken aback, the tutor explained the lively interest on the young boy's part for weapons and military ornaments. The startled King could not believe what he heard. On the occasion of a solemn banquet with the greatest lords of the kingdom gathered about him, the King put the boy to a new test. He gave him a choice between a magnificent crown, enriched with gold and jewels, and a helmet. "Which would you prefer, my son? To be crowned king with this one, or to go and expose yourself to the dangers of war with that one?" Without hesitation the boy answered: "My lord, I should like the helmet better than the crown." The King could do nothing but submit to the evidence, while the guests were amazed at so precocious a calling, in which more than one of them had recognized himself. Charles therefore cheerfully offered his son the helmet he coveted, and made an additional gift of the sword the boy had glimpsed earlier. The sword would hang at the head of the Dauphin's bed, and the father would order weapons forged on a more manageable scale for his delighted heir, who thanked his father from the bottom of his heart.

"Is this my son, then?" the King asked himself. An accident of heredity, or the natural reaction of a small male confronted by too great and weighty a genitor, whose prowess overwhelmed him? The boy refused to deal with the obstacle, forfeited the game, and, doubting he would ever be able to match his father, sought and found a path on which he would not run up against the colossal shadow of Charles V.

We could say that the boy's reaction was a healthy, vital one. Unless, going back to the mentality of those days, we realize that such a taste was common to any feudal baron worthy of the name, and not particularly surprising. It is rather the father who appears out of place, with his love of jewels and his taste for study. The son merely falls within the norm for his contemporaries. It is in any case unsuitable to draw premature conclusions from the event.

Besides, nothing said then that with age and proper advice his mind would not open.

FEARS AND TEARS

Some time later—the Dauphin was barely eleven years old—he sat by his father's side at a solemn reception for the pontifical legate of His Holiness Clement VII. The boy was visibly agitated and, turning pale, he explained to the entourage the feelings he was experiencing, too strong to keep silent about: "Don't you see, as I do, the personal Devil who walks at the Cardinal's side and informs him of things past and yet to come?" The King, dismayed, ordered the boy removed from the room. No more illusions. After that his mind was made up. His son was "light-minded." From that time on, he was convinced—despite redoubled efforts, as he felt his own death approaching, to anticipate and organize his succession (which, alas, would pass to a minor!)—that the future had slipped out of his control.

On such a subject, the chroniclers of that time, with a single exception, kept silent. But that silence does not preclude the fact that the heir to the throne seemed to have publicly displayed the symptoms of an unsettlingly unbalanced mind. It would have been nice to believe that what happened that day was a fortuitous incident which would not reoccur. But the witnesses to this little drama realized that the brief hallucination was only the expression of a state of anxiety which had reached such a degree of intensity that young Charles could no longer bear it. Despite all the affection with which his parents surrounded him, they had been unable to prevent his early years from containing certain elements of insecurity; his father, so fragile-looking and constantly in pain, with that awful open sore on his arm; his mother, stricken for an entire year with an illness thought incurable, immured in an inner world from which he was excluded—had she rejected him, then, her own son? And already those images of peace and happiness in the garden of the palace of St. Pol belonged to the past.

The month of February 1378 had brought only mourning. At the Cathedral of Notre Dame, at the convent of the Cordeliers, at the abbey of St. Denis, the Dauphin had stood in the first row of the funeral processions which carried off his mother and then—

perhaps more shocking still—his sister Isabelle, five years old and a child like himself. The following year, the plague ravaged the kingdom. His father grew weaker day by day. And the child was afraid. He felt disarmed, vulnerable, alone, facing death—death which was encroaching, threatening . . . threatening him.

Death was that mysterious and terrible Beyond to which priests were the ferrymen. God knew that during those last months they had been kept busy; God knew that he, Charles, had seen them haunting the palace with their crucifixes and holy water, and that the great of this world had felt abruptly reduced to the rank of simple creatures whose earthly powers looked derisory from the vantage point of eternity, as compared with the powers at the disposal of the Church.

Death was also hell, and the Devil, the worst enemy of humanity, the one who knew everything about your past and future life, and who would demand an accounting from you. Perhaps the sight of the papal legate in that solemn setting had recalled to Charles the funeral ceremonies of the month of February, still so fresh in his mind, when death had taken precedence over life, and the priest over the king, when he had found himself, heartbroken, fear in his belly, miserable, in tears at the sound of the *Dies Irae,* in the first row of the church where the nave had been draped in black, clutching the hand of his brother Louis, stumbling down the dark steps which led to the crypt and the open tombs waiting to take what he held most dear. For this child, the priest was the one who could (if he wished) send you to the Devil or to the angels— to the angels if you had been good, and to the Devil if you had been bad.

The legate had stepped forward majestically, his head held high, the pastoral ring on his finger. He might have been God the Father appearing for the Last Judgment. The child had imagined that his face was the burning face of wrath, when in all probability what his lips addressed to the King and his innocent offspring was the most unctuous of smiles. On seeing him, the young Charles suddenly slipped away from the present moment, plunged into the past, where a flood of images unfurled, images of the previous winter, distressing images which obsessed him and drove him to distraction. Wounds barely closed were reopened, he was gripped by anxiety, there were knots in his throat, and confused thoughts collided in his head. He was still a little boy, barely over the shock of the cruelest of separations, and he was "light-minded" to boot, as they said. What if all those things were his fault, all those deaths, those misfortunes? To the Church, everything was always someone's fault. Charles had never felt so bad as when those indescribable fears took bodily form in the Devil he saw following the legate.

Charles was still wandering in the stone universe of closed spaces, Gothic arches and flagstones, of cathedrals and tombs, a labyrinth of tears and steles, a labyrinth without an Ariadne's thread, and with the odor of ashes. February was a dark month, a month of unhappiness and mist, almost November, with a low sky, freezing rain, the Seine swollen. Charles felt cold, chilled to the very bone, chilled to his heart. At Notre Dame, no sunlight shone through the great rose windows of the transepts. He trembled. He needed air, to rediscover the living. But all roads led to St. Pol, to the Louvre, to Vincennes, to Beauté, all of which royal residences and castles, so many kingdoms for Charles, were empty: empty the Queen's apartments, empty Isabelle's room. He spent his days there as well as he could. But when the sun sank below the horizon, abandoned to the forces of the night, yielding itself to the threatening shadows, motherless children choked back their tears.

Fleur-de-lis princes, motherless children, lost children, into whose hearts there rose, never more to leave them, never to depart, the great sense of abandonment, the great, perennial grief, wherein abided the greater grief of the world, how, little princes, will you recover? Who will console you, inconsolable, incurable, stricken, marked for life, by this loss?

Less than a year and a half went by until Charles and Louis, in great mourning, followed their father's bier, while before their astonished eyes, in the cortege which brought the body from Beauté back to Notre Dame, the men of the provost of Paris and the doctors of the university fought over the first places in the procession.

THE FLEUR-DE-LIS PRINCES

It was at this point that the uncles entered the historical scene—the dead King's three brothers, Anjou, Berry, and Burgundy, who were joined by Bourbon, the late Queen's brother. The latter, it is true, will not be mentioned very often. He was a sweet, pacific man.

The late King had always wished to be on good terms with his brothers. He had shared the exercise of power with them and had been able to count on their aid in difficult circumstances. They had done the kingdom signal services and were entitled to their slice of the cake—quite a big slice. It was normal, therefore, that the monarch, when he felt his end was near (and with doubts about his eldest son besides), should have thought of his next of kin to look after the commonweal until such time as his heir should be of age and capable of taking charge himself. In order to forestall anticipated dangers, he had arranged for his son's minority with a series of ordinances in which he judiciously meted out responsibilities among princes of the blood and administrative or political personnel.

But Charles V had hardly been buried, the dear departed was hardly cold in his grave, before his wise edicts were put on the shelf. "*I'll* be the Regent and guardian," Anjou decided, "since I'm the eldest now." "Not at all!" exclaimed Burgundy and Bourbon. "The guardianship reverts to *us* by right." Arbitration was required to settle their contested claims. They were brought into agreement by deciding that there would be neither a royal minority nor a regency, and that the Dauphin would be crowned King on All Saints' Day, little more than a month having intervened since his father's death on Michaelmas. At that time the new King would do whatever he wished. If his lordship the Duke of Anjou insisted on the title of Regent, he could keep it until the coronation, or even afterward. But the guardianship of their nephew would remain as foreseen with their lordships of Burgundy and Bourbon. As for the government, it would be left to a Council of twelve members, our four dukes among them. Anjou as the eldest received the presidency of the Council, but he was obliged to promise in writing that "for grave and weighty matters, such as the marriage of the King and the signing of treaties, his opinion would not prevail over those of the other members."

No one could harbor any more illusions in regard to the princes of the blood, who at that period were called the fleur-de-lis princes. From now on each would play his own hand, cards on the table—and besides, what did they have to hide any more? And if

they were seen sobbing uncontrollably at the King's funeral, they
felt they were already too involved in the responsibilities he had
left them to accompany his heart to a tomb in Rouen. The past
was the past. They had no desire to return to it. They had never
been able to see above or beyond themselves, and the essential
thing for them was their own dreams. For twenty years, or nearly,
they had been there, fidgeting impatiently in the shadow of their
elder brother, enduring second place, a quite uncomfortable spot
when you are so near the sun; and on certain evenings, when sleep
was slow in coming, there was no end to the number of "what ifs"
and other unmentionable desires. Twenty years of castles and celebrations, of luxury and respect, of "happenings" as well—their
epoch had undoubtedly given them a taste for such things. Twenty
years of taking on orders, responsibilities, and missions of trust, titles and goods, money and lands. Twenty years of being wards
and children, kept in check, on a close rein. Of obeying, and saying thank you—with dignity, but with a bent back. They had had
enough, and more than enough, of the will of the King and the interest of the realm. For, after all, had they been anything more
than officials like the others; simply better born, undoubtedly better paid, and with places of honor at official ceremonies? But now
that was over. The great man was gone now and lay at peace in
the family vault. Now they were going to enjoy themselves, and
nothing, no one, could prevent them from acting as they pleased,
dropping their masks and declaring quite openly that they recognized nothing in this world but power and money—for them.

The first-born, Louis of Anjou, a man of forty-one, began by
unscrupulously confiscating the ready money which his brother
had gathered so laboriously, some ingots and gold bars valued at
fifteen thousand crowns, which the late King had evidently put
aside in the tower of Vincennes, or perhaps at Melun or even at
Beauté, in secret hiding places concealed in the walls for this purpose. A few intimates who knew about the gold had promised to
keep it secret and had sworn oaths to reveal its existence only to
the young King when he had attained his majority. But Anjou
didn't see it that way. He was no man to let such sums lie sleeping
when so few people were aware of their existence. As for discover-
ing the hiding place, he did not beat around the bush, nor did the
choice of means frighten him, as we shall see. He summoned Sir

Philip of Savoisy, whom he believed to be in on the secret, and put the question to him boldly; Savoisy, with dignity, avoided answering. Requests, flattery, promises, even threats came to nothing. Savoisy persisted inflexibly in his silence. Then Anjou had the executioner brought in, with the appropriate instruments. Before such arguments the chevalier capitulated, while Louis snatched up the small fortune with dispatch.

Nothing about Louis's behavior would have surprised the dead King. Charles V had known that he was greedy and unscrupulous; but also that he had a head for politics, ambition, energy, tenacity —in other words, ability: qualities necessary to assume a regency. Thus he had set aside a dominant place for his brother in the government he anticipated. Anjou was accorded the presidency of the Council, a position he could have filled brilliantly. But he must have judged it too envied and insecure a role for him, and he must have taken into account that to keep the position he would have had to maneuver between a child king, his overly clever brothers, intrigues and quarrels, and that in the last analysis he would never exercise more than a fragmented, temporary authority.

Then in the month of June of the same year, 1380, Louis woke up one fine morning to find himself King of Naples, Sicily, and Jerusalem. His aunt, Queen Joanna, had just died, the same aunt who as a result of long and complicated negotiations, in which his late brother had intervened, had taken him as her adopted son. The bequest included the county of Provence to add to his possessions of Maine and Anjou, and a kingdom to conquer, the kingdom of Naples way down in the south—acres of pebbly soil, scorched lands, volcanoes, miles of beaches, bays, islands, a thousand suns, white seas, enraptured evenings, the weather of the world's first day. And an old dream, of which he had despaired, miraculously realized: a crown of his own. At last the final responsibility, at last the power. A new life suddenly beginning when his life seemed already behind him. He felt himself in his prime, ready for a new departure. Somewhere else. Adventure at the gates of the Orient. The fascinating, different, and dangerous games of Mediterranean politics. Those prestigious titles . . . how could he hold out against mirages, how could he live with himself between the Loire and the Seine—the same horizons, the same faces looking at him—quarreling over scraps of power? He no longer wanted to share. He dreamed of nothing but leaving. Pockets full, up on horseback, a few troops and above all some money provided by his wife, whom he left without excessive grief. But the adventure ended midway. He died of a fever at Bari, in the month of September 1384, after his army had been decimated by hunger and an epidemic. At the end he was completely destitute, and reduced to wearing, in place of his coat of arms of spun gold, a simple canvas painted with yellow fleurs-de-lis.

The second brother, Jean of Berry, was just forty, and without doubt the greatest hedonist in a family which did rather well in that field. Nor is there anything pejorative in the description. The pursuit of pleasure, so resolute and so constant, coupled with a facility for drawing on the public treasury, had turned him into one of the most remarkable patrons of the arts in the medieval West. But such a pursuit hardly seemed compatible with the virtues of action. So the dead King had arranged for his younger brother to be excluded from the government during the Dauphin's minority, and Jean was hardly mentioned in the division of spoils. During his lifetime, if the truth be told, Charles had authorized his brother's possession of Berry, Poitou, and Auvergne. Which did not prevent Jean from taking offense and complaining to such an extent that his brothers added to this smart collection the administration of Languedoc and Guienne. And so Berry found that he had at his disposition a third of the kingdom.

He did not have a head for politics, it is true. But he had long teeth and holes in his hands, which is to say that he was both greedy and a spendthrift. He was also a bandit and a pillager, who did not hesitate to send his men out after travelers and convoys of merchandise, with instructions to strip them to the last stitch. Every means was fair for him to get money and he never had enough of it—he was following, he claimed, the example of those above him. But on days when manna failed to descend, he declared sensibly enough: "Finances always come and go." All the same, let us do him justice. For if he robbed and pillaged, he did so to satisfy the lively and violent passion which any work of art inspired in him, a passion at least as ardent as his late brother's for the kingdom, or his two other brothers' for power. "Commission" was a key word in the life of Jean of Berry, and out the commissions went: to painters, sculptors, master craftsmen, illuminators, weavers, embroiderers, goldsmiths, jewelers, what you will—the money wasn't squandered. They came from everywhere to practice their art in the Duke's workrooms: from England, Germany, northern France, Flanders especially, and, it was said, from Spain and the Orient, to work on his castle at Bicêtre. The best artists in Europe flocked to his call, men like John of Liège and Jean Beauneveu, the architect Guy de Dammartin, the painter John of Bruges, and so many others.

We are indebted to the Duke for truffles and for seventeen dream castles: La Nonette, Gien, Montargis, Étampes, Concressault, Lusignan, and Mehun-sur-Yèvre near Bourges, his favorite haunt. All of them emerged from the earth on his order and were swiftly destroyed by the misfortunes of the times. But they were saved from oblivion by his illuminators, who turned them into legendary castles. One has only to contemplate the *Très riches heures,* the Book of Hours containing prayers to be said at the canonical hours, commissioned by the Duke.

The Duke of Berry lived to a ripe old age—too old an age. Too many misfortunes, responsibilities, and crises would interfere with the end of his long life. All or nearly all of what he constructed, assembled, and raised was scattered, ruined, reduced to nothing. But some wonders remain, some echoes, and a dazzling memory.

As for the third brother, Philip, Duke of Burgundy, called "the Bold," at the age of thirty-eight he was preparing to become the real master of France, and he remained so for a quarter of a century, except for a brief interregnum. We shall speak of him again in his place.

From this point on, the chips were down in the court of France. Each of the brothers was ready to take all, and each was concerned with himself alone. The page had been turned, and he who held the reins no longer dreamed only of the well-being and grandeur of the kingdom, lived only for his people, who would honor and cherish his memory, braiding floral crowns for him while he lived and laying flowers on his tomb. From now on the people existed only to obey and pay.

VIOLENCE

So Charles VI began his reign at the age of twelve, a cardboard show-king, forced to pronounce, when problems came up in Council, decisions dictated to him in the wings. It was Burgundy who governed, with the aid of Berry. But Charles was nonetheless obliged to be present and to speak; and such was the political crisis of the times that life became an endless series of dramas for this docile but ultimately untalented adolescent.

Everywhere there was disorder, trouble, and death. What did he feel about hearing such things and dealing with them, this boy-king who tried to do his best in the position where he found himself, and who was forced to take responsibility for the bloodiest orders? A good deal of anguish, probably.

Indeed, the people of France had proved no wiser than their princes. The late King had hardly been buried when they took up arms and broke out in rioting across the land. The occasion for the rioting was the public announcement on church porches and in even the tiniest towns of the dead King's last wish: the abolition of the *fouages* ("hearth taxes"). Now, as beneficiaries of King Charles V's measures, which they interpreted to include all kinds of taxes, the people refused to pay the tax collectors, saying that they would die a thousand times rather than submit to humiliating exactions. "What!" cried a Parisian rabble-rouser, "shall we see forever and always the growing greed of the lords who crush us with their constant unjust exactions, and have reduced us to such a state of poverty that, hobbled by debts, we are forced each year to pay more than we earn? Do you understand, dear fellow citizens, the contempt they have for you? If they could, there's no doubt they would deprive you of the sun's light. They are angry that you are allowed to breathe, to speak, that you have human faces and mingle with them in public places. They say: 'Why mix heaven and earth?' No doubt these men, to whom we pay a forced homage, over whose welfare we keep a constant watch, and who feed themselves on our substance, have no other thoughts than to sparkle with gold and jewels, to surround themselves with retinues of servants, to build superb palaces, and to invent new taxes to weigh down this capital. The patience of the people has tolerated this plague of vexations much longer than it should have, and if we aren't freed of this unbearable yoke soon, it is my opinion that the whole town should take up arms. For we all must wish for death rather than suffer such dishonor."

The princes were therefore confronted with a difficult situation, which disturbed all the more as it spread to England and Flanders. They put it to an end in less than five years by measures of extreme severity. Now, these measures were supposed to have been taken by the young King. The dukes dictated the orders to him, but they were carried out in his name. This boy, who was now almost fourteen, appeared in person wherever his will was to be accomplished, in Paris and outside of it, no matter how far he had to ride: wherever peace had to be re-established by physical punishment and violence; wherever he had to impose his justice by sentences and executions which took place most often before his eyes: beheadings, hangings, gibbets with cadavers dangling upon them, nothing was spared this adolescent, who saw immediate and terrible effects proceeding from words which were inspired in him by others, but which were nonetheless his own. Under such conditions, it must have been hard for him to sleep peacefully at night, even if he was convinced that the welfare of the kingdom demanded such actions. He would have to have had a very stable constitution not to be overwhelmed by such sights even if there were raised between them and him, like a screen, the reassuring stature of the men who were really responsible, and who had his full trust. It would have taken solid shoulders to move without transition from an ordered, peaceful, protected existence to a universe of struggle and violence, and to acquire the habit, at an age more proper for games and treats, of dealing out life and death. Charles, as we know, was sensitive and impressionable. The type of life imposed on him does not seem very suited to the undeniably weak state of his nerves.

At the outset of 1382 the crisis was serious. Popular uprisings, riots prompted by hunger and misery, broke out almost at the same time in Picardy, Normandy, the Loire Valley, Lyon, and the south—in short, really everywhere. At Rouen the coppersmiths, drapers, and other poor people sacked the town over a three-day period. So the uncles decided that the King should go and preside in person over the punishment. On the first of March, Charles left his château at Vincennes and took to the road. At St. Denis he turned back. Messengers from Paris had overtaken him with disturbing news: a royal tax collector, operating in the market place, had tried to demand taxes from a woman selling watercress. Immediately he had been stabbed in a thousand places and stretched out stiff on the ground. At once the whole populace had filled the streets. More than four thousand demonstrators had marched on the Hôtel de Ville, where they seized weapons, daggers, swords, and, above all, twelve thousand lead mallets (*maillets*). Thus armed, the Maillotins hunted down all over Paris the tax collectors and Jews who lived under royal protection. Not content with taking these men's lives, they plundered their homes, robbing, breaking, destroying, ransacking, foraging in their cellars, glutting themselves on their wine barrels; the riot turned into an orgy. Besotted, howling mobs stormed the prisons of the king and the bishop, freed the prisoners, and burned the records. As soon as Charles was informed of these events he retraced his steps and prepared to starve Paris into submission. But in the meantime the burghers took fright. In three days order was more or less restored by their efforts. Now it was up to the prince to impose what he wished. He therefore ordered the usual reprisals: arrests, beheadings, hangings. They proceeded at such a rate that he had to recruit two additional executioners.

Once Paris had been calmed, Charles set out again for Rouen. He entered it as one enters a conquered city: the city gates were torn off and lying on the ground, the bells stilled, the arms sequestered in the castle, the prisons full, while the severed heads of the townsmen of Rouen stared at him hollow-eyed above the ramparts. For two months he remained there in an atmosphere of the aftermath of a riot. On the first of June he returned to Paris, but only for two months. He left again in August. Not satisfied with pacifying a kingdom still in the ferment of revolt, he flew to the aid of others. The Count of Flanders, at war with his rebellious subjects led by Philip Artevelde of Ghent, had appealed to his son-in-law, Philip of Burgundy, and Burgundy's royal nephew could refuse him nothing. The young man loved arms, the life of camps, and he was going to get a taste of them. On August 18, Charles took up the oriflamme of France against the Flemish.

On November 27, at the head of an army of forty thousand men, he participated in the battle of Roosebeke. He was going on fourteen, to be sure, but age did not seem to matter in the fourteenth century for those of royal blood, when there was fighting to be done. His brother Louis, who was twelve, was at his side.

Charles lived through the anguish of waiting that wintry St. Martin's Eve, in a drizzle, in the thick fog of Flanders fields, icy and gray, with their heavy clay sticking to the horses' hoofs and the men's feet. He knew the trying silence before the fray, a silence pierced by the croaking of ravens gathering in flight formations, and by the neighing of the horses, left at a distance to remove all possibility of the soldiers' fleeing the field. No doubt he started when the fearful, confused din of the battle's beginning suddenly erupted, magnified by surrounding echoes, and in fear he commended himself and his men to heaven. For several hours he awaited in a deafening tumult the outcome of a battle which was hard and uncertain. Suddenly the fog lifted, giving way to a sun bright enough to hamper the enemy, and he could see the most awful violence being perpetrated before his eyes. Men with open wounds, smothered, decapitated, their organs burst, their limbs torn off, lay expiring. In certain spots their corpses formed lance-high piles. A field of slaughter. On the fertile earth of a Flanders field, the blood congealed in blackish puddles.

"Why do we not relieve our soldiers, who are facing mortal danger for our sake and prefer our glory to their own lives?" exclaimed the royal youth, who in his generosity of soul was dismayed at what he saw.

"Don't worry about it, my dear nephew," answered his uncle Burgundy, who didn't care to take the risk of another Poitiers. "And remember that a king must aspire to conquer as much by his wisdom and prudence as by his sword."

After the victory a count was made. The French losses were not severe. All the same Charles was informed that Sir Flotte de Revel and their lordships Antoine and Guy de Cousant, illustrious knights whom he had known well, were no more. And when he left his tent he could see, dangling on a branch, the naked body of Philip Artevelde, which had been retrieved from among the corpses by his orders. One manuscript tells us that when he drew near the Fleming's unclothed body he trampled it underfoot in a rage, cursing Philip for a villain. But the story remains dubious, for the manner little resembles Charles's.

On December 1 he was at Courtrai, another city in rebellion. He entered it after all of its gates had been knocked down, and had the four leaders of the rebellion executed before his eyes. After his departure he learned that, despite his firmly expressed wishes, the city had been pillaged, burned, and destroyed. Bloody but by now familiar images must have haunted his mind at that time. On the way home he tasted the sweetness of glory. Picardy acclaimed him victor in cities adorned like temples, and its people proclaimed their respect and devotion to him, while laying the richest presents at his feet.

Still Charles did not allow himself to be moved. Crowned with the conqueror's laurels, he was now in a position to carry out pitiless repression in a land where public order was still a fragile thing. On January 11, 1383, he entered Paris as its judge. The army had been divided into three companies, while he rode in alone. The burghers of Paris came out to greet him, as was the custom, to offer their homage to him. They were sent back brutally. "The King and his uncles could not forget recent offenses," they were told.

Then the barriers were smashed, the city gates torn off their hinges, thrown on the ground, trampled by the procession which moved slowly forward toward Notre Dame, where the King offered the Blessed Virgin Mother a banner, sewn with golden lilies, in thanksgiving. Then, while the King returned to the palace, the Lord Marshal, Sancerre, and the Lord Constable, Clisson, occupied the Petit Pont and the Grand Pont. With those bridges occupied, troops were stationed at every crossroad and armed men quartered in the citizens' houses. During the next few days more than three hundred burghers got a taste of the damp straw of the dungeons, while others were hanged high and low. All the chains used to close the streets at night were removed and transported to the grounds of the forest of Vincennes. The inhabitants were obliged, under penalty of death, to turn in their weapons at the palace or at the Louvre. The St. Antoine gate was knocked down, and the work of completing the Bastille hastened. For two months, punishment followed on punishment. "Every day," reports the chronicler Juvénal des Ursins, "three or four heads were lopped off." Enormous fines were imposed on the taxpayers; Paris, subdued now, kept quiet.

The repression was extended with equal severity to other cities guilty of the same crimes; when these cities were taken in hand once again, they followed the example of the capital. But the King did not rest easy for all that. After Easter he went on a pilgrimage to Chartres and passed through Orléans, where more punishments were inflicted. On the second of August he set off again for Flanders at his uncle's request. From this new campaign the kingdom drew no benefit.

The eighteen months which followed were calmer. The harshly throttled cities kept silent. The less dramatic period thus permitted the sixteen-year-old King a little relaxation. He could call a halt, put time's oblivion between himself and those dreadful years, and devote himself without constraint to his favorite pleasures: hunting in the forests of Ile de France, and all of the physical exercises, especially jousting, in which he excelled.

FEMALE BODY, THOU ART SO TENDER . . .

For some time Charles had been showing a rather lively interest in women. He delighted in their company, sought them out, and couldn't take his eyes off the ones he found to his liking. A new problem, then, well within the natural order, which the uncles had to resolve as soon as possible. At Charles's age, his royal ancestors had already been married for several years. In fact, the princes had already given this matter some thought. They had remembered their brother's last will (for once! it was not their usual habit as we know) and all the more willingly since in this particular instance it coincided quite exactly with the interests of Duke Philip. Charles V, on his deathbed, had ordered that the Dauphin be married to a princess of the Germanies, where (for the good of the realm) greater alliances needed to be made. The King of England had benefited greatly from his marriage in that country. So the uncles had thought first of the powerful Wittelsbach family. The Wittelsbachs were, to be sure, divided into four branches, but they stood out from the multitude of princely houses beyond the Rhine. They owned Bavaria and the upper and lower Palatinate.

Moreover, they had just established themselves in the Netherlands.

Now it so happened that three years earlier, one of the Wittelsbachs, Frederick, had joined up with the King of France's army on the occasion of the first expedition to Flanders. He was treated as his rank demanded, as a noble baron and as a man of good company. When the opportunity for such a question presented itself, the princes asked him straightaway: did he have a marriageable daughter? "Not I, my fair lords," he replied. "But Duke Stephen, my elder brother, has a lovely one." "And how old is she?" the uncles inquired. "Between thirteen and fourteen," was the reply. "That's just what we need," they exclaimed. "When you return to Bavaria, speak of the matter to your brother, and bring your niece on a pilgrimage to the shrine of St. Jean at Amiens. The King will be there. If he sees her, perhaps he will desire her, for he always likes to see beautiful women, and to love them. If she captures his heart, she will be Queen of France."

As soon as he had returned home, Frederick called on his brother. But Duke Stephen was strongly opposed to the plan. "Dear brother," he replied, "my daughter would be quite lucky if she could attain so high an honor as to be Queen of France. But there's a long way to go and too much to consider to make her Queen of France and the wife of a king. I should be extremely angry if my daughter were taken to France and then sent back to me. I prefer to arrange a marriage for her at my ease in my own country." Duke Frederick accepted his brother's opinion and answered the uncles accordingly. The matter had rested there.

The months passed. Nearly three years later the Duke and Duchess of Burgundy and their family were gathered at Cambrai, in all their pomp and attire, to ally themselves by marriage to a branch of the Wittelsbach clan, whose domains bordered on their own. Their two children, Margaret and John, the Count of Nevers (later known as "John the Fearless"), were marrying William, the Count of Ostrevant, and Margaret of Hainaut—the son and daughter of Duke Albert of Bavaria, the Regent of Hainaut. The celebration was magnificent. King Charles and the Duke of Berry had lent their golden dining service and their jewelry. Charles, who could not restrain himself where tilting lances was concerned, was unafraid of making a spectacle of himself and, although a King and in defiance of custom, went down into the lists to take on simple knights in combat.

The Duchess of Brabant, an aunt by marriage to Philip of Burgundy, brought up the matter of the marriage again. "What a pity," she said, "to give up such a plan deliberately. Duke Stephen plays an important role in the Empire—he is as great as, or greater than, the King of Germany."

"My lady, it is true," the uncles answered her. "But we hear no news about our project."

"Be still, now," exclaimed the Duchess, "I'll get on with it. You'll have your news this summer without fail."

She kept her word. At Whitsuntide, Duke Frederick did bring his niece Isabella to the shrine of St. Jean at Amiens on the pretext of making a pilgrimage.

"Bravo, dear nephew, but how did you manage it?" the Duchess asked him, happily surprised.

"I had a lot of trouble, my aunt," was Frederick's comment. "All the same, I pushed and pestered my brother so much that my niece has come with me. But when I was taking my leave, after he had kissed his daughter he took me aside and spoke to me like this: 'Now, Frederick, Frederick, dear brother, you are taking my daughter Isabella off with you without any guarantees, for if the King of France does not want her, she will be humiliated for as long as she lives. Think on this too as you leave, for if you bring her back to me, you will have no enemy worse than I.'"

In fact, what was not to Duke Stephen's liking in this matter, besides the chance of a refusal, was the thought that his daughter would not be able to escape the French custom whereby the future Queen appeared before an assembly of matrons so that her virginity and her fitness to bear children might be duly established.

Young Isabella was rather simple by the standards of the French court. She savored of her native mountains, and, what was more, she did not know a word of French. But she was fifteen, with a lively eye and a fresh face. The Duchess of Brabant indoctrinated her protégée every day in manners and behavior, provided her with ornaments, jewels, and attire, and saw to everything. In a matter of weeks the little German princess could outshine any lady of the court, in all save the speaking of their language.

On the specified day, Isabella was taken amid great pomp to Amiens. King Charles was visibly frustrated with waiting. He neither ate nor slept any more, and, much to the amusement of the ladies in his entourage, he was unable to conceal his impatience. On Friday the meeting took place. The Duchesses of Burgundy, Hainaut, and Brabant brought in the girl, who sank to her knees before the King in a low curtsey. He raised her up again and stared at her silently. She kept quite still, knowing "neither to move her eye nor her mouth."

The lords and ladies in attendance held their breath and looked on with the liveliest attention and the most perfect indiscretion, as they scrutinized their prince's face. Already the duchesses were taking the girl away. "This lady will stay with us," whispered Clisson to Lord de Coucy and Lord de la Rivière. "The King cannot take his eyes off her."

"Try to find out about the King's impressions, Bureau," asked Burgundy. "It is you he confides in the most."

The lad did not make a mystery out of it. "Yes, Bureau, she pleases me mightily. We want no other. Tell my uncle of Burgundy, in God's name, that the arrangements are to proceed apace."

"May God take a hand in it," exclaimed Philip, who was straightaway informed, "for we wish it too." And he rushed off to the Hainaut household to bear the news.

Plans had been made to leave the very next day for Arras, where the wedding was to have been celebrated. But Charles refused. "Fair uncles," he said, "we wish to marry here in this beautiful church of Amiens. There is no reason for further postponement."

Once more the Duke invaded the lodgings of the Duchess of Brabant and amid much laughter informed her of the changes to be made in their travel plans: "Madam, my dear cousin, my lord has shattered our resolve to go to Arras. The matter touches him too closely. . . . He has let me know that he cannot sleep for thinking of the one who will be his bride. So you will take your ease today and tomorrow in this city, and Monday we shall cure these two invalids."

That Monday, July 17, 1385, Charles was wed in the cathedral at Amiens to this little princess of a great house, who, though sprightly and desirable, had a dry, rapacious soul, which was to cause his undoing. But who suspected it then?

The honeymoon was brief. Barely a month later Charles set out once more for Flanders, still on behalf of his uncle, Burgundy. The siege of Damme was hard, trying on his nerves, cruel, a repetition of all the obtrusive violence he knew well. Four months later he returned to celebrate Christmas at his fair one's side. For the first time the fighting had seemed long to him, for obvious reasons. The departures, the absences, the warriors' expeditions had lost their charm for him, especially when the results achieved were seen to be less and less fruitful.

During the two following years the uncles concentrated all of their efforts on attacking England. Their plans failed. The third year, Charles's uncle, Philip, dragged him off to war against the Duke of Gelder, who had in any case insulted the young ruler by calling him in letters of defiance "Charles, who believes himself King of France." After four months of bivouacs and long rides under torrents of rain and in mud waist-deep, out of which once again no advantage was drawn, the prince went home, weary to his bones. On the first of November 1388 he celebrated All Saints' Day at Reims.

There, in the episcopal palace, at the Council, a sudden surprise: he declared his will to rule alone, thanked his uncles, with the greatest respect for their good offices, and politely dismissed them. For a month they hung on, laying claim as a reward for their pains to Normandy and Guienne, respectively. But Charles held the upper hand. It was useless for them to insist. And so they respectfully took leave of their sovereign at Pontoise. Stupefied. Their nephew was no longer the same; someone, something, had changed him. But who or what? Was it their brother's old advisers, who were replacing them now in the Council and whom they had scornfully dubbed the "Marmosets" on account of their humble origins? Perhaps he had simply become a man over the years and, in accord with the old, barbaric desire, had just taken out on them the common need to symbolically murder his father.

ANOTHER VALIANT KNIGHT

Charles VI was twenty years old. He was a splendid lad, with an athletic body and a handsome face, tall, blond, and fair-skinned. His features were regular; his glance, lively. Physically vigorous, he was also goodhearted, loyal, considerate, and impulsive. He was quite capable of loving, and his emotions were strong. But he was devoid of judgment, or nearly so. The King was lightheaded and frivolous and had no interest in affairs of state. He pursued them out of duty, as conscientiously as he could, but preferred to shift the burden to others whenever he thought he could. Perhaps he was weary from having been made responsible for affairs of state at such a young age, like a thoroughbred forced to run too soon. Perhaps he lacked the requisite faculties. His father might have perceived the situation clearly when he confided to his brothers, "The lad is light-minded." The father had hoped to set all to rights by a serious education. "It will be necessary," Charles V had remarked, "for the Dauphin to be guided and governed by sound doctrine." Now, we know what Charles's adolescence had been: a perpetual departure. No one had thought to develop his capacity for work and concentration, his faculty for reflection and judgment. Thus he was found to be weak and easily swayed, a king who could not say no. As the monk of St. Denis, his biographer, explained it, "His mind was accustomed to yielding to the advice and the reasons given him by other people."

No great intellectual resources, then, or intellectual curiosity or artistic sensibility either: the young King was out of place in his dynastic line. Without sharing the exceptional endowments of a Charles V or the extreme refinement of a Berry, all of the Valois had been men of taste, open to all thought, all culture, sensitive about artistic objects and books; they had been collectors, builders, patrons of the arts. Nothing of the sort in the case of the current bearer of the name. Had the bloodline become impoverished? Charles retained the love of extravagance, of luxury. Habit or necessity? Decoration and attire enhanced the grandeur of his rank, or so at least he believed. The King was thirsty for honor and renown. And so he removed the old knightly ideal from the strongbox where it had been slumbering for years—obsolete, superannuated, but quite tenacious—and brandished it like a standard. "My father is dead," said he; "let's turn the page." And surely the page had been turned.

Nearly forty years had gone by, but nothing seemed to have changed. The good old days of King John had returned—the old, destructive dreams of valor and glory, of heroism and inefficacy, of honor for honor's sake, of the spiked breastplate which hid both from others and from oneself one's weakness, immaturity, under the steel and feathers of one's plumed armor. Charles was burning with a neophyte's zeal for a laughable ideal. "To rule, in reality, is simple enough," he thought. Hearts were won by appearance. You had to know how to dazzle from the beginning of the game to the end, to create a gigantic charade. All was in the verb "to show": to show your strength, your wealth, your generosity, your noble, magnanimous heart. Power, for Charles, consisted in displaying a princely image that would delight his subjects: an image that had Charles's own private dream woven in —a delirium of honor and glory, of peace and justice, of plumage and standards. His people must have been naïve and credulous if they were satisfied with that. They must have felt an inner weakness, a need to see themselves protected and to admire their protector, if they demanded in a monarch this magnified image of a superman, a hero. Between this child-king and his children-people there flowed affinities, connections, and currents—up to the time of his death, after all the years of his illness, he would be known as "the Beloved" on that account.

So once more upon the throne of France we find a knightly King, after Philip, after his grandfather, John, whom he strangely resembled, to such an extent that he seemed to be much more John's spiritual heir than his father's. Charles V had left no mark on his son. Charles took after him in no respect and in fact appeared to be his living antithesis, to the point that these two men, so near in blood, seemed two strangers. It would be necessary to go back to the grandfather to find the least family resemblance.

Charles had not yet created the Order of the Star, but that would come soon; he had not yet been taken prisoner on the battlefield. He had shown the world he was not afraid to fight, but his uncle, Duke of Burgundy, had always taken great pains to protect him during battle. His capture would probably have resulted in a spectacular catastrophe for the country's cash reserves, which Burgundy often confused with his own. With no other outlet, and in order to show his valor and his remarkable skill at arms, Charles threw himself entirely into tourneys, jousting against any knight who presented himself. He ignored the gossip of the dowagers who said a king should not make a spectacle of himself, especially when his opponent is of humble extraction. Charles could not have cared less.

Today he would have been a record holder in swimming, horsemanship, or tennis, in ice hockey or polo. He was surely of international class, a good horseman, a good fencer, a fine shot.

His hand over his heart (and he was sincere), he dreamed of peace and justice, a grand dream. But he loved war above all things—for its fine sword blows, for glory, and for adventure. And it mattered little to him whom he faced. Too bad about "good policy," provided he entered the lists. In his boiling enthusiasm, the hyperactive prince discounted the enemy's strength, and had a boundless desire to carry abroad the glory of his name, his prowess, and his exploits, to see distant and unknown lands. And here, resurrected, was the idea of a crusade—departure, the faraway—which Charles V had laid to rest.

Courtesy is the necessary counterpart to the strength of a true knight. Here, too, the King excelled. He treated everyone in the grandest manner, with exquisite civility, extreme affability. These qualities were truly spontaneous; they came from his heart. They might be considered his favorite luxury. Besides, he took pleasure in regarding the weak man as the equal of the strong, the poor man as the equal of the rich. Courageous, courteous, the monarch must also show he is generous. In keeping with the lack of moderation which characterized him, Charles was insanely generous, astoundingly munificent, so that his generosity could be considered as high as the throne he occupied, the crown he wore, his royal self. Whenever he received ambassadors from foreign lands he treated them sumptuously, considered their stay his personal expense, and sent them home loaded down with gifts. When his brother Louis got married, it was Charles who paid for the wedding. Petitioners swarmed about him, and he was unable to refuse them. "Where his father had given a hundred sous, he would grant a thousand." The royal treasury found itself completely drained at regular intervals. By now the members of the Chamber of Accounts, knowing who was ruling them, took the precaution of entering on the royal account books, beside the names of the donees, "He has had too much" or "Let it be recovered." Moreover, it was decided to stop keeping gold coins in the coffers, to melt them down at once into a good-sized stag. Unhappily these intentions fell short. For lack of time, the plans never materialized.

Such was the new King, the worthy grandson and continuator of King John. For the third time in less than half a century, a valiant knight occupied the throne of France. That meant a great deal, as we shall see, for the prosperity of the realm.

THE FOUR HUNDRED BLOWS

In order to celebrate the ideal he proclaimed as his own with the greatest brilliance, the King, in the course of a magnificent celebration, dedicated the first five days of the month of May 1389 to chivalry. The occasion was the departure of his young Anjou cousins, Louis, King of Naples, and Charles, his brother (aged thirteen and eleven at the time), for their distant kingdom whose possession was threatened. The King wished to sanction their journey by proclaiming before the eyes of the world his friendship for them.

First, couriers and messengers were dispatched through the entire kingdom and abroad, in the Germanies and in England, to invite the nobility of both sexes to the ceremonies and feasting at St. Denis. The place had been wisely chosen: the great personages of the court could lodge in the abbey, and the sacred rites would take place in the church. All that was needed, then, was to add a hall for the banquets and an enclosure for the jousts. These things were done. In the principal courtyard a wooden pavilion was erected, sixty-four paces in length by a dozen in width, whose exterior surface was entirely covered with bolts of white toile sewn together. Inside, gold and silk tapestries bedecked the walls, and silks of white and green the ceiling. At the upper end of the hall a dais marked the spot where the monarch would take his place. Finally, the space outside the hall was laid out as a jousting field.

The soil was leveled out over a length of one hundred and twenty paces, surrounded on three sides by ribbons representing the outer bounds, the fourth side being taken up with wooden galleries reserved for the ladies.

On Saturday, May 1, the feasting began. At sunset the King with all his attendants went to St. Denis. He was followed shortly by his aunt, the Queen of Sicily, in a covered chariot, which her sons escorted on horseback. The princes of the blood, her brothers-in-law the Dukes of Berry and Burgundy, the Duke of Touraine, the King's brother, and the Count of Nevers, her nephews, followed her. After them, in a long procession, came the invited nobility.

In keeping with the ancient customs of chivalry, taken up again in honor of the occasion, the young princes had dressed in the costume squires wore on the eve of being dubbed knights. It was an austere sort of dress, consisting of a dark gray robe, long and quite ample. There was none of the customary gold on their garments or on their horses' harness; behind their saddles they carried a roll of the same gray fabric. They left their mother in the abbey, then went on to the priory of Estrées, where they were expected to proceed to the first rite, the bath.

They were stripped of their clothing and plunged into tubs filled with purifying water, out of which they emerged, according to the Ordinance of Chivalry, "without taint and without blemish, having left in this water all foulness of sin and dishonest life." Silently they were dressed in white garments, like the catechumens of the primitive Church, for "if they wished to attain to God" they had to be "as pure in their soul as in their flesh." Finally they were reclothed as knights: in double garments of red silk lined with fine squirrel fur—a long, rounded robe falling all the way to their feet and a cloak, blood-scarlet in color, symbolizing the blood they would have to shed to defend the Holy Church. To this garb was added black hose, "signifying that from earth they have come and to earth they must return for the death which awaits them, whose hour they do not know, and for which they must put all pride beneath their feet." Lastly, they were girded with a white belt, "signifying that their bodies were completely encircled with chastity and cleanliness." Then they were ready.

For their souls it was meet "that they should be confessed and repentant of all their sins, and that they put themselves in the proper state to receive the body of Our Lord."

Night fell on St. Denis, fresh early May night, dark, almost cold. At sunset the birds suddenly fell still. Here and there screech owls shrieked and mists rose. The air smelled of new greenness, the leaves were half open. The lords gathered by torchlight about the little princes. Fantastic shadows played upon the stone of the walls. Each took his place according to his rank, Louis of Anjou between his uncle, Burgundy, and his cousin, Touraine; Charles, his brother, between the Duke of Bourbon and his cousin, Navarre. "Let us go pray together in the basilica," proposed the King.

In the light of the nave illuminated by tapers, the opaqueness of the mute church windows, the odors of incense and spring flowers, the dampness of the crypts, the echo of footsteps on the flagstones, the procession halted, and silence settled in, while the monarch and the two young boys fell on their knees and prayed before the saint's relics. Then they moved on to the brightness of the great hall, hung with gold and silk, to take their supper. The King had placed at his right his aunt, the Queen of Sicily, the Dukes of Burgundy and Touraine, and the King of Armenia, who had fled several years before to the French court, where he was treated with honor. To his left were the two aspirants. The ladies young and old, according to their rank, occupied the rest of the table. Once the repast was over, the boys went back to pray before the altar of the martyrs. In consideration for their tender age, they would be spared the traditional vigil of arms, in which the future knight spent the night in the church. They would rest, then, but dawn would find them once again prostrate before the saint's tomb.

On that day, the second of May, in the course of a solemn mass, the King personally conferred on his young cousins the order of knighthood. Charles, in a long royal cloak, and the two princes of Anjou made their entry into the church by the cloister door. Two squires led the procession, each holding in front of him a naked sword, which he bore by the point. On the hilts of the swords were the ritual spurs of pure gold. A crowd of noble lords followed. They halted before the altar of the martyrs while the procession of the ladies of the court, led by Queen Isabella and the dowager Queen of Sicily, came forward to join them.

The church was full. Monks in black tunics, immobile, their heads tonsured, their cloaks thrown back, in the choir stalls. In the nave and the lower sides the barons with their scarlet, vermilion, or pink capes, blue velvet mantles embroidered with pearls in fleur-de-lis and hawthorn leaf patterns, green satin greatcoats, woven with gold leaves. An iridescence of gems and spangles on Cypriot cloth of gold, on the headbands, the whiteness of the headdresses; the sparkling of jewelry in the rays of sunlight; heavy fabric slipping over stone, the rustling of silk, footsteps, and a discreet jangling of weapons—everyone took his place, remained immobile while on the King's order the chanting of the introit rose toward the vaults, *Misericordias Domini*. Next, the choir came to life, and all glances converged upon it. The Bishop of Auxerre, Ferry Cassinel, officiated. The ceremony continued with a solemn Sunday mass, sung in accord with the ordinary for double feast days. Chanting, murmured prayers, signs and gestures, a sermon— the universal rites were carried out and then yielded their place to other rites, reserved for only one caste. On their knees, the two young princes asked their King to be admitted among the knights. Charles had them take their oath, then girded them with the two-edged sword, "that with one edge they may smite the rich oppressor of the poor, and with the other punish the strong persecutor of the weak." And he ordered Lord Chauvigny to place the gold spurs on their boots, "for the knight must be as obedient to the spur of the divine will as his horse will be to the blows of the material spur." Then the bishop blessed them.

Taking place under the sign of God and of consecrated power, the ceremonies had been exemplary. A feast for the soul, in the contemplation and joy of promises, for the child who made bonds, or the man who remembered his recent youth, in the mothering security of the Church. "Go in peace," said the bishop at the conclusion of the mass. Go and celebrate, he could have added. The celebrations were to last more than three days. And what celebrations! Make room now for the body, for demonstrations of strength, room for games, for the body's pride, for its pleasures, room for physical prowess.

It was the ninth hour of the day, Monday, May 3, 1389. Twenty-two knights chosen by the King for their proven valor joined him in the courtyard of the abbey, each of them followed by a squire bearing his lance and helmet. The freshness of May mornings. The haughty allure of the riders on their plumed horses, with gilded armor, green shields bearing royal emblems; the noise of hoofs on the pavingstones, the whinnying of held-in steeds. A gesture of courteous welcome, a sovereign's affable smile. Again, the sound of riding. Looks turned with one accord to the twenty-two ladies who emerged into the courtyard, sitting quite straight upon their richly caparisoned palfreys. Bright cheeks, bright eyes under the thin stroke of plucked eyebrows, perfect complexions, smooth skin, not a wrinkle on those foreheads, bound with linen headdresses set off with jewels. The white of their hands against their dark green costumes embroidered with gold and precious stones. Tiny feet under heavy fabrics. Soft velvets, polished saddles, glossy-coated mounts. Slender, light arms, drawing colored ribbons from their bosoms and holding them out to their partners. Smiles were exchanged. The men took their place to the right of the women. The minstrels ran up with viols and jigs and gamboled behind them like a flight of blackbirds. Music, hubbub, the pawing of horses; a double procession formed and set off for the nearby lists. Each lady led the knight who would be fighting there for her honor until the end of the day.

Evening fell on the combats. A pure sky, a red sun on a pale horizon, dust from the lists. Victors and vanquished dismounted, and the squires were busy collecting the lances and casques, unlacing the cuirasses, leading off the mounts.

In vaulted rooms paved with flagstones, steam rose from tubs of warm water. Vapor, moisture-saturated air to soothe dried-out membranes. Valets undressed the lords and helped them into the water, which splashed everywhere and then became more or less calm again. A rippling noise, silence, the well-being of muscles stiffened by effort, relaxation, sighs of contentment, vigorous yawns, the passage of time. And then suddenly the loud noise of massive dripping bodies, so slippery no hand could hold them, freeing themselves all at once from the sluggish liquid. The dull thud as they stepped to the ground. The beauty of clean naked athletes. The servants waiting with warm linens. Rapidly they applied the linens to the damp skins, rubbed vigorously, then presented their masters with clean clothes and helped them return to

their rooms. There the lords would dress for the night, a very long
and propitious night.

Their garments had been taken from the chests and laid out on
the beds. The men put on their great robes of state, hung golden
chains across their chests, slipped on their rings, and prepared
themselves for games other than those of strength and adroitness,
for hungers other than those for glory and renown.

For the King was twenty-one years old, the Queen nineteen,
their brother eighteen, and the courtiers were scarcely older—they
were the sovereign masters of the first kingdom of Europe. To
have at the same time supreme power, money, and youth was intoxicating. The royal hands of Charles, Isabella, and Louis
clutched at fruits which burned their fingers. Fascinated, dazzled,
enraptured, they couldn't stop biting them, hungrily, with their
fine teeth, so violent was their savor. The rejuvenated world was
peopled with delights, and it belonged to them free and clear. What
a journey they would take to the outer limits of revelry and into
the night of the body, in quest of the ineffable, the moment!

There, delinquent children, they would play the *four hundred
blows,* followed enthusiastically by their whole entourage, here
and elsewhere, wherever they found themselves, even on these two
evenings in the Benedictine and royal abbey of St. Denis, which
innocently offered them hospitality, and where they abandoned
themselves to every pleasure, every excess.

This taste for feasting was very Valois. Charles had inherited it
from his grandfather, John, as well as from his great-grandfather,
Philip, and his father had appreciated it from time to time. But
these early feasts had always been *decent*. Those days were past.
Under the present holder of the throne, celebration would lose all
sense of propriety. The era was a libertine one, it is true; it was so
with impunity and the court set the tone.

Nonetheless, on the fifth day, they were all gathered in the basilica, bright-eyed and eager in full panoply, to render homage to
the memory of the High Constable, Du Guesclin, and through
him, to all knighthood.

Charles devoted the next three years to living with an incon-
ceivable ardor. He burned the candle at both ends, as the expres-

sion goes, only to devote thirty years to dying as a result. Did he have a presentiment that his days were numbered?

The year 1389 was a veritable whirlwind. On May 17, at Melun, his brother Louis married the beautiful Valentina Visconti, daughter of the Lord of Milan, Giangaleazzo Visconti, known to the French as Jean Galéas. The wedding, celebrated as we have said at Charles's expense, was sumptuous. On August 28 his wife, Queen Isabella, made her solemn entry into Paris to be crowned there in the midst of unforgettable revels which lasted for five days. All the chroniclers talked about them.

Ten days later Charles left in great pomp for Avignon. Not content with taking his usual entourage with him, he had retained for the journey the nobles who had come up to Paris for the crowning ceremony, "wishing to cause talk even in foreign countries of the magnificence he would display."

We may imagine this long procession as it crossed the whole of France, passing through Nevers, Norvan, Burgundy, Lyon, and Vienne. Triumphal entrances, presents, tournaments and banquets, going to bed at dawn, long stages, little sleep, lots of dust and excitement. All that took two months. On October 30, Charles arrived in Avignon. His Holiness invested Louis, the young Duke of Anjou, with the kingdom of Sicily, and solemnly entrusted him with the scepter, the crown, and the royal ornaments. The new King then received homage and oaths of loyalty from the barons who were there. The King and his entourage were given magnificent lodgings and entertained in like fashion: the highest lords and the princes of the blood served them at the banquets held in their honor. Nothing befitting the magnificence of a pope and the majesty of two kings was lacking. They also talked business—politics, schisms, the bestowing of privileges. And on November 4 they set off again, toward Aquitaine, where Charles had to put an end to the exactions of his uncle, Berry.

Before his departure, deputies from Berry's duchy had come to throw themselves at Charles's feet and beseech him, with tears in their eyes, to save them from the Duke's persecutions: "their compatriots," they had added, "no longer held any hope except in him, and if his support was not forthcoming, they would see themselves reduced to following the example of the forty thousand Aquitanians who had gone off to Aragon, and leave their native land to seek exile in whatever place they could. Any fate seemed preferable to them compared to the tyranny of Duke Jean."

The King took three weeks to reach Toulouse, by way of Béziers and Carcassonne, and remained for a week in that southern metropolis. He went on an excursion as far as the county of Foix, where Count Gaston Phoebus treated him splendidly, and made Charles a gift of his domain. Afterward, when all affairs had been settled and justice had been done, he headed back toward the north.

Suddenly, at Montpellier, time began to weigh heavy on him. He missed his palaces, his wife Isabella, and his sister-in-law Valentina. He wanted to be home at any price, to see them within the hour. He could wait no longer, and in his impatience he revealed his feelings to Louis:

"My dear brother, I wish that you and I were in Paris now."

"My lord," the latter answered him, "there is too long a road to travel from where we are."

"You are right," the King replied, "but it seems to me that I could be there in a trice if I wished."

"Indeed, by dint of what your horses can do, and not otherwise, my lord. So could I, too, and my horse would carry me there."

"First," said Charles, "which of us will be there sooner, you or I? Let's make a bet."

"So be it," replied the Duke, always short of money. "Shake hands on that, my good brother. Five thousand francs to the first man who reaches the capital."

The following day, at dawn, each escorted by one arbiter only, the two rivals departed: with the Duke, the Lord of Garencières; with the King, the Duke of La Vieuville.

Riding non-stop, hastily gulping their food in the saddle, pushing their horses at full gallop night and day, the young men drove on. At Troyes, the King could take no more. He collapsed onto a bed and caught eight hours of rest. Eight hours too many, during which time Louis, equally exhausted but much more astute, regained his strength without losing the advantage by doing so. He was taken by boat from Troyes to Melun. There he jumped on a horse and reached St. Pol. Four hours later Charles burst in. Louis sprang forward, saying: "My lord, I've won the bet. Have

me paid." "You're right," Charles admitted, "and you will be."
And paid Louis was, in hard cash.

They had covered a good four hundred and fifty miles, one of
them in 104 hours, the other in 108. A rather pretty performance.

Did that first year of Charles's personal reign, devoted to feasts
and to pomps, bear its fruits? Without any doubt. People's minds
had been struck by this display of splendor. The entire world
looked to the court of France and asked for the help, if not for the
arbitration, of the King. Now it was the Genoese, imploring aid
against the Turks; now the Bolognese and the Florentines, in
conflict with the Lord of Milan. One day it was an impostor, Paul
Tagari, the poorest Greek of the poorest of the islands of the
Hellenic peninsula, who was called (and was believed to be) the
Patriarch of Constantinople. Charles gave the warmest reception
to all. But there was none to equal the welcome he arranged at the
outset of 1391 for the ambassador from England, the Duke of
Lancaster. He defrayed the entire cost of the Duke's stay, decided
that the interview would take place at Amiens, and ordered lodgings readied in the different quarters of the town, the magnificence
of which was to be proportionate to the importance of the guests.
He pressed delicacy to the point of having hung above the entry to
those traveling quarters escutcheons struck with the coats of arms
of the one who was lodged there. He invited the whole court to
Amiens, and for once his uncles, above all Burgundy. It is likely
that he was hoping, amid the contagious joy of the banquets, that
the conflict with the English which had lasted for more than half a
century would find its solution. The King was naïve, as we know.
Courtesy and good manners did not prevent the English from
making exorbitant claims. After several days of vain discussions,
they parted empty-handed and limited themselves to extending the
cease-fire for one more year.

But within that year the course of affairs had time to change,
the winds to turn and misfortune to cut down in the prime of
youth the man who ruled France.

CRIME

It is the bloody business which informs thus to mine eyes.

Macbeth

We know that there were warning signs: the little statuette of the Blessed Virgin Mother, which belonged to the treasury of the cathedral of Le Mans, began to spin on its own pedestal for about half an hour, without anyone having touched it. There was the typhoid fever the King caught and from which he had not completely recovered. And then a series of unpleasant circumstances which we shall attempt to relate.

The heat of an August noon in the sand pits of the forest of Le Mans. The royal army was making its way toward the estates of the Duke of Brittany, who had treasonously offered asylum to another traitor, Pierre de Craon. The latter was guilty of an attempt on the life of Olivier de Clisson, the Constable of France and a most devoted servant of the Valois dynasty.

Pine trees, green oaks, moors, dry brittle earth, and not a puff of wind. Blue everywhere: the blue of the sky, the blue through the rows of tree trunks, the blue atop the dark green of the plumed foliage, the intense blue of the sky. Tree trunks reddish, ocher, scaly, withered; congealed drops of resin; pale, grayish soil; faded green mosses and somber green furzes with velvet cones; pink clusters of heather flowers; the silvery blue of thistles; the faded yellow of strawflowers hanging on dry gray stems over the pale earth; the faint scent of sandflowers and the warm scent of pine trees. The heat of the air, the heat of the ground, the heat of the horse against its rider's leg, the heat of the lance in the armor-bearer's hand, the heat of cloth on damp skin. The dull sound of the horses' hoofs on loose earth. The army advanced, horses and lances swaying. The forest moved past on either side, the shadows brushed past gently, slowly; the forest weighed heavily, no birdcalls, a dead silence. The army came to the edge of the forest and passed onto the sandy plain. The daylight was dazzling, the air trembling. Not a shadow. Sunlight, on men and on horses, on casques and on crests, on steel helmets and bucklers. Dazzled glances, blinking eyes. A fiery air, on skin, hands, lips. Fire from heaven.

Small groups broke ranks and rode off separately in order to avoid raising too much dust near where the King was to ride. The Duke of Bourbon, the Lord de Coucy, Sir Charles d'Hangiers, and the Baron d'Ivry rode ahead, and behind them came the uncles, Burgundy and Berry, who conversed amicably. The Count of la Marche, Jacques de Bourbon, Philippe d'Artois, Henri and Philippe de Bar, and Pierre de Navarre moved off to one side. There were men-at-arms everywhere.

The King rode alone, in a jerkin of black velvet, with a hat of vermilion. Around his neck he wore a rosary of large white pearls, which Queen Isabella had given him when he left. His two pages rode behind him, one carrying a steel helmet and the other a vermilion lance, trimmed with a silk banner.

Under such circumstances, we can imagine what this man was thinking to himself, overwhelmed by his fears, his troubles, his indignation, his fury, in the growing solitude of the journey, in the regular, monotonous swaying of his mount, in the crushing heat of the day, after several nights of exhausting fever, now that the cares of office, crystallized by the shock of events, had become obsessions with him.

The King was somber. He had forgotten the heat, the sunlight, the long road. He had forgotten the forest of Le Mans and the sand pits. He had forgotten the season. It had been only yesterday, at this very moment, on the night of June 14, that it all started. . . .

For the Corpus Christi holiday, he had given a tournament and a ball at St. Pol. The last of the guests had just departed, and he had gone back to his apartments. The night was limpid. The darkness of the room, the soft glimmering of the torches near the bed, the windows open on the gardens, the pale moonlight shed in large bright pools on the flagstones, silver boxes filled with sugarplums thanks to Isabella's attentions, crystal wine bottles with vermilion stoppers, cool water in the water jugs, the lukewarm air, the silence, the echoed croaking, the calls, the water running from the basins—it had been a lovely June night. His body felt heavy, ready for sleep. Suddenly, in the empty corridor, the noise of footsteps and weapons. Some words were spoken, the door was opened, and men burst in out of breath, in a state of agitation. Misfortune hovered in the air.

"Ah, sire," they finally began, "we don't dare conceal from you the great mischief which has now befallen in Paris."

"What mischief?" exclaimed the King.

"Your Constable, Lord Olivier de Clisson, has been murdered."

"Murdered?" Charles started. "How? Who has done this deed?"

"Sire, we do not know, but he's been the victim of foul play, right near here, in the Rue St. Catherine."

"Right away, bring torches, bring torches!" the King cried. "I will go see him."

Charles set out just as he was, barely taking the time to let shoes be put on his feet. The way there, between St. Pol and the large street called St. Catherine, seemed endless. He was overcome with anguish and rage. In what condition would he find his Constable? Who could have dared do such a deed?

He arrived at the bakery where the wounded man had been taken. Clisson was still alive, lying where they had left him, bloody, half clothed, breathing painfully. His wounds were already being inspected. The King stooped over the old man and spoke to him:

"Constable, how do you feel?"

"Dear sire," the wounded man whispered, "I feel very faint and very weak."

"And who put you in such a state?"

"Sire, it was Pierre de Craon and his henchmen—traitors who caught me off my guard."

The King sent for his personal physicians and surgeons. They arrived in great haste and bowed to their master, whose features grew calmer on seeing them.

"Examine my Constable for me," the King declared, "and tell me in what condition you find him, for I am much grieved by his discomfort."

The doctors went to work. Time hung suspended in the silver hourglass. Like blood, like expectation. Charles anxiously drew his men aside and asked:

"Tell me, is there any danger of death?"

"Certainly not, sire," they reassured him, "there is no danger of

death at all. God willing, we'll give him back to you within two
weeks, and able to ride again."

Charles sighed. "God be praised. This is rich news." He returned to Lord Clisson and told him:

"Constable, think of your own needs, and do not embroil your
blood or concern yourself with anything. For never was there a
misdeed so costly, or so likely to rebound on the traitors who
committed it, as this one will be: for it is my affair."

And upon that promise, he left Clisson's side. . . .

The heat of an August noon in the sand pits of the forest of Le
Mans. Fire from the earth. Fire from heaven. Vengeance. Vengeance for you, my friend. Let's get on. Let's get through this pitiless
furnace, vengeance is waiting at the next stage. His horse slowed
down, stumbled, snorted, trembled. Charles spurred him on,
sweating. The animal started and, forced on, set out again.

To have dared to attack his Constable, who was pure as gold
and loyal. A traitor, this Pierre de Craon, a disreputable, vicious
traitor, a swindler, a piece of filth. He had a number of crimes already on his conscience: indelicacies, thefts, embezzlements of
funds, and blood on his hands. Not only Clisson's blood, but
Valois blood: the blood of a prince of the fleurs-de-lis, the King
of Sicily, Charles's uncle, who had died of a fever on the journey
to conquer his distant kingdom. Louis had died while awaiting the
return of his dear cousin, Craon, whom he had sent to his wife
Marguerite in Angers to collect the funds he desperately needed.

The princess had entrusted Craon with huge sums. And while
Louis I of Anjou was expiring, wretched and alone, in a tiny village of Apulia, his cousin took the money and lived in grand style
in Venice. Having learned there of his cousin's death, Craon returned, with a large retinue, to Paris. Such cynicism touched on
insensibility.

He had been ejected from the palace of the kings of Naples.
After which, he disappeared; it was safer. Time passed, and he
was forgotten. He returned. He was tolerated at the royal palace,
and afterward at the residence of Louis, Duke of Orléans. A mistake. He started saying the most disreputable things about the
Duke of Orléans. The Duke was a sensualist (as he would tell
anyone willing to listen to him), a rake, who loved only dancing
and women. In this respect, we are obliged to admit, Louis was

not above reproach. But Craon extended his audacity to the point of accusing Louis of sorcery, of practicing such abominations as necromancy; and he whispered that Louis cast spells with dead men's bones. There were people who believed him. We know how courtiers sweeten their discourse with tidbits of this sort, especially when they have to do with their princes. Once again Craon had been ejected from the royal and princely residences, and he had taken refuge with his relative, the Duke of Brittany, Clisson's mortal enemy.

It would be useless to seek any further for the motive behind this latest crime or for the choice of its victim. The business had been carefully worked out. Craon kept a house in Paris, near the St. Jean cemetery, for his visits to town. He had sent his servants on to the house to lay in a store of wine, meat, salt, and flour; and he had ordered his steward to purchase furtively some armor, coats of mail, gauntlets, and archers' headgear. Then he had sent for forty fearless and outrageous Bretons, whom he installed there without giving them a clue as to what precisely he expected of them. When the moment came, he joined them, incognito. The rest we know. . . .

Ah, the wretch! One would see, they would all see, those unbearable nobles, what the King of France was capable of when anyone dared strike at him! As they had already seen, on the night of the attempted murder, Charles had not slept. At daybreak he had summoned the Provost of the Châtelet.

"Provost, take some men, well mounted and armed for the task, and pursue the traitor, Pierre de Craon, over roads and highways. By his treason he has wounded our Constable and put his life in danger. You can do no service more welcome than to find him, capture him, and bring him to us."

"Sire, I shall do all that is in my power," the Provost had answered, "but what road might he take?"

"Inform yourself about it, Provost, and be prompt."

But Craon had already crossed the Seine, and had seen to it that the ferry lines were cut, so as to forestall all means of pursuing him. They sought him nonetheless, all the way to Chartres, but in vain. The traitor had reached his castle of Sablé, in the west. Not feeling secure there, he took refuge at Susinio, at the residence of the Duke of Brittany.

Unhappy the man who went to his aid.

Four of Craon's men who were found in a village seven leagues from Paris—two squires, a page, a man-at-arms—plus the steward from his town house were arrested, tossed in the Châtelet prison, and beheaded; their truncated bodies were exposed upon the gallows. A canon of Chartres, who had given the fugitive fresh horses, was imprisoned and deprived of all he had. All of Craon's household goods were seized in forfeiture to the royal treasury (and Craon was a rich man); all of his real property—the Parisian residence where he had prepared his coup, his castle of Porchefontaine (a very lovely dwelling), and his castle of La Ferté-Bernard, where he and his family resided—was razed to the ground. His chattels and valuables were confiscated and they were worth forty thousand gold crowns; his wife and daughter were evicted without the slightest deference and found themselves on the street with only their nightclothes on their backs. Charles's brother Louis received La Ferté-Bernard in perpetuity, and the income from Porchefontaine. Heralds proclaimed with a trumpet blast through all the towns and hamlets in the kingdom that Craon and his henchmen were outlaws. Finally, the Duke of Brittany, Jean de Montfort, was summoned and told to hand over the guilty party under pain of the crime of lese majesty.

The Duke was instantly evasive. He had indeed seen Craon, and even received him. But his cousin had since left the country, and he, Brittany, was not able to say where he was.

Nothing about Jean de Montfort's attitude ought to be very surprising. He had laid an ambush for the Constable five years earlier, the same year in which he sabotaged the expedition Charles's uncles had gotten up against England. He had lured Clisson to his castle of Hermine, on the pretext of inviting him to dinner. There his men had laid hold of the guest, showered him with blows, heaped insults upon him, and thrown him, chained, into an underground dungeon. Clisson had gotten out only after he had promised, under threats and torture, to deliver to his overlord three fortresses and the treasure hidden in them. (Clisson had a large fortune, which is why they were so jealous of him.)

Montfort had spent his life betraying his countrymen and intriguing constantly with the English. Why should he have stopped doing so now? But he had gone beyond the limits a king can tolerate in a vassal. This Breton was going to be compelled to loyalty by force of arms. And, since he refused to understand this, there would be fighting.

He would see, that Duke! He would be made to stoop. His fief would be taken away and he would be replaced by a governor until his sons attained their majority.

And Charles had summoned the host, that host which was marching now on Nantes. His uncles had expressed their opposition, to be sure, but the decision wasn't theirs to make. Charles would not compromise. He had shown himself patient, amicable, and generous long enough, and he had taken the path of understanding and clemency as far as possible. And with what outcome! They would see, then, what the power of Charles VI of Valois was, what his anger was, and what his army and his soldiers were like when they billeted themselves upon a place to live off its inhabitants—something to give you a taste for loyalty and obedience.

Suddenly, Charles felt extremely weary. This heat, these thoughts: and they claimed that the Duke of Brittany was for nothing in this affair. Come on, then! I realized long ago you can't take the word of a nobleman. My father himself never depended on any but people of modest origins. Following his example, I've had to call on my dear Bureau de la Rivière, on Jean Le Mercier, on Pierre de Chevreuse, on Jean de Montaigu, on some churchmen as well. They are competent, efficient, helpful with their advice, reliable, loyal. Don't imagine that I was able to dismiss my uncles lightheartedly. I was fearful of incurring their rancor and their resentment. I've always felt affection for them. Naturally, I would prefer to be able to count on them, as I can on the "Marmosets." That's what they call my people contemptuously. But whom can I trust in this world, if not them? Those of my blood are vain and fickle, they give way, like the sand in which my horse is laboring.

I'm unhappy, I'm alone, among these submissive, friendly faces, these hostile hearts, these hands which dream of nought but taking and me giving, giving, giving, but never enough. Not the slightest gratitude, the slightest affection. To fight, and go on fighting, against a masked enemy . . . To be constantly on guard against one and all; and today, at this very moment, more than ever, ah, the traitors . . .

Traitors . . . The word penetrated and spread out inside him like a poison, causing his heart to pound and his veins to burn. His sweating temples began to buzz, again and again, every time the word made the rounds of his skull. He had really been holding on all by himself since that night of June 14 and he no longer ate or slept, consumed by fury and fever. His doctors talked to him of rest. But how could he put up with inaction in the green lands of Gisors or Melun, when they were betraying him? They were betraying him. They were betraying him. The phrase came back to him again and again.

His uncle Jean, a traitor, who for twelve years had thought of nothing but filling his own pockets at Charles's expense and had systematically seized and squeezed more than a third of the kingdom, to the point of forcing his own people into exile. A traitor, too, his uncle Philip who, for his own ends, had led Charles at the most tender age from war to war, from punitive expeditions to useless armaments, without the kingdom's ever having reaped the slightest advantage. Who now was systematically opposed to every enterprise of his ministers and dug pitfalls behind them at the country's expense. A traitor Ostrevant, son-in-law of that traitor Philip, who despite Charles's orders had not joined the host. A traitor the Duke of Brittany, and that base Pierre de Craon. Treason, treason, Yolande de Bar when she wrote him that she was keeping a noble knight prisoner—could it be Craon?—and asked someone to identify the knight, trying, for certain, to gain time— for whom? For Craon's accomplices, a lot of them, it seemed. Treason. Even Louis, even Isabella, Louis who was deceiving him, Isabella who was deceiving him, as he well knew. And as everyone knew. Even that beggar in rags who had been waiting for him in front of the leper house and had followed him for more than half an hour, calling out to him in a jarring voice the phrase which was haunting him: "Do not go farther, noble King, they are betraying you."

They are betraying you, they are betraying you. These sand pits were interminable; he would never get out of them. And the sun, still at the zenith. Not a puff of wind or a cloud in the sky. This black velvet was very warm. They shouldn't have let him put it on.

They were betraying him, they were betraying him. Even the brilliance of this day, even this blinding light. If only a little rain would fall to settle the dust, a little rain to moisten his hands, a little rain on his skin, his forehead. How good it would feel to lift his face to the rain. But no. Always this heat, implacable, unchanging, which did not let up. Like Brittany. They were betraying him, they were betraying him. My uncles, my noblemen, Louis my brother and my wife Isabella. Everyone knows about it. . . .

Charles twisted around in his saddle, casting uneasy glances from one side to the other. This land, all things considered, was far from safe. A western land, profoundly silent, secretive; and he was crossing it for the first time. Beneath its calm appearance, it concealed many dangers: wild inhabitants, hardly loyal, their Duke's subjects first of all, not his own, and war had been raging here for a very long time.

And what if the Duke were suddenly to loom up in front of him? What if he were waiting at the edge of the sand pits, with his army lying in ambush in the copses, in the green meadows, with his forces intact in the shadows? For they were hard, aggressive men, these Bretons, remarkable soldiers, Du Guesclin's countrymen, remarkable wrestlers, strong of back, solid, grappling, with enough energy and endurance for any ordeal. What if Montfort were waiting there with a large escort of Englishmen? With the double disadvantage of the heat and the road, it would be a disaster, a new Poitiers, who knew? But they wouldn't get him like that, not Charles, he'd fight, he'd defend himself, he was going to defend himself because they were getting ready to attack him, as soon as he passed the sand pits, and already he could make out their shadows. "They are betraying you, they are betraying you, noble King." Yes, they were lying in wait, they were preparing themselves. How had he not foreseen it?

And suddenly, a terrible noise rent the air, a noise of clashing arms that traveled across the silence of the sandy plains to the edge of the heath, without meeting an obstacle, until it struck the curtain of trees and echoed back. A chance occurrence. One of the two pages following Charles had dozed off. His moist hand, which had been holding the vermilion lance with the silk standard, fell open. The weapon he dropped struck the other page's helmet in its fall. The long steel of the spear against the round steel of the headdress. A fortuitous shock, intolerable for the lonely man in the black jerkin riding along under the blazing sky. A horrible noise. It transfixed him, overpowered him, spread undulating, wave upon wave, echo upon echo, through his head and body, overpowering him with anguish, with terror and rage, tearing apart his soul, which a single word had already filled to bursting: treason. An affront, a wound, a running sore at the very center of his being, a glowing iron, a fire. Where to flee? Where to escape, if not into a reality which he reconstructed as he wished, into which he projected (his only way out) the one word which obsessed him, from which he would deliver himself by giving it form and body in those traitors he was going to destroy in his turn, a just revenge against the word which engendered them and which had been torturing him for hours, for days, for months, to the point of exhaustion, destroying him. But not quite.

Charles drew his sword and spurred his horse on. "Forward," he cried, "forward upon those traitors!" And he turned, charging after pages, who fled before him, screaming.

The whole host, dozing with the heat, gave a start. Terrified, they saw the King directing his mount upon his brother Louis, whom he no longer recognized. "Flee, dear nephew of Orléans," cried out the Duke of Burgundy, "flee! My lord wants to kill you!" Orléans galloped off in dismay. Gesticulating, high on his stirrups, brandishing his sword, the King pursued them at a full gallop, raving madly. Louis barely escaped the charge. Charles wheeled his horse, spotted him again and charged. Orléans avoided the charge and set out in the opposite direction. The King turned his horse around and struck out in pursuit: "They want to hand me over to my enemies, to hand me over to my enemies!" And he struck wherever he could, at baron, knight, page, or groom, all so many traitors who were defying him. Four men fell under the blows, the bastard De Polignac among them. Finally Orléans managed to get out of danger.

No one was able to stop the King. Out of breath, beside himself, he came and went, turned and returned at a mad pace, amid clouds of dust within an improvised jousting field, bounded by rows of armed men who eluded his assaults every time he charged, letting themselves fall to the ground as soon as he was upon them. They exhausted him, they wore him out like a hunted animal.

At last his chamberlain, Guillaume Martel, jumped on Charles's horse's croup, seizing the King's sword arm and immobilizing it. The poor madman was subdued, disarmed, taken off his horse. He put up no resistance. Exhausted, panting, dripping with sweat, he recognized none of them and did not speak. But his eyes rolled wildly.

A mortal silence fell over the sand pits. A burning sky, fiery sand, weapons cast on the ground glittering beneath the sun, the dark blur of a body stretched on the ground, the whiteness of shoulders, of the torso being undressed, pages stooping to fan the King. Squires curbed the horses. Orléans, off to one side, caught his breath, while the lords, struck with consternation, conversed in low voices. The princes conferred. "We must return to Le Mans," the Duke of Burgundy commanded. "The journey is over for this season."

SO LONG A DEATH

Henceforth the King would be *in absentia*. The condition would last for thirty years, thirty years of crises and remissions, thirty years of deliriums, screams, prostrations, long convalescences leading to relapses. There would be forty-two such attacks in all, some lasting several months. For thirty years the life of Charles VI would be reduced to a few cruel words: anguish, terror, frenzy, loneliness, abandonment, and one that sums them all up: unhappiness.

Temples buzzing, heart pounding, a knot in his throat, the prince would follow the rising curve of the disease that possessed him. Aware of what awaited him, in the grip of an inexpressible anguish, he would weep, demanding that his dagger be taken away, commanding his uncle Burgundy to have his entourage disarmed. Already he was no longer the master.

Stricken by the growing instability of his motor impulses, he would become agitated, pacing up and down in his chamber, gesticulating, talking, coming and going restlessly. Then a dull mask would freeze his features, and shortly he would show no further signs of recognition, while before his eyes would take form, for him alone, a world of terror, sound, and fury. Terrified and fascinated, he would watch it through empty eyes. A vision of hell, of the apocalypse. They were leading him into the empire of death and confining him there. Who were "they"? The question was already irrelevant. Ghastly creatures would draw near him, more and more of them every instant, till they formed that crowd, that horde, that tide converging on him, wretched and lonely, to destroy him without pity. Were they men, specters, or monsters, or a single knight, huge and outrageous? No matter; they were assailing him.

Then he would groan, sob, beseech, howl, want to escape—consequently all the doors of St. Pol were walled up. Or else his courage would have carried him away. A king did not flinch from battle. Charles would rise to attack, take off at a run, screaming through the corridors of the palace, seeking and pursuing his enemies, the traitors who were threatening his life. Everyone was dismayed at the tumult of his demented pursuits. His servants hid, out of fear that he might pursue them and cudgel them—it had happened. They did not dare defend themselves or raise a hand against the sick man, who in his disgrace still remained the Lord's anointed.

Panting, in a sweat, Charles would stop, catch his breath. But not for long. His fury would turn on the objects that surrounded him. Goblets, water jugs, golden bowls, basins, silver cups would fly through the room, striking the walls full force and ricocheting off the ground. He would hang from the draperies, tear them down, and rip them to pieces. With wild gestures of rage he would pull the sheets of fine Reims or Morigny linen off his bed and tear them to shreds. He would break chains, throw napkins, boots, and clothes into the fire, and attack the lining of his cloaks. Sitting on the ground, he would carefully pluck the fine squirrel skin or Prussian sable off his sleeves. There would be nothing left to do, once the crisis had calmed down, but to gather the damaged objects and linen and send them to the furrier's, the embroiderer's, to the shop of Jehan and Guillaume Balle to be repaired.

Or else, passing from tears to laughter, from extreme tension to a beneficial relaxation, Charles would run around naked, trampling his possessions and casting them to the winds, singing, laughing at the top of his lungs, abandoning himself to obscene cavorting.

Of a sudden terror would seize him again; he would freeze, neither blinking nor budging, for fear of falling and breaking into pieces, since he was made of glass, didn't they see that? "Don't touch me!" he would scream. "Don't anyone touch me!"

In order to calm these terrors which came back in cycles, his servants would dress him in clothes with iron stays to support his limbs, which he thought were about to crumble.

Sometimes Charles would fall into a state of torpor which necessitated constant assistance for the simplest acts of life—assistance which he would refuse. With a straggly beard, lice- and vermin-ridden, covered with boils, he would remain for months at a time prostrate in a corner of his room; or else sitting on a bed he allowed no one to touch, barely feeding himself, sleeping little, not speaking, except violently to forbid anyone to try to administer the most urgently needed assistance. His servants did not dare contravene what they took to be his orders.

We are at the end of the month of November 1392. The situation had lasted for four months. The taboos against interfering with the Lord's anointed remained so strong that the uncles did not dare take upon themselves alone the responsibility for restraining the King, who despite his condition was still the King. They needed the Council's permission in order to adopt a course of action in regard to their sick nephew. And even then they would not have thought it possible to oppose the deranged man's will without resorting to a stratagem.

Every evening, as night fell, Charles's usual entourage would leave him. Other servants, ten in all, new faces with which the King was unfamiliar, would enter his lodgings, disguised for the occasion. They would surround the patient, lavish on him sweet words, advice, even reproaches, and try thus to get him to do what they wished. It took them three weeks to convince him to undress for bed, to change his sheets and bedclothes, to bathe, to let the barbers shave him, and finally to sleep and eat at regular hours.

Thus appearances were kept up, and no one could say that the King had not acted of his own free will.

But he was no longer himself, no longer King; he called himself a simple knight, named not Charles but George, and his coat of arms was a lion transfixed by a sword. Never has a fantasy uttered in delirium more closely encompassed reality. For in effect he *was* no longer King, nor did he assume the royal responsibilities any longer. All that was left him were the combats which were the knight's stock in trade, the trade of the patron saint of the order whose name he had taken in this new life fate had assigned him, and who fought against monsters, as he was doing now. But St. George, as an archangel, escaped the human condition, whose rule is to suffer. Not "George," an earthborn man, who had chosen as a symbol of himself the most precise and just of images, the king of the forest, struck deep in the heart, stopped in his tracks by the murderous force of a sword, blindly directed by some unknown hand. What could better express the cruel fate of King Charles of France, mortally struck, reduced to the level of a beast by the world's wrong, than this heartbreaking symbol, this cry?

For delirium, like dreams, does not lie. It takes precise account of a cruel, ambiguous, difficult reality, which no one dares admit, let alone formulate. How could Charles tell his wife Isabella that he hated her for having deceived him with his brother Louis, whom he had wanted to kill in those sand pits? That he no longer trusted her, and even doubted that their children were his own? That he knew she had no heart, that she was selfish and greedy, that she had no love left for him, nor he for her? That she was of no help to him in his distress, that she bored him, that he did not like to be near her and by now had nothing left to say to her? But in his crisis he expressed in broad daylight feelings as unavowable as his desires: he claimed not to be married, not to have any children. When Isabella approached him he did not recognize her. If she insisted, he did not conceal the revulsion she inspired in him. "Who is that woman who is constantly in my sight?" he would ask his retinue. "Find out what she needs, and deliver me any way you can from her persecution and her importunity, so that she stops dogging my footsteps like this." At other times he would ragefully attack the blazons in which the arms of France were quartered with those of Bavaria, and everywhere he observed them, he obliterated them, on the walls, on the glazed windows, on the golden dining service. But he would cry aloud for his sister-in-law, Valentina Visconti, Duchess of Orléans, calling her his "beloved sister" and seeking her company every day. Only she could appease him. He loved her and made no secret of it.

But when he returned to his senses and was asked about these things, he knew nothing. The truth about what he had just lived through had already evaded him. He was no longer anything but a poor, broken thing with no memory, who brought nothing from the hellish world out of which he had just emerged but a feeling of unutterable anguish, unbearable grief. He would take fright: might he be the victim of poison or spells? And he would weep: "In the name of Jesus Christ, if there is any among you who are accomplices in the evil I am enduring, I implore you not to torture me any longer but put me promptly to death." And he would hold himself guilty. Before those troubled faces, that floor strewn with broken objects and tattered garments, he would beg pardon. He would try to redress the verbal excesses that had revealed the secret depths of his heart—excesses he did not remember, but which were most likely reported to him. At such times he would shower his brother Louis with favors, chattels, gifts. He would do his duty by his wife, with whom he spared neither money nor children—six in ten years.

He was still believed to be a responsible person because in the course of his remissions he came and went, sat in at the Council, participated, seemed to lead a normal life; and because the belief that he was the Lord's anointed protected his sacred majesty. The epoch could not allow itself to see a consecrated king as a man among men, weak, vulnerable, obedient to the same laws of nature as ordinary men. It refused to declare that there was a much diminished and perfectly irresponsible being occupying the throne of France, a very sick man, incapable of controlling his own mind. His memory and sensitivity were impaired; his perception was deficient. His attention wandered, and his handwriting was permanently altered. He could no longer remember or exercise his will. If his entourage were neither sufficiently advanced to realize that a psychotic is in no condition to assume the burden of power, nor sufficiently honest to draw the logical conclusions, they were nonetheless quite able to adjust to the situation. From the top to the bottom of the hierarchy, everybody helped himself with impunity. Uncles, brother, wife, cousins, courtiers, down to the humblest valet, all thought only of extorting the most they could from the sick man, who was unable to say no and, what was more, no longer recalled, the instant after a decision he had just made, what he had or hadn't said, what he still owned or had given away. Two examples among so many others: within the same hour, Charles granted the same vicarage to two different priests. If the position of Master Regnault de Bussy was vacant, and eight people were hankering for it, by the monarch's command it would be granted to each of the eight. The realm had become lands up for grabs, to be auctioned off or handed over to the most rapacious.

Even more sordid, some—probably lowborn knaves—didn't even hesitate to steal the King's personal effects. They stole and looted even in his private rooms. Clothes, jewels, gold and silver vessels, all disappeared. One day they got into his wardrobe and helped themselves to two pairs of his boots; another day, it was the gold trimming on his belt. Within a period of two months his gem room and his Hall of Lion Tapestries received visitors who skillfully went about cutting off the cloth-of-gold furniture backings. Charles saw nothing or, if he noticed what they had done, he promptly forgot.

Everything got blurred and dulled, even his capacity to love—up to that time his best quality. His heart, affected by his illness, had no room for other people. This type of deterioration must have begun early on. It had been noticeable from the time of the "Ball of Flames," six months after the Le Mans episode. To celebrate the wedding of one of the Queen's bridesmaids, Catherine of Germany, and a knight of the Vermandois, the King had given a party for the couple at St. Pol. As a joke and in order to surprise the ladies of the bridal party, six lords of the court, the King himself among them, had disguised themselves as savages. They donned linen coats covered with pitch and unraveled flax, shaped and colored like human hair, cut to their measurements and sewn on to look like part of their own bodies. Their entry caused a sensation. There were exclamations and wild laughter, guffaws, and excited cries of "Who is it?" The Duke of Orléans approached the six, with a torch in his hand, in order to determine the identity of the mysterious maskers. At that moment, before the terrified eyes of the party, our heroes were transformed into living torches.

Four of them died in horrible pain, while the fifth threw himself into the great tubs of water which were customarily located in kitchens, and thus barely escaped death. As for the sixth, he owed his life only to the presence of mind of the young Duchess of

Berry, who smothered the flames by tossing her court robe over him. As chance had it, this sixth masker was the King.

The next day he had scarcely mourned for his dead friends. Such a shock ought to have marked him; instead, it hardly affected him. Such indifference was construed as strength of soul—in fact, it was a sign of the greater affliction which was consuming him. It confirmed the mental deterioration which was to display itself in more and more peculiar behavior as time went by. In 1408, Charles showered favors on his brother's murderer. In 1416, on the death of his uncle, Berry, he gave a tournament, since ambassadors from a neighboring country were paying him a visit, and he had to honor them in accord with their rank. In 1420 he ratified the most monstrous decisions, disowned his eleventh child (the future Charles VII), whom he declared a bastard, and gave the child's kingdom to the English. A madness which at this time he turned against himself as well, tolerating the worst license:

> In his wardrobe he has no jewels
> For treasure is not kept by fools. . . .
> And if perchance he gives away
> His favorite shoes or clothing gay,
> With much ado he'll come by more—
> Of that, at least, we can be sure.
> And it is three whole days he's been
> Without a belt that I have seen
> For want of coming by another;
> And equally he lacks a light
> Beside his bed when it is night. . . .

That is the way a contemporary pamphlet, *The True Dream,* evoked him at the end of his reign. It is hard to believe that the "he" in this text is the King of France.

Charles, a prisoner of his illness, let everything slide. He was no longer capable, between attacks, of doing any more than playing at cards or tarot with his pages, Robinet and Cerise, laughing at the farces performed before him by Fatras and his company, and attending the festivities which up to the time of his brother's murder entertained the court incessantly, and which he himself esteemed so highly. Only his physical life escaped disaster; his kinetic faculties remained intact. Was this a coincidence? It corresponded to his liveliest enthusiasm. Till the end of his life he hunted, aimed his crossbow at targets in the Bois de Vincennes, played court tennis, and participated in tourneys—the last one of which the books preserve a mention dates from 1415.

What mental aberration made the contemporaries of the unhappy Charles VI think they had to keep at the head of the kingdom a man in so deteriorated a condition? Nowadays such a psychosis, defined, studied, and catalogued, is treated and mended. But then, nothing at all was known about it.

The royal family spared no effort in attempting to set Charles free of his madness. He lacked neither medicine nor physicians, we may be certain. But doctors soon showed the impotence of their art in such matters. Bleedings, purgatives, fresh air, entertainment, music, flowers whose scents had curative powers, all of these things were tried. In vain. They had to admit that the remedies prescribed were proving wholly ineffective.

At that point the King's subjects turned to the sovereign physician, Jesus Christ.

At first they prayed to Him in private chapels, in palaces and castles, in convents, in churches where courtiers and common folk thronged together, brought there by the same misfortune. Church bells summoned the faithful with their loud pealing. Would God hear them with favor? Hope is so strong. And the number of observances increased, with processions furrowing the land, carrying the bodies and relics of saints from church to church, through towns and villages, by roads and highways. On the first Sunday of January 1396 three thousand people followed the monks of St. Denis who, on the order of the King's uncles, were transferring the relics of St. Louis and the Blessed Virgin Mary from their convent all the way to the Sainte Chapelle. Dalmatics, silken copes, reliquaries of unburnished gold heavy upon the shoulders of their bearers, symbols of the passion, the cross, thorns and nails, banners, the white road, the cold light of winter. The city's contours etched out against the clear horizon: round towers, rough wooden walls capped with pointed roofs, crenellated ramparts. A slow progress, a gathering of God's people, who made their way, barefoot, tapers in hand, with chants, responses, the murmuring of prayers. And God was moved. The King recovered. But not for long.

And promises were made: that the gate of Paris, previously known as "Hellsgate" because it led to a meadow where the Demon dwelt in the form of a lovely courtesan, would be renamed in honor of St. Michael the Archangel; that a confessor would be granted to all criminals condemned to death, whatever their crimes, as in other countries; that blasphemies would no longer be uttered on penalty of being branded with a hot iron, paying a fine, or losing one's worldly goods. This prohibition was a royal edict.

And vows were taken: by the Queen and her daughter, Marie, born almost a year to the day after the drama of Le Mans—always on condition, however, that the King regain his health. The Queen's word could be taken back otherwise; but it would not be taken back on the wishes of the little girl.

And gifts were offered. Among others there was a crystal reliquary, bezeled with gold and decorated with precious stones, supported by two sculpted angels, clasping hands with St. Thomas the Apostle—a priceless gift if ever there was one, for it had been given to the prince by Pope Clement, who had gotten it from Gregory the Great, who had discovered it in a reliquary containing the heads of Sts. Peter and Paul.

A waste of effort, it seems, these prayers, these observances, all this travail. The King recovered only the better to relapse again afterward. Then people despaired, and turned their glances away from an unyielding heaven. The wildest notions invaded their minds. What if the King were a victim of witchcraft and spells? The Almighty would have nothing to do with it, and they would have been knocking at the wrong door.

So they turned to the Devil by way of sorcerers. For a start, they went to Guienne to seek out a certain Arnaud Guillaume. Loutish and unengaging in appearance, this Arnaud nonetheless offered certain assurances of authenticity: he lived as a hermit, practicing fasting and asceticism. Hence the absolute power which he claimed to exercise over the four elements. He obtained his knowledge from a book, the *Smagorad,* which had been handed down to Adam by an angel, so that he might regain by reading it what he had lost by sinning. Whoever had possession of this book could direct the stars in their courses. Thus, if a planet were to appear whose influence was causing many deaths, Arnaud could cause an opposing planet to ascend in the heavens, one unknown up to that time by astrologers, which would neutralize, at least in part if not entirely, the evil action of the first planet. The folly of relying on Arnaud was quickly perceived. What Charles needed was a healer, not a star maker. Arnaud was sent back, and others rounded up—from the same country as it happened.

There were two of them this time, Lancelot and Pierre by name, who professed to be hermit friars of the Order of St. Augustine. They were taken at their word and installed in the royal castle of St. Antoine, where they were treated with the customary generosity; and they set to work. They began by prescribing a decoction of powdered pearls and distilled water which was to be mixed with the King's food and drink. When this remedy produced no miracles, they wanted to resort to magic. But they were forestalled in this design. Only divine grace could cure the King. Thereupon followed a new relapse. An explanation was demanded of them, and for want of a better scapegoat, they accused two men of black magic. One was Charles's barber, Mellin, who had dressed the King's hair the day before; the other was the doorkeeper of the Duke of Orléans's residence. A mere touch by these men, the mountebank friars declared, would be enough to cause someone to lapse into dementia. The accused barber and doorkeeper were thrown into prison at once, but their arrest did not cure the prince. Still, the two acolytes remained for some years in this sinecure, nurtured, sheltered, glutted with precious coins, leading joyful existences and engaging in seditious talk which, smelling excessively of brimstone and all of a piece with the total ineffectiveness of their various therapies, finally got them sent to the block. Their books were burned, their limbs were torn off, and pieces of their bodies were scattered to the four corners of the city walls.

Yet for all that, those who had sought out the so-called friars did not give up on resorting to others of the same calling. In the month of October 1402, Charles relapsed into one of his "absences." Two sorcerers, Poinson and Briquet, called on the Duke of Burgundy. Let the means be procured for them, they told the Duke, and they would discover what was eating away at the King. The bargain was struck. Philip set them up in his duchy, not far from Beaune, at Sanvignes, and began by paying out lots of money. The two confederates chose a thick wood as the site for their practices. They erected in that wood an iron ring of enormous weight, supported by columns of the same metal, as tall as an average-sized man. A dozen chains were attached to these columns. Then Poinson and Briquet called for the co-operation of a dozen persons chosen from among the notables of the city of Dijon.

For two whole months the experiments were carried forward. The witch doctors carried on their incantations while their twelve assistants, each chained to a column, took their places within the ring. No more than the *Smagorad* or the powdered pearls did the tactics of Poinson and Briquet succeed in curing the deranged King. In their turn these sorcerers were pitilessly burned at the stake.

Nothing, then, would work. The King would bear his cross for another twenty years, while the folly of his blood relations would cause a whole people to feel its weight. The "great sorrow of the kingdom of France" had begun.

The King wandered endlessly in cruel dreams. From then on "the great abandonment," the great everlasting pain, would be all he knew. Night and silence, Charles the King, alone, moving slowly through what abysses, what despair, condemned without appeal to the irremediable, a death so slow, so long, that there was no end to waiting. And what of the weight of his merits, in the angelic scales at the gates of eternity? Had God turned His countenance away from the first of His servants, and from the country which He had entrusted to His servant's preservation?

CHAPTER VII

Chronicle of the Great Sorrow

ORLÉANS AND BURGUNDY

And what was happening to the kingdom during this time? For ten years the situation remained stable. The fleur-de-lis princes simply sent the Marmosets packing with many thanks and took up their former roles. Berry plundered, horded, and built. Orléans and the Queen amused themselves; Valentina Visconti had to leave Paris for rather obscure reasons; Burgundy reigned. The world ambassadors of the time paraded through the French court, which still remained the most brilliant in Europe, and also the most dissolute. But the country was at peace. And that was the work, it must be admitted, of the man who made himself the real ruler of France, Philip the Bold. There wasn't a prince in the Council who didn't recognize the authority, cleverness, and wisdom of this last son of John the Good. Not a one who didn't fear him either. For this man who took as his haughty motto "I am impatient" had built up a veritable nation in the east of France in less than forty years.

To the duchy of Burgundy, inherited in 1363, he had added his wife's inheritance—the counties of Burgundy, Nevers and Rethel, Artois and Flanders. He had also bought with hard cash the county of Charolais from Bernard, Count of Armagnac, and from the Duchess of Brabant he had bought Limburg and the land whose name she bore. These dominions thus constituted two distinct groups, to the east and the northeast, and he governed them remarkably well. His iron authority had created order and prosperity there. For the task of confirming and solidifying the power of his own kingdom and of working out the innumerable problems it presented (if only by its geographic configuration), Philip found his means increased tenfold when he began governing the greatest kingdom of the time—France, with her prestige, her alliances, her considerable resources in men and currency, and her finances, which he dug into at will. One can easily imagine the importance the first seat in the royal Council had for old Duke Philip. During his long and fruitful life he used and abused his place and certainly intended to continue to do so as long as he lived. This was not to everybody's taste. But where to find the necessary means to oppose the ambition and the maneuvers of this powerful man!

As it happened, another prince, just as powerful, just as ambitious, and, possibly, of even better birth, attended the Council—the only brother of the King, Louis d'Orléans.

Orléans was young, handsome, elegant, affable, spoke well, and had a good feel for situations: quick-witted, brilliant, he understood everything, knew everything, was interested in everything, and wanted everything. And that was where the shoe pinched.

He had the King's ear, the King's money, the power of the King, whenever the King was not "absent," and, when available, the Queen's bed, at least that's what people believed. He loved women and women couldn't resist him. He loved gambling at least as well, was "always interested in playing dice and loving whores," according to a grumpy scribe. He loved luxury too, dressing up, fine objects, books, buildings; he loved the night and celebrations, he was a real Valois. But he surpassed his ancestors in his abuse of excess. Although a lover of pleasure and a rake, like his uncle Berry, unlike his uncle he was never a patron of the arts and never even dreamed of hiding his excesses from the masses, ignoring prudence and disdaining the common herd. He was an aristocrat. With his own people, he was seduction itself—his wife, who adored him in spite of his constant infidelities, was the proof of it; toward everyone else his behavior was despicable.

He was an object of scandal too, frequenting occultists, seeking out necromancers and magicians, but finishing his nights of debauchery in the convent of the Célestins where he had his own cell and preferred to rest. Orléans was pious, even devout. No need to add that money flowed through his fingers. The young Duke was insatiable, at least as much so as his uncle Burgundy. Cupidity and generosity went well together in any case, both being excesses.

God and the Devil, love and money, power and saintliness, luck, Monseigneur d'Orléans carried within him a thousand lives, a thousand desires which sleep extinguished, but which reappeared at sunrise, intact, full of vigor. My lord of Orléans forced all, attempted all. But did he know how to will anything? My lord of Orléans was flighty, undependable, fanciful, with a roving imagination, a penchant for squandering money, and crazy ideas—less, however, than one might think.

Thanks to his brother's generosity, he built up a dispersed but important domain across from Burgundy's on the Loire River. The duchies of Orléans, of Touraine, the counties of Blois and of Dunois belonged to him, and in the southwest those of Angoulême and Périgord. He added to that the county of Dreux in the northwest and to the northeast the counties of Valois, Beaumont-sur-Oise, and Vertus. It was impossible to count the fiefs that paid homage to him: Pierrefonds, Béthisy, La Ferté-Milon. . . . Valentina Visconti had brought him the rights to Asti in Italy as a dowry. And finally, he capped the lot with the purchase of the duchy of Luxemburg. None of this pleased his uncle Burgundy in the least. Nor did his attitude in the Council, where the two men always argued. But as the years passed, so did the age of folly; ambition settled in and the taste for power began to offset the taste for women.

Since the beginning of the century, animosity had been growing between the nephew, "greedy for all the delights and estates of this world" (to borrow the phrase Froissart used to characterize his wife, Valentina), and the uncle who had firmly decided never to concede to anyone the smallest parcel of his power or anything it depended on.

As it happened, on the twenty-seventh of April 1404 the uncle died, leaving his place to his son John. Like his father, John seemed determined above all to stake two claims: one on the state of which he was the master, and the other on the King's Council, where he intended to take control in his turn.

Between the two cousins of similar age, Louis and John,

conflict seemed inevitable. Moreover, they were different in all respects.

Burgundy was ugly, small, dressed badly, spoke poorly. Misleading appearance, which he knew how to use when necessary. He was extremely courageous, having been dubbed "John the Fearless" after his heroic conduct against the Turks at Nicopolis, had boundless ambition, stubbornly demanding what he believed should come to him by right. His cold and vicious will was well served by the qualities of intelligence, energy, and cleverness. In obtaining what he wanted, he was not encumbered by scruples. He proved it: one year to take hold of his estates, two years to set in motion his plan for the conquest of power. The result was not long in coming; both sides began to arm for war. Insults and challenges multiplied in the entourage of the princes. They themselves rivaled each other in insolence. Louis took a knotted staff as his crest and *Je l'ennuie* ("I vex him") as his motto. John answered by choosing for his symbol a rasp with the Flemish inscription *Ik Houd* ("I've got him").

Violent words would soon give way to violent deeds. They would continue for nearly thirty years.

MURDER

On the evening of November 23, 1407, Orléans was with the Queen. She no longer lived in St. Pol, having moved to the Hôtel Barbette, in the Rue Vieille-du-Temple, a house which she had asked her husband to give her, since they lived almost entirely apart. Was Orléans there that evening to discuss the current political situation or simply to comfort Isabella with his presence because she had just given birth to a dead child, his own perhaps? No matter. Suddenly the King's valet, Thomas Courteheuse, entered: "Your Highness, the King is asking that you come to him without delay; he must speak urgently with you about something which concerns both himself and you."

Louis quickly took leave. He went out into the courtyard of the house where he was silhouetted against the light shadow of the threshold. Valets were running back and forth, bringing the saddles, opening the heavy wooden gate. The prince jumped on his horse; riders holding torches were waiting ahead of him. As he rode away, two young pages mounted the same horse bareback and took off after him. A few more men closed off the procession. Clattering hoofs, creaking hinges, the hollow sound of the closing door, the clanking of the enormous key being turned with care; the prince had left the house of Queen Isabella.

Dark night, dark street, dark bulging façades, perforated with pale lights, overhanging upper stories and verandas, not a soul. Silence had settled on the city, the silence of a November night, silence of the mists of time, silence of the winter of time. Anguish and cold, precarious life, misery. Behind these closed façades, the little people of Paris were asleep, several in a bed, men, women, and children together. Beaten-down sod floors, unhealthy air in the rooms, all the windows closed, burned-out hearths. But in the homes of the powerful, entire trees were being burned for warmth. The street smelled of wood fires, of the resin which oozed from the trunks in slow tears. Paris was only good for rich people, for this prince who traveled without a care in the world, whistling, from the home of the Queen to that of the King his brother, from the Hôtel Barbette to the Hôtel St. Pol through the Rue Vieille-du-Temple, in the city of his childhood, this Paris familiar to him, where he knew every alley, every street stall, every house, in this city which belonged to him, in this night which belonged to him. Night pierced at head level by the flickering light of the torches which preceded and followed him. Night suddenly cut with cries, peopled with menacing shadows, two, ten, twenty men who were attacking Orléans, with swords, daggers, knives, hatchets. "Kill him, kill him!" He scarcely had time to be surprised, still thinking that everyone loved him: "I am the Duke of Orléans!" "That's what we want to hear!"

No reprieve. A few seconds left to feel, to breathe, after that cry of hate, the last words he heard; no cross to kiss, no pardon to ask for and to receive, no body of Christ, but arms which tore him from his saddle, throwing him on the pavement, boots kicking him and heavy clubs hammering him, swinging axes and falling maces, breaking his flesh and bones, weapons invading him, lacerating him, cutting off his hand, slashing open his head.

His young page, Jacob van Melkeren, tried to save the prince by lying on top of him. But he was killed. The two pages who

were following on the same horse didn't even have time to put
their feet on the ground, the crazed animal carried them off at a
gallop in spite of themselves. "Murder, murder," they screamed at
the top of their voices, followed at a distance by the torchbearers.
"Fire, fire," took up the killers, setting fire to the house which had
hid them during their ambush, the better to protect their escape.
Their leader esteemed his duty accomplished: "Have manly
hearts," he said to his accomplices, and they took cheer, some
leaping onto the horses brought to them, others swallowed up into
the Rue des Blancs-Manteaux. In order to stop any pursuit, they
scattered iron traps behind them.

A dark inert mass intermittently illuminated by the ghastly
flames of the burning house, Prince Louis of France, younger son
of Charles V, lay in the mud and the night of the Rue Vieille-du-
Temple, losing his blood and his life. Alone he relinquished himself to his Creator, with no one to help him through this rough
passage, this body full of grace, this brilliant mind, this soul that
had so burned for the "delights and estates of this world." What
weight would its merits carry with the masters of the Invisible?

All these cries, galloping hoofbeats, and violent lights had
brought out the inhabitants of the quarter. Quickly, feeling their
way, they slipped on breeches and coats of mail, grabbed their
greatcoats, and dashed outside. In an instant the street was full of
people. Some attempted to put out the fire while others, curious,
clustered around the corpse. Quietly they questioned each other.
Judging from the luxurious dress, it must have been a prince, but
the face was unrecognizable. They hesitated to identify him. Suddenly there was a ruckus at the other end of the street. It was people from the Duke's house who, alarmed by the witnesses to the
murder, had come running. Parting the crowd, they took the mutilated body of their master out of the mud and carried it to the
nearest house, that of the Marshal de Rieux, and pounded on the
door. A few seconds of waiting. Someone was coming. Slowly,
creaking, the heavy wooden gate opened and then closed on the
dismayed group.

In the dark room the men placed their burden—already stiff and
gray—on a table which they moved to the stone fireplace. The
master of the house had been summoned and entered in haste,
asking for light, held his torch up to the body, discovered the cut-

off hand and the gaping skull, the mask of blood, unrecognizable, the broken limbs. Not a single hope for life, it was really all over. At the horror of the spectacle, faces paled, looks were averted, lips trembled, throats were tied in knots, the people from Orléans's house burst into tears and imprecations. Marshal de Rieux imposed calm, got busy sending for the priests and the family, and informed the Provost of Paris.

A silence of catastrophe hung over the room. The women gathered together ewers and linens, two of them unfolded the long white sheets, took away the robe of black damask from the body of the handsome Duke, washed the unhealable wounds, enfolded them in the useless freshness of the linen, then redressed the ghastly body, which they covered with the death shroud. The room filled up with priests, dark-robed, capes pushed back, rosaries in their hands. Four men brought a bier and placed the Duke gently on it. A procession was formed, taking off in the night for the Church of the Blancs-Manteaux nearby, entering the sanctuary, and placing the prince in the center of the nave.

Gray floor, gray space punctuated by ogives, the long white form under the shroud, hedges of candles in the four corners around the corpse, black shadows moving on the walls of the aisles at the passage of the priests and the family, which took its place in the chancel.

The King of Sicily had just arrived with several princes, dukes, knights, and horsemen, overwrought by the horrible crime perpetrated on the only brother of the King. They bowed down before the remains. On their knees they cried and prayed. They put the body in a lead casket. Lord have mercy, Holy Mary, pray for him, let the whole assembly pray for him. Come to his aid, saints of God, run to meet him, angels of God. Accept his soul, may the angels offer it to the view of the Most High. Hymned prayers like appeals for the repose of the soul. Lord have mercy, Christ have mercy. The night passed on. In the tepid half-light of the church, vacillating, uncertain life resumed among these men assembled, united by one feeling, life triumphed in those orations which spoke of eternity and pardon, the comforts of the soul; fear dropped away. But, at sunrise, when they brought the cut-off hand and a part of the skull found in the mud of the street and joined them to the body in the coffin, anguish and horror again seized everyone.

The princes of the blood, the Marquis of Pont, the Counts of Nevers and of Clermont, Vendôme, St. Pol, Dammartin, the High Constable of France, all Paris had to offer in the way of important people, men of the Church as well as nobles, with great multitudes of common people, were now packed into the Church of the Blancs-Manteaux. The street was black with people. In the gloomy early morning of November, the procession took off at a slow pace. With torches in their hands, in black robes and crying, holding aloft the arms of the house of Orléans, the dead man's pages preceded the coffin. The four princes of the blood, the Dukes of Berry and of Bourbon, the King of Sicily and the Duke of Burgundy, John the Fearless, accompanied it, each holding a corner of the pall, crying and wailing. After them came the nobility and the clergy, all asking God for the repose of the soul of the King's brother. Through the Rue Vieille-du-Temple, the Rue Roi-de-Sicile, the streets of Pont-Perrin and Petit-Musc, they made their way among tears and prayers up to the convent of the Célestins, near the Seine. Freezing wind, thick fog, dampness piercing the bones. The funeral was celebrated with all the royal pomp due such a high personage, and the body was placed in the chapel which Louis had founded while alive in order to purge himself from the Flaming Ball disaster he had caused by his own imprudence. After the absolution was pronounced, everyone hastily returned home, stupefied, dismayed, upset. Dry-faced, heads cleared, they had to discover who was responsible for the coup as soon as possible. As for the "absent" King, he was oblivious to it all.

A STUNNING CONFESSION

The King of Sicily summoned to his house the princes of the blood, members of the Council, the men of justice and the Provost of Paris, Guillaume de Tignonville. He also had all the gates to Paris closed, so that nobody could leave without his knowledge. The investigation was officially opened.

The Provost worked diligently. The very next day he followed up every lead and asked for permission to enter the princes' homes. "Let him in anywhere he deems necessary," ordered Sicily,

Berry, and Bourbon. At that, John the Fearless looked worried. He took his uncle Berry and his cousin Sicily aside, and they heard from his own mouth this stunning confession. "I myself caused the crime," explained Burgundy. "The Devil inspired me to have this homicide committed by Raoulet of Anquetonville and his accomplices."

The princes were speechless. The two men hated each other, that was known, but from that to this horrible act . . . Torn between sadness, indignation, and fear, all they could do was reproach the powerful Duke for his abominable deed. Burgundy let the storm pass, sure that he wouldn't be punished. The following day he went to the Hôtel de Nesles, Berry's Parisian residence, to attend the Council, as though nothing had happened. But the old prince had given the order to close all the doors. He waited for John in front of the chamber and forbade him to enter. "Good nephew, don't go into the Council this time; it isn't anyone's pleasure that you be with us." And with these words he took leave of the Duke of Burgundy.

Would John be treated by his peers as a common assassin? Doubt slipped into his quick mind. His cousin, Count Waléran of St. Pol, was present at the scene. Worried, John asked him for advice. "Good cousin, what should we do about what you just heard?" "My lord," replied the latter rather dryly and with complete politeness, "you must retire to your house since it doesn't please the lords that you be in the Council with them." But when John asked his cousin to be his escort, the latter turned away from him. "My lord, excuse me, I am going to join our lords of the Council, who have sent for me."

So the Duke began to realize the feelings brought about by his act, which, despite the fact that its author was a prince of the fleur-de-lis, might not go unpunished. Prudently, he chose without delay to escape. He returned in great haste to the Hôtel d'Artois, his Parisian domicile, took six men and a good horse and headed for his estates—Lille—to wait for people's feelings to calm down. The people of his house, afraid they would have to pay in his place, did likewise. It was a helter-skelter flight. In a few hours the house was empty. Everyone, by various means, headed for the road to Flanders. With the help of disguise, the killers escaped the king's justice, and on Burgundy's order took refuge in his castle of

Lens. As for John himself, he assembled scholars of law. Since it appeared that he was going to be asked to account for his actions, it was important for him to have the law and legitimacy on his side. It remained to be proven that he had been right in ordering Orléans's murder.

ON THE PROPER USE OF ASSASSINATION

While the brain trust was settling down to work, spies left in Paris communicated with John daily on the state of public opinion. And what he learned confirmed that his plan was well founded. As he had foreseen, the Parisians had not all felt unparalleled grief after the announcement of the crime. They hadn't really liked the Duke of Orléans. The dead man had crystallized in his person the general discontent of the populace. Symbolizing the excesses of court society in the face of the hard existence of the laboring classes, he had been at the same time the archetype of the bad prince and the scapegoat for the people's complaints and their aggressions. They blamed everything on him, suspected him of everything—pillaging of the public treasury, responsibility for crushing taxation, scandalous immorality. . . . In short, they hadn't mourned him for very long. The first feelings past, the clergy, the university, the bourgeoisie, and the people retained the sympathies Burgundy had inspired in them over the past two years.

His air of directness, sometimes of familiarity, so unusual in people of his class, his well-advertised disdain for celebrations, luxury, and clothes had earned him a solid popularity. People appreciated his seriousness in business, his taste for work—didn't he closet himself for entire days with his counselors in order to study a problem?—so many details that John, with a keen eye for public opinion and a totally modern sense of propaganda, had taken care to publicize. And finally, they needed him. Faced with a bad government, the thinking elite of the capital had devised a program of reform that could only be realized with the help of the King or, failing that, with the help of a member of the royal family. As it happened, of all the princes, the Duke seemed to them to be the only one who might listen to them and understand them. Thus the disappearance of the unpopular Orléans, even in such unfortunate circumstances, would hardly cause them to turn against the man they hoped would help them. From the people, John of Burgundy had nothing to fear.

However, at court, indignation was acute. The nobles demanded an exemplary punishment. Emotions ran at their highest when Valentina Visconti and her entire entourage arrived in Paris in carriages hung with black and drawn by white horses. The princes and the highest barons came to greet her and escort her to St. Pol. She brought with her her last son, the Count of Angoulême, and her daughter-in-law, Madame Isabelle, daughter of Charles VI, widow of Richard II of England and now the wife of her eldest, Duke Charles. She had sent the young Duke and his brother Philip, Count of Vertus, to Blois under heavy guard. Louis had left five orphans between the ages of thirteen and one, including a bastard, brought up by Valentina and named Dunois; we shall return to him later. She threw herself, she and her two little ones, at the feet of the King, weeping and crying for justice. The King, in tears, raised her to her feet, assuring her of his affection. Not for long.

Already the King, dulled by his illness, didn't remember ever having loved either Louis or Valentina. She had to settle for vague promises. If Bourbon and the young Brittany still remained ferociously hostile to the murderer, those who counted in the government, Berry and Sicily, were already showing themselves to be less inflexible.

Berry feared the responsibility of ruling, and Sicily, completely absorbed in his Mediterranean kingdom, didn't wish to devote too much energy to his position in the Council. Burgundy thus had time on his side. Nobody was capable of facing him down at the court. So the kingdom of France, like the house of Orléans, fell to the womenfolk—Valentina and Isabella, who detested each other. So Burgundy could begin immediately to prepare for his return. If he played his cards right, he would be back in power soon.

He called a meeting of the three estates of Flanders and the highest lords of his relations in the second half of December. Explanations were in order. So he had his chief advocate, Jean of Saulx, explain to them the circumstances of the crime and what had motivated it. He hadn't committed murder, he had done justice, delivered the country from a dangerous enemy and thus accomplished a deed for which they should be grateful. Not an assassin but a champion of the interests of the King and of the kingdom, thus appeared Duke John in the light of his act of courage.

Copies of his statement were made available for those who wanted to familiarize themselves with it.

The audience acquiesced without a word to the arguments presented by the Duke. And when he asked "if they would willingly come to his aid for any of his eventual needs," they committed themselves immediately.

Sure of the cohesion and fidelity of his subjects, Burgundy waited for reaction from the court. It was immediate. Steps were taken hurriedly to re-establish contact. Old Bourbon, sickened by such proceedings, retired to his estates. Berry and Sicily asked for an interview. Burgundy was glad to consent and fixed a meeting in Amiens. The cold was rigorous, the routes impracticable, and the peasants would have to clear the snow in front of the horses in order to make way for the procession. But Berry, in spite of his age and the season, gave in. He was afraid. He feared his nephew's whims. He knew John's ambition, his lack of scruples, his power also. What if he marched on Paris? Or made an agreement with the English? This conflict had to be settled as quickly as possible.

It didn't take long for Berry and Sicily to realize that they were dealing with someone much stronger than they. Ironic, presumptuous, without the slightest remorse, their relative had the upper hand and knew it. Without waiting, he laid down his conditions at the outset: he would go to Paris and explain to his peers and the King the reasons for his conduct. Berry and Sicily didn't even have to give their opinions. When they suggested consulting the monarch, the Duke declared in a haughty tone that he would appear when it was convenient for him. That's what he did, one month later.

The twenty-fifth of February 1408, he arrived at St. Denis, followed by all his nobles, "in order to be stronger if the occasion arose," entered Paris as a liberator, went to the Louvre, kissed his son-in-law the Dauphin Louis, husband of his daughter Marguerite, dined that evening with Berry, and went back to his Hôtel d'Artois where he took the precaution of having workmen construct a greatly reinforced "chamber fortified with stone, well cut in the manner of a tower in which he slept at night." One never knew.

On the eighth of March the great hall of the Hôtel St. Pol was crowded, as on a great day. Against the far wall two daises had been set up. On the left one, around the orator Jean Petit, were the greatest names of the court of Burgundy. On the right one, the Council of the King, the Parlement, and, as a security measure, the Provost of Paris and his sergeants. Facing them, in the first row, the Dauphin, replacing his sick father, and the court. Behind them the delegations from the university and the bourgeoisie of Paris. In state robes of red velvet embroidered with gold leaf, furred with calaber, with open sleeves and a stand-up hood, John the Fearless made a majestic entry, head held high, with a sure step. He took his place between the Dukes of Berry and Brittany. Should he have been afraid? The glimmer of his coat of mail was visible through the opening in his sleeve. The session began.

Jean Petit stood up and prepared to vindicate both the murderer and the murder in due form according to the law. After four hours he concluded: "It follows clearly then that the aforementioned Lord of Burgundy should not be in the least blamed or punished for the deed committed on the person of the criminal Duke of Orléans, and that the King our lord should not only be happy about it but should find Lord Burgundy and his deed agreeable to him. He should also pardon him and remunerate him with love, honor, and riches . . . and should have the good word of his loyalty and good name spread over the whole kingdom, and outside the kingdom. God grant that it be done so, Who is blessed in the world without end. Amen."

A justification for murder, delivered under the auspices of God with the benediction of the University of Paris and the clergy in Christian France, its like had never been seen before! It convinced no one who hadn't already been convinced however. But the dissenters kept silent: "There was no one so bold who would dare to speak against it," said a chronicler. Audacity had paid off.

THE CHILDREN OF ORLÉANS

John the Fearless emerged victorious but returned home under heavy escort. In the days that followed, he obtained from the King total absolution and ratification of his crime: "It is for the safety and conservation of us and of our line, for the good and utility of our kingdom, and to pay us the devotion and loyalty which he owes us, that our Dear and Beloved Cousin the Duke of Burgundy put our brother, the late Duke of Orléans, out of this world," the unfortunate madman explained in his text. But the Queen fled to Melun, taking the Dauphin with her, and numerous lords followed suit and returned to their lands. As for the Orléans, they hadn't given up. They replaced their old motto, "I vex him," with another whose meaning was clear to all—the word "Justice."

How could the victim's wife, his children, the people near to him, his friends, those who had loved the Duke of Orléans, those who had watched him grow up in his father's palaces, those who had taken care of him when he found himself an orphan, those who had served him, all of those who had remained faithful to his memory, how could they tolerate such an outrage, the unimaginable affront made publicly to this dead man, how would they be able to forget, to pardon?

John the Fearless had set out on an irreversible path. Braving heaven and hell, he had advanced so far in crime that he could no longer go back, even if he wanted to. Prisoner of the murder accomplished under his order, chained to the perversity that hardened his soul a little more every day, John the Fearless had himself let loose the infernal cycle of hatreds and disorders that would bring him to his end, through the death of thousands of men, the destruction of the kingdom, until justice was done. But from the height of his power, arrogant, coldhearted, he would play his hand to the end and never lose a trick.

Humiliated, jeered at, disarmed, with burning hearts and closed mouths, the children of Orléans could only remain silent, suffer, accept the unacceptable, and turn the other cheek. They were forced to forget, pardon, promise love and alliance, swear to preserve the peace in the presence of the King and the court, assembled for the occasion at Chartres cathedral. One of the victim's sons, Philip, Count of Vertus, was betrothed to the assassin's daughter. How could the children of Orléans bear such infamy? Their hearts were full of despair and shame when, weeping, hiding behind the King in the middle of the choir at Chartres, they were pushed out to greet the Duke of Burgundy, who was going to ask for their friendship. They saw the mutilated body of their father, the cut-off hand, the open skull, lying in the mud of the Rue Vieille-du-Temple; they heard the humiliating declarations of Jean Petit; they relived their mother's pain when she heard the news at Château-Thierry, that long year that she had spent in tears, asking for reparation, raising money, running hither and yon, having a part of her jewels melted down—but not the diamond ring set in the form of a "forget-me-not." She had never parted with that. They saw her dead, at thirty-eight, from a languorous sickness, from sorrow rather—it was possible then—one year practically to the day after her husband's death. Would it be in their manly hearts to forget the injury? They had to obtain justice. A day would come. . . . But they had to remain patient until then.

As it was, a large fraction of the nobility hadn't been able to accept the crime committed on one of its peers, or the impunity which its author enjoyed, or the vindication of such an act. Already numerous, they had left the court and gone back to their lands. They too were waiting. A whole powerful party existed around the children of Orléans, ready to defend their cause, but dispersed, without cohesion, lacking a leader. Then, through the chance of a marriage, the Count Bernard of Armagnac entered on the scene. In 1410 he gave his daughter Bonne, granddaughter of the late Duke of Berry by her mother, in marriage to the young Charles of Orléans, widowed husband of Isabelle of France. Bernard was a remarkable soldier who held a superior position in the Pyrenees of the Midi. He procured impressive forces for his son-in-law, who had settled in the Loire Valley. The Dukes of Bourbon and Brittany, faithful to the house of Orléans from the very beginning, came running. Berry, Clermont, Alençon, and Albret followed. The west, the center, and the southwest of France were now united against the east where Burgundy held sway. The Orléans party was ready. They were called "Armagnacs," after the name of Count Bernard. They took for their motto "The Narrow Path," and as their livery a two-tone violet jacket embroidered with silver leaves with a white cross on the chest. On July 11, 1411, the three Orléans brothers sent letters to Burgundy laying down the challenge: "To you, John, who call yourself Duke of Burgundy . . . for the most horrible murder done by yourself in great treason by planned ambush by hired murderers on the person of our father, we send warning that from this hour forward we will harm you with all our power, and in every way we can. . . ."

Burgundy immediately picked up the gauntlet, signifying that he was "very happy in his heart. But," he added, "from the excesses contained in these letters, you and your brothers have lied and are lying falsely, evilly and disloyally, traitors that you are . . . we will bring you thus to punishment in the end."

Both sides lined up their allies, recruited, armed themselves, and began the campaign, that is to say, they plundered. From the Loire to the Somme with Paris as the stakes, the two sides confronted each other. Raids, engagements, skirmishes, cities besieged and taken, only to be besieged by the other side, flat lands on fire, "Orléans," "Burgundy," shouted wildly by the attacking troops, the violet livery and black and red hoods of the Armagnacs against the jackets with St. Andrew crosses and the green hoods of the Burgundians . . . The civil war had begun.

CABOCHE

Paris, faithful to her old love, declared herself for John the Fearless with increasing passion. Curious fact, the political action in favor of this prince was led by the powerful Corporation of Butchers, more Burgundian than the Duke, and the trades which gravitated around it, skinners, pelters, tripe handlers, tanners. At their head were several men of low stature: John le Goix and his two sons, butchers; Denys de Chaumont and Simon Caboche, cow skinners at the St. Jacques butcher shop; John de Troyes, caretaker at the palace, sworn surgeon of the city, and two of his sons. At the sound of their voices, the citizenry got excited, tension mounted, people took sides, donned green hoods, put them on their wives, their children, friends, neighbors, on the old wooden saints which protected their streets, on the statues of the same saints inside the churches. If someone wasn't wearing a hood, people were surprised, and they convinced even the lukewarm or recalcitrant to wear one through reason or by force.

The clergy followed along. It excommunicated the Armagnac party. It refused the last rites to those whose convictions were susceptible to the slightest doubt, baptized and buried only those sure to be orthodox, assembled relics from all sources and organized many processions in favor of the cause. Barefooted, candles in hand, the people filled the streets of the capital and walked singing canticles and carrying crosses, relics, and statues to conjure the favor of the Almighty in favor of their idol, who, except for a brief stay with the English, whose help he was courting, resided in Paris at his Hôtel d'Artois and nourished the ardor of his supporters with his presence, his fine speeches and warm handshakes.

The university, in sympathy with these popular movements, fell into step. Could it ever have found a better opportunity to put into operation its old dream of reforming the kingdom? Never had there been so much talking among the scholars, never so much staying up late on the Montagne Ste. Geneviève, nor had the world and society ever been so well remade, for lack of power to remake human nature. Codes of reform were drawn up in feverish haste. The people expected miracles from them. But did they realize that the reforms weren't at all innovative? They were simply new formulations of the ideas put forth by Charles V, fifty years earlier. The monk of St. Denis commented with indignation: "I wondered how the university and the bourgeoisie would accomplish their endeavor. I remember having heard it said by several important people that it was very strange that those people dared to meddle in affairs which should only be handled by the secret councils of the King and by the princes of the blood. It is absurd that people who are speculative and live among books habitually, that merchants, artisans who only think about money, should think they can govern the kingdom and regulate to their pleasure the magnificence of the princes and the state of the King."

Paris was in the hands of an unusual alliance: the university and the slaughterhouse. The former put words together, the latter cut up carcasses. Paris obeyed Simon Caboche, the butcher, son of a tripe seller from the courtyard of Notre Dame. Paris recognized the dictatorship of the slaughterhouse.

Caboche could do anything. He held burghers for ransom under the pretext of collecting taxes for the English war. He burgled their houses, stole, plundered, started fires, armed the city, made her people come down into the street, led his troops outside the city walls to ransack the beautiful castle of Bicêtre, which belonged to the Duke of Berry, a supporter of the Armagnacs. Caboche rounded up twenty-four thousand men and marched against the Bastille. Caboche dared anything, forced his way into the Hôtel St. Pol, summoned the Dauphin, lectured him, demanded recognition, seized the Dauphin's counselors, broke down the doors of the private apartments, penetrated into the Queen's rooms, captured her brother William of Bavaria and members of her entourage, and threw them into prison. On his orders, people were exiled, banished, drowned, massacred—the mob was let loose. The Duke of Burgundy invited Caboche to call, listened to him, committed himself to shaking the butcher's hand in public. Caboche's party was ready. He chose his color, white, had two thousand hoods made, and insisted everyone wear them—the princes, the Dauphin, the King himself, the people, the burghers, and the artisans, even the vegetable vendors in the market. In Ghent, the Duchess of Charolais, born a Valois, daughter-in-law of John the Fearless, wore Caboche's color. He had triumphed.

"If you rebel, you will be destroyed," prophesied Christine de Pisan, always practical, in her *Book on Peace*. She was right. The Parisians, tired of so much violence, began to demand peace. John the Fearless decided it would be safer to go back to Flanders with Caboche on his heels, while the court, afraid, called back the Orléans clan. Within a month, Paris was converted, swapped the green hood for the cape of violet cloth, the cross of St. Andrew for the white cross of the Gascon. Paris turned Armagnac in the interest of self-preservation. The roles were reversed; repression took over. Disguised as vagrants, pages, or harness sellers, the most compromised of Caboche's friends fled to Flanders, to the Holy Roman Empire, even overseas. Banishments and executions proliferated, terror reigned again. John the Fearless, called back by the butchers, tried to make an offensive re-entry.

For fourteen days the city remained closed, with its doors nailed up and its bridges guarded. Nobody entered or left, not even to work the fields. Burgundy gave up. The war oscillated be-

tween the Loire and the Somme. It was at that moment that a
third thief decided to enter the scene. The King of England, Henry
V, claimed the kingdom of France for himself and, joining acts to
declarations of intention, crossed the Channel.

THE SLAUGHTER AT AGINCOURT

The King of England landed on the Normandy coast at nightfall
on the twelfth of August 1415. He camped with thirty thousand
men on the plateau of Ste. Adresse: objective Harfleur. Feelings
were high at court. But things turned out better than had been
thought. Although the siege of Harfleur lasted only one month, the
English lost half of their men: five thousand dead from dysentery,
five thousand sick and evacuated, and numerous desertions. The
conqueror was now thinking only about getting back home in great
haste. But the weather was unfavorable. Equinoctial storms were
raging. Where to go? the prince asked himself, blocked on the
shore. To Calais, the only English enclave in this enemy land that
he said was his, but which burned his feet. He left his artillery and
his wagons and headed toward the north by forced marches.

The opportunity seemed beautiful to the French nobles, swash-
bucklers by nature as well as education. An easy prey, this King of
England, so proud of himself, who was now fleeing, harassed,
starving in swamps, under pouring rains, through this unknown
country with such a small following, ten thousand archers and two
thousand armed men. Intoxicating chase, and reduced risks, or at
least so the French nobles thought. And they threw themselves
into it wholeheartedly; they followed Henry, they worried him,
they harassed him, they guarded all the rivers, and to the last little
passage, they blocked all the fords on the Somme, they forced the
English King into exhausting detours, finally forcing him into the
battle he was so afraid of. When, on the evening of the twenty-
fourth of October, thinking the road was clear, he reached the
small village of Maisoncelles, nine leagues from Calais, he found
the French, in impressive numbers, barring his path. Now he was
trapped. So he parleyed, promised the impossible; he relinquished
the unheard-of demands, the unbelievable pretensions he had been
putting forward for two years, on the sole condition that they let

him go home. But the French remained inflexible. Tomorrow they would fight at dawn, one against five, he realized. Little hope then of survival. Without waiting, he assembled his troops and harangued them, as the Roman emperors did in olden days in this same Gaul.

"Brave companions in arms," he cried, "and you, my faithful subjects, here we are reduced to taking our chances in a battle full of danger. Let us hope for the assistance of God. . . . Let us remember that often He gives victory to a handful of men rather than to the most dreadful armies. . . . We must stop here, gather up all our courage, wait for the enemy, and hold our ground. . . . Remember the courage which our ancestors showed when they caused Philip of Valois to flee, when they conquered and took prisoner King John, his successor, when later they crossed France six times without being stopped. Now you must bring forth all your daring. Necessity must augment your courage. Far from being afraid of having to meet up with so many princes and barons, you should be firm in the hope that their great numbers will turn to their great shame and eternal confusion, as in the olden days." They all promised with great feeling to fight until death.

Henry of Lancaster bivouacked in the place called Maisoncelles where his destiny seemed to be written. In the village and the surrounding orchards, the watch began. During the night the sounds of church songs, men's voices, the deep notes of trumpets and horns, and the twang of strings were heard; Henry V and his people prayed to the Almighty for the repose of their souls, which tomorrow, perhaps, would leave their mortal bodies. Priests confessed, absolved, and distributed communion. The songs began to die out. Vielles and viols fell silent. Quiet reigned. Sleep brought forgetfulness.

On the other side, three bowshots away, the French were celebrating wildly. All the nobility were there, having come running enthusiastically to fight against the secular enemy—knights and barons burning to avenge on the Englishman the injuries which the King, like themselves, had received from him.

They practically had to restrain Charles VI and the Dauphin at Rouen by force. The Duke of Burgundy, left out of the affair "because he wasn't liked by the other dukes," had forbidden his vassals to answer the royal call, and especially his son Charolais, whom the herald of France, Montjoie, had come in person to summon. But the most powerful had disobeyed and joined the host: his two youngest brothers, the Count of Nevers and the Duke of Brabant; his vassals, the Duke of Bar, the Counts of Blâmont, of Fauquembergues, of Roucy, and the Lords of Croy. As for Charolais, confined in his castle of Aire, he cried hot tears at not being able to take part in the battle while his governors, Roubaix and La Vieuville, stood guard over him.

As they arrived the nobles pitched their camps in the open country by whole companies. They planted their banners next to those of Constable d'Albret, who had received supreme command of the operations. Everyone took his place as near to the Constable as possible. There were continuous comings and goings of men, with their horses, wagons, harness and battle gear. Old friends met, hugged with great demonstrations of friendship, compared arms, mounts. All over fires were lit.

The princes had assembled under the tent of Constable d'Albret and were discussing the battle plan. Optimism was obligatory. At one to five, they were playing without risk. The young maintained one charge would suffice, if executed with speed and boldness. The enemy, terrified at the sight of so many princes, would surrender immediately. And everyone demanded the honor of leading the front line. Arguments started, voices were raised, were they going to quarrel? As well as he could, Albret divided them up. They would all be holding the first line, he promised. There would be no crossbowmen to protect them from the bowmen on the other side, as had been envisaged. Those villains would be sent home. It was beneath gentlemen to mingle with the common infantry. Then Marshal Boucicault turned the horsemen over to the Count of Nevers and to the young Duke of Orléans. The night was short.

Already dawn was breaking. Pale morning light, cold charred tree trunks, blackened, the smell of ashes from the night fires, mist covering the ground in thick layers. A heavy rain was falling over the camp. The valets and pages had gone to wake their masters, bustle around them and help them put on the silk-lined undergarments of linen, canvas, and silk which would protect them from being bruised by their armor: the blouse, the breeches, the under-

coat, the hose, the leather shoes, and the hood over the head.
Then they brought out the armor. They attached the sollerets to
the shoes, placed the greves and the cuissets on the legs, the
genouillères on the thighs and continued on to the upper body—
forearms, upper arms, and gauntlets—and the leather overgarment
painted with the subject's coat of arms, then the visored helmet
covered with a hood of mail.

Now for the weapons: the dagger placed on the right side, the
battle-ax, the mace, finally the great wooden lance, three or four
yards long, tipped with a metal blade.

The pages led in the horses, protected by metal and leather
armor, slipping and sliding on the muddy ground, sinking into the
rutted earth up to the ankles. Then, with great difficulty, they
hoisted into the saddle the heavy metal statues into which they
had transformed their masters, piece by piece.

The battlefield where Constable d'Albret had lined up his battalions was a narrow plateau of interminable length. The barons,
in spite of their ardor, took several hours to get to their places,
each under his own banner. The miry soil, gullied by rain, trampled all night by the comings and goings of the troops, was now a
great swamp. Slipping, faltering, slogging, the French formed up
in rows behind each other to a depth of forty lines, divided into
three corps. The first, or shock brigade, commanded by the Constable included the Dukes of Orléans and Bourbon, the Counts of
Eu and of Richemont, and Marshal Boucicault. The second one, a
reserve unit, commanded by the Dukes of Alençon and Bar, the
Counts of Nevers, of Vaudémont and Blâmont. The third under
the Counts of Marle and Dammartin, with the eighteen thousand
men of the communal militia.

On the other side, the English were waiting, holding their
ground, having heard mass and received communion. Henry V
formed his troops into a single corps on his right; the front lines
were under the orders of the Duke of York. On the left, the rear
guard, directed by Lord Camois. The wagons were placed nearby
to avoid having them plundered during the fracas. Barefoot,
breeches pulled up, without hood or armor, hatchet or dagger by
their sides, their great longbows of yew in hand, the archers
formed up in each battalion. They were in the center in the first
line, with the dismounted men-at-arms behind them. Great staffs

sharpened at both ends had been planted in the ground in front of them to break the knights' charges. At the rear, on horseback, the priests were praying.

The French nobles once again, after Crécy, after Poitiers, always one war behind the times, were prepared for a set-piece battle of the type that hadn't been fought for ages. They probably thought that placed the way they were, sixty thousand strong, they were going to pulverize the twelve thousand English who faced them. However, to do that they would have had to be able to move quickly. Rain was falling on the churning ground. With each horse carrying the weight of his own armor, his rider, and his rider's armor, the load per square inch was considerable. The horses sank into the mire where rain was digging gutters a little deeper with each step. And even if the knights had to give up their horses, they would be riveted to the ground like towers of iron by the weight of their armor and become harmless living targets for the mobile archers who would run after them and whose arrows would strike them down, visors in the mud, from one end to the other of this field where they would be trapped by the shape of the landscape.

Suddenly the plateau of Agincourt was silent. All around the name of the Lord was being evoked. Then this cry: *"Now strike!"* The old knight Thomas Epinhem threw his staff in the air. Trumpets and horns sounded the attack. With a tremendous shout, the English mounted to the assault. The archers braced themselves, pulled their bows taut with all their strength. Ten thousand arrows riddled the sky, which grew dark. A whooshing murderous night fell suddenly on the front lines. The first ranks bowed their heads with one movement to avoid the arrows, which could injure them by penetrating their visors. They fell back, off balance, managed to straighten up again and tried to start their horses off at a gallop, lances in hand. In vain. The next ranks were so tightly packed that no one could lift his arm to "strike down the enemy." Hit by the projectiles, the animals went mad, tried to run away, stumbled, bringing their riders down with them. The din was deafening: arrows, cries from the soldiers, whinnying of the crazed horses; the front lines were put to flight.

Light, bounding, agile, energies multiplied by the stakes, the English archers charged the mastodons of iron who were stuck in the soft ground. It eluded their foothold; they slipped, tottered, always off balance, and, at the slightest bump, collapsed over each other like card castles.

Leaving the bow for the hatchet, the mallet, the mace, and the pike, implacable and resolute, the archers progressed toward the second corps of troops, cutting down everything in their path. One would have thought Death itself was advancing. The flower of chivalry of the first and second French battalions was scattered on the ground. The third was on the run. The battle was lost. Lords and knights surrendered by the hundreds. They were relieved of their headgear and waited for a decision on their fate. Then a tumultuous noise was heard. The third battalion—French, Bretons, Gascons, and Poitevins—were returning to battle. "We're not taking any prisoners," ordered the King of England, who feared a counteroffensive. Stupefied, the English soldiers hesitated. To kill a prisoner was a sin; a dead loss also since prisoners brought ransom. "We're not taking any prisoners, orders of the King," shouted a gentleman sent to the spot with an escort of two hundred archers. With the exception of the dukes and counts, who were led to the base camp, all the French nobility was massacred, quickly, but in cold blood. Since they no longer wore their helmets, they were hit on the head, the body remaining invulnerable under the steel armor. The English cut them down like cattle, clubbed them with maces, slit their throats, opened their jugular veins, and "smashed their skulls and faces." It was a great pity.

The French deserted the battlefield of which Henry, our runaway of yesterday, remained master. Prudent, fearing a counterattack, he let the hours pass. Already people were running over the field, searching for their own, and also looking for booty. The knights-at-arms were searching, counting, identifying. For the French the list was long: ten thousand dead. On the English side, not even sixteen hundred. Henry V called the French herald, Montjoie. Would the English King be moved by the horrible spectacle to which he had been subjected for hours? Would he feel responsible for this carnage, thus guilty? Addressing himself to the French, he made this curious remark: "We haven't made this massacre, but God has been almighty, we believe, through the sins of your people." Then he had Montjoie confirm that the victory belonged to him and asked for the name of the castle he noticed

on the horizon. In possession of the name, he declared: "And
since all battles should carry the name of the nearest fortress, village, or good city where they were done, this one from now on
and forever will carry the name of the Battle of Agincourt." He
stayed until nightfall.

The English took their dead and their booty over to their bivouacs of the day before. They pulled out the bodies of the Duke
of York and the Count of Oxford from among the corpses and
had them boiled in order to be able to carry their bones back to
England. They kept only those objects that were easy to carry—
gold, silver, precious clothes, hauberks of great value—then they
shut the harnesses and bodies in a barn and set fire to it.

The next day, at sunrise, they left for Calais. Going alongside
the battlefield, they noticed some survivors, hurt, haggard, wandering, still in shock from the battle. The surrounding woods were
full of them. None escaped alive, except for those of very high
birth who were taken away for ransom: the young Duke of
Orléans, Charles, the Duke of Bourbon, the Count of Eu, the
Count of Vendôme, the Count of Richemont, brother of the Duke
of Brittany, the Count of Harcourt, Master Jean de Craon, Marshal Boucicault. From there to Calais, no one dreamed of trying to
stop the English.

As soon as they were out of sight, the peasants of the area, of
all ages and both sexes, swarmed in. In an instant the dead were
as naked as the day they were born, completely stripped by the
common folk they had so despised. Armor, helmets, lances, and
swords, but also linens, hose, leggings, blouses, hoods, shoes, everything was carried away in less time than it takes to tell about it.

Low sky, pale sunrise, bitter wind, ten thousand naked corpses
lay scattered over the plain of Agincourt, ten thousand Frenchmen, two thirds of them knights, the fine flower of the nobility.
Not a family that wasn't touched. Officers of the King: Constable
d'Albret responsible for the disaster, Admiral Jacques de Dampierre, the grand master of the crossbowmen John d'Hangest, the
Count of Hornes, hereditary grand huntsman of the Empire.
Princes: the two brothers of the Duke of Burgundy, the Duke
Antoine of Brabant and the Count of Nevers; Duke John of Alen-
çon, Duke Edward of Bar and his brother John the Lord of
Puisaye, their nephew Robert, Count of Marle, Count Ferry of

Vaudémont of the house of Lorraine, all cousins of the King of France, Count John VI of Roucy, descendant of the old Counts of Reims, and recognizable by an old wound which had left him with one arm shorter than the other, Master Louis of Bourbon, son of the Lord of Préaux. And barons, as many from the borderlands of Picardy as from other provinces, the Lord of Croy and his son Heilly, the Lord of Dampierre and his son, the Lord of Roche Guyon and his brother, Master Regnault of Créquy and his son Master Philip, the Lord of Maunies and his brother Lancelot, Matthieu and Jean d'Humières, Master Oudart of Renty and two of his brothers, the Lord of Agincourt itself and his son, the Lord of Offemont and his son Raulequin, the Lord of Coucy, the Lords of La Tour d'Auvergne, of Béthencourt, of Combourg, Masters Bertrand of Montauban and Bertrand of St. Gilles, Masters Lancelot of Rubempré, Perceval of Richebourg, the three Noyelles, Jean, Pierre, and Lancelot, Palamède of the Marquais, Le Borgne of Noailles . . . The names of the knights killed at Agincourt fill up whole pages of the chronicles.

The following days saw a long parade of families and households. They came to look for the remains of their own, often several from one family. They looked, identified, washed, and buried with great tears the blood of France, the flower of the nobility in the chapels of their fiefs or in nearby churches. They carried their dead away to rest in native soil. Nearly six thousand were left unclaimed. Moved by pity, the Count of Charolais had them buried at his expense in great trenches surrounded by hedges of thorns to protect them from the wolves and the dogs, and the Bishop of Guines came to bless the graves. All of France wept for her dead.

Agincourt didn't have any immediate consequences. When the campaign was finished, Henry V went home; he would be back. The Armagnacs and the Burgundians went on killing each other. Most of the princes on Orléans's side had taken the road to London—they wouldn't be coddled there the way their ancestors had been sixty years before. But Bernard of Armagnac had taken a step up. He ruled Paris with an iron hand. Terror reigned. The treasury was empty, the luxury of the nobles insolvent. From the height of the pulpit, preachers thundered and scolded. Death struck repeatedly in the entourage of the King. The greatest patron of the arts in the West, the old Duke of Berry, passed away in his Hôtel de Nesles at the age of sixty-three. He had lived a long time. But the King of Sicily, first cousin of Charles VI, who died all swollen from St. Quentin's disease—dropsy—was exactly forty, and the two sons of France, two Dauphins, Louis, Duke of Guienne, and John, Duke of Touraine, both of whom tuberculosis carried off in less than a two-year interval, were respectively eighteen and nineteen. The situation was extremely grim. Was the Valois dynasty in danger? Would the third Dauphin, the very young Count of Ponthieu, who in this month of April 1417 succeeded his brother John, be able to put on the crown at Reims? Would he inherit the kingdom of his fathers?

CHARLES VI'S LAST SON

The Count of Ponthieu, Charles, was the next to the last of the twelve children which the King had had by his wife Isabella, the last of the eight who lived and the only one of the six sons to survive. Aside from the first and the last, who died at birth, the three others had been carried away by tuberculosis; one, Charles, at the age of nine, the other two, Louis and John, before twenty, as we have seen. The daughters showed more resistance. Other than Jeanne, who disappeared at the early age of two, and Isabelle, who died in childbirth at the age of twenty (she had married Richard II of England, dethroned and assassinated by Henry V, then Charles of Orléans, her first cousin, five years younger than she), the others had a life span which, though short, was just about normal for the times. Michelle, Duchess of Burgundy, died the same year as her father—1422—in the bud of youth, at twenty-seven; Catherine, Queen of France and of England, at thirty-seven in 1438, the same year as her sister Marie, abbess of Poissy, carried away at forty-one by the plague; Joan, Duchess of Brittany, died at forty-two. Only he who was King lived into his fifties, fifty-eight exactly.

On the night of February 22, 1403, the first day of Pisces, Charles was a very tiny newborn baby who had just come into the world and was resting in an annex of St. Pol, in the Hôtel du Petit-Musc, in the big ceremonial cradle refinished for the occasion, after having been used for Charles and John. In the corners, pommels of golden copper decorated with coats of arms of Bavaria in enamel work. At the head, two large screens to protect the baby from drafts. The season was still cold, it was only February. The nursemaid rocking him stopped her singing. Nothing made a noise or moved. Out of the silence rose regular breathing. The little prince was sleeping.

The royal children had come to look: Louis and John, six and five years old, and Catherine the baby, in the arms of her nurse. Marie was in her convent at Poissy. The other sisters, married at the age of eight, had already left the palace and were living with their husbands: Isabelle was in London, Jeanne in Nantes, and Michelle in Burgundy. Standing up on tiptoes, grasping the pommels, their noses at the level of the bed, the other children surrounded the bassinet. Three pairs of curious bright eyes stared at the newborn baby tucked up in his swaddling and bibs, his head covered with a little bonnet, who, with his closed lids, half-open mouth, and clenched fists, didn't notice anything. Silence reigned. Already it was time to leave, but they would come back.

If they could. Because in order to do that they would have to persuade Jeanne the nurse or Ozanne the nursemaid, or Margot the chambermaid and especially the governess, Dame du Mesnil. Sometimes by chance it happened that they came at the perfect moment when the baby was having his porridge or when he was having his bath in the big two-handled brass basin in front of the fireplace. Wasn't he adorable at scarcely six months, with his scarlet vest, his bonnet and his bib of Reims linen, with a large green coat on top?

And what fun to look through the tiny clothes in the coffers—the scarlet jackets furred with squirrel, the bright green coats from London, the long, full overcoat, in grass green, from Brussels. Later there would be red, green, black or gray surcoats—vermilion from Brussels, bright green from London, black or gray from Montvilliers—some of which, furred with marten or squirrel breast, hung down to his feet. He would also have pourpoints of black satin with scarlet linings of embossed velvet brocaded with gold, hoods of green damask, breeches half white, half red, hats of white material with black silk borders, decorated with a feather or silk piping and gold from Cyprus. No surprise moreover, the other children wore the same clothes, several sizes larger.

It was really fun to poke about in this room, to open the dish cupboard where the six cups and the six porridge bowls in white silver were placed side by side, the two silver pots for the milk, and the ewer of glazed silver, all engraved with the arms of the Count of Ponthieu.

The children could be helpful. Was he crying? They could shake his silver-gilt rattle. Was he out of sorts? They could amuse him with his little brass caldron. Soon he would get a harp. When he was peevish, excited, they would play on it. The effect would be immediate. Right away he would perk up his ears, lie still, relaxed, attentive, happy, watching fingers move over the strings. Listening was very nice, a real pleasure. Almost as much fun as sucking rose sugar, candied orange peel or lemon of which Lord Charles received monthly provisions, and which they never got enough of. The children would snatch some of his anise and coriander, grab a sugared nut and, with an air of innocence, walk away.

Those were the pleasures of the first years. Did they compensate for the tenderness of a mother never seen? They had to. For most children, the mother is the one who cares for them, but for Charles it was Jeanne, Ozanne, or Margot. It sufficed that they were goodhearted and healthy-minded. For a time he would be protected from himself, but not from others, not from the world. And the latter was in uproar. Scarcely able to stand, already he received its bitter mark. At the age of two and a half they took him and his brothers away from St. Pol. Practically a kidnaping. Thrown into a boat, they went up the Seine to Vitry where their maternal uncle, William of Bavaria, was waiting for them. Together they were on the road for Pouilly to meet up with their mother and the Duke of Orléans, when John the Fearless suddenly appeared with a strong escort. "Back," cried Burgundy, "you can't come through." "We shall see about that," shouted Bavaria. Crouched down in their wagon, the royal children heard their uncles confront each other in violent terms. Were they going to fight? Then suddenly there they were, thrown to the bottom of the litter. With a slash of his sword, Burgundy had cut the traces which held the horses in harness. He took the three little princes back to Paris, this time placing them in the Louvre under the guard of old Berry. That was only one of the first episodes of the Orléans-Burgundy struggle which was soon going to take the shape we have seen.

Once Uncle Louis had been assassinated by Cousin John, there were nothing but furtive departures, secret comings and goings, abruptly shortened stays, a perpetual shuttle between St. Pol, Melun, and the Marne residences. And Paris changed her aspect. Her streets were blocked off with chains in great haste at nightfall; she put down her portcullises, pulled up her drawbridges, doubled surveillance on the gates, strengthened her rampart walks. She filled up with armed men. She was heavy with threats and echoed with cries of fear. She was afire with outbursts of hate. Human limbs exposed as examples, the sky barred with gallows laden with corpses, furious hordes let out into the streets. Death was a pageant on view every hour of the day in that month of May 1413, with Caboche and Capeluche, his hangman, in the lead role and Burgundy doing the stage direction.

Horror and blood, violated palaces, a kingdom adrift—the child was afraid. What could you do when you were ten, other than take refuge in the arms of your guardian angels, your father and mother, so that they would reassure you? But Charles's parents were worse than dead, they were weak, fallen into disrepute. He felt it already, although he knew only evasive replies, embarrassed silences, averted looks by which the women who cared for him deflected his questions, not to mention the hidden meanings which he was not supposed to understand and the things he overheard when they thought he was elsewhere. What would Jeanne, Ozanne, or Dame du Mesnil say about this father who was always "absent" and who in his crises didn't even recognize his son, and this mother of whom he saw even less and whom rumor accused of every sin?

She was now nothing more than a fat old woman crippled with rheumatism, infirm and heavily made up, more selfish and pleasure-seeking than ever, whom he saw from time to time. "How long has it been since you've seen your mother?" the King asked the Duke of Guienne, one day when he was in his right mind. "Three months ago, my lord," replied the child. Isabella thought only of parties and luxury (had she thought of anything else since her marriage?) but she also thought of possessing, accumulating things. She had persuaded her husband to give her a veritable fortune in land, furnishings, in gems and liquid assets, and never ceased to demand more. She felt no tenderness for this lunatic from whom she lived apart or for these children she had had by him in such great numbers. Where was Isabella of Bavaria's heart? Had she ever had one, except for the possession of those goods which inspired her with such violent covetousness? Except also for fear? Isabella of Bavaria was alarmed by the slightest thing, a thunderclap, a street to be crossed, the rumor of a possible epidemic; Isabella of Bavaria was phobic. But she was only fearful for herself.

The reality of pain. By now the child gazed at the world and other people with sad eyes. How much did he know about what was weighing on him? Nothing or practically nothing. He was quiet, he submitted, he waited. At the Hôtel du Petit-Musc, Charles was bored. His brother John had gone to live in Valenciennes with his father-in-law, the Count of Hainaut. He hardly ever saw the Dauphin Louis, who, mad about music, women, and luxury, turned night into day, got up at noon, lunched at four, had supper at midnight, and went to bed at the break of dawn. There remained his sister Catherine, who was twelve, the age for princesses to marry.

As it happened a real little scandal had just taken place at court in that month of November 1413. The King of Sicily, Louis II of Anjou, had definitely opted for the Orléans party and had sent the young Catherine of Burgundy back to her father, John the Fearless, complete with dowry. She had been engaged to his eldest son a few days before the murder of the King's brother and had been living with his family for five years. Louis didn't want the daughter of an assassin as a wife for his son, he declared emphatically, albeit a little late. Now he was looking for alliances in the royal family, which up to now had found spouses among the Burgundians. It happened he had a daughter, Marie, almost two years younger than Charles. And the King of Sicily, having descended from Valois kings, believed he was not raising his eyes too high by thinking of the last son of the house of France as a husband for her. So he sent his wife, the Queen, to the castle of Marcoussis, where she was to make his offer. The business was soon settled.

To seal the bargain Isabella sent her cousin six gold goblets enameled inside with bright red, a beautiful pointed diamond
mounted in a ring for his son the Count of Guise, the future King
René. The groom had received for his portion an ewer and a
golden goblet. What the bride got, we don't know. She surely
wasn't forgotten. The engagement was celebrated in the Louvre in
the last days of December, in the presence of the immediate family
and intimate friends, the Queen, and the Dauphin Louis representing his sick father, the Anjous, the two young Orléans, Duke
Charles and his brother Vertus, the Count of Eu and the formidable Bernard of Armagnac.

But the Queen of Sicily was a woman of great common sense.
She had no intention of placing her daughter in the company of
Queen Isabella, as was the custom then. The court of France
wasn't the place for a princess in those days. Moreover, she
wanted to take the Count of Ponthieu home with her. Better to get
him away from his family. That would help him grow up.

The Queen of Sicily was a very beautiful woman. She spoke ad-
mirably: "This princess captivates everyone's glances by her rare
beauty, by the charms of her face, and by the air of dignity surrounding her whole person," the monk of St. Denis had written
fifteen years before. "Nature blessed her with all perfections. She
only lacks being immortal," he concluded, ravished. She hadn't
changed. Time had matured and refined the face, fixed the features. But her powers remained intact. The charm still worked.
The child succumbed to it. Happily.

Without regret Charles of Ponthieu turned a page in his short
life. A sad page. He took leave of the King his father, of the
mother of whom he had seen so little, of his brother the Dauphin,
of his sister Catherine. He tenderly kissed his nursemaid Jeanne,
his nurse Ozanne, and his chambermaid Margot, made a last tour
of the Hôtel St. Pol, raised his little white hat lined with black silk
and decorated with a braid of gold to the passing lords in reply to
their greetings, laughed once more at their extravagant costumes,
visited the horses, the dogs, the falcons, leaned out his window to
contemplate the ravaged city, and said good-by to his childhood.
He would try not to think about it too much.

One February morning Charles left for the castles of his cousin,
the King—the castle of Angers with its eighteen towers, the castle

of Saumur, the white castle of Tarascon on the Rhône. For the moment, he was protected, out of harm's reach.

Through the February mists, on the most radiant of mornings, the child rode toward large, gray rivers, toward the gentleness of the Loire and the violence of the Rhône, a freezing wind, a burning sun, toward the desertlike, stone-studded Crau, toward Camargue, half sky, half water, where the wild game took refuge, toward Aiguesmortes and Les Saintes, toward the Mediterranean Sea. A new life awaited him, and with it no more of False Seeming and Sloth, Anger, Murder and Greed, but Order, Vigilance, and a mother's tenderness. There he regained strength and life. It lasted nearly four years. Then duty called him. With the death of the Duke of Berry, the King of Sicily took a dominant role in the government. He was a capable man. He thought it was time for the Count of Ponthieu, who for more than three years had been living with Sicily's people, to be initiated into business. He had to go back then. On the third of September 1417, Charles (having become Duke of Touraine in the meantime) started attending Council meetings.

No doubt the King of Sicily found exceptional qualities in the adolescent. No doubt also, he wanted to push his future son-in-law, a choice trump for his house. And then Agincourt had decimated the class of princes. The rising generation had to be trained without delay. A task he was not able to accomplish. He died on April 29, leaving alone on the political stage the boy whom he had been able to father only too briefly, and who at the same time, by the death of his brother John, found himself Dauphin.

UNHAPPY THE LAND WHOSE KING IS A CHILD

His Highness the Dauphin, as young as he was, nevertheless had very good sense and understanding.

Juvénal des Ursins

The Dauphin was intelligent, courageous. Conscious of the duties in his charge, he took his role seriously. But he was fourteen years old. In the Council, Bernard of Armagnac had replaced the King of Sicily. So it was he who governed. But Charles had his own Council whose members had been chosen with care by Queen Yolande of Sicily, who continued to watch over his education and whose opinions guided him. Charles VI's condition grew worse by the day. His wife's behavior was scandalous. Her lovers didn't even bother greeting the King when he came to visit her. So they exiled Isabella to a nunnery at Tours while the lord through whom the final scandal occurred, Boisbourdon, was thrown into the Seine, sewn up in a leather sack bearing this inscription: "Respect the King's Justice." As for the young princesses who were living in the Queen's company, exposed to too many temptations in such a dissolute milieu, they were asked to return to their mothers.

The Dauphin knew exactly what to expect of his own mother, who, by disappearing from the political stage, left him in the forefront. He was worthy of it. Active, conscientious, enthusiastic about what he did as well as about what he saw, he spared no time or effort to give the best of himself. His good will was whole-hearted. As much as he could, he participated, attended all the Council meetings, listened, observed, spoke when he was asked to, showed himself wherever he was asked to go, in brief, little by little, through contact with events, he was learning the rudiments of the job. He showed himself to be very capable. Under the circumstances, you couldn't have asked for better behavior from a young boy.

In devastated France the struggle between the Armagnacs and the Burgundians went on. It was going full force, you might say. The advantage was with Burgundy at the moment, in whom half of the country saw a savior. The Queen, having been exiled, threw herself into his arms. What a prize! Burgundy was overwhelmed, took her from the nunnery in Tours, and gave his faction a veil of legality by covering himself with her authority. By dint of a text decreed by Charles VI for temporary use fourteen years previously, Isabella, installed in Troyes with her chancellery, her sovereign court, and her officers, titled herself "Queen of France by the grace of God having the government and administration of this Kingdom." Thus the government of Burgundy and the Queen openly opposed that of Bernard of Armagnac and the Dauphin, who both declared they were governing in the name of the mad King.

Then John the Fearless marched on Paris, entered it without

bloodshed thanks to traitors within the town, and moved in with his cousin Isabella. In his baggage train, some old acquaintances: Caboche and Capeluche. Riots, settlings of accounts, members of the opposite faction hunted down; three thousand Parisians met death during the bloody nights that followed. Count Bernard, betrayed by the artisan in whose house he was hiding, fell into the hands of the once again all-powerful butchers. They massacred him, threw his nude body into the courtyard of the palace. For three days the crowds amused themselves with it, carved out a piece of his flesh in the form of a St. Andrew's cross (his emblem) before throwing it to rot on a dung heap in the courtyard of the priory of St. Martin of the Fields.

The Dauphin owed his life to the presence of mind of the Provost, Tanguy du Châtel, who, seeing the danger, hurried to the Hôtel du Petit-Musc where Charles was staying, rolled him up, sleeping, in a dressing gown and carried him to the Bastille where he locked him up—the best way to keep him from the rioters. At daybreak he would have the Dauphin taken from Paris in great haste. After attempting unsuccessfully to retake his capital, Charles retreated to the province of Berry, which, by the same title as the Dauphiné, Poitou, and Touraine, was part of his inheritance, and established his government there. From there, valiantly, he continued the struggle to re-establish his authority, contested by Burgundy, but also by the English. He might have expected that.

On the thirteenth of August 1417 Henry V of England once again claimed the crown of France from those who had worn it for four generations, and began applying himself with dynamism and method to making his desires become realities. The Norman cities fell one after the other in the face of the invader's rigorous cruelty. On January 2, 1419, at the end of a determined siege, one of the worst in the Middle Ages, Rouen capitulated. And then the goal was Ile-de-France. On July 31, Pontoise, in the hands of a Burgundian captain, opened her doors to him. The capital fell under the direct menace of the English King. Confusion was at its height, the country was bled white: "thus you might better say the deserted land rather than the land of France," the chronicler moaned.

Judging that between two evils he should choose the lesser, the

Dauphin tried to approach John the Fearless. He would need all his subjects finally reconciled and more to force an adversary of the determination of Henry V to go home again. Negotiations were opened. A meeting was arranged for September 10 on the Montereau bridge.

TRAP OR RISK?

John the Fearless was not anxious to go to Montereau. He had already met the Dauphin earlier that year, in July, at Pouilly. After three days of sterile negotiations the Dauphin had managed to extract a promise of peace from him. Since then he had been putting off for as long as possible a new encounter. Now the boy was harassing him with envoys, with letters. And if it were only his. But Paris was getting involved too. Paris, which had always followed him, was sending one ambassador after another in the hope of restoring peace—a peace which was being called for everywhere. Such insistence. How to get away from it?

Up to then, circumstances had faithfully served him. His talents too, it is true. On the days following the murder of the Rue Vieille-du-Temple, he had been able to turn opinion in his favor by his crafty maneuvers. His enemies had for the most part left the political scene in a timely fashion: Valentina Visconti was no longer alive; the party of the Orléans princes had been decimated at Agincourt and the children of Orléans were rotting in London for lack of ransom; Berry had died; Sicily had died; Constable Armagnac was lying under seven feet of earth. The road to power was finally open; Isabella at his disposition. But there remained the Dauphin . . . the one obstacle no one had expected.

How to avoid this alliance against the English? Not that Henry V was an easy ally to be led around as you pleased. But John felt strong enough to resist the Englishman's ambitions when the time came. From that point of view, the game seemed relatively easy. But this upstart Charles bothered him. The Dauphin seemed to promise a future less rosy than the past had been for John and, in spite of his young age, held a rather different position on the political chessboard from the Armagnac chiefs of yesterday. Would luck change?

John of Burgundy felt his game was not working out. He stalled, wanting to gain time but becoming more gloomy by the hour, hesitating, gathering other people's opinions: should he go to the rendezvous or not? John didn't want to admit it to himself but he was afraid to go to Montereau. In the meeting at Pouilly, he had recognized among the men in Charles's entourage some faces that hadn't pleased him at all, old partisans of the Orléans clan. When they saw him, the hate had been rekindled in spite of the twelve-year interval, like embers still warm, coming to life with a breeze. Suddenly it had been as if Louis were among them again.

Somber presentiments John didn't know how to define made him anxious. Those people, his avowed enemies, numerous in his cousin's entourage, were the ones who were going to organize the encounter. How could he not be suspicious of it? "If you go, you'll never return," his Jewish astrologer Philippe Mouskès repeated to him every day. Which made him think. . . . And then they would ask him to account for things. Had he kept his promises of a few weeks ago? What could he reply? John the Fearless saw himself caught in a trap, confronted, driven back to the ineluctable. Fears and premonitions assailed him; that wasn't customary for this skeptic: no, he wouldn't go to Montereau.

The Dauphin, as agreed, arrived there on the twenty-fourth of August. John, in Troyes, was stalling. He assembled his men-at-arms, ordered his captains to join him with the greatest possible number of soldiers, and told them not to hesitate under the circumstances to keep messengers moving night and day. Nonetheless, he was taking his sweet time while the Dauphin, at Montereau, was waiting on the pleasure of his father's vassal. Finally, on the twenty-eighth, John set out. At five leagues from Montereau, at Bray-sur-Seine, he stopped. Was he going to change his mind? The Dauphin sent more ambassadors: on the thirty-first of August, on September 1, and on the third. Without success: "The Duke was the slowest man in all of his enterprises that one could ever find," wrote the anonymous chronicler known as the Burgher of Paris. On the seventh of August, John made up his mind. He would go in three days. But he had conditions. The two factions at Montereau would keep apart, the Dauphin in the city, himself in the castle. They would meet on a bridge set up for the occasion so that all the guarantees of security would be respected. As a security measure, the city and the castle of Moret would be given over to him. The Dauphin consented immediately.

On September 10, John the Fearless heard morning mass in the church in Bray-sur-Seine and then set out with three thousand men. At three o'clock Montereau was in sight. He didn't enter the castle but arranged his troops in battle order in the fields around the fortress. Would he go? Hesitation tortured him. He had little desire to encounter the Dauphin, who had had every opportunity he could have wished to set up killers in ambush, since he had come to Montereau with a veritable army; some said fifteen thousand soldiers. He, the prudent Duke of Burgundy, wasn't well enough informed about his cousin's manpower. He was taking chances and felt it more than he thought it. All his being, all his blood told him that, but not his reason, on which he had always relied, and his counselors, who had never seen him in such a state. "I must have additional guarantees of security," announced John. "I will not budge unless I get them." St. Georges, Navailles, and Champlitte left to make contact with the Dauphin. While they were gone Pierre de Giac made sure that the entrances to the bridge were clear and that no armed men were near it. When they returned, their report was definite: nothing they had seen gave rise to suspicion.

The Duke took three hundred men with him, left the rest on a war footing in the immediate proximity, and decided to enter the castle. A table had been set up for him in the dining room and wine and meat laid out. He consumed the food in silence, his face impassive. The time for the interview approached. Anguish seized John the Fearless. Again, he expressed his fears, his suspicions, asked the same questions over and over. Like a tracked animal, he paced the room. The master's unrest spread to his entourage. They had never seen such despair in the proud Duke of Burgundy. Disconcerted by his unusual attitude, some of them fell silent, bereft of further arguments; others pleaded: "Don't go there, Your Highness, you're risking an ambush." "You aren't risking anything, Your Highness," affirmed Navailles and Vergy, for whom the reality of what they had seen had removed all fear. "The Dauphin is in good faith. We wouldn't hesitate to accompany you there." Finally the Duke took the plunge: "Let's have confidence in our cousin's loyalty," he cried out as if relieved.

By now it was five o'clock. The Duke had bade farewell to his people, entrusting his jewels to his faithful Jossequin (following the custom of the day, he took them along with him on all of his journeys), and left the castle with a small escort.

The Montereau bridge where the encounter was to take place had been entirely closed off for the occasion. At each end there was a barrier guarded by the Burgundians on the castle side and by the Dauphin's men on the city side. In the center was the space reserved for the meeting, entered through a narrow gate. Each party had to leave his escort at the entrance to the bridge and could enter with only ten gentlemen whose names had been decided on in advance. With Burgundy, Charles of Bourbon, Navailles, Fribourg, Neufchâtel, Montaigu, Vienne, Vergy, Dautrey, Giac, Ivret de Pontarlier. With the Dauphin, Tanguy du Châtel, Narbonne, Louvet, Beauvau, Noyers, Avaugour, Escorailles, Frotier, Lairé, and Le Maçon.

The Duke arrived at the agreed-upon spot where Beauvau was waiting for him. He left his mount and his escort, gathered the ten designated men, and presented himself at the barrier. Then there were the usual formalities, exchanges of promises, and searches. Everything was in order. In accordance with the agreement, the men retained only their coats of mail and their swords. John the Fearless went out onto the bridge, the ten lords from his entourage close behind. The Dauphin's counselors went to meet him, and together they covered the few yards separating them from the meeting place. The Burgundians were on their guard. The atmosphere was heavy. The Duke saw his nephew Du Châtel and his tense face brightened. With a friendly gesture, he took his nephew's shoulder: "Here's the man I can rely on," he cried to his people.

The reserved area was a rectangular enclosure covered with a light roof. In one corner, leaning against the wooden wall, stood the Dauphin, armed, his sword at his side. Was it because of these fifteen days of waiting or did he fear an ambush? He had been warned to "be careful because the undertaking was set up to his disadvantage." The young man looked grim; he had a hard time showing a good face when John the Fearless, taking off his black velvet biretta, came to kneel in front of him.

"My very honored and respected lord," began the Duke, "I pray God that He grant you a good evening and a good life."

"Good cousin, be very welcome," came the reply.

"My very honored and respected lord," continued Burgundy. "I have come before you by my sovereign lord the King your father, may God keep him, to serve you both and to give you my aid against his enemies, yours and also mine, the English. I offer you my person, my fortune, my family, my vassals, my subjects, my friends, my allies, so that we can all aid, in whatever manner you care to order us, in the restoration of the domain of His Highness the King, and of yours, and for the driving out of his enemies."

The Dauphin took him by the hand: "Good cousin, you speak so well that one could ask for no better. Stand up and put your hat on. But you wouldn't be a good priest at all," he added.

"And why not?" inquired John.

"Because you don't keep to your word."

"How is that?" he asked, surprised.

"Because the last time we spoke together you promised to clear out all your garrisons in a month. You haven't done this. You also committed yourself to our meeting that same month in Montereau, to talk about the business of the kingdom and to organize the resistance against the English. Now I've been waiting for you here for two weeks. What kept you? You were less than twenty leagues away."

"My very honored lord, I came when I could," interrupted the Duke.

"No doubt," continued the Dauphin quickly, "but you forget the state of the kingdom. I beg of you, good cousin, do not delay bringing your help. I consider peace to have been made already between you and me, as we promised and swore at Pouilly. Let us together find the way to resist the English."

"May His Highness excuse me," evaded Burgundy, "but we can't decide anything without the presence of His Highness the King. You must promise me to betake yourself to him within the month, wherever he may be."

"I am better here than with him," replied the Dauphin, irritated. "And I will go to His Highness my father when I feel like it, and not at your will. But I am surprised at you, you were supposed to challenge the English, but you haven't done so."

"Your Highness, I have done nothing but what I should do," replied John in a peremptory tone.

"That's not so."

"Yes, it is."

"You're lying through your teeth," exploded the Dauphin.

The Duke blushed with anger. Navailles took a step forward: "Your Highness, you must come along now to your father," he said, taking the Dauphin by the shoulder and pulling out his sword halfway, while the Duke started for his sword.

"Will you put hand to your sword in the presence of His Highness?" cried Lairé.

In an instant Avaugour, Frotier, and Du Châtel had placed themselves in front of the Dauphin: "Get back my lords, back. Are you going to lay hands on your King's son?" and they advanced, menacing.

Clanking swords were drawn, blades flashed, Tanguy du Châtel pulled the Dauphin out of the enclosure at breakneck speed, and troops pushed their way in through the half-open gate. "To arms, to arms," they cried. "Kill, kill," they shouted. The Dauphin's men, with the old servants of the late Duke of Orléans in the first rank—Beauvau, Lairé, Narbonne—surrounded the Duke of Burgundy. He had only a few more instants to live. Of his men, only two came to his aid. He fell. Vergy, Navailles collapsed in their turn. The others fled but they didn't get far. They had scarcely passed the gate when they were captured, while, at the barriers, the escorts were battling to the death.

On the rough planks of the Montereau bridge, under which the capricious Yonne followed her course, John of Burgundy, his hand cut off, his skull bashed in, his chin torn off, lay spilling out his life and his blood just like twelve years earlier in the mud and the night of the Rue Vieille-du-Temple his cousin Louis, whom he had assassinated—crime being for him the last resource of hate. No men of his household came to carry him to a friendly house. No women in tears washed his mutilated body by torchlight, folding fresh linens over his wounds. Instead, until midnight the Armagnac soldiery came to insult his bloody remains, his fixed eyes, to strip the robes, the coat of mail, and the rings right from his body. They didn't dare strip him naked. At midnight they dragged him to a windmill near the bridge and laid him out on a table. At daybreak they placed him in a cheap coffin with only his cape and leggings on, his biretta pulled down over his eyes, and they put him under a slab of the church of Notre Dame in the town where his soul was committed to the Most High with twelve masses said quickly.

John of Burgundy shouldn't have agreed to meet his cousin. He hesitated too long in deciding. He shouldn't have given in to the insistence of his own reason. He should have had faith in his intuitions, refused to go to Montereau. What happened in that closed space, away from the sight of impartial viewers, that scene played out under such fluid circumstances that even today no one has been able to establish each man's responsibility, was never any help to anyone. "Why did they do it?" cried Barbazan, one of the Dauphin's counselors, arriving just after these occurrences. "They have put the throne of France in great peril." But Orléans had been avenged. Now it remained to avenge Burgundy. That would take another sixteen years.

VENGEANCE

The news spread like wildfire through the country. The army of the powerful Duke had not exactly shown dauntless courage. At the news of its leader's death, "it split up and wandered, each one pulling out and going off without order or reason wherever God counseled him." But the family and of course the hangers-on put on spectacular demonstrations. Valentina Visconti, the wife of Orléans, had not behaved any differently. "The bereaved young prince," reports the chronicler Chastellain on the subject of the heir, Philip of Charolais, "vanquished and laid low with grief, throwing up a loud and fearful cry with all manner of lament, flung himself on a bed. And lying there, suddenly his face became disfigured, he couldn't speak, and his spirit was completely deadened. His eyes began to roll, his lips blackened, his teeth gnashed, his arms and his legs to stiffen as in death. Pity was so great in the house that their hearts melted in tears, in outcries and in beating their fists, as though they had seen the whole fabric of the world come apart in front of them. His poor ladies came streaming in from everywhere, all upset, crying, sobbing, and falling to the ground in heaps, one on top of the other."

As for the lamentations of Madame Michelle of France, wife of Charolais, they came from ancient tragedy:

"Miserable wretched woman," she cried, "adorned on the outside with a resplendent title, and on the inside the most unhappy creature that ever lived, unfortunate daughter of a king, sad and lamenting creature, bearer of pain and slave of fortune born to live in confusion, and living to die in reproach, a woman, not a lady, a servant ashamed before the world and fallen from a high and glorious throne into a filthy puddle of tears, there where the remainder of my days, which will be too long, will be lived out in clamors and in agonizing discomfort, may the hour of my birth be damned, if only I hadn't been engendered or conceived in the womb of a queen, when I myself abominate my being, despise living, go in horror of my own self, and desire, against nature's will, extreme malediction of misfortune."

Paris fell into step. The news of the event plunged the capital into a state of frenzy which incited her to avenge the victim within the hour by pursuing, sword in hand, every partisan of the Dauphin, certainly the instigator of the crime. A blood bath was barely avoided.

As for Queen Isabella, she vowed inexorable hatred of her son.

But in fact, what had happened in Montereau? A murder by premeditation, proclaimed the dead man's family. The late Duke John had been the object of an abominable plot concocted in advance down to the last details. And the Burgundian versions of the assassination, written with a vengeful pen, but with very approximate truth, were dispersed throughout the kingdom: While the Duke was kneeling in front of the Dauphin "making a sweet and humble bow, offering body, horsemen, and friends, several armed men rushed up and struck him with axes, and inhumanely killed him against God, justice, reason, faith, and law."

Not true, protested the Dauphin's partisans. Our prince was provoked by the well-known deceit of the Duke in a state of legitimate self-defense.

The Dauphin himself explained it in a letter addressed to his brother-in-law, Philip of Charolais. He pleaded with Philip to understand how greatly he had been wronged by John, Philip's father. Did Philip know that John had taken all measures to seize him, Charles? Did he know that the Lord of Navailles had pulled out his sword and tried to injure Charles's person with it?

Neither side listened. By a strange aberration of mind, the Dauphin became in the eyes of the mob public enemy number one. As it happened, at that very moment he was busy in many directions, sending out ambassadors, endeavoring to reconquer the cities and fortresses that had fallen into the hands of the English. It didn't matter, he had become the man to strike down.

By order of Isabella, the public criers filled up the streets, proclaiming: "By the King's order, it is forbidden to give Charles any title whatsoever, Dauphin, Duke, or Count, and to call him anything but Charles the ill-advised, self-proclaimed son of France."

Against this monster, only one recourse—the English.

On December 2, 1419, the son of the victim, Philip of Burgundy, signed a pact of alliance with Henry V. On May 21, 1420, they met in Troyes, this time in the company of Isabella; Philip appeared on his own behalf, but also as the representative of the King of France, whose place he held on the political scene at the special request of the Queen. The three conspirators prepared to sign the scandalous Treaty of Troyes.

Peace was made between France and England. Henry V married Catherine of France and was recognized as a son by the royal couple. As a consequence, declared Charles VI, "as soon as we are dead from that time forward the two thrones of France and England will remain together and will belong to one and the same person, King Henry our son and after him his heirs, perpetually and forever.

"Our son King Henry will work to bring back under our control each and every city, township, castle, land, and person hostile and rebellious to our authority being for the party vulgarly called that of the Dauphin and of Armagnac.

"Taking into account the horrible and enormous crimes committed in our kingdom by Charles the *so-called Dauphin of Vienne*, it is understood that neither we nor our son Henry nor our dear son the Duke of Burgundy will in any way talk of peace with the aforementioned Charles.".

At the news, the people of Paris sang, danced, and formed many processions of thanksgiving. The university exulted, foreign courts congratulated the French, and Henry V had coins struck bearing this legend: *Henricus rex Anglie, heres Franciae.*

So this dream of a double monarchy took form, to the profit of the Lancastrian dynasty, bringing an end to the secular struggle between France and England, but also constructing in the Christian West a state without a counterbalance, a power predominant to such a degree that hegemony would fall to it immediately and quite naturally.

A grand and old dream was thus in a strong position to be fulfilled, at the expense of the French.

On June 2, 1420, Henry V married Catherine of France. On December 1 he made a stately entry into Paris in company with Charles VI and moved into the Louvre. At the end of the same month the Dauphin was banished. A year later, on December 6, 1421, Catherine brought a son Henry into the world. But on the thirty-first of August 1422, Henry V died at Vincennes, to be followed a few months later by his father-in-law, Charles VI, who died on October 21 of the same year.

They were buried with royal rites. At St. Denis, when the deacons had finished reciting the prayers for the dead, all of the dead King's servants held their maces and their swords upside down to show that they were no longer in office. They broke their staffs and threw them into the open grave. Then Berry, the King-at-arms, cried, "God have pity and mercy on the most high and excellent Prince Charles, King of France, sixth of that name, our natural and sovereign lord." And then immediately continued, "God grant long life to Henry, by God's grace King of France and England, our sovereign lord." Then the sergeants-at-arms turned their maces upright, fleurs-de-lis on top, and cried out with one voice, "Long live the King! Long live the King!"

THE WAR ACCURSED OF GOD

> I do not believe that since King Clovis, who was the first Christian
> king, France has been as desolate and divided as she is today.
>   The Burgher of Paris

The new King of France and of England, Henry VI, was in
swaddling clothes, but his interests had been taken in hand by his
paternal uncle Bedford, Regent of the two realms, a man of energy and stature. For the first time in history, a foreigner governed
France. Only a part of it, but its heart—the capital, the great governing bodies, the intellectual elites, the university. Blinded by
partisan passion, swearing only by Burgundy and behind by one
war, they swung toward repudiation and gave the double monarchy the support of their prestige. In other words, they collabo-
rated.

Normandy bent under the superior strength of the new monarchy. Conquered town by town, despite a sometimes heroic resistance, she bowed to the inevitable. But not for long. Soon her
partisans would people the Norman nights with their determined
groups. "Brigands, peasant filth," cursed the intruders whom they
harassed. That, in itself, was proof that the partisans were feared.

The house of Brittany, which for more than a century had always been English with half its heart, the other half remaining forever Breton, recognized Henry, even though the present Duchess
Jeanne was the daughter of Charles VI.

To the east, Burgundy had waged war in collaboration with
Charles VI, in the Ardennes, in Champagne, and at one point
threatened Lyon. The Duke had been the cornerstone of the English foothold in the realm, and Bedford tightened those ties by
marrying the Duke's sister Anne. That is to say, France north of
the Loire was controlled by the islanders.

The Regent's policy was pursued on two levels, one administrative: to install his dynasty in the conquered lands—Normandy
and Ile-de-France; the other military: to extend what was called
the land of conquest, which in plain language meant relieving the
Dauphin of all that remained to him. He sought to associate the

French with his administration and distributed public offices among them. But he entrusted the war to his countrymen: Salisbury, Warwick, Le Pole, Falstaff, Talbot—names to conjure with.

As soon as he learned of his father's death, Charles took the title of King of France, on October 30, 1422. But his partisans, surnamed "Armagnacs" or "Dauphinois," greeted him always by the simple title of Dauphin, for he had not yet been consecrated, Reims being inaccessible to them. For the moment history designated him by the pitiable name of King of Bourges, with the country south of the Loire for his realm. Not even all of it, moreover. The southwest seceded. We know to whom Guienne belonged, and the house of Foix, ancient rival of the Armagnacs, hence Burgundian, allied itself to the invader. In consequence, here was Charles encircled, at bay between the Loire, the Garonne, and the Rhône, rejected by the great families of the land, the peers of France, those very ones who, at the coronations at Reims, had assisted the kings, his ancestors, to don the emblems of their office. Only the Anjous remained faithful. Those who might be so, the Orléans, the Duke of Bourbon, the Duke of Alençon, were being kept in London by Henry until such time as he was paid the ransoms of Agincourt, which were exorbitant.

The masses knew only their misery. Again the man-at-arms was king. Let him be called Burgundy, Armagnac, or Lancaster, or merely a freebooter working on his own account, he pillaged, raped, burned, and killed. The flat land was deserted, the refugees crowed together in the towns. Work, but where? Eat, but where? Epidemics were spreading. All was fear and barrenness.

And the war must be paid for, paid to Bedford, dearly and without delay, if one was Parisian or Norman—since he, as a good leader of the occupying army, intended to raise the funds required by his administration from the occupied land; Burgundy, Brittany, or Foix must be paid, the King of Bourges must be paid, but his courteous, legal demands were set forth through the Estates. The Dauphin traveled ceaselessly, from Bourges to Chinon, from Poitiers to Tours, from Selles to Puy, presenting the royal purse. There again, how could one refuse?

As for national sentiment, it remained an anachronism, but not for much longer. Patriotism, in that first quarter of the fifteenth century, meant fidelity to the legitimate prince. Now, there were

two who claimed this legitimacy. Which to choose? Especially
when one had been declared a bastard by his own mother; a certainty for the Burgundians, a moral dilemma for the others, including the interested party.

This was the great sorrow of the realm of France. We find ourselves carried back to the worst hours of the regency of Charles V.
But the man who had taken his place possessed neither his broad
shoulders nor his winning hand. Destiny was working against the
Valois dynasty in these early years of the fifteenth century. One
misfortune followed another. Destiny knocked with repeated, with
traitorous blows. Would it gain the upper hand over the man it
tormented?

THE FINAL BLOW

"Our surest protectors are our talents," the philosopher Diderot
would write in the mid-eighteenth century. And Charles of Valois,
Count of Ponthieu, Duke of Touraine, Dauphin, did not lack
them. Intelligence, energy, and courage were his master virtues.
Since the time when the King of Sicily placed him on the Council
at the age of thirteen, confronted with a terrifying predicament, he
had not for a single day ceased fighting. . . .

But misfortune had pursued him ever since. Today, it overwhelmed him. The tally of his short existence? Violence, battles,
failures . . .

Then the springs, so solid, so well constructed, which seemed to
support his being, ceased to work. The dynamism and the vitality
of adolescence disappeared. Charles of France became a somber
and a weary man, overwhelmed by events. Something within him
had broken.

He had become again a small sad boy, the boy at whom his
mother Isabella did not look and who waited, in a Paris gone
mad, for the Queen of Sicily to take him with her to the Loire
country.

Why should he bind himself to the past? What mattered the
mother by blood, since fate had arranged for him another who
was a hundred or a thousand times better? From then on he did
not lack affection. He married Marie. She gave him a son, Louis.

Bonfires were lighted in Paris to celebrate the truce between the Dauphin and the Duke of Burgundy. *(Bibliothèque Nationale)*

Charles VII. *(Archives Photographiques)*

Marie of Anjou. *(Photographie Giraudon)*

The Battle of Harengs, 1429. *(Photographie Giraudon)*

After the French victory at Castillon, the English were driven ou[t]
of France, and the French entere[d]
into Bordeaux.
(Bibliothèque Nationale)

Louis XI was a realist. He believed in fact, in actions, not dreams. He was the son of necessity, and urgence was his master. *(Photographie Giraudon)*

Charles VIII. *(Bibliothèque Nationale)*

This carving of Charles VIII shows him wearing an ordinary day-time headpiece—far removed from the splendor of his grandfather Charles. *(Archives Photographiques)*

Anne of Brittany. *(Bibliothèque Nationale)*

The Queen of Sicily left her château on the Rhône to join them in Berry. But reason was not enough. Following the repeated shocks which fate dealt him, and which were named Montereau, Troyes, and quite recently La Rochelle, where he had nearly met his death —the room where he was holding court having suddenly collapsed, hurling him to the floor below, while his cousin Bourbon expired before his eyes—Charles foundered in a melancholy from which nothing could distract him. The field of his consciousness and interests was reduced under the influence of a neurotic inhibition. That is to say, he no longer found pleasure in anything. Everything weighed upon him, everything seemed vain to him. He, so active, so vibrant before, became slow and easily tired. Discouraged before he began, incapable of desiring, of refusing or wishing, he was merely passive and indifferent. Vacant, submissive to all things and all people, he regarded the world of noise and of furor with a weary air as it tore itself to pieces before his eyes. He remained behind glass. Out of danger, or a prisoner? What did he think of what he saw? For he saw all. Yet he had trouble in formulating it, his thoughts were slowed, his attention was fixed with difficulty, his ideas were too heavy to manipulate. He wrapped himself in silence. Not a gesture which was not dictated to him, not a word which was not whispered to him. Until he turned away from a spectacle which he could no longer endure and until, out of sight, hidden in his châteaux, he fled the company of others, no longer tolerating any but himself in a sterile tête-à-tête from which he emerged more weary than ever. His face in turn took on the mark of the malady, his features were drawn, his forehead became wrinkled, the signs of debility were evident. With leaden complexion and a saddened eye, he had a dreadful visage.

"The enormous offenses committed in our realm by Charles the ill-advised, so-called son of France, so-called Dauphin of Vienne," a bastard, hence; this cruel word did not leave him in peace. By these declarations in the Treaty of Troyes, Queen Isabella was able to achieve a result which went beyond her hopes. Since Montereau, she had pursued her son with an implacable hatred for having killed her old lover John the Fearless—unless, worse yet, she had already cursed him to hell for having permitted the pillage of her coffers and her exile to Tours. Now she had thoroughly destroyed this hated son. Henceforth the world was a desert to him.

Why didn't he hate her? This would be far healthier, far simpler.

But the taboos were there, and the mysteries, the incomprehensible problems before which he must bow, the laws of evil. The son had been wounded to the quick by the mother. This hate, this rancor, these reproaches, all the feelings which oppressed him so and which he held inside, penetrated through this open wound, enthroned themselves in the night of the being and there distilled their poisons. They gnawed at him. The stifled cry turned in on Charles and inflicted a thousand deaths on him. He felt awful. The weight of a gigantic fault, The Fault, weighed upon him, inhibited him. But what fault? He did not know, and he trembled. And he was permanently afraid, afraid to cross a bridge, as at Montereau, afraid lest the floor of the room which he entered collapse beneath his feet, as at La Rochelle, afraid of a man alone whose presence caught him unawares, afraid of an unknown face, afraid lest he be stabbed, afraid to die of it. Afraid.

If only he could name it, this fear, in order in some way to exorcise it. If only he could recognize that he experienced it, that anxiety tormented him, beset him, that he was no longer its master. But he found alibis for it, camouflaged it beneath good excuses, accused the bridges and floors of being worm-eaten, the crowd of hiding spies in the employ of the enemy, the unknown men of seeking his life. He multiplied the precautions, ordered that the bridges which he planned to cross and the floors of his residences be inspected, went about only with a strong escort and armed to the teeth.

And he demanded reassurance. Whence this confidence which he granted with a ridiculous ease, the heart of a child; a vital need, since in exchange he was tranquilized. Whence the importance and the influence of the entourage.

Thus channeled, masked, the anxiety lost some of its destructive force. This phobic neurosis which Freud, distinguishing it from the obsessions, called anxiety hysteria, was actually providential. It would save him from the worst, prevent him from totally losing his reason. His faculties were intact—and they remained what they were in the beginning, exceptional—his access to reality, total. Only his relations with others, and particularly with himself, were disturbed. This abandoned him, disarmed, to the torments of the heart, to misery of soul. The world had lost hope. Tomorrow would never come. For Charles, bound to the fatality of his past, time had taken on the visage of misfortune and of death.

It was not very surprising, in fact, that after so many repeated shocks a depressive state should be manifested. But let it last, and the pathogenic factor entered into consideration. It would now last for more than fifteen years and would disappear miraculously, with no one able to explain the cure. There was, of course, a predisposition to such an episode. Let us not forget that the King of Bourges was the son and the grandson of psychotics. If he was not the son of his father, as his mother claimed, he remained no less born of her, that is to say, Wittelsbach and Visconti, two very heavy names to bear, which by themselves justified the appearance of the neurosis. The heredity factor, the predisposition of the terrain, had, then, surely contributed to bringing about the result that the preceding years had had such unfortunate and long-lasting repercussions in Charles's psyche.

The excesses and the perversions of the Wittelsbachs, and especially of the Viscontis, all this was carried along in blood, and Isabella of Bavaria was not responsible for it. But the rest suffices for her to be called before the tribunal of history, placed in the prisoner's dock, and forced to account for herself. I accuse. This son, what then had she done to him? Doubtless he bore within him the pathogenic seeds which centuries of exceptional destinies and of consanguinity passed on to him. They would not have sufficed. The child was of great intelligence, hence still more fragile. It took these few sentences formulated by the mother to turn him into the unrecognizable man, the neurotic who, for so many years, would drag his sadness and fatigue from castle to castle, in a realm which his state did not permit him to assume. One unbearable word obsessed and destroyed him, took from him even the joy of living.

Do not ask bastards to love, they can no longer do so. Do not ask them to be happy, for them life has the taste of ashes. Do not ask them to feel at ease in their skin, or sure of themselves either. They are permanently ashamed, believing themselves to be vaguely guilty. Betrayed, excluded, denied, rejected by their own blood, they no longer exist for anyone, or for themselves. Only the nostalgias of the soul remain to them, a difficulty in living, in breathing a despair. Bastards carry in their hearts a wound of which they cannot be healed, "the great abandonment," which must be placed in the feminine, like betrayal, like hatred. Hate is a precious source of energy; with perverse ends, it is true, but a force, a hardy flower, voracious, a crabgrass, a desert flower. A desert, this heart in which nothing can survive, a desert, this soul from which storms no longer rise, from which nothing rises any longer. Not a cry. When he ought to be screaming with rage. Not one word louder than another. The impossibility of speaking. No more words. The impossibility of acting.

He had been disavowed, struck from the living. It had been declared that he never existed. No child. No father, then. How could he exist? How learn about the world? How distinguish white from black, good from evil? Who would teach him of men, who would form his mind, his heart? Who would love him?

Mothers lost their beauty, their tenderness, their voices, and their laughter. Their skin was no longer smooth as silk at the hollow of the neck, at the bend of the arm, near the blue veins of the wrists. Their body had never been his. He had never belonged to them. Never slapped, never spanked, never scolded. No cries, no storms. He had never permitted them everything, he had never had to accept everything from them, expect everything from them, and give everything to them, for they never asked anything of him. Never sad because they were, never happy because of a smile, never in peace in the shelter of their arms.

Mothers had left the earth, they peopled hell. They slept side by side in great empty rooms, like the dead in a morgue, reduced to hard and cold bodies, which henceforth haunted his dreams.

Here was Charles, forever inconsolable, a lost child in quest of the impossible, through the wearinesses of his heart.

Cry, my lord, rebel, cry scandal, fight! But the prince could not. He had no more voice, no more blood. His confessor reproached him for it. He reminded him of the three virtues which would do his soul good: faith, hope, and charity. Take heart, my lord, a bit of will power. But the prince's soul was sick. He could no longer either love or hope. But it wasn't his fault, whatever the priest might think. Behold the sin, my son, the sin of despair. It didn't help to add the weight of guilt to that of despair.

Charles could still pray, which he did for hours at a time, locked in his oratories; he heard three masses on his knees every day; he also took communion every day. The aid of religion permitted him to survive the desolation of his soul.

The journey through night, the slow climb back toward the day across a thousand obstacles, so much effort and the great sorrow of the kingdom. *Quare obdormis Domine?* cried the people to their King. All he could do was stifle his cry inside.

THE GAME OF PLUNDER-THE-KING

Let kings be on guard as much as they can . . . from being enslaved to their servants in order to conquer their enemies.

Jean du Tillet

It must be recognized that Charles contributed to the ruin of the kingdom. This sick man, in his constant demand for consolation, felt a neurotic need to take people into his confidence, and he did so with little discernment or moderation. That is to say that at the court of Bourges the favorite governed. And what favorites! The less they were worth, the more they pleased. (But later on, Charles being incapable of refusing or of willing, all the guile of his entourage would consist in replacing an annoying favorite with one who pleased or, rather, who did less harm, since all the favorites sooner or later became pests.) Without hesitation an undesirable was exiled, or soon killed, even in the presence of the prince, who cried and stormed. One bowed his head and went on to the next. The court of Bourges became a place of intrigues and palace revolutions.

In 1422 the favorites were those who had been faithful from the beginning: the former Provost of Paris, Tanguy du Châtel, who had twice saved his life; the president of Provence, Louvet, former servant of the Dukes of Anjou; and a gentleman of petty extraction, Frotier. Charles abdicated all his power into their hands. He showered them with favors. Which wasn't enough for them. They made money from everything, from the soldiers' pay, from the currency, in which they speculated, from the crown jewels, which they pawned. So Charles sold his most beautiful diamond, "the Mirror," had new sleeves sewed to his worn doublets, wore out his old boots because his shoemaker refused him credit, and borrowed

from his cooks. "If only this lasts," thought Louvet, who cloistered the Dauphin and jealously protected his influence over him
by every means great or small. The court of Bourges was transformed into the cave of Ali Baba. Would to God that there were
forty thieves there! The worst of it was that they made the prince
persevere in old quarrels. The core of the Armagnac clan was at
Bourges; they made any reconciliation with Burgundy unthinkable.

There is a famous saying about this kingdom: "Ruined by a
woman, saved by a woman." The woman was not Joan but Yolande. I am talking about the mother of his wife Marie.

Yolande, by marriage Duchess of Anjou and Queen of the four
kingdoms—Sicily, Aragon, Cyprus, and Jerusalem—was the daughter of the King of Aragon, John I, and through her mother, Yolande de Bar, the great-granddaughter of John the Good: thus a
Valois. The death of Louis II in 1417 left her a widow with five
children, not yet of age, and the guardianship of an important but
dispersed domain: Maine and Anjou in the Loire country, Provence in the Rhône Valley, and Naples across the sea.

She had maintained her scattered domain from the Loire to
Africa, consolidated it, augmented it by the inheritance of Lorraine, when the events in the kingdom began to demand all her attention. Granddaughter, wife, and mother-in-law of Valois
princes, she was too close a relation to tolerate the idea of victory
by a Lancaster, who at that very moment was menacing her Angevin possessions. Until now she had limited herself to protecting
her territories and keeping her eye on the situation. But now everything was going too badly. Her son-in-law was so changed, the
court of Bourges a place of such disorder and the English so
strong that she made up her mind, used her daughter's confinement
as a pretext, and came to live at court.

This princess would play the role of a gray eminence there—
hard to notice, but very influential. Who else could have conceived
of the plan that was put into effect at Bourges as soon as she arrived there and was carried on until her departure—a plan that
made it possible to hold the invader in check for four more years?
Not the sick Dauphin, and even less so his entourage of thieves.

This policy was at once simple and ambitious, and it bore the
marks of intelligence and energy: bury the past and with it the Armagnacs, make peace and an alliance with Burgundy; at the same
time reconstruct around Charles the unanimity of the country—

which meant, rally the princes around him (it is known that the principal ones had made allegiance to Bedford) in order that, by a consensus of the entire kingdom, the English would be routed out of France, and the Dauphin re-established in his rights.

In one year the situation was reversed to the advantage of Charles. If Burgundy remained stubborn, Brittany payed homage and the high nobility returned to the Council.

For a moment, everything seemed transformed. The miserable court of Bourges, only yesterday the lair of bandit chiefs, filled up with knights and great lords, and assumed an almost royal style.

But all of these princes and soldiers had to be paid. No money, no troops, and above all, no princes. It had cost a pretty penny to bring about this unhoped-for festive atmosphere. From so much spending the prince had nothing left. The tradesmen refused to supply on credit. The most basic necessities were lacking.

And it all began again, pillaging, intrigues, crimes. It was the game of the plundered King, of the scorned King too.

Yolande had to admit the obvious: everything had been going from bad to worse for the prince ever since the return of the great feudal lords. Decidedly, the throne had never been able to count on those people. The Queen of Sicily left the court. The English redoubled their efforts, and while Burgundy pushed his advantage in Mâconnais, they laid siege to Orléans. Charles was adrift. Enclosed in his chapel, he wept and prayed for nights on end. Destiny was showing him: he was not the son of the King of France. His bastardy was certain. He would leave for Dauphiné, or even farther, for Castile, or Scotland.

It was then that God the Father spoke out in that desolate kingdom of France through the voice of a peasant maid.

THAT MAD GIRL POSSESSED BY THE DEVIL

He wants it known that it is neither by the sword, nor by the lance that he saves the people, and that he is the arbiter of the wars.

II Kings

Joan was a simple village girl, from Domrémy, on the borders of Lorraine and Barrois, of old rural stock, implanted in the Frankish earth. Her father was named Jacques d'Arc and her mother

Isabelle Romée because her family had made the journey to Rome.
They were farmers, then, honest and brave, not very rich, but with
a good reputation and a healthy look. Nothing but good was ever
heard of them.

Joan was gentle, hard-working, active. What she did, she did
well and with good will. She had lived until now the life of the
girls of her village—the same as Mengette, her neighbor, and as
her friend, little Hauviette—working at a very young age on the
farm, helping in the house as well as the fields, sewing and spin-
ning, attending to domestic chores, feeding the animals, going with
her father to plow, to harrow, or to reap, guarding the flock in the
communal pasture when her turn came—this was her life: a life of
labor marked by feast days, Christmas, Mardi Gras, and, for the
young people, the Sunday of *Laetare Jerusalem* or Fountain Sunday, as it is called. The young folks trooped off together to the
Fairy Tree; they brought garlands, rolls, wine, nuts; they drank at
the nearby springs, frolicked at their ease for a few hours. An in-
terlude in this time of sorrows.

The kingdom's trouble did not by-pass Domrémy. The village
was for the King. But the surrounding country sided with Burgundy. The village urchins came home bruised and scratched from
fighting for their loyalist opinions against those of Maxey, Burgundians. The people lived in anguish, under the constant threat of
the arrival of soldiers. Just recently they had fled to Neufchâteau
and had to wait there for two weeks, wherever and however they
could, before returning home.

Is this the reason why Joan prayed more than anyone else in
Domrémy? "You are much too devout, Jeannette," her friend
Mengette would say. And the others would make fun of her. Joan
herself was slightly ashamed not to feel that she was the same as
Hauviette and Colin, the son of Jean Colin, or as Simonin Maus-
nier, whom she had comforted when he was young and always
sick.

Joan was a pretty girl, solidly built, robust, with a good figure.
She had neither birth nor education and could not read or write.
Like Martha in the Bible, she tended the humble chores of the
body all day long, but the heavens were open to her. Saints and
angels visited her; they talked to her and she saw them. The things
she heard and contemplated enraptured and amazed her. How

could she tell Mengette or Hauviette? In whom could she confide? Not even her parish priest. She would be taken for a madwoman or one possessed by the Devil.

She was about thirteen years old. It was noon, in her father's garden in summer. Suddenly she heard someone speak to her. She looked but saw no one around. Suddenly to her right, toward the church, in the direction of the voice, a great brightness appeared. Fear gripped her. But the voice was repeated three times; it was a good voice, a worthy voice, speaking the French language. She understood that it was an angel. And from then on she waited and prayed.

Her first vision was of St. Michael. A heavenly host surrounded him. He brought her a message from God: two saints from heaven would visit her, St. Catherine and St. Margaret, who had received the order of our Lord to lead her and to counsel her. She must believe them and obey them. Joan made a very deep bow. Already he was leaving her, dazzled, gratified, in her hunger. She kissed the earth where he had stood. She cried. She would really have liked him to take her away with him.

St. Margaret and St. Catherine came in turn. They always took the same form. They wore gorgeous crowns, spoke well, with distinction, in beautiful soft voices. They told her to behave herself well and to go to church often; they heard her confession. Joan asked them to take her to paradise. Then the saints revealed to her that in order to go there she must accomplish the mission which God had assigned to her: drive the English out of France.

For five years they stayed with her. Sometimes it was an angel who spoke to her about the great sorrow of the kingdom. Often she saw St. Michael and his companions in the presence of Christians. She was the only one to see them. Joan lived for these encounters. "When I hear the voices," she said, "I am overjoyed and I marvel, and I would like to be in this state always." She fasted, went to confession, multiplied her good works. "You are too devout, Jeannette," said Mengette her friend. Too devout? If she only knew—Mengette did not suspect anything; neither she, nor Hauviette, nor Joan's family. But the father had dreams about his daughter which he remembered in the morning and which always upset him. He dreamed that she went off with soldiers. Joan a camp follower; he shuddered. "If I ever thought that what I dreamed about her would happen, I would like you to drown her; and if you would not, I would drown her myself." Because of this or something else, Joan's parents did not let her out of their sight.

However, she had to leave them. It was the year 1428. The English had laid siege to Orléans. Two, three times a week, the voice told her to come into France to deliver the good Duke's city. Joan could not sit still. And her father? He would know nothing. She was nothing but a poor girl who didn't know how to ride a horse or make war. "Go to Vaucouleurs," said the voice, "and find the captain of the place, Robert de Baudricourt. I will tell you how to recognize him, and he will give you the men who will go with you. Twice he will push you away but the third time you will get what you ask for." And Joan went.

She was a very young girl of eighteen. This was not a case of some kind of medium, rich in psychic gifts, who heard voices. She was, by special grace, tied to God, sent, a messenger chosen by the celestial forces to accomplish on earth a precise and urgent mission.

Mystical experiences are by nature ineffable. Those who live them conceal them. Joan conformed to the norm as long as it was a question of conversing with the voices. But now she had to act. Thus only when events constrained her did she speak, did she raise a corner of the veil. A hazardous enterprise, even in that century when people were quick to believe. Robert de Baudricourt began by answering that she should be given a spanking and taken back to her father's home, and he sent her away. She returned and argued her case. "The kingdom does not belong to the Dauphin but to my Lord, and my Lord wants the Dauphin to become King, and wants him to take command of the kingdom. In spite of his enemies the Dauphin will be made King anyway, and it is I, Joan, who will lead him to his coronation." "Who is your lord?" asked Robert. "The King of Heaven." The prudent Robert ordered an exorcism; she became indignant: "Don't you know that there is a prophecy which says that France will be lost by a woman and saved by a virgin of the marches of Lorraine?" But Baudricourt remained stubborn.

Joan was worried. She was staying in Vaucouleurs with some

acquaintances of her family, a couple named Le Royer. And as
she spun wool in the company of Catherine, her hostess, the fear
of not reaching her goal made her break out of her silence; she
revealed the reasons for her presence. Vaucouleurs was not a big
town. In less time than it took to tell, all of Vaucouleurs knew
about it. And they all ran to see her; they questioned her, they
approached her in the street. It was all the more a burning issue
since Vaucouleurs, like Domrémy, was a small loyalist island in
enemy territory, and since it had just heroically fought back an assault by Anglo-Burgundian raiders. Vaucouleurs didn't want to
become English. "My dear, what are you doing here?" inquired
Jean de Metz, a nobleman of the town. "Must the King be chased
from the kingdom, and must we become English?" "I have come
to this royal town," Joan answered, "to speak to Robert de Baudricourt, so that he will deign to take me or have me taken to the
King; but he pays no attention to me or my words; however, by
the middle of Lent, I must be before the King if I have to wear
my legs down to my knees to do it. No one in the world, neither
king, nor dukes, nor the King of Scotland's daughter or anyone
else can recover the kingdom of France. There is no help but
through me. Even so, I would much prefer to spin near my poor
mother, because this is not my place; but I must go and I must do
it, for that is my Lord's pleasure."

The inhabitants of Vaucouleurs did not hesitate. They saw and
they believed. This maiden must get to Chinon and all the way to
the Dauphin. They decided to help her. They chipped in to buy
her men's clothes and a horse. Baudricourt finally let himself be
convinced and gave his support. A small escort was formed, the
first believers—two gentlemen, Jean de Metz and Bertrand de Pou-
lency, their two servants, a royal messenger, and an archer.

On Sunday they assembled at the Porte de France ready to leave.
Baudricourt came to wish them a good trip. He gave his messenger credentials for the Dauphin, avowing that this woman came in
his name. He emphasized besides the difficulty of the journey undertaken, as much for the enemies who might be encountered as
for the rivers to be crossed. He was visibly moved at leaving Joan.
"Swear to me that you will take good care of her," he said to the
men. "Go, go, go, come what may," he cried as a farewell.

In the Name of God, she said,
Gentle King, I will lead you
To be crowned at Reims, whatever they may wish,
And the siege of Orléans I will lift.
    Martial d'Auvergne, *The Vigils of King Charles VII*

They were on the road for eleven days, sometimes by day, sometimes by night, across the war zone, through lands infested with Anglo-Burgundians. "Don't be afraid," said Joan, "my brothers in paradise tell me what I have to do." On February 23 they arrived in Chinon.

Everything is simple for those who are simple. There was no hesitation, no doubt, no fear in the spotless soul of Joan, who knew no evil. As soon as I arrive, I'll be received, she thought, coming from so far away, carrying such a message. She also took care to warn them of her arrival. From St. Catherine de Fierbois where she stopped, she wrote to the Dauphin to announce herself. But now the prince was making Joan wait. For how long? Every day King Charles V used to receive anyone who requested to see him, however humble. We are far from those times.

But what she didn't know, what her council didn't tell her, was that the actual master of the kingdom of Bourges wasn't the prince to whom Heaven had sent her but the favorite, Louis de la Trémoïlle. He had only one goal—to maintain things as they were. Every change that might intervene could turn out to his disadvantage. He decided therefore to act with circumspection toward every newcomer. The welfare of the kingdom mattered little to him.

"When you appear before the King, he will receive a good sign to let him know he should receive and believe you," the voices told her, "so go ahead boldly." In the shabby inn where she was staying, Joan began to pray.

For two days Charles hesitated. Who is she? What does she want? Who sends her? He assigned his clerks to find out information. She only wanted to speak to the King. They questioned her in the name of the King. In truth, they harassed her. So she agreed to state the reason for her trip: "I have two commissions from the King of Heaven: one, to lift the siege of Orléans, the other, to lead the noble Dauphin to Reims to be crowned."

There was much commotion. In the Council opinions clashed: This girl is tricking us, she's deluded, a madwoman. This whole story is nothing but foolishness. Let her go back from whence she came. She says, however, that she is sent by God, argued the others, including Gerard Machet, the King's confessor. Perhaps it would be advisable to see her and hear her out.

Charles, anchored in his passivity, remained silent. Every decision cost him. He wondered if he must see her, if he must encounter a new unknown face, this alarming girl. Anxiety gripped him just thinking about it. Charles was phobic, as we know. He had, however, half given in. Joan had already entered the castle. Her name had been on everyone's lips for the past two days. Dunois, who defended the city, sent to the court two of his lieutenants, the Lord of Villars and Jamet du Tillet, to find out what it was all about.

In the commotion the lords waited. Coarse warrior faces of tanned leather, athletic bodies pressed into leather vests, haughty faces, long robes and cassocks, the best names of the region, princes of the Church, among whom was the Archbishop of Reims, Regnault of Chartres. The Maid had entered the guard room. But Charles still hesitated. Night fell. The servants brought in torches. They projected dark masses onto the bright walls. What would the prince decide?

Now they told him about a letter which, until now, had been carefully kept from him, the one that the Vaucouleurs Captain Baudricourt had addressed to him. He recommended the girl. He wrote also of the dangers she would have to overcome in order to get to him. In the present circumstances her presence was a near miracle. Charles was moved by this proof of devotion on the part of an unknown girl. He gave in and let her be shown in. Was it for tactical reasons—to save himself an eventual way out—or was he playing a game—slightly cruel—with this peasant girl who dared to venture among these high lords and pushed audacity to the point of teaching them a lesson? He hid himself among his followers.

Joan, dressed all in black in her men's clothes—doublet, long hose, short plain gray robe, hood—appeared in the doorway. The freshness of her face and her eighteen years shone out against all that black—bright eyes, a fresh mouth, brown hair cut around, like a page's, a strong body. A presence. There was ease also in this shepherdess. No timidity.

Joan advanced through the crowd and made her way directly to the prince. She stopped before him at the length of a lance, took off her hood, and performed the customary salutations as well as if she had been raised at court.

"May God grant you a long life, gentle Dauphin."

"I am not the King," answered Charles. "There is the King," and he designated one of the lords next to him.

But Joan did not let herself be deluded:

"In God's name, gentle prince, you are he, and no one else."

And all in one breath, she delivered her message: "Most illustrious Lord Dauphin, I am called Joan the Maid. I have come, sent by God, to bring help to you and to the kingdom of France; and the King of Heaven commands through me that you be consecrated and crowned at Reims, and that you be the lieutenant of the King of Heaven, who is King of France."

Charles's expression changed. He took the young girl aside. She spoke to him, he listened, he asked questions. This went on for two hours. La Trémoïlle and Clermont wanted to come near, to listen, but he sent them back.

Her words astounded him. He asked her to explain, to say more, also to give some proof. He wanted so much to believe her. "Sire," asked Joan, "if I tell you things so secret that only God and yourself know them, would you really believe that I have been sent by God?"

"I will believe you, Joan," he promised.

"Sire, do you not recollect that last All Saints' Day, while you were in the castle of Loches, all alone in your chapel, you asked three things of God? . . . The first, that if you were not the true heir of the kingdom of France He would deign to take from you the courage to pursue it, so that you would not be the reason for sustaining the war from which so many evils befall the kingdom.

"The second, that if the great adversities and tribulations that the poor French people suffer and have suffered for so long originated from your sin and if you were the cause, that He would deign to relieve the people and to make only you be punished and carry the penance, either by death or by any other penalty that would please Him.

"The third was that, if the people's sin was the cause of their adversities, He would deign to pardon the people and to appease His anger, and to take the kingdom out of the tribulations in which it has been for eleven years."

"That is exactly right, Joan," pronounced Charles.

And Joan added solemnly: "I tell you on behalf of God that you are the true heir of France and the son of the King."

And Charles wept. His father had a name, a face. So he was the old, sick man in the Hôtel de St. Pol. Now he was attached, joined to the chain of men, a link inscribed in the security of a family line. Never again alone, a child without a master, a child without a name, who couldn't take after anyone. There were so many faces in which to recognize himself now. Blood of true blood, soul sprung from the manifold souls of the race, the pride of the name, he was Charles, son and grandson of Charles, who was himself the son of John and grandson of Philip, great-grandson of Charles, who was not King but the son of the King, and descended like himself from St. Louis.

Charles looked at the young girl. Hope itself stood before him. Joan the Maid—she was the end of doubt, his people brought together. The double monarchy crumbled, Lancaster no longer had any rights. The Treaty of Troyes was brought down to its true value: a low vengeance. The blood of France remained Valois. The struggle continued. Charles turned a face transfigured by joy toward the crowd of staring courtiers.

The Dauphin installed Joan in the castle under the surveillance of Captain Guillaume Billier in a tower in the third enclosure, named the Dungeon of Coudray, where at the time of the trial of the Knights Templars the High Master of the order, Jacques de Molay, and some of his companions had been imprisoned for a while. On the next day he saw her again at mass. After such long torments, hope could not be relearned in one night. Doubt again had taken over; again he questioned, opposed with arguments. Joan did not contradict herself: "Gentle Dauphin, why don't you believe me? I tell you that God has pity on you and on your people, for St. Louis and Charlemagne are on their knees before Him, praying for you."

Was it on that day that the mysterious episode of the sign intervened? At her trial of condemnation, Joan dated it in March or

April, at Chinon. Was she afraid that her words were not enough to triumph over the skepticism surrounding her? In her will to convince her judges, she revealed the other side of things, unveiled the miracles. At her call, Heaven came down to earth and appeared to humans. Did she receive the power to do this? That must be the case, for otherwise she condemned herself to eternal damnation. We will not try to describe what remained hidden but will give the stage to Joan and to her judges.

"The sign, what was it?" questioned the judge on March 13, during the third supplementary interrogation.

"The sign," answered Joan, "was that the angel certified to the King, by bringing him the crown, that he would have the entire kingdom of France with God's help and through my work; and that he must give me work, that is to say, he must round up warriors for me; for otherwise he would not be crowned or consecrated for a long time."

"How did the angel bring him the crown? Did he put it on the head of your King?"

"It was given to the Archbishop of Reims, I think, in the presence of the King. The Archbishop received it and gave it to the King. I was myself present. It has been put in the King's treasury."

"And in what place did the angel appear to you?"

"I was still praying when God sent the sign to the King. I was in my quarters, which were those of a good woman of the castle of Chinon, when he came; and then we went together to the King; he was accompanied by other angels, whom everyone did not see. If it hadn't been out of love for me, and in order to stop the suspicion of the people who were harassing me, I really think that several of those who saw the angel wouldn't have seen him. . . .

"When the angel came, I went up the stairs with him to the King's chamber. The angel entered first, and I said to the King, 'Sire, here is our sign, take it.' When he arrived before the King, he bowed before him . . . with this he reminded him of his great patience in the great tribulations that had happened to him."

"Did everyone with the King see the angel?"

"I think that the Archbishop of Reims, the Lords d'Alençon and de la Trémoïlle, and Charles de Bourbon saw him. As for the crown, several churchmen and others saw it, who didn't see the angel."

"Those who were with the angel, did they all look the same as he?"

"Some of them looked alike, but not others, according to what I saw; some had wings, some were crowned, others not; and in the group, there were Sts. Catherine and Margaret, who were with this angel, and the others also, all the way to the King's room."

But of the strange spectacle that has just unfolded before us, Joan was the only one to speak, as if she were the only one to have seen it. Why her contemporaries remained silent remains an enigma. Could anyone forget such an encounter? Doubtless such a revelation of the holy was less astounding five centuries ago than it would be today. Nonetheless, the silence of those who witnessed the scene, or, like the Dauphin, were the center of it, makes us queasy. Besides, Charles did not appear entirely convinced. A bit shaken up, benevolent, he still kept a cool head. In such an area, one can't be too careful. Also, his followers were there, and ever since the first day they had been working hard to undermine the shepherdess. The prince therefore tried to surround himself with every possible human guarantee in order to determine the nature of the mission with which Joan claimed she was invested. "Is she from God or the Devil?" To answer this, he needed the opinions of the clerks. As it happened, the fraction of the university who joined his cause had come to Poitiers and were in session there. He took Joan there as soon as possible. For three weeks theologians, doctors, inquisitors, harassed her with interrogations. At the same time, two monks were sent to Lorraine to inquire about the so-called Maiden. Finally, since no demonic work was compatible with virginity, matrons checked her state, which appeared to be virginal.

From all of these inquiries, it resulted that there was no evil in the Maiden but only "good, humility, virginity, devotion, honesty, simplicity." And Charles officially recognized the divine origin of her mission. In his Council he declared that, "considering the great goodness that is in this Maid, and what she had told him, that she was sent by God, and that from now on he would use her aid in his wars."

Joan had triumphed in the most delicate part of her task: to make the powerful and learned accept that her message was from

God. It remained to accomplish it. It took her one year. No more was allotted to her. "I will last one year, no longer," she said.

Therefore she hadn't a day to lose. On the twenty-second of March she sent to the English the famous letter:

"King of England, and you, Duke of Bedford, who call yourself the Regent of France, you, William Pole, Count of Suffert, John, Lord of Talbot, and you Thomas, Lord of Scales, who call yourselves lieutenants of the Duke of Bedford, do justice to the King of Heaven. Return the keys of all the cities you have seized and violated in France to the Maid. She has been sent here in God's behalf to establish the royal blood. She is completely ready to make peace, if you wish to do her justice, on the condition that you render up France, and pay for having kept her. And among you, archers, companions of war, men of arms and others who are before the city of Orléans, go back to your country, in God's name; King of England, if you do not do this, I am the war chief, and in whatever place that I find your men in France, I will chase them away, whether it is their wish or not. And if they don't wish to obey, I will kill them all; I am sent by God, body for body, to rout you all from out of France. . . . And think not otherwise, for you will never hold the kingdom of France from God, the King of Heaven, Son of Mary, but Charles, the true heir, will keep it, for God wills this, and this has been revealed to him by the Maid. . . . And make answer if you wish to make peace in the city of Orléans."

From Poitiers, Joan returned to Chinon. She did not stay there. Charles sent her to Tours, built her a military force, and gave her the rank of captain. Now, by the prince's will, she was ready to enter into legend—with her shining armor, her sword found in the Church of St. Catherine de Fierbois in the place indicated by her voices, her white standard with silk fringes on which she had painted at her saints' command the image of our Lord sitting in judgment in the clouds of heaven, and an angel holding in his hands a lily which God was blessing.

"Daughter of God, go, go, go. I will be your aide, go," said the voice, and Joan went.

On the tenth of May 1429, Orléans was delivered. The Loire was swept clean—Jargeau, Meung, Beaugency: on the twelfth, fifteenth, sixteenth of June—on the eighteenth of June, the victory of Patay: two thousand English killed, Talbot taken prisoner, Falstaff in flight; on our side, two dead. The English garrisons in the Beauce country fell back on Paris. On the twenty-ninth the Dauphin, preceded by an enthusiastic army, took the road to Reims, in the middle of the country loyal to Burgundy. Auxerre closed its gates, but on the twelfth Chalons gave up its keys to Charles, on the sixteenth at the castle of Sept-Saulx the notables of Reims offered him "full and complete obedience as to their sovereign." That same night he slept in the city; on the seventeenth he received in the cathedral of his forefathers the royal anointments while Joan, sobbing, clutched his knees. "Gentle King," she cried through her tears, "today God's wish that I should raise the siege of Orléans and lead you to this city of Reims to receive your holy coronation has been realized, showing that you are the true King and he to whom the kingdom should belong."

The two orders that Joan said she had received from the King of Heaven had now been carried out.

But the offensive on Paris failed on the eighth of September, the coronation army was dissolved at Gien on the twenty-first day of the same month. La Trémoïlle regained his power. The King fell back into a torpor and would not leave Berry. He no longer listened to the Maid. The charm was broken. The voices, in their turn, ceased, or at least their counsel became less decisive. Had her mission ended? She persevered, however, and left to fight alone. In May of 1430 she joined her good friends at Compiègne, under siege by the Burgundians. On the twenty-third, during an excursion, she was taken prisoner and in December sold to the English for John of Luxemburg for ten thousand pounds and a pension for the bastard of Wandonne.

Charles, King of France through Joan's work, had become once more the King of Bourges. Everything Charles VII owed to Joan—the denial of his bastardy, the confirmation of his royalty, the coronation, the enemy in flight, this happy, recent past—he turned away from. He would pay for it dearly and for a long time.

Charles had forgotten the robust young girl who, one March night, approached him with a firm step in the great hall at Chinon. He had forgotten that gentleness, the candid look, the lively voice: "I tell you on behalf of the Lord."

She was certitude itself, for him who always doubted; determination, boldness, for him who had so little, always hesitating, slow to act. She was courage for him, who was nothing but fear; hope, for him who lacked it; confidence, all that his sick soul lacked, Joan brought him. How was it that he was not cured by her presence? But he assented to her departure for La Charité. Left afterward out of action, she went to help at Compiègne. And now she was in prison.

Absence is the worst of evils for the anxious, a type of abandonment, a frustration in any case. Joan had disappeared from his reality; now she was nothing but an image, abandoned, without help, to the destructive forces of his being. Reproaches and grievances arose and took form, above all when a jealous following set themselves to tear down the absentee at the slightest occasion. And the King abandoned her, as he had been abandoned before. Once more depressed, tired, returning to his old demons, his eye lifeless and his expression sad, Charles left Joan to the English.

The Maid, having worked, having suffered, had accomplished her destiny. She took her place among the heavenly hosts. Her terrestrial mission accomplished? It didn't seem to be at all the case in the sad years that followed Rouen. And yet everything was changed. God had settled the debate by means of Joan. He had declared himself for Valois against Lancaster, for Charles VII against Henry VI, and by so doing had gone back through the course of time to the year 1328, when it all had begun, for Philip against Edward. Also the problems raised by bastardy appeared, with the passing of time, to be of less consequence than those posed earlier about the validity of the rights of a nephew of the male side compared to those of a grandson on the female side. The lawyers and soldiers who had worked upon it for a hundred years had not succeeded in settling this point of litigation. Heaven was needed to rescue the subjects of this prince from the mire of impossible choices. The blood of France was authentically Valois, the Lancasters had no right to the fleur-de-lis—such was the ruling of the stake at Rouen.

So, by clear logic, since a master was needed for this people, and even for the great vassals, all of them French at last for the first time, united in their hearts around a chief who would be great, they cried all at once: Go back from whence you came,

English, Godons,* cruel and hated oppressors, the affair has lasted far too long. To the quarrel of kings now in its hundredth year had been added the bloody quarrel of the princes. The quarrel of fathers, worn to a frazzle, but whose sons could not finish with it.

In the face of the offender—empty cash-boxes, "the kingdom at its lowest"—the son of the offended rose up at the height of his power. Philip the Good, also called the Magnificent, had pursued the task undertaken by the Fearless. He finished the edification of the veritable nation-state that he had put together over the past fifteen years—the Burgundian state—by adding to it considerable territories outside of the kingdom. The opportunity was granted him by the impossible situation his overlord was caught in during those years. In 1433 the goal was reached. He was now the Count and Duke of Burgundy, Duke of Lotharingia, of Brabant, and of Limburg, Count of Flanders, of Artois, of Hainaut, of Holland, of Zeeland and of Namur, Marquis of the Holy Empire, Lord of Frise, of Salins, and of Malines. Both his glory and his self-interest made him magnanimous today, consenting to this peace, which for sixteen years his cousin of France had been begging of him as a favor, and now as a pardon, on bended knee. Peace today necessary for the conservation of his work, in the same way that war was yesterday. He had always held the key in his hand.

He granted it at Arras, on the twenty-first of September 1435, at the majestic and superb assizes that brought together the Christian West. More of a king than the crowned King, more Valois than all the Valois up to that day—at one and the same time he could thank Charles, the ancestor, for his military talents, Philip IV for those of feasting and piety, John the Good for vigor, fine presence, and the chivalric ideal in the name of which he created the Order of the Golden Fleece, Charles V for good government and culture, Berry for luxury and the taste for fine things, and his grandfather, of course, from whom he inherited his name, who had already embodied a good number of these qualities, which he was able to bring to their height. Not to forget the hereditary enemy, his late cousin Louis, formerly Duke of Orléans, for escapades—Philip would have seventeen official bastards by his thirty mistresses. And at last he threw the veil of pardon and ob-

* Nickname given to the English during the Hundred Years' War.

livion over the past. Did this gesture, magnanimous and triumphant, point to the end of the great sorrow of the kingdom of
France?

Those who attended the ceremony in the abbey of St. Vaast
d'Arras accepted it as an omen. It would take Charles more or
less a quarter of a century to succeed in putting an end to it.

CHAPTER VIII

Charles VII the Victorious
(*Born 1403; reigned 1422–61*)

Do not be afraid, I will not knuckle under . . . , I will give them orders. . . . I will remain alone. . . . There is this war to wage, and
I will wage it.

J.-P. Sartre, *The Devil and the Good Lord*

SINCE I MUST

Closely shaven by a careful barber, without a hair, his eyes narrow, his look marked with reserve, reproach, and a wistful air, he
held himself stiffly. Meeting his dark glance, one felt ill at ease.
You who stare at me, it seemed to say, if you only knew what I
have endured, if you knew what has befallen me—you who have
only yourself to answer for. There is neither presence, nor radi-
ance, nor charm in this painting of the man whose name has been
inscribed on the frame in gold leaf, but instead something obstinate. The very victorious King of France, Charles, the seventh of
this name, was a man to be reckoned with.

Clearly, he did not like posing. He little relished having to
remain still for the desired time, as painter Jean Fouquet respectfully asked him to. His old sad demons assailed him. His difficulty
in being himself shows again in his lips. The King did not open

himself. He held himself on the defensive where he put himself reluctantly. A certain lassitude left its mark in the circles of his eyes,
it can be seen in the wrinkles of the smile and in all of the features, which droop. Within this triangular face, only the mouth—
wide, thick, which the chin underlines with a transversal—remains
in place. It is the sign of the life that the forehead hides from us. It
says that this life is intact, powerful, in the nocturnal sources of
being which alone attach the prince to the world, maintain him
there and reconcile him with the Creation, if not with himself. All
the rest of this portrait is camouflage, the work of the tailor and
the hatter, the painter's bread and butter. The costume is part of
the art and politics—arranging, make-up, elaboration, transfigura-
tion. But when Fouquet took on the man, he did not cheat. He
showed him to us in his truth, naked. Charles VII, the very victorious King of France, was above all this face inserted among these
costly materials. Let us leave the heavy, bulky robe and the hat,
marvelous we must admit, and let us keep only what refers to
Charles. Let us carefully cut out this face with little scissors, not
forgetting the neck or the ears, and let us slip it into our album
with the family photographs. It is the only impartial testimony
about the King which time has left us.

For the man is hidden behind this sullen look, behind his
weaknesses, his infatuations, his inexplicable surrenders, his un-
explained changes. He is hidden behind his detractors, for posterity has not shown itself tender. He had after his death—beginning
with the sixteenth century and for reasons which have remained
mysterious—a good number of biographers. They bore him, in
spite of the concern for honest information which should have
guided their pens, a genuine grudge. They painted him black,
without the least sense of nuance—this man, full of half shades
which are ill suited for brutal lighting, this being which was com-
plex and incomprehensible. Psychiatry gives us certain clues with
its depressive and phobic neuroses, but it cannot explain to us
how, in times when neither psychotherapy nor cures existed, the
salutary transformation which chroniclers report to us as beginning in 1439 could have occurred.

Little by little the King came out of his torpor. Anguish and fatigue delivered him from their destructive influences. Returned to
himself, his faculties intact, his energies freed, he finally had ac-

cess to reality. The hex was broken. He dared, he acted, he ordered, he fought. Doubtless events came to seek him out, to look for him deep in his castles, to compel him even in his bedroom. Urgency took him by the throat. But now, he faced it, he came to grips with it. A sleep, a sickness, which lasted twenty years, and from which, without any apparent reason, he escaped. Why? How did life make itself suddenly less burdensome, the air lighter, the difficulties endurable, other people less overwhelming? How did he escape from the heavy necessity, which he himself created without being conscious of it, to trust anyone but himself? How was he once again able to believe in the soundness of what he felt and thought, to move into himself, find his peace, accept himself, love himself, and thus be able in his turn to love? No more doubt, no more refusal. New eyes, new strength, a new heart, and the gifts that he had received in the cradle once more a part of him. Charles became another man. The mysterious changes which would permit the prince to realize himself had occurred. By what means? That is without a doubt the biggest mystery of the life of Charles VII.

This return to activity did not mean a real change, but stabilization, progress. A slow maturation had occurred in which he had help. Joan and the peace of Arras permitted him to heal the wounds of the murder of Montereau and of the Treaty of Troyes. The unctions of the coronation consolidated the improvement which occurred. But it required ten years for him, marked as he was by a past that was too heavy, to be capable of assuming the formidable responsibilities of kingship.

Now Charles left his castles to make war, on horseback at the head of his troops, laid siege to rebellious fortresses, crossed the moats of cities, and led his soldiers to the assault. But still the fears remained. "Nowhere sure, nowhere strong, and able to be watched by no one," the chronicler Chastellain said of him. His fears haunted him still, ready to reappear at the first sign of weakness. Although he relegated them to the background, they did not disappear.

As for his relations with others, they were never normal, but remained a function of his attitude toward himself. His old sad demons, the throbbing need for reassurance and for love, self-doubt, and doubt of others were still there. The whole problem of the King came from a lack of love. This strikes to the heart of the question.

The chronicler wrote: "He maintained three major vices: insta-bility, distrust, and, the worst of them all, envy of others." As long as Charles mistrusted what he felt and thought, he could feel for others only mistrust and envy. It is true that he lived in a jungle where you could scarcely permit yourself relaxation, confidence, and friendship toward your neighbor without risk, but nonetheless his mistrust became so profound that it crippled him emotionally.

He felt he had accounts to settle with humanity. People had mocked him, deceived him. He had been weak and naïve, allowed himself to be used and abused.

He was a practical empiricist. From now on, he would use other people. He would no longer give his favors except to extract some advantage in return. And even then, only after it had been begged for on bended knee. And he would never accord it except in the name of the common good.

In his heart of hearts, the King had not changed. He was still dragging his childhood around with him. He was too structured in his neuroses to see them disappear as if by a charm. Remission is a more accurate word than "cure," since for the long term Charles resolved nothing. But everything became possible. He was build-ing on sand, but building nonetheless. Once again he was able to live.

And he took the plunge. The step had been taken, the step for-ward, the decisive step, from *No* to *Yes,* from refusal to accept-ance, from nothingness to positive action. Not real reconciliation with himself and with the world. Not that great, salutary definitive upheaval of the soul. Not love. Not the gift. But a hopeful step.

It was thus that King Charles threw himself into action—eyes blindfolded, forgetting what had once seemed to him indis-pensable. He fled into duty and work.

But still went on believing, like his great-grandfather John, that the King of France could live for himself alone. He did not under-stand that a sovereign does not belong to himself and that he has no choice but to sacrifice himself and to place himself in the serv-ice of the kingdom. Nor did he understand that, when you gave, you gave all, like Joan, and never grudgingly or by halves. For him to save his sick soul, he would have had to offer his life to God and to his country, to consecrate his works, to transcend them through a gift, a total gift. That would have been the only means to bring into his life that Absolute whose absence left him inconsolable. And even though he turned away from these fantasies, put a bridle on Pegasus, prepared to accomplish fruitful and necessary works for other people (whom he still did not love, any more than he loved himself) and acted like a very great king—he remained, at the source of his being, in danger.

FIFTEEN YEARS, NO MORE

In 1439, at the age of thirty-six, Charles had satisfactory health, insofar as it neither restrained nor inconvenienced him. He also had a sweet, unobtrusive, proper wife, Marie, who in contrast to her late mother-in-law, Isabella of Bavaria, held the advantages of respectability and a most authentic virtue. Queen Marie seldom did anything to call attention to herself. Still, she played her part in this inexplicable remission of Charles's illness. Hers was a role which no one spoke of but which can be inferred from the frequent mention of her presence at the side of her husband during those terrible years, even to the point of neglecting completely her first-born, Louis. Later she would prove to be an extremely attentive mother. What we know about her in other respects confirms that she had a hand in the prince's mysterious transformation.

She was not a brilliant woman. She did not intervene in political life. She is said to have had no influence at all. But she gave him something which no one at that time was able to give him: a peaceful heart in exchange for the divided one he had before. She neither demanded nor reproached; she did not judge him but simply honored him. In such a presence, he slowly recuperated. Did he ever appreciate what he owed her? Did he forget her? Ultimately he was bored with her, and their union became nothing more than a long-standing habit.

This King, in the prime of life, manifested little vitality, few needs, and no excesses. He rose early, ate little, did not drink, was content with two meals a day. He did not do much exercise, except for shooting the crossbow, at which he excelled. Silent, taciturn, he liked peace and quiet, games and tranquil pastimes, chess, studies, religious observances, the silence of his study, and his chapel and the pleasure he received when the musicians of his chapter played and sang in the evening stillness.

He also enjoyed the society of a small, well-chosen circle composed of a few faithful and reliable men he had known for a long time, and of those who were good at reassuring him about a body which might betray him and against stars which might control him. His physicians and astrologers never left his side—Pierre Beschebien, Miles de Brégy, and later Adam Fumée and the renowned Simon de Phares. By the end of his reign, their names were legion.

He did not like Paris, although on November 12, 1437, he made a triumphant entry. He did not linger there despite a delirious reception. He returned as soon as he could to the regions of the Loire and the Centre: Amboise, Loches, St. Aignan, Tours, Blois, Bourges, and rarely left them, although he moved from one to another of his residences incessantly.

With prudence and a few precautions, the King had arranged for himself, against the fury and the assaults of the century, a padded world where he regained his equilibrium and recuperated. It was with this life style that he had to come to terms in order to become King. It was essential for him to set about his work, to apply himself to it and to stick to it.

To be sure, Charles had all the qualities necessary to ensure a great reign: intellectual vigor, a fine political mind, sound judgment; "very wise in council," said his contemporaries, who repeatedly emphasized his "great good sense," explaining moreover that he was a man of character. He had some talents according to the chroniclers: "a fresh and lively memory," the eloquence of the Luxemburg line, "fine speech that is very pleasing and subtle," an impressive education, "great historian, good latinist," along with a taste for intellectual matters. In more propitious times he could have proven as brilliant a patron of the arts as any other member of his family. Such factors, at least, speak for his consanguinity with Charles V.

· He learned to exercise power the hard way, by experience. He was always closely watched. Always on the lookout. He realized he must be strong and that he must be obeyed. He proved all the more jealous of his authority, because he remembered what it was like not to have any. He was not an impulsive man but, rather, one who carried things through. He mastered at his own expense the rules of this game of power.

Now he understood that the authority he was so jealous of was based on information, precise knowledge. He therefore played the card of personal effort. There was no mystery to it. Apart from hard labor there was no certainty. Now he showed "diligence and a fitting solicitude for his affairs." Now, before counting on anyone else, he relied on himself. And he set himself to work. Diligence, regularity, orderliness, strict schedules, sustained activity; the King took his kingdom in his hands, or at least what was left of it. Indeed, he never stopped. King Charles's "marvelous industry" was noted by the Burgundian chronicler, Chastellain, who was scarcely to be suspected of any fondness for the sovereign. What higher praise than this?

This "industry" is no myth. The King divided his time between sessions with the Council of State and the audiences in which he received certain of his subjects for the purpose of obtaining firsthand information. Among the members of the Council were the princes of the blood, Orléans or Anjou, whoever was in favor, and we know that from 1445 Dunois played an increasingly important role, as did some lords of lower degree, such as Foix, Harcourt, Estouteville, Bertrand de Beauvau (an old servant), and several bourgeois whose names will go down in history: Guillaume Juvénal des Ursins, Jean Bureau, Jacques Coeur, Étienne Chevalier.

The King devoted Monday, Tuesday, and Thursday to judicial affairs, in the presence of the chancellor and of his Council. Wednesday was reserved for studies of war and finances, with the High Constable, the marshals, the captains, and the treasurers. Friday and Saturday were for finances also; Charles was quite good at them. In parallel with these sessions he held hour-long private interviews, by category, with all sorts of people: clerics, noblemen, foreigners, even artisans. He devoted his full attention to the makers of cannon, armor, and projectile weapons, for their advice was precious to him at a time when he had a kingdom to win back and when the techniques of war were changing. This explains his insistence upon firsthand information. To learn what was happening, he relied on no one but himself. The same went for giving orders. He kept the outgoing correspondence under constant surveillance, studied it personally, read it word for word, signed it in his own hand, and did not surrender to anyone else the responsibility for affixing his seal. This was a far cry from the era when his dear Louvet had unlimited access to it. He listened, asked questions, supervised. "He had his eye on everything."

As for the men who had humiliated him so, he found it advisable to utilize them according to their competence and to demand the maximum.

No one knew better than Charles how to define men in terms of usefulness—What is he worth? How can I use him?—to detect talents, to weigh their merits exactly. The King was a good judge of men. His contemporaries knew this. And as Chastellain says in his delectable prose, "He became so adept that he drew to himself the most excellent men, and availed himself of each one according to his vocation, one in war, one in finances, another in the Council, others in the artillery or in various undertakings and productive holdings; and he gave to each authority in the area of his competence so as to enable them to become the tools he needed to hammer and forge in the edification of his glory."

Thus Charles set out to reign, and in this way the King of Bourges would become again the King of France. He kept his courtiers in a state of perpetual competition, in a contest for his favor, which he doled out in shrewd doses, holding it up as a bright prospect to be coveted, granting it "just long enough for it to extract from the man whatever was in him," only to take it back and bestow it upon the next one. That was his way of keeping men under control.

And the "curials" scurried and danced attendance, imagining themselves indispensable, hatching intrigues and entangling themselves in quarrels such as no one had ever seen at the court of a French king. Truly, they surpassed themselves. And the poet who captured them in action sharpened his pen on the spectacle they presented at court.

> He who cannot hide his thoughts,
> Who cannot bray cajolingly,
> Who knows not how to flatter lords
> And has not learned hypocrisy
> Or when to turn a deafened ear
> Has little business being here.

The King was not duped by these pretenses; he made use of them when necessary. He was the most subtle player of all, and it was he, by these methods, who would win the game. So he "brought law and order to his kingdom" and "accomplished so much that all gave way before him."

Fifteen years sufficed for him to achieve this success—for Charles the Well Served to become Charles the Victorious. Fifteen years with limited means at his disposal, during which he had to fight for every inch of ground against considerable problems. He met each difficulty patiently, one after the other, knowing exactly what he wanted and how to command and compromise so as to arrive at a solution for each. But there were evenings, no doubt, when this man must have despaired of ever being able to put an end to all the anarchy and misery: greedy, perfidious feudal lords, slippery as eels, hands perpetually outstretched, always ready to switch to the opposing party; a land where no one could travel any more; the roads full of potholes, the rivers clogged with mud, unfit for any traffic, fords where one was fleeced before crossing; wolves that come into the village streets in search of food; starving subjects in rags; at every moment new reports of migrations toward what were hoped would be milder climes—Brittany, Spain, the banks of the Rhine. Rouen's population had shrunk from fifteen to six thousand souls; Avallon, which numbered sixteen solvent households and thirty-six poor ones, shrank to five solvent, thirty-six poor, and eleven destitute. Toulouse had lost half of its population. Lyon went over to the Empire. There were five inhabitants left in Limoges. The northern parts of Poitou and Angoumois were deserted, Quercy was abandoned. Charles must have been saturated with reports like these, brought to him day after day, and to which he could only offer again and again, to save face, the same reply, an admission of helplessness: "I shall take note of it."

The naked truth is not pretty, but he had to see it; King Charles had to hear it, endure it, and change it. One grows accustomed to such spectacles, one becomes inured and adapts. But one has to get up in the morning and not deceive oneself as to the proper application of remedies.

In this unending battle to transmute hunger into abundance, anarchy into order and labor, war into peace, a land bled white into a country where men could start a new life, you had to be a pretty good alchemist. The King poured all of his virtues into the task: tenacity, courage, realism, ingenuity, moderation, doling out his favor and his anger judiciously and using that great good sense of which the chroniclers speak.

The kingdom of France was a threadbare fabric, so worn out that it crumbled when touched. No sooner was a hole patched than one appeared somewhere else. Nonetheless, the attentive master painstakingly continued to fit the scraps together.

In 1435 the English occupied the north of the Loire and Paris, with all of their dynastic claims intact. Bands of hardened mercenaries swept across the land like locusts in a grain field. The populace called them by the eloquent name of "Écorcheurs" (Skinners), because they stripped whoever fell into their hands down to his shirt. They were old acquaintances from the preceding century, when they were known as Free Companies, "seeking food and adventure for sustenance and for gain, neither recognizing nor sparing the lands of the King of France, of the Duke of Burgundy nor of other princes in the kingdom." They had just formed themselves into a society and with a remarkable sense of efficiency and justice divided the country into a certain number of conscriptions —so many sectors that they had apportioned among themselves to pillage. Bastards of noble stock, quite numerous in these troubled times, occupied advantageous positions among them: the two Bourbon bastards, and the bastard of Armagnac, who were joined by illustrious captains, like Antoine de Chabannes, by companions of Joan of Arc, La Hire and Poton de Xaintrailles, and finally by the formidable Rodrigue de Villandrando. It was the golden age of banditry. The Englishman Talbot is said to have exclaimed: "If God came down from Heaven, he would become a plunderer."

It would take ten years to get rid of them. The King led the majority of them out of France, just as Du Guesclin had done with the mercenaries of the fourteenth century, and he integrated the rest into a renovated army.

If the noble bastards had been the only ones upholding anarchy, Charles would have come off relatively unscathed. But the legitimate heirs themselves were not about to leave him in peace either. For years and years the great feudal lords had been thriving on his weakness. His overcoming it was not something that they resigned themselves to willingly. Conspiracies, coteries, intrigues, there was no end to the rebellion, which had two superb men as its guiding spirits: Duke Charles of Bourbon and John of Alençon, Joan of Arc's "handsome Duke." Others rallied to their cause, to various ends, always at the expense of the King: now the Duke of Brittany, John V, now the Duke of Armagnac, John IV, and King René of Anjou (1437), now the Lord of Trémoïlle and Dunois himself (1438), then the Duke of Burgundy and the Duke of Orléans two years later. Doubtless the worst was the uprising of 1440 known by the name of the Praguerie because of the goal that it set for itself: to take the government away from Charles VII and to transfer authority to his son Louis, ruling as Regent. Louis was himself a member of the conspiracy. It failed. Charles was able to show his force at an opportune moment and to purchase allegiances—at a very high price. In these circumstances, the houses of Orléans, Anjou, and Brittany came over in 1442; those of the Midi, Foix, and Albret understood that it was in their own interest to make peace with the *"rey franses"* (the French king). Bourbon knuckled under. Relations with Burgundy continued to be strained and at the end of the reign had declined to such an extent that the houses just missed coming to blows. Indeed these relations bore a closer resemblance to those which customarily arose between two sovereign states than to those which governed suzerain and vassal.

As for those who didn't come around, Charles treated them with the utmost severity. The moral order of the kingdom was at stake. Scandals and treason were rife, and it was essential in these unfortunate times to stanch this tide of spiritual dissolution.

It appeared the Devil was honored in the same right as God the Father. Men were so power-hungry and avaricious, they turned to the Father of Lies, the Tempter, the Prince of This World, Legion. "I am your heaven; there is no other hope," said the fallen angel. People left the Church in droves and delivered themselves up to occult practices issuing from the depths of the ages; they flocked to the witches' sabbath. Worse still, a great lord perpetrated human sacrifices: Gilles de Rais, the dean of the barons of Brittany, a valorous warrior, an old companion of Joan of Arc, a marshal of France at the age of twenty-five, also known as "Bluebeard." He had his men abduct children of both sexes and bring them to his castles, Tiffauges, Machecoul, and Champtocé, where he abused them in the course of bloody orgies before immolating them on Satan's altar. He was burned.

John V, Count of Armagnac, lived with his sister Isabelle as a concubine; she bore him three children. He married her. Not content with violating taboos, he decided to be independent and conspired with the English. He was banished from the kingdom, and his estates were incorporated into crown lands.

As for the "handsome Duke," John of Alençon, he planned an attempt on the life of his sovereign and procured a powder intended to leave him "completely dried out." He assembled a formidable artillery and took preliminary steps toward an invasion of France by calling upon the English, who had been driven out scarcely three years previously (in 1453), for help. Although of the blood of France, he was condemned to death, and the duchy of Alençon was annexed. The King, however, postponed the execution "until such time as he pleased," and imprisoned him at Loches. The Dauphin Louis, his godson, granted him his freedom when he became King.

Black bread, hard bread—there was no end to this fare, not very appetizing, but such was a monarch's daily fare in feudal times. The glory of our monarch lies elsewhere. Was there any king, any Valois king, with a more prestigious record than that of this reign? Through Charles's decisive actions the English were driven out of France, the Hundred Years' War was ended, the menace which hung over his dynasty and his lands was eliminated and the way was now clear to re-establish the kingdom's prosperity upon new foundations. Who could top that? Not Philip VI, who ushered in the conflict, not John the Good, who was captured on his own territory by an outnumbered enemy, not even the great Charles V, but this man whom an English dramatist of the 1930s irreverently nicknamed "Charlie, the bastard," the King of Bourges, now became the first king of Europe.

To be sure, a combination of circumstances was in his favor: Henry VI was challenged in his own country, the War of the Roses was imminent, the people of occupied Normandy had begun an underground battle. But would that have sufficed if Charles had not turned to the best account the truce secured at Tours in 1444 and stretched it out for five years while organizing

a completely modern army? An army principally made up of horsemen, but one in which the problem of armaments has been carefully re-examined with regard to a century of defeats, and also in
light of recent evidence: to win battles, courage alone and skill
with arms were no longer enough; war was not a tournament. And
so the King, trusting more what he had learned from experience
than in an accumulation of traditions—a surprisingly bold attitude
in these scholastic times when the authority of the ancients prevailed over what you saw with your own eyes or proved by your
own reflection—the King concentrated on what was then the latest
novelty in the art of war: firearms.

He was wise enough to delegate the responsibility of intro-
ducing this new weapon to some remarkable organizers who were
at the same time metal founders, engineers, and captains, the
brothers Bureau: Jean, appointed in 1437, was well informed
about artillery, and Gaspard, who succeeded Pierre Bessonneau
in the office of great master in 1444. The arms race began. Great
bombards and culverins, and other breech-loading guns of smaller
caliber—veuglaires, serpentines, crapaudeaux, and ribaudigues—
piled up in the arsenals "in such great number as had never in the
memory of man been seen to belong to a Christian king." The old
catapults were put aside and replaced at the tops of towers and on
the city ramparts by cannons and by small bombards made out of
copper and iron and mounted on gun carriages. Nothing was over-
looked in this campaign to maximize the effectiveness of what was
coming to be the finest artillery in Europe. Foreign inventors were
called in, Genoese, German Jews, whose knowledge helped to im-
prove all of this war matériel even more and, most importantly,
solved the problems of transporting it in the field, and so made it
an instrument capable of reconquering France.

Finally, this spearhead weapon was complemented by a reor-
ganization of the army: regular monthly pay lessened the tempta-
tion to live off the land, and strict discipline was enforced. Plundering and extortion were actually punished by death.

Charles VII was now in possession of an invincible army. From
now on, when confronted with his bombards and culverins, what
good were all the swift bowmen of England, who were so quick to
shoot from behind the palisades of stakes they planted before
them? A new leaf had been turned.

The results were stupendous: one year to reconquer Normandy. And this eloquent bulletin of victory in the Battle of Formigny, which concluded the campaign: four thousand dead and twelve hundred prisoners among the English, as opposed to insignificant losses on the French side.

As for Guienne, in spite of its loyalty to the princes from across the Channel, who ruled the province for almost three centuries, she could not, whatever she might have thought, resist for very long. The cannons of Jean Bureau were responsible for the massacre at Castillon in 1453, in which old Talbot, who hurried to the aid of the city despite his eighty-one years, perished.

THE ENGLISH ARE DRIVEN OUT OF FRANCE

Victory, then. The match had been won. A grueling contest, but over now. This war, which had lasted more than a hundred years, became an old story, like the plague or the Crusades.

In 1453, at the western end of Europe, we find the conclusion of the century-old conflict. At the other end a thousand-year-old civilization was sinking under the wave of barbarians. The Turks had sacked Constantinople: the Greek world was crumbling. But at the heart of the old continent, at Nuremberg in the land of Germany, there was the promise that another civilization would carry the torch further: Johann Gutenberg, knight, "a man adroit in cutting characters on stamps, had brought to light the invention of printing by means of stamps and characters." Meanwhile the survivors of the massacres in the Orient had fled to the West, to Venice. Among their belongings were remnants of a learning which was wisdom itself. These were enough to shake the foundations of medieval occidental thought, and they would force it to cast off the old man and to attempt, like the phoenix, a rebirth from its own ashes.

Back in France, who perceived that such changes were in progress? Perhaps the prince, who was always on the watch, continually in search of innovations which could be of use to him and which, who knew, might change life, change this all too familiar world that had not stirred in centuries, which shackled him with irrefutable truths and age-old violence; a closed, static, monotonous world, all things considered, suffocating with boredom. In

1458 he secretly sent one of his men, Nicolas Jenson, over the Rhine with orders to make inquiries, or if possible to bring such a treasure back to France. (Nicolas, however, was a traitor and left France for Venice, where he set up a print shop and did splendidly.)

Did he already sense that he was leaving the universe of St. Thomas behind and setting out toward the Gutenberg galaxy?

AGNÈS

> All the walls are red.
> Not one word stirs. . . .
>
> > Aragon

Was it because he thought that he had reached the end of an era, that he was once more overcome by distress, that he rediscovered his fears and was overtaken by them again? Agnès had been dead for eight years now, that woman whom he had loved passionately. Ever since then he had been looking for her in the others they brought him and on whom he grew dependent. Opinion was shocked; he took no notice. No more than he had before when he took Agnès as his mistress and publicly flaunted her.

For Charles loved Agnès more than he could ever love himself, in a way that few are able to love. Maybe it was because she happened to be there when he needed her, in the year 1443, when he had been battling incessantly for four years, in a relentless situation where nothing was pardoned or forgotten, where everyone acted with an eye to personal gain and generosity was unheard of. And he needed to pause and take a deep breath; he needed someone to show him that the world was beautiful.

The gray days were growing longer, their skies gloomy with familiar obligations, when, in the month of February 1443, the prince, passing through Toulouse with the Queen, received a visit from his brother-in-law, King René, accompanied by his wife, Isabelle of Lorraine. Warm, friendly, lavish, the Anjous carried all the signs of luxury and good breeding along with them. The Queen of Sicily came to bow before the sovereigns, followed by her suite of ladies and maids of honor. The King affably bade the princess rise, embraced her, then beheld the pleasing assembly which was presented for his admiration. His eyes came to rest upon a person of great beauty. He inquired. They told him that her name was Agnès Sorel and that she was the daughter of John, Lord of Coudun, near Compiègne in Valois.

The King looked at the girl. In an instant the bond was made fast. Everything that could be said, he read in her glance: his dreams, his most secret longings, he perceived them in her voice. She was the one whose image he carried within him. He recognized her. And, looking at her face, he knew that a long, long night was ending.

And he burned with love for her. He existed only for those hours when he saw her, for the words he heard from her, for the feasts to which he invited her.

Words no longer served, Agnès had opened her benevolent arms, the beautiful arms of a fallen maid, Agnès, who cannot say no, receptacle of energies and dreams. Agnès led him to the source, eager, dazzled, completely happy; until then he had lived in expectation, disconsolate. Agnès the Blonde gave him mastery over the moment. And now, burning with the fire of the ineffable, he was reconciled with his own image. He became a new man, in harmony with a world where all find their place, their true dimension. Agnès was the Other encountered at last, confronted, admitted, recognized as indispensable, the complete abandonment of self to trust. Love given and received. The earth had stirred, the world had changed; it was decked out with promises. And because he found her very beautiful, he gave her in seigniory a castle by the name of Beauté, which his grandfather, King Charles, had had built on the edge of the forest of Vincennes as a resort. It is not clear any more whether it was because of this castle or because of her countenance that she was thereafter called *la Dame de Beauté*.

It all seemed simple to him now. All of the defenses, the barriers erected around him lowered by themselves like so many bridges leading away from self toward others. There was no more withdrawal, no more rebuffs. Neither conditions nor prerequisites, openness.

Agnès was not a mirror. She existed, she was. And that was why he loved her, this magnificent creature, this beautiful plant, this big, sturdy, happy girl with her simple joy of living. Agnès was fond of luxury, pleasure, and festivity; Agnès loved finery, jewelry, golden necklaces, diamonds which he had cut as novelties. Agnès loved costly fabrics, gold brocades, silks, furs, perfumes, which her friend the silversmith Jacques Coeur brought back from far-off lands and offered for sale in the Hôtel de Bourges. Agnès, thanks to royal generosity, liked to enhance her dazzling beauty, almost to flaunt it. She arrayed herself in gowns with long trains which lent majesty to her bearing, daring décolletés which revealed her shoulders and breasts. Agnès plucked her eyebrows and her hair, so that her forehead looked larger under a coif or a steeple headdress. Agnès was accused of immodesty, indecency: "On the Day of Judgment the Archangel Michael will place those gowns in the balance, and their weight shall condemn her to everlasting damnation." Thus the Chevalier de la Tour Landry thundered out against her memory in the book he dictated for the education of his daughters. But Agnès paid no heed; Agnès, who never left the King: "At table, in bed, in Council, she is always by his side," the chronicle informs us. In addition, she bore him three more children—three daughters.

Charles, captivated, showered her with gifts, heaped favor upon favor. "She had the most beautiful bedclothes, the best wall hangings, the best linen and coverlets, the best plate, the best rings and jewels, the best cuisine and the best of everything," Chastellain notes with considerable shaking of the head. For such excesses, far from being discreet, occurred with the Queen's knowledge, under her roof, before her very eyes. She, "that she might keep peace and secure her state," endured everything and kept her countenance. Never in the memory of man had there been such a scandal at the French court.

In this respect the King was unforgivable. Nevertheless, he had some excuses. Even if his mistress was beauty itself, she proved to be extraordinarily gifted in addition, and her unorthodoxy in matters of dress did not necessarily imply that she had the heart and the brain of a bird. Agnès was all sweetness and elegance, generosity toward those who had not; she had intelligence as well. She was cultured and discerning; she soon developed the taste for power. Because her lover was King she conceived a passion for politics, just as she would have for horses or tournaments if Charles had been King René, or even for rondeaus and virelays, if he had been a versifier like his cousin Charles of Orléans. She held opinions on what policy to follow, what options to take, and which men to urge on. She had her friends, her supporters, her own clan. And it must be said that she chose well, that she, too, had "great good sense." It may be surmised that men like Pierre de Brézé, Jacques Coeur, and Étienne Chevalier were introduced into the government through her influence. Was she led or did she lead? What does it matter? They were, at any rate, remarkable men.

If Charles was King, Agnès was Queen. He was completely at her command. Under her dominion, rejuvenated, transformed, he played the gallant, entered the lists, broke lances, and began to enjoy company, luxury, festivities, and to govern in the grand style as a great king. Was it coincidence? Agnès' reign corresponded to the most fruitful years in the reign of her royal lover.

Charles, day after day, lived for Agnès, wanted what she wanted, selected and engaged whomever she advised, admired whatever she admired, shared with her his joys and cares, great schemes, hopes and fears. Together they made one. They were madly in love; theirs was an insolent happiness, the kind that tempted fate. On the eleventh of February 1450, Agnès, who in spite of her advanced pregnancy, had joined the King in Normandy, which he sought to reconquer, died of dysentery somewhere near Jumièges.

Do we hold the key to the mystery? Did Agnès remake the King? Agnès, whom he could not do without thereafter and so replaced with another woman, the closest, most similar one he was able to find, her cousin Antoinette de Maignelay; he being one of those disconsolate people who, in accordance with the natural order, cannot, once they have experienced such benefits in a bygone union, wait very long before forming new bonds.

THE INEVITABLE ENCOUNTER

> The strength of Charles VII
> will be that prodigal son. . . .

Charles lived on for a few more years, still working, holding Council, giving audience, listening, putting the affairs of the kingdom in order, developing not just the knack but also a lively interest in his work, which he performed to the last. But the final upheavals were already beginning. Charles turned away. He prepared to return to those places known only to him. A refuge of delight and distress where bit by bit his fate dwindled, like the time he had left to live. The remaining days flowed in a painful tête-à-tête, from which henceforth nothing or no one could protect him. He was once again a prisoner of himself, of his whims and fantasies, for there they were, tenacious, indomitable, indestructible, his old acquaintances, the faithful companions of long ago, the anxieties of yesteryear, which had lain dormant for a decade and a half. They were still there, quite alive, baneful, ensconced within him, ready to well up, burst out, and destroy. Duty, the kingdom, affairs, the company of his loyal subjects, the consolations of religion, the tranquillity of music, the luxury with which he had surrounded himself in his last years, the joy he experienced at the birth of his last child, Charles, who was nicknamed the Little Lord, the respect enjoyed now by a monarchy renewed in power, nothing and no one could deliver him from the fear which gripped him. Except, to be sure, the women who were procured for him, with whom he shut himself up in his castles, whose presence created such a furor. Was it the lost Agnès he searched for and rediscovered in other women who were young and beautiful like her and who became mere bodies as time blurred the image? This restless desire which wandered from face to face, seeking satisfaction, what was this but the other side of his fear?

Woman was the fountain of youth, the source of life. Now he felt it departing from his worn-out body. Life left him fatigued, illness moved in; for four years his leg was covered with a suppurating sore. Did he recite for his enjoyment the lines of the troubadour Guillaume of Aquitaine? "I wish to keep for myself the most beautiful woman to refresh my heart and to renew it so well that it can never grow old." People were indignant, talked about his harem, called him an old lecher, a man ruined before his time by carnal excesses. The King, completely indifferent, anxious primarily about his own peace, nonetheless pursued his quest among these bodies which continued to be his ultimate refuge.

"Betrayed, you are betrayed, King Charles." Terrible words, familiar words which resounded for his father at high noon on a certain day in August 1392, in a forest to the west of where he led his army, and now for him, the son, in a chamber of the castle of Mehun-sur-Yèvre, where sickness had confined him for several weeks. "Betrayed, you are betrayed; they have designs on your life." Traitors were everywhere in the kingdom, and at court even more numerous. He knew it. And at his orders men were arrested, imprisoned, tried and executed. But the net was drawn tighter, the threat grew more and more serious. He imagined that he could read a name on everyone's lips: Louis, his son, the Dauphin, whose only thought, since the age of sixteen—and he was thirty-eight now—had been to rise up against his father.

Louis had fled the province of Dauphiné, which had been entrusted to his governance. He had requested asylum of the powerful Duke of Burgundy who, all too glad to vex his French cousin, conversed with him and regaled him. Louis swore his unrelenting hatred of Charles. He would not return to his country until the day when Charles was no more. And he devoted his energies to hastening that time. He was informed about it, and kept posted through letters. His spies prowled about, on the lookout for the smallest bit of information, for the slightest sign that could give hope to Louis.

The King had shut himself up at Mehun. He buried himself there. He did not fight, as his father Charles did against the Duke of Orléans. He did not kill the bastard of Polignac with his own hands. Worn out by so many terrible years, King Charles gave up. Huddled in his fear, he was caught in the vise of a permanent suspicion of everything and everyone. Whom could he trust, this great King, this weak and miserable man, who had become after long and arduous efforts the monarch of Europe? On whom could he lean for support? The world was a desert. What had he done? What was this grudge they bore him? Now he had reached the end of his life, enslaved again by the vice of his youth, insensible to everything but fear and pain. The wounds of his soul, which time had never managed to heal, had opened again; they tormented him even more than the wounds of the body.

And so a cruel sport commenced, a man hunt in which a son in the prime of life pursued an aging father. It was the base triumph of an armed victor over a defeated man on the ground. A most pitiable and futile settling of accounts between two contenders who confronted each other in every chamber of every castle, in their oppressive fantasies of vengeance and self-destruction.

Charles screened his entourage, tolerated none but his most reliable men, his cousins, the last son of the late Queen Yolande, Charles, Count of Maine, the Count of Duncis, Foix and Estouteville, Bueil, Brézé, Gaucourt, Chabannes, Chancellor Juvénal des Ursins, Étienne Chevalier. But his physician, Adam Fumée, became suspect and was placed in safe custody in the great tower of Bourges, while one of his surgeons sensed that a threat hung over him and took flight posthaste.

Charles, consumed by his obsession, thought only of Louis. His loyal supporters wanted him to call back his cruel son; they wanted the King to see him, speak with him, and above all to restore to the proper hands the country that would henceforth belong to him. And there, in this tête-à-tête between peers, between the King who would die and the one who would be born to his new state, there would finally be concurrence. The ties which had been broken for so long would be renewed for the love of the kingdom. And the King, set free, could think of his soul and prepare for death.

It was Midsummer's Day. Spring turned to summer in a single night. A warm night of festivities, filled with fire, laughter, and embraces. Clouds were adrift in a bed of wind, in the stream of time; the grass was high, the grain was ripe, the harvest ready. The hour had come for men of the earth to bring the scythes and pruning hooks out of the barns and to sharpen them with pieces of flint. It was a good time, a happy time, the glorious, uncomplicated time of reaping, of promises fulfilled, the terrible time of judgment.

It was the ninth of July 1461. The King, in a state of extreme debility, kept to his bed. His leg, corroded by tubercular osteomyelitis, was one large wound. His mouth was on fire; necrosis affected his jaws. His throat burned. The taste which saturated his mucous membranes worried him so much that he was afraid to take the smallest bit of sustenance. He became suspicious. King Charles had the fever. He was delirious. King Charles had his wits about him. He saw everything, had premonitions of everything, even the deadly drugs that his son Louis was having administered to him by his agents who populated Mehun. And in a final burst of energy, since they had designs on his life and he could not trust anyone, he decided that from then on he would not touch the suspicious food that was placed before him. Immobile, stubborn, at the end of his strength, immured in denial and despair, the King, for seven days, refused to consume anything.

Louis had nothing to do with this state of affairs. Except that he was impatient. But he had no hired assassins at all in Mehun, at the very most a few zealous informers.

The courtiers begged the King to take some food. They insisted, heaping argument upon argument. They tried to shore up the pervasive fear, to fix it upon an individual. Let him point out, let him name the man responsible for his sufferings: "If he mistrusts someone," his loyal Chabannes insisted, "let him have the man tried and drawn asunder by four horses."

But the King no longer wanted to defend himself or to exercise his authority. Summary punishment seemed pointless to him. "I leave it to God to avenge my death," he whispered in a husky voice.

He knew that he was nearing the end. His body failed him. A phlegmon obstructed his throat. The infection won out. He now had only a few days left to live, a few hours at the height of summer. What must those hours have been, all the while the disease, a form of blood poisoning, was invading him?

July 22, 1461. Mehun-sur-Yèvre. The King's chamber. Early morning. Charles was resting under the sheets, his features distorted, eyes half shut, a rosary in his hands. The priests and other clerics knelt down at his bedside and began to pray. Standing about the chamber were his relations, his entourage, his servants, those who had remained faithful in these last days. They joined in the prayers of intercession. The watch began. The silence was heavy with petitions and clouds of incense which ascended toward the Almighty in hopes of averting His anger and invoking His mercy. The man turned away from his past life, which was now inscribed in the book of days.

The cheerful light of this summer morning streamed in at the windows; it was time to go: to admit, recognize, and accept—difficult words—that the body which was himself must return unto dust. He must renounce life, tear himself from those faces which were his good companions, from this region of the Loire which he made his own, from the kingdom. He must leave the world to which he clung with every fiber.

Like a slow, inexorable tide, death took possession of this body. When all things are abolished, one must forget what is left behind and anchor oneself in a present where each word and each thought count. He said, in a sickly voice, that he wished to be laid to rest, not in the Loire Valley, which was his native land, but at the royal abbey of St. Denis, alongside the others of his stock, his father, Charles VI, and his grandfather, Charles V. He wished to confront eternity from his place in the regal line. It would be the fulfillment of the fondest desire that can dwell in the heart of a bastard—and it is well known that he believed for a long time that he was one—to join in death with those of one's own blood.

From that moment on nothing mattered but the passage to those regions whence perhaps he had come. Suffering again besieged him. Amid the groans and tears he remembered nothing but his own offenses. Forgetting his merits and his glory, his sufferings and the troubled times, he feared for his soul. Nothing remained in these final hours but the awareness of his sinfulness. On this bed of pain he was no more than a man overwhelmed by the transgressions of an entire life: it was the wages of sin he dreaded. He could not believe in the forgiveness which was offered to him, which is the manna of the New Testament. How idle his works appeared to him now.

"What day is it?" he inquired. "It is the feast of Mary Magdalene, sire," was the reply. "Ah," he said, "I praise God and thank Him that He has been pleased to let the most sinful man on earth die on the day of the sinful woman."

The priests interceded for him, comforters and mediators, familiar and fraternal faces that would see the soul across to the other shore. On his behalf they petitioned the Almighty to take pity on his suffering, to deliver him from all affliction, to permit him to share in the mystery of Reconciliation. Charles was brought round; subjected to the power of the Word, he listened to the prayers, the promises. The consolation of the words, "Yea, though I walk through the valley of the shadow of death, I will fear no evil: for thou art with me, O Lord." The fortification of the last rites: these were provisions for the perilous voyage, the

viaticum, the body of Christ, which would protect him from the
malevolence of the Archfiend. Now the anointing of the eyes, the
ears, the nostrils, the lips, the hands, and the feet, "that Satan may
have no more power over thee . . . and that by this holy oil and
His great mercy, God may forgive all the sins thou hast committed
through the frailty of the senses." Go forth upon thy journey from
this world, O Christian soul; the time of exile and suffering is
come to an end. . . . "I commend thy soul to Him who hath
created thee, so that having atoned by thy death for the guilt thou
hast incurred, being man, thou mayest return to thy Lord and
Maker."

The morning drew to a close, the sun approached its zenith, the
incense burned itself out in the censers, the kneeling priests continued their incantations, while the prayers called up images before the eyes of the dying man. The whispered words, so passionately attended to, took on substance; the presences which had
been promised and invoked drew near, the heavens opened.

King Charles, conveyed by the priests, had completed the passage. Faithful, they have closed his eyes and now kept vigil over
this body which was a temple of the Spirit. Released, absolved, at
peace now with God, he was on the way back to his original fatherland.

Soon afterwards his close relatives—the princes of the house of
Orléans, Duke Charles, the Count of Angoulême his brother, and
Dunois the bastard, who was his most faithful servant—escorted
his worldly remains from the Loire region to St. Denis in France.
They made the long voyage on black horses. Then when all Paris
resounded with the calls of criers saying: "Say your paternosters;
pray for the soul of the exalted, the mighty, the most excellent
prince, King Charles VII by name," at the hour of vigils, the nocturnal city glimmered with the bright and fragile flames of thousands of glowing candles, like so many petitions sent up to the
Almighty. Let the people arise, put on the robe and then the hood
of mourning, let them leave their rooms and their houses, each
taking a torch weighing three or four pounds, and let them accompany him, who had toiled so faithfully to serve them, to his final
rest.

May the holy angels, mentioned by the priests in their promises, guide his poor soul through the spaces which the heart may cross but our eyes can only question; may they take with his spirit, to be weighed with it in the scales of justice, the heavy destiny of King Charles VII, and bring both to the dwelling of eternity where one sees God face to face.

CHAPTER IX

Louis XI the Restorer
(*Born 1423; reigned 1461–83*)

PRECOCIOUS BOY, RETARDED DAUPHIN
THE SEAL OF EMERGENCY

Louis XI was born in 1423, at about three or four o'clock in the afternoon, in the archiepiscopal palace in Bourges. His father, Charles, was barely twenty years old, and the kingdom he would eventually inherit was contained between the Loire, the Garonne, and the Rhône. It was land up for grabs, threatened and devastated by the English, the feudal lords, and the men-at-arms.

His godfather was a young fool, the Duke of Alençon, whom the King at the end of his reign tried to purge of his taste for intrigue and crime. His godmother was Catherine de l'Ile Bouchard, a licentious woman who was successively the spouse of two favorites of sinister repute, Giac and La Trémoïlle. No first name had been decided upon in advance. The child was there; they were still making up their minds. Would they call him John, like his godfather, or Charles, like his father? It was judged most politic to appeal to the preceding dynasty, which had furnished two renowned saints who held the same first name, Louis. The mother and grandmother were especially gladdened by this. And when, the day after his birth, he was christened at the cathedral by the

Duke-Bishop of Laon, Guillaume de Champeaux, he was invested with the Christian name of Louis.

Though Charles rejoiced to see his descendance assured, he had little time for the boy. The mother expended all her energy on the fragile King and she too had little to do with the child. There was too much anxiety in each of them for the joy to be complete. Although messengers left to announce the happy event as far as Castile and Scotland, and bonfires were lit in the most out-of-the-way cities, the fact remained that the minds of the parents were elsewhere. Could this newborn infant sense all of this as he was carried off by his nurse, Jeanne Pouponne, a peasant woman? A sign of the times: until then, the sons of the King had been entrusted to the care of noblewomen.

Nor was there any security. At the end of that same month of July the troops of his father—still called the Dauphin—suffered the harsh defeat of Cravant, an English raiding party was marching on Bourges, and after eighteen months civil war threatened. They decided to place the young Louis in the security of the donjon of Loches, far from the noise, far from his family. For eight years the child lived there alone, in the hands of common people with the exception of Dr. Guillaume Léothier, who remained with him always. At the end of four years, in 1429, they finally thought of providing him with a governess, his beautiful godmother, who married the murderer of her first husband. Along with the governess they hired a tutor, Jean Majoris. Whom did he find to love, who loved this prince without a father or a mother, this child of royal stock, raised by peasants and who shared the games of the little village children? Will he be able to love in his turn, for want of being loved in his time? A time of emergencies, scarcely propitious for childhood, for fragility, a time that crushes, destroys, or ruins.

He was well trained, and possessed a well-exercised, robust body. In fighting and in running he bested all the other boys. The body was formed in such games. Watched, but not cared for, he was allowed to frolic freely from the hour of matins to the sounding of the Angelus in this country in the heart of the Loire with which he fell in love. The trees, the river, the sky, the dawn, the scents of the earth, the evenings, the seasons, and the forest, which already absorbed him, were a refuge, a haven, a pleasure

for him. They helped him to forget the fear, the sadness that probably oppressed him on certain days.

Alarms, penury, disappointments, monotony, even humiliations
—this was the stuff of life at Loches during those years 1425–33.
Did he experience his life as the history of events pass it down to
us? In 1427 he was forced to leave Loches and flee to Vivonne,
since the castle was one of the stakes in intrigues being carried on
by the favorites of the day, Richemont and La Trémoïlle. In 1429
it was the turn of the English; they approached, crossed the Loire,
besieged Orléans. Meanwhile, the kings of Castile and Scotland,
solicited by the King of Bourges, refused the hands of their
daughters for his heir.

What echoes of these afflictions reached the child? What kind of
screen did the adults set up between him and the events so that the
sound and fury of the world did not come to shake him? Did he
himself, through his people, already understand the precariousness
of his condition and the threats that clouded his future as the days
went by? Did he perceive the ever present anxiety? Did he partici-
pate in it or did he simply become used to it? Did he know how
to harden himself to it? It is probable that he then felt so weak
and poor, humiliated in the depth of his pride as the eldest son of
a king that in his eyes from that moment on one thing alone took
precedence: power. To be feared, respected, that was the essential thing. In the hierarchy of values that he was creating for himself he placed one idea at the top—power: something whose lack
he felt most sharply in his childhood. And from then on a
truth imposed itself upon him—in this valley of misfortune, the
fear that one inspires and the respect that one commands are very
important. But who can say? Perhaps he was entirely absorbed in
his games and the pleasures of learning. Perhaps he didn't have
the time to think about issues of power.

He was going on eleven when, leaving Loches for Amboise, he
was reunited with his family. The place was taken. Radegonde, six
years old, Catherine, four, and Jacques, two, clutching their
mother's skirts, take from him what he never had.

Marie was no more present to him now than when she bore
him. Constantly pregnant, self-absorbed, in her own world, she
would bear two children over the next two years: Yolande, then
Philip, who died. Did Louis suffer over this? What dream during

these ten years attached him to his mother, to the Queen? Hoping for nothing, giving nothing, keeping to himself, the question of his mother duly resolved in the negative, all sources of love dried up, he turned away from this woman with the permanently deformed body to whom he had nothing to say. The voice of blood did not speak. Could it? As for his father, always on the road, the boy glimpsed him from time to time.

Little interested by the world of women, not yet admitted into the world of men, Louis found himself alone in the midst of strangers. He was used to it. He compensated for it by becoming absorbed in Donatus, Cato, and Priscian, from whom he learned his grammar, in the sciences of the quadrivium, in sacred history and the lives and legends of saints. He was passionately fond of history, the *Chronicles of St. Denis* that reported to him the feats and deeds of his royal ancestors. His father, who remembered the beautiful books of the royal library and who was disconsolate at the idea that they were in the hands of the Duke of Bedford, had some books bought for the use of his son. He also loved the physical life into which his tutor Guillaume d'Avaugour initiated him; horseback riding, jumping, climbing, the bow and javelin, the sword and the lance, no weapons held any secrets from him. Here was his world, he was happy with it. He left it only when his father, between two journeys, stopped by for several days at Amboise. The castle, now a royal court, was suddenly animated by the sound of affairs of state. The young boy became enthusiastic at the spectacle of the life suddenly blown into those usually silent rooms. For him, truth was there. Decidedly, relationships with other people counted less in his eyes than the activities to which he would soon accede.

Then, after these ten lean years that probably left irreversible traces in the man, life decided to spoil him: two fat years, two easy years. Tours welcomed him; he resided there and thus celebrated his new and joyous accession. He discovered pleasures hitherto unknown to him: linen, robes of gold-wrought velvet, silver objects, and a woman brought to him from Scotland—a very young, pretty, intelligent, refined girl of twelve, Margaret, who was taken away from him as soon as the celebration was over and entrusted to the vigilance of the Queen; while he was put out of his lodgings and a household was created for him. He retained his chaplain, his doctor Léothier, and his tutor Jean Majoris (passed off as a confessor for the occasion), but now he was assigned a first chamberlain, a first house steward assisted by two aides, a squire, a treasurer, and a comptroller, as well as a guardian for his silver plate, all topped by the authority of a new governor, Bernard of Armagnac, Count of La Marche, son of the late High Constable who had been chief of the Orléans clan, and called by Chastellain for his piety and the austerity of his morals "that singular mirror of every good life." It is not certain that the young prince appreciated his manner, as it was severe, if not harsh.

All these good things did not displease him; nor did they convince him. He did not linger over them. The gifts, the beautiful objects, the gowns, and the female companion they had conferred upon him, all those pleasures assigned to him were blurred and forgotten in the movement of days, cities, and faces.

But, whether at Loches, Amboise, or Tours, what he discovered, what he realized, was the importance of the title he bore. Yesterday for the young village scamps, today for the noblemen of the court, as for the people of the good towns—wherever he was, wherever he went, he was His Royal Highness the Dauphin, he dominated. Which pleased him. Alone, perhaps; not loving much, perhaps; but first. Not for long.

His father had declared that it was high time to initiate him into affairs of state and took him on a long and complicated journey across France. Good-by, Madam Mother, good-by, Madam Wife, good-by, my dear studies. Good-by, childhood, without regret. It was mid-August 1436. The Dauphin was exactly thirteen. In fact, he was already almost a man.

THE LAST OF FATHERS

And they left, for eight months: Berry, Auvergne, Lyon where they celebrated Christmas, Vienne and Dauphiné where he was at home, finally Languedoc, for a stay of eight weeks. Horseback rides, the cities' enthusiastic receptions, presents, five hundred gold francs for Louis, at Lyon, a free gift of ten thousand florins at Romans, sessions of the Estates in Clermont, Romans, Montpellier. However, the King was not there to celebrate but to make himself known and to reform abuses. Nothing was hidden from him: complaints, grievances, petitions were added to avowals of misery. It was a somber journey in spite of appearances preserved here and there with great difficulty and against which the scourge of the times, the pillaging Écorcheurs, who forced the monarch to shorten his voyage, stood out as the most urgent problem.

The Dauphin did not need to hear. To see was sufficient for him, as he rode from province to province. Untilled lands, ruined hamlets, burned towns, his father's heritage was a disaster in these terrible years.

Amboise, Tours, even his sad donjon at Loches were in the pleasant Loire Valley. Inside the castle or the town, he had imagined that an ounce of power still belonged to his royal father. In the field this illusion was quickly dissipated. At Montpellier it became necessary to return home with all possible haste; Rodrigue de Villandrando, known as the Emperor of Pillagers, had dared to march on Tours where the Queen and the princess (the Dauphin's wife) were staying. These women were reduced to begging him to divert his rampage away from the town of his own good will. The brigand yielded to their wishes but carried his fire and blood elsewhere. And when his men met the King's men on the way north at the castle of Hérisson de l'Allier where they were preparing his lodgings, they did not hesitate to pillage the baggage after having thrashed his servants.

The Dauphin observed and took stock of the reality of the kingdom. It was a hard experience to which was added the even more trying confrontation with his father, who was almost unknown to him. And Louis considered him with the same surprisingly lucid eye with which he surveyed his future estate.

The King appeared to him as he then was, sad, silent, indecisive, a plaything in the hands of a coterie of nobles. This grown-up son who seemed to have fallen out of the sky hardly appeared to attract or cheer him. He didn't make a single gesture, a single effort toward him—only the necessary, nothing more. Louis remained alone, lodged alone, lived alone with his servants and never approached his father unless he was surrounded by a horde of importunate followers. There was no intimacy at all—neither possible nor desired. You would have thought that the King was unaware of him, or else that he was suspicious or vaguely jealous of this lively, precocious boy who seemed to frighten him. In his adult perversity, forgetting the superiority of age and measuring himself against the child, dependent by definition, might he not have already feared to see himself surpassed?

Charles's transformation of the 1440s had not yet taken place. A prisoner of his neurosis, he found himself quite incapable of winning Louis's heart, which was already mutilated on the emotional level. As in 1423, his mind was elsewhere. Thus he could give nothing to this thirteen-year-old son whom he was seeing for all practical purposes for the first time. Neither was there anything in this tired man that might excite admiration and enthusiasm on the part of an adolescent.

For the Dauphin, it was a bitter experience—a father whom you had never seen and who came with a morose expression to impose his law upon you, to remind you at every instant that you existed only after him. This hardly prompted concessions toward the person considered responsible for a situation as unpleasant as it was then. Not to mention the burden of what Louis heard people say in regard to what had happened and what was still happening in this court. Filial love was once more put to a rude test. It didn't withstand it. And from that moment on it was all over between Charles and Louis. If the father was totally oblivious of his son, the reverse was not true. Louis scrutinized Charles and judged him with a vigor that became at the slightest fault a pitiless judgment. Nothing escaped him. Divided between spite and despair, he formed a distorted, exaggerated, angry image of his father—like those fabricated by rejected lovers. He saw his father as a weak man who allowed everything to happen and was incapable of making even a minor decision by himself, who tolerated a band of greedy men around him and let them impose their points of view and prejudices. An impotent man. Or worse, a coward. Who doesn't know and sneer at the King's fears?

Louis was ashamed both for his father and for himself for thinking these thoughts. He was ashamed of his father's family, of his crazy grandfather, of his grandmother Isabella of unhappy memory. Only his maternal grandmother, Queen Yolande, survived in this desert. It was a cruel discovery for an adolescent, and a more influential one than he realized, since the faults in his model made it extremely difficult to build a personality. Everything was mixed up, all points of reference were inverted. ·

As for his fear, he shielded himself against it, as against something abject, he turned away from it, he ignored it, he denied it, he tried with furious strokes to cross it out within himself. And if he ever happened to experience fear, he would die rather than let the least sign of it show. He reacted in his own way—which revealed his violence, his impulsiveness, his inner resources—to this first real experience of men, which he lived through his father. His way was not to complain or brood, but to act, to face the difficulty squarely and to show others what he was capable of, that he feared nothing and no one.

In July 1437 the King departed to battle the English, who were entrenched in the upper Seine. He took the Dauphin with him and, dispatching the various corps of his troops to assault the neighboring towns, settled in Gien-sur-Loire, which he made his general quarters. Louis's governor, aided by four thousand men, distinguished himself at Charny but found himself held in check at Château-Landon where the siege had been dragging on for eleven days. This was the state of affairs when the Dauphin arrived, doubtless exasperated by a father who was incapable of placing himself at the head of an army and who was waiting out events, cloistered in Gien, where he limited himself to ordering processions and thanksgivings upon the announcement of the slightest advantage gained.

Thus, with fury and shame in his heart, the Dauphin took his revenge on his father and his fears, on the weakness of his name and the misery of the kingdom, on the object he hated and feared the most in the world, the English. He ordered the attack on Château-Landon and led the assault at the head of his men. The town fell. Louis demanded reprisals of an unheard-of severity. Attempts were made to soften his anger. They pleaded with him, but Louis stood firm. All Englishmen found on the premises were hanged, all traitors were put to the sword. But he knew how to thank those who had served him well, he regaled knights and squires, and rewarded loyalty and good service.

Perhaps because of his son's example Charles made a risky decision. He left Gien, took command of his troops, and behaved at the siege of Montereau with great courage. He sent Louis to rest

at Bray-sur-Yonne. He did not want to owe his laurels to the boy.
He recalled him only for the capture of the last bastion. And there
(surprise!) when the fate of the prisoners came up the son begged
for clemency against a father desirous of punishment. The Dauphin begged: "Let the English be permitted to withdraw safe and
sound with their goods; as foreigners conquering territory, they
did not come to France under their own authority." What did he
want to accomplish? To calm public opinion. Was he trying to obtain pardon for the excesses at Château-Landon that had caused
so much talk? This concern for others' opinions was no longer visible when he was a man. Or perhaps he wanted to adopt an attitude contrary to the King's just for the pleasure of it. At least he
proved that he was not afraid to contradict himself.

Better days finally came. On the twelfth of November 1437,
with the streets "draped to the sky," fountains of mulled and regular wines, mysteries, discourses, and wishes for a long life, Paris
opened its gates to Charles and greeted him as a victor. Dressed in
shining armor, his head covered with wrought gold, Louis, who
was less ashamed during these days, followed him into Paris like a
shadow, impressed, but envious.

A GOOD BEGINNING

Charles entrusted Louis with an important mission in Languedoc, a province "almost fallen into extreme poverty and total
destruction." In April 1439, Louis was invested with the title of
the King's lieutenant general to bring relief to the misery of his
subjects afflicted with "mortalities, plagues, floods, the payment of
large subsidies, ransoms, and losses to men-at-arms," subjects
whose only hope rested in the aid of their sovereign. Prudently,
the King supplied his sixteen-year-old envoy with a Council whose
members—both laymen and prelates—had been carefully chosen.
The King did not deem it wise to separate him from his governor,
the Count of La Marche, whose presence surely weighed upon the
young man. What is most surprising and makes one question the
motives of this departure is the fact that, aside from the usual revenues for his household, he was given no money to deal with the
expenses that would not be long in surfacing. No money, no

means, thought the boy, who had his feet on the ground. The coffers were empty, of course, but hadn't the Estates of Languedoc voted to give the King a hundred thousand pounds *tournois,* with the request that "part and parcel of this be reserved to provide for His Excellency the Dauphin and for others who would be charged with defending the country"? Charles VII had responded with an evasion, pretending to have provided for his son as appropriately as possible. Thus, all that was left for Louis to do was to live well with the little he had. This accorded with neither his ideas nor his character.

And the interested party, rather inclined by nature to brood over contradictions and already possessed of a desire to justify by facts his animosity toward his father, could not prevent himself from seeing in this attitude a distressing lack of good sense suggesting glaring professional deficiencies on the part of the man who governed him.

Either the King needed his son to do useful work in Languedoc or he did not. But this strange commission with no money behind it was confusing. What did this journey mean, a promotion or an exile? Or did Charles simply want to send Louis off to fail, in order to cast discredit upon him? Louis was indignant.

It was not unlikely that the father saw his son's good start as a threat; that this man, who had just barely surmounted his own problems and who was accomplishing with great difficulty at forty what his son of sixteen achieved easily was jealous. He might have felt himself lowered by all this precocity. But the boy, who was at the age when young people question their parents, and even rebel against them, needed a target for the anxieties he felt, so he analyzed each of his father's acts.

Decidedly, Charles, in this respect, was handing out switches so as to be beaten; for the boy, it represented another piece of evidence to add to the dossier of the permanent case he was working up against his progenitor.

Nevertheless, Louis was happy. Here he was free. He had put days of riding between himself and paternal tutelage. And the homages of the crowds at Albi, where he entered under a gold canopy on May 17, and at Toulouse, on the twenty-fifth of the same month, where the municipal magistrates came to meet him on horseback, were for him alone. For him alone, the towns were decorated and children in processions waved pennants and banners. They hoped in him alone. He was finally the first—which had not been the case for a long time, for three years, since his father had decided to take him along with the baggage.

The young man made good use of this power to which he acceded for the first time. The same precociousness that he displayed in war was shown again in the exercise of his responsibilities. And he already affirmed his manner in this first attempt at government, limited to a province. With seriousness and with passion he set himself to the task.

In the first place it was important to procure some cash; he set about it, and found the help he needed locally. Caught up in the joy of his arrival, the Estates spontaneously voted to give him important contributions.

And if anyone showed himself to be less than punctual, or perhaps forgetful, Louis demanded that the allocated funds be paid up to the penny, even if it entailed the prosecution of the defaulting parties. The money came in; it would not be wasted.

The money that made power at first gave him power over others. Now he feared others because he was only the sixteen-year-old Dauphin and because he represented a monarchy in a failing state, and must at any cost conciliate these others if he wished to succeed. Three years spent near the sun had taught him that power was often bought, and that it could be sold like any object. So he earmarked for this use the portion that the Estates set aside for his pleasures and personal needs. This prince was not prodigal. He rewarded, never to please but rather that he or the kingdom might be served—which for him were one and the same. In his business affairs the prince was regular and without illusions about men's motives. The servants upon whom he knew he could count, and the great nobles of the province whose loyalty was important, received fine sums from his hands.

His peers duly conciliated, Louis went out into the countryside to take stock of the problems by contact with the people. He went from town to town, listening, questioning the burghers, receiving directly from them, without intermediaries, the information that would clarify the issues. This concern for direct information was doubled by a very sharp concern for his authority. This was no pious vow but a desire born of the humiliation of the years past which already expressed itself in the most severe measures against pillagers and marauders, who were relentlessly pursued—to serve as an example, he said.

These were the immediate problems that he had to confront— problems of the times, identical to those that were confronting the rest of the country. He bought off the mercenaries and sent them away. By negotiation he succeeded in putting a stop to the feudal wars that divided the houses of Foix and Comminges and brought the two parties to "certain agreements and settlements." In order to block the road to the English, who were preparing to descend into the southwest, with remarkable pertinency and efficiency he put Languedoc in a state of defense: he found money, fortified the boundaries, and appointed the Count of Foix, the Lord of Albret, and the Viscount of Lomagne captains general. Meanwhile, he had informed his father, whose only response was to recall him. He returned. Six months of effort for nothing. In Languedoc, the mercenaries reappeared, Foix and Comminges resumed tearing each other to pieces. Only the English were keeping still. Louis was fuming.

THE GREAT INTRIGUE

He had been swindled. What was the reason for these pressing injunctions, "to return in all haste for whatever task *the prince's pleasure* might want to employ him in the future"? These words made the young man feel bitterly his inferiority in relation to the aforementioned prince.

At sixteen he had discovered his truth during his voyage. He now knew what he loved and what he wanted. Louis conceived a passion for the exercise of power that would not cease to grow for the rest of his life. It would not be possible for him to satisfy it before the age of thirty-eight. It was a drama for this impatient, headstrong young man who wanted everything and wanted it immediately, but who nevertheless found himself condemned to wait for it for twenty-two years. That seemed a long time to Louis of France, especially since there was no sharing.

Why did he feel this jealousy, this hatred? He was scorned, jeered at, neither his efforts nor his successes were taken into ac-

count. He was opposed and persecuted. It was a cruel game and
easy to play against a boy who had nothing. Everything was going
to rack and ruin. Decidedly, that man's incompetence no longer
needed to be demonstrated. Louis plotted to replace Charles with
a regency whose power would reside in himself, the Dauphin.

The sirens appeared to him in the form of three princes of the
blood. Jean of Alençon, his godfather, the Dukes of Bourbon and
Dunois, joined by the former favorite, Louis de la Trémoïlle, supported him in his dream.

The Dauphin stopped at nothing—his governor was dismissed,
his servants put in a position to choose between their master and
the King. There were manifestoes, calls to revolt, promises, letters
to the southern provinces, convocation of the Estates, even force.
He drew back from nothing, even opening negotiations with the
English, with that same Hundington against whom he had expended so much effort in Languedoc. There was fighting in
Touraine, in Poitou, in Bourbonnais. In rebellion Louis demonstrated the same prodigious activity as he had formerly in lawful
activity.

The father had taken to the field; he led the counterattack with
decision, and prevailed. It was a narrow escape, however. Following the great ordinance of 1439 on the reform of the army, the
King controlled only a small number of organized companies,
while the rebels, who did not hesitate to enlist the wandering
troops of Écorcheurs and bands of marauders, had considerable
forces at their service. It took him five months to bring the plotters
to the point of surrendering, which Louis delayed as long as he
could. Right up to the last moment he asserted his rights, thereby
delaying any coming to terms, and pushed his presumptuousness
to the point of stating conditions in such a way that one would expect concessions. He demanded land, revenues to assure the expenses of his retinue; he demanded that he be permitted to exercise his rights over the Dauphiné: he must have a large
government, Languedoc, Guienne, or Ile-de-France, and amaz-
ingly he requested that his wife be provided for—his wife of whom
he had never spoken! The King answered his son by telling him to
present his requests in person. Cleverly, from the start he had
minimized his role in the uprising: "The actions of the princes
were undertaken under the cloak of our son, who is still young,

as everyone knows." The Dauphin persisted and requested that
the three Estates be assembled. He would go to the court of his
father accompanied by all of his partisans and, once there, he
would demonstrate his justifications and theirs! "If the three Estates should so advise, he would make reparation according to
the King's good pleasure."

In addition he requested the presence of the Duke of Burgundy
at this meeting of the Estates, and declared that "if it would please
the King more, he would submit to the Duke's arbitration alone."
Insolence could not be pushed any further. The King responded
with a demurrer and took up arms once again. In the course of his
triumphal onslaught, Alençon surrendered. Louis's troops abandoned him. Burgundy confined himself to the offer of hospitality,
nothing more. Louis was thus forced to go home, head held high,
without a twinge of remorse, and to live close to a father at whose
feet he must prostrate himself, imploring his pardon three times.
The next day he was made to understand that he decidedly was
not the strongest and that he must remain under the royal thumb.
When one last time he insisted upon and sought to obtain satisfaction on at least one point, amnesty for his followers, he heard
himself brought irrevocably back to reality: "Louis, the doors are
open, and if they aren't wide enough for you, I will have thirty or
forty yards knocked out of the wall for you so that you may pass
where you deem fit; you are my son and you cannot oblige anyone
without my leave; but if it is pleasing to you to go, go in this manner, where God pleases, for we will find others of our blood who
will help us maintain our honor and authority better than you
have up to the present time."

The humiliation was great. Louis was deprived of his household. Only his confessor and his cook were left to him. He was
forced to appear behind his father during the triumphal return that
he made as conqueror through those same provinces that he,
Louis, had tried to stir up. But he was granted his Dauphiné and a
monthly pension of eight hundred pounds.

After the Praguerie, Louis stayed quiet for a while. Through action, it seemed, he had emptied himself of his revolt, lived it out.
He was behaving himself. He was watched closely. For three years
his father didn't let go of him and took him everywhere with him:
to the front, to Chartres against the English, to Champagne

against the Écorcheurs, to the siege of Pontoise, in the southwest, to Tartas, to Toulouse. He used his capabilities, but under strict supervision, until he judged him sufficiently calmed to have him carry out missions, rather short ones at first, in which he could give tokens of his good faith. Eventually, following the Treaty of Tours, he received the order to lead the Écorcheurs out of France. Undoubtedly his capacity for command must have been outstanding for him to be entrusted with responsibilities of such magnitude, responsibilities that in the preceding century fell to no less a noble than the tenth champion, Bertrand du Guesclin, who had led the Free Companies across the Pyrenees.

CONFERENCES AND MASSACRES

The strange adventure began at Langres, into which mercenaries had been thronging for several months. They were a mob of dismissed soldiers of fortune who were wanted by no one. Twenty thousand men-at-arms and ten thousand useless mouths, valets, pages, women, distributed among seven hundred wagons. Their equipment consisted of huge bombards, the Pas Wollant and the Pas Rose, cannon, veuglaires and culverins, herring barrels filled to the brim with cannon balls and powder, boxes for lead and iron and piles of halberds, bows and arrows, shovels, pickaxes, siege ladders, body shields, and rockets. In this array they left Langres and headed for Switzerland. Captured towns, full-scale battles, massacres, terror—it was physically a very hard year for the Dauphin.

He was wounded at the siege of St. Hippolyte when his knee was pinned to the saddle by an arrow. His father had ordered him "to clear and put out of the kingdom all captains, mercenaries, and other men of war scattered throughout the land . . . so that pillaging might cease and the poor people and subjects might rest and live in peace." Henceforth, all dreams were permitted, including the dream of the imperial crown. Through embassies and delegations, he wove from one side of the Rhine to the other a web of intrigues, never before seen, which astonished everyone. It produced results that no one, not even he, had expected. Although he left to give military support to the Emperor against the Swiss, he returned armed with a treaty assuring understanding and firm friendship between the cantons and the kingdom. The King of the Romans thundered, the Duke of Burgundy demanded reparations. Louis was barely able to fight his way home with a handful of men through hostile populations who pillaged and burned his baggage. But his mission was accomplished. Now he had to face the anger of the Duke of Burgundy at the Châlons conference in the form of thunderbolts delivered by Burgundy's wife, Duchess Isabelle. Louis showed himself there in a not very favorable light, by turns amiable and aggressive, flexible and violent, a quibbler, in bad faith, taking pleasure in aggravating the quarrels. He already had his own policy, which was not that of the King. The paternal advisers foresaw solutions based on a viewpoint contrary to Louis's, which revived his bitterness. His heart was invaded by regrets. He felt alien, even hostile to all that surrounded him. He had to give in to the obvious—there was nothing for him to do at the court of France as long as his father was alive. He was too dissimilar in mind and character to second him in his political policy. He felt he would always be confined to playing secondary roles. He would never hold any position but that of an executor of others' plans.

WIDOWER WITHOUT TEARS

Isolated, under suspicion, put out of phase by his year of adventure, Louis was unhappy at this court at Châlons where for the first time unaccustomed luxuries were being enjoyed. He did not like the luxury, or the feasts, or the parade of tourneys, or the people he met there. One and all irritated him. His wife to begin with; a wife whom he never saw very much, whom he hardly loved, whose tastes, expenses, and associates he despised, who enjoyed all the things that excited boredom and disdain in him, and who both pleased and was pleased by this court. Quick to suspicion, he had her followed by a certain Jamet du Tillet, who spread the most vicious tales about her. At this point she died of galloping consumption on August 16, 1444, pronouncing these desolate words: "Fie on life and this world, don't speak to me any more about it." The King, who had much affection for his daughter-in-

law, opened an investigation on the famous Jamet. It was hardly
to Louis's honor.

OUTBURST

A year went by. Louis was using up his resources in various
plots. He borrowed money everywhere. He was on bad terms with
King René. He fell out with Dunois, with Louis de Bueil, with
several of his familiars. He detested Pierre de Brézé, quarreled
with Agnès, slapped her in the face after having tried to gain her
good graces by gifts. He was running around in circles, losing himself in conspiracies, unable to contain himself any longer. He
wanted the throne—right away. A first conspiracy against his father's advisers failed without giving him much trouble. A second
one, this time directed against the person of the King, was discovered. Exasperated, Charles banished him to the Dauphiné for four
months: "By this head which does not wear a hood," shouted the
undaunted Louis when he heard the sentence, "I will avenge myself on those who have thrown me out of my house." He would
keep his word.

DEPARTURE

The Dauphiné was that region between the Rhône, Savoie, and
Provence that had been bequeathed to the Crown a century earlier
to serve as the personal domain of the eldest sons of France, together with the title: Dauphin. Louis, who had been governing it
by procuration for seven years, again found himself obliged to reside there. The plot had failed. For want of a kingdom, he had to
content himself with a province. It served as an outlet for his
dreams of power. He took possession of it, passing through
Romans, Valence, Montélimar, all the way to Grenoble where he
made his entrance on August 12, 1445. He would remain there for
ten years. He didn't have a bad time of it.

His first acts speak clearly: the Dauphin was the master in his
Dauphiné, consequently, he behaved as a sovereign; he demanded
within the month the homage and oath of fealty from all noble

holders of fiefs. He added new recruits to his team of collaborators. He fixed the rules of his chancellery in the image of the
great chancellery of France. He organized a regular army. He held
his Parlement in Grenoble. In short, he gave this province the aspects of an independent principality, or at least one that intended
to be so and did not recognize any higher authority. The Dauphin
intended to act according to his own good pleasure.

Events had killed all trace of love in Louis and set up in its
place one of those obsessive, inextinguishable family hatreds. He
did not know how to rid himself of it. That was why he hunted big
game—bear, deer, boar—with such violent impetuosity, disappearing deep into the forest for days on end with a few of his men, tiring his body and hoping to wear down his pain.

At the heart of this hatred was the kingdom he waited for which
he could attain only through his father's death, which he longed
for, he admitted without pretense.

Louis denied his father any authority over his own person. He
wanted to be free. He wanted to be his own master. He was a
rebel. Every time he could he baited his father, enveloped him in
a web of intrigues, rumors, suspicions. He spread rumors, disturbed the King, kept him in a climate of insecurity. Which leads
us to wonder whether this permanent provocation wasn't really
the sign of an almost infantile search for confrontation in which
the son attempted to prove to his father as well as to himself that
he was truly the stronger.

Faultless in his work when it was a matter of administering his
Dauphiné, encouraging commerce, creating industry, covering the
Jewish bankers with his protection, establishing a postal service,
creating a university at Valence, he lost all sense of restraint when
it came to his suzerain lord, whom he openly treated in such an
offhand manner that he practically ignored him.

And the grievances piled up, swelling under the influence of
time and the courtiers on both sides who believed they were serving their masters by dramatizing the already poisoned atmosphere.

Louis wished to remarry and, deeming himself old enough to
make his choice alone, informed his father that he would marry
eleven-year-old Charlotte, the daughter of his neighbor the Duke
of Savoie.

The Dauphin did not limit such scandals to his private life. Pol-

itics enjoyed its share of them. Fascinated by the Italian imbroglio
—we are in the midst of the *quattrocento*—he had firmly decided to
play his part in it, be it against his father or his father's allies. He
experienced no qualms at all.

Furious, Charles stormed and threatened. He was the master
and he had all the power. He would take away the Dauphiné and
disown Louis in favor of his younger brother, Charles. Louis had
already provided him with seven counts of indictment of the fourteen necessary to legitimate his decision. Louis quibbled, implored, promised, while behind the scenes he plotted with the feudal lords of the opposition, Brittany, Alençon, Armagnac, in this
year of 1454. Once again he armed his forces.

The King moved into the Bourbonnais in full strength.

Louis sent more dispatches and promises which no one
believed. Charles became indignant: "He is neither honest nor
wise to haggle with his father in this way," and he remained firm
in his demands.

FLIGHT

Louis then went into a panic. He believed, or at least he said he
believed, the worst. His father wanted his life. He was going to
march on Grenoble. A little longer and it would be too late. He
was caught in a trap, blockaded in his mountains, surrounded
from Oisans to Vercors, "trapped like a mouse in his hole." He
would be arrested and "secretly expedited in a sack filled with
water." He had to flee in all haste the Alps and the kingdom. He
did, under a small escort, gripped by a "wild" fear. But his choice
of retreat betrayed only too well the desire to provoke once again
the rage of the King. Louis sought refuge with his uncle, Philip of
Burgundy. Why this scandal? Was he pretending? Was he sincere?

His uncle received him with all the marks of respect due to an
eldest son of France. He feted and comforted him, he placed at his
disposal the residence of Genappe, he had a pension of thirty-six
thousand gold *écus* counted out for him each month through the
good offices of his treasurers, and never showed the least reticence. Louis could be his guest, a guest of honor, as long as neces-

sary. Meanwhile, the issue of peace between himself and the offended father grew more and more frayed.

It was nevertheless exile for Louis. A gilded exile, a comfortable desert crossing, a forced rest which suited him poorly.

And from that moment, spying and having others spy for him, listening to the news, watchful, he counted the days and consulted astrologers. He fretted, ruminated over his resentments, plotted the revenge to come. To try to calm his impatience and to satisfy the need he had to know what was happening, he maintained a web of informers. And, to kill time, he hunted, read books, improved his mind, and, above all, he observed. The court of Burgundy was quite a spectacle at the moment of its apogee! It provided him with food for thought for five more years. Another trump card in his hand.

CHAPTER X

King at Last

FROM THE BEGINNING, HE THOUGHT ONLY OF VENGEANCE

> This man will not reign in peace long without having a prodigiously great trouble.
>
> Philip the Good

The Dauphin had achieved his long-awaited goal. He was crowned King at Reims on August 15, 1461, recognized by all the grandees of the realm, as well as by the nobility which had arrived en masse from the provinces to affirm their fidelity. All that was noble and elite in France made the trip to Reims. The dynasty had nothing to fear. The feeling for it had survived the vicissitudes of the Great Sorrow and converged, reinforced by the Trial, upon this new representative of the race to whom they entrusted their destiny. Acclamations, shouts, crowds—for Louis a rejuvenation; the cathedral was full to bursting. If the houses of Anjou, Foix, and Brittany hadn't seen fit to disturb themselves, the Bourbons, the Orléans were there, the Counts of Eu and Vendôme, and especially the Duke of Burgundy, his son, his entire court, had come in state to escort the new King to Reims.

At the coronation, Philip the Good was everywhere. He officiated as dean of the peers. He bestowed knighthood on the King as well as on an important number of lords and gentlemen. And he especially gave to Louis the homage that the Treaty of

Arras had allowed him to refuse to his predecessor. Along with the other peers he took an oath. "My very feared lord, I pay you homage for all the lands that I hold from the noble Crown of France and hold you as lord and promise you obedience and service; and not only from that which I hold from you but from all my lands which I do not hold from you and from as many lords, noblemen, soldiers, and others as can be found therein. I promise to serve you with my own body and also with as much gold and silver as I can take from them [the lands]." One could not help wondering if this oath of loyalty had finally turned that page of history so deadly to the realm, of fratricidal wars between Armagnacs and Burgundians? Had the death of the father definitely imposed the seal of forgetfulness on the old quarrels, the base vengeances, the animosities of man toward man? In the joy of the coronation, the past no longer counted. An ill for a good was how the flight to Genappe was described. It renewed links between the two families broken for half a century and brought the prodigal Duke back to the vassalage of his suzerain. The new reign began with auguries of hope. Would an era of peace be opened up by the new King?

To think so was to misjudge him badly. "Promise me, my lord," pleaded Duke Philip, one knee on the ground in the great hall of Tau, once the coronation dinner was over, "promise me, in honor of the passion and the death that our Savior Jesus Christ endured for all men, that you will pardon all those whom you suspect of having sown discord between you and your late father, to leave in their posts the officers and governors that he named, unless by true information and good justice they be found guilty." "Sweet uncles," replied Louis, "I promise, all but seven."

There was a great upheaval. Not a complete renewal of the personnel holding the sixty-four thousand offices of the kingdom, a project he had toyed with in the furors of exile, but an incredible waltz of offices, a rearrangement of employees, some thrown in prison and others showered with gold and sinecures: a settling of accounts, a price set on the head of the two most intimate counselors of his father, Chabannes and De Brézé, the return of the exiles (among whom was a dangerous conspirator, Jean V of Armagnac, condemned for incest), a liberation of political prisoners who were immediately replaced by the supporters of the losing faction: "To some he gave, to others he refused, some paid by deeds, others by words." Then, the abscess lanced, the furor purged, he got down to work, or rather he threw himself into it. He wanted to do in one day what his dead father would have taken a month to accomplish and to take point by point the opposite position in political matters. "He embraced so much at the beginning of his reign that a very prudent and a very powerful king reigning a long time could scarcely have brought it all to a good end."

After four years of being led at this hellish pace, the nobles armed themselves in the name of the League of the Common Good. Then twenty-one houses with fifty thousand soldiers proposed a candidate to the succession, Louis's brother Charles. Would the drama be relived?

BAD MANNERS

Without a doubt such a conflict was written in the order of things, but it might have been avoided or, at least, put off, were it not for a problem of language the importance of which should not be minimized, given the uncommon personality of the new King.

Scarcely had Louis taken up his duties than tongues started wagging. The gossips chattered and spread tales. Bad words true and false flew from mouth to mouth, starting with the prince, for God knows the prince was generous with words, to seduce, caress, or convince. So many stupefying, contradictory rumors circulated about him that in 1462 the ambassadors from England were pleased to get an audience with Louis so they could speak "by true account to their master after a multitude of people who invented things each in his own manner." For this man astonished, he upset, he displeased, he caused anxiety. First off, there was nothing kinglike about him. His fashion was detestable; he dressed in short when the fashion was long. He wore poor cloth and a poor hat ornamented with a lead portrait. He had a poor horse and few attendants. From the bottom to the top of the social scale, he shocked. And the common people asked, when in 1462 he entered Hesdin at the side of the Duke of Burgundy: "Where is the King? Which one is he?" And, duly informed, they concluded:

"Good God, is that the King of France, the greatest king in the world? He seems more a valet than a knight. All this is only worth twenty francs, the horse and the clothing." And they chattered. It was only a beginning.

Scarcely had Louis taken possession of his office than his "new behavior" furnished gossip to the chroniclers: immediately after the coronation, he made a brief stay in Paris in the company of the Duke of Burgundy, then returned to the Loire country and settled in at Tours. He didn't stay there very long. He left, without giving his destination, for Guienne, as was later discovered, to spend the season. He had it cried out with trumpets sounding that no one, under penalty of death, was to try to follow him. He took five companions with him, and dressed them like himself, in coarse gray cloth with a wooden rosary around his neck. One would have thought them six pilgrims except for the escort of a hundred and twenty men-at-arms who, on his order, destroyed the bridges behind him. What did he fear? When on the road, he always stayed with little people: canons, choirmasters, clerics, receivers, or town councilors. Was this the behavior of a king?

At court there was the same "strangeness," poor style, little expense. The King hated luxury, "pomp and arrays of fancy dress." He went so far as to forbid it, and allowed no one to try to contravene his orders. One day he saw a young squire dressed quite fashionably, wearing a velvet doublet. "Whose man is this?" he inquired. "Sire, he is yours," they answered him. "Mine?" he cried. "By the passion of God, he is not mine. I disavow him. And he will never be mine. By God, he is dressed in silk, he is prettier than I!" The squire had to leave his post. Henceforth when someone received the King, he avoided the least pomp. They knew he could not abide it. No more than the feasts and the jousts. The exploits in the lists left him cold, bored him. He was, however, an excellent soldier and a great hunter, a point in common with the class from which he came and for which he showed so little concern. Not at all. Point of dispute. He proclaimed everywhere a law forbidding hunting, to the great and the humble, without his grace and leave under penalty of corporal punishment: on his order, all nets were burned. If someone broke his edicts, he punished with an unbelievable rigor. A Norman gentleman who had trapped one or two hares on his own land without the King's authorization had his ear cut off.

Neither was he polite or self-effacing. He showed himself most often very rude and gratuitous. "There was little love and softness in his company. They praised little his house and his followers, being away from him was more desired than being in his presence." He never left his residence without his dogs or his birds, he installed them where he wished. If they ruined everything, he didn't care. The good people who received them had to keep their mouths shut and not take it into their heads to protest. The King allowed protest from no one, not even from the best people, like those from the University of Paris. One day when they had come to present their respectful objections to his politics regarding the Holy See, they heard themselves dismissed with these coarse words: "By God, you are foul people and lead bad lives, with the fat bawds you nourish. Go away, for you aren't worthy for me to bother with."

As for the generosity, which would be fitting to his role as king, it appeared to be totally lacking except with regard to his protégés: "He gives nothing, spends less, cuts corners on everything and takes from everywhere." Not satisfied with withholding favors, he amassed money. Never had a king of the realm taken so little trouble to hide his lust for money. Was it greed? There again, his subjects had no room to maneuver. Neither by prayer, excuse, nor pity could anyone ignore his demands. He simply took money. By gift, restitution, borrowing, or fine, the *écus* landed in his coffers. The man was pitiless. Nothing stopped him, and in him "will has more credit than reason." Here was the cause of uneasiness. For a will on which reason had no influence could not be bent by anyone. The father governed with the high officials of his Council. The son abhorred them, asked no opinions, made decisions alone, did only what he wanted.

The King was false, impenetrable, "a sweet talker" certainly. He was generous with words, "very pretty words, but feigned," under which "envy lies hidden." "How he spoke with a sweet tongue, but always with craft." Was this the worthy descendant of King John?

THE KING IS LIKE GOD

We know the importance of a man's word to the knightly ethic. It was grave and troubling if the King broke this essential rule of honor; it instilled a feeling of insecurity quickly followed by indignation. "Since there cannot be certainty in the word of a king and in his orders, it is difficult to expect truth from a man of lesser condition, and thus faith and confidence will no longer be on earth, and there will be nothing between men which they have in common." Besides, how could one love the King when the King did not love his nobles, treated them harshly, and aimed only to be feared, while eating away their power?

King Louis was a realist. He believed in acts, in facts. But he forgot that power does not sustain itself with money, wheat fields, and men-at-arms. He was wrong not to recognize one aspect of his power which was always important. Because the political action which he undertook was unusual: he could have used the traditional kingly role. The nobles may have accepted capricious behavior from a magnificent and ostentatious prince leading a sumptuous life, making known his desires for glory, loyalty, and justice, a king in whom they could have had confidence, men like his vassals the Duke of Brittany or the Duke of Burgundy: "That sun of a man, that image of a high personage," as the chronicler Chastellain enthusiastically calls the Duke of Burgundy. "Here is a human prince," he cried, "and may he be blessed, and all those whom he loves. If only our King were thus who only dresses in a pure gray dress, ill belted and ill made, around him a mean cape, and who hates nothing more than joy."

The royal image as the nobles of the time carried it in their hearts had elements of both St. George and King Arthur. The father combined with the hero. This image had to exalt them and give them security. The King should be like God. One must be able to believe in him, but also to disobey him from time to time. There were taboos that could not be broken, signs that could not be obscured, rules to follow with respect to the royal religion as well as the Christian religion. Louis was wrong not to heed this.

The great feudal lords of the kingdom did not see themselves in this King. They could neither follow him nor willingly give him their goods and their suspects when he requested them, as the oath of fidelity sworn at the coronation required of them. They could no longer die for him. The trade mark appeared falsified, the dice were loaded. They no longer played. The Duke of Bourbon, whom he removed from the governorship of Guienne for no reason, served notice on him: "It seems to me that our friendship and our service are very dear to you. If you want to be so rude to us, you will give us small cause to love you and even less to serve you." But the King cleverly brazened it out. Feelings mattered little. He wanted to be obeyed, and he threatened: "Good, good brothers that you are, it would seem that you are looking for trouble, but when it comes to that, we will do the best we can." A grave error in calculation on the prince's part. It would cost him dearly.

KEEPING HIS PLACE

Had they understood nothing, these nobles? Whatever his words, whatever the appearances, this man with all his faults, his bad manners, never let up, worked without stopping for the kingdom and the general interest. True, these grandees certainly had genuine complaints: Duke John II of Bourbon had been removed from his government of Guienne, Count Gaston IV of Foix was deprived of Mauléon and the land of Saule, the Count of Dunois was removed from power, the right of Duke Francis II of Brittany to enjoy revenues from his bishoprics was contested, the interests of the houses of Orléans and Anjou in Italy were argued by the prince. But they would have had a better right to complain if they had thought less of their own interests. For during fifty years of the country's misfortunes they had gathered their honey, had their sunny days. They had profited by it. At the worst hours, they had not hesitated to sell their services to the late King very dearly, requiring exorbitant pensions for a loyalty which was too often of short duration. The nobles had fed on the misery of their King. They had increased their power at Dijon, Moulins, Aix, Angers, Nantes. There they had their palaces, their courts, their domestic and foreign policies, their government, their administration, their finances, and their army, superimposed on those of the monarch, whose authority they evidently wanted to continue to undermine and whose power they wished to control. They had seen that the newcomer had great ability, and that although he had had a heavy hand at the beginning, he nonetheless had the making of a leader. This was where the shoe pinched. The man was too big. They had to put him down. Down with the tyrant! Hadn't this been the slogan he used against Charles?

Thus this visceral hatred that Louis had for the princes was ultimately justified. They constituted more than a threat to him, a danger to the kingdom. Louis XI took the country in hand at a time in its history when, in the balance of forces, those of the King did not sufficiently outweigh those of his vassals (all, by the way, of Valois blood, by the men or the women) for peace to be preserved. Unless he found a way. His father had. But he was a levelheaded man. And since then there had arisen against the power of the sovereign a confederation of princes. They would eventually meet head on with equal arms in the course of a life-and-death struggle. The King of France would have to play his cards close to his chest and play them well if he wanted to retain his place. It was a game of double or nothing. He could lose everything. But if he won, he took a decisive step for the dynasty. The stakes were high. The importance of the game placed the French monarchy at a turning point and made this reign a key one.

It was an exhausting fight. From the north of Flanders, Charolais, Regent of Burgundy, was constantly calling up his leagues, placing enemies on every border. His best ally was the Duke of Brittany. As extras, there were two conspirators from the preceding reign, Alençon and Armagnac. A hostage of royal blood was used as a scarecrow, the King's own brother, Monseigneur Charles, "a man who did little or nothing on his own, but who was led and manipulated by others." For him they demanded either the crown or a province. Normandy, which would link together Brittany and Burgundy, the two wheel horses of the conspiracy, or Champagne, which would simply extend Charolais's borders. The English pretensions to the crown of France remained intact and the nobles did not hesitate to appeal to England for help.

The War of the Public Good, which lasted six months and cost

the King daily, finally came to a painful end. The King had
learned at his own expense the importance of opinion; now he
thinned his wine with water, showered everyone with smiles,
caresses, and money. He took pains with his dress when he entered the cities: red and white doublet worn over the armor in the
Italian way, velvet damask, a scarf with great silver leaves, a mantle of gold thread woven with a horned deer, and his dress sword,
"the beloved." His entourage was dressed the same. What was
more, he created a knightly order which he placed under the patronage of the head of the heavenly militia. The Order of St.
Michel was to be the complement of the Golden Fleece established by Philip the Good, "this sun of a man" who so pleased
the crowds. He sought to rally to his cause the greatest number of
subjects. He thus won back his father's useful supporters, of
whom he had so foolishly deprived himself at the beginning of his
reign. And he coped. Battles were fought only when necessary, negotiations were always undertaken again, truces were sworn with a
kiss and broken no sooner than signed. King Louis labored. His
good cities were for him, the small and middle nobility were of
fragile loyalty, public opinion had to be won over and over again.
He was not sure of his people. It seemed a serious problem, when
in the east, in his ambition and power, the new Duke of Burgundy
rose up. "How to get him to submit?" worried the King.

THE GREAT DUKE OF THE WEST

When he came to power on the death of Philip the Good, on
June 15, 1467, Charles, the only son of the dead man and the
fourth representative of this remarkable line descended from John
the Good, was nearly thirty-five years old. Fifty years of peace
were behind him. He had five to seven million subjects, fiefs rang-
ing from the Rhône to the North Sea, which correspond in present-day Europe to Belgium, Holland, and Luxembourg, plus the
northeast corner of France, with the exception of Champagne, Al-
sace, and Lorraine. The richest cities of Europe were his, an active, industrious, solid population, armies, money, palaces, a royal
standard of living, ambassadors everywhere. He who would be
called the Great Duke of the West no longer counted his riches.

Or his dreams. An ambition without limits, an anxiety which made him think more of what he lacked than of what he possessed, an energy equal to his desires. Unrealistic, however, he demanded that the world resemble what he wished it were. Pride held him. He was called "the worker," "the terrible"; he declared to his enemies: "I prefer your hatred to your scorn"; he was all violence, extremes. But he burned.

King Louis wrung his hands: "Woe to my life! What does this Duke of Burgundy want who always runs on the heels of his sovereign, his king, from father to son? Let his seed be cursed and never let a royal woman bear his child! Didn't they join with the English against us and bring them into the kingdom to destroy everything? Does he want to have the crown and scepter in hand? He who has so many castles and possessions, and is so powerful in Ghent and Bruges, what does he want? Does he also want Paris?"

He wanted a crown for this duchy which was now worth a kingdom and which, in this patchwork Europe of the fifteenth century, was a great power. He wanted to implant himself between France and the Germans, to push one toward the ocean and squeeze the other back along the Rhine. He would gladly build on the ruins of the realm the Burgundian state of his dreams. He would extend it to the Mediterranean, thus reviving the old domain of Lothar who, at the division of Verdun, received these lands and the title of Emperor.

As for Louis, "he loves him so much that in his place instead of one king he would like to see six." That is to say, he detested him. Perhaps for having in his adolescence shown Louis a friendship he usually refused, never having had need of a confidant or friend. He only trusted his mother, Isabelle of Portugal, and his second wife, Isabelle of Bourbon, whom he loved and who died of tuberculosis, leaving him a daughter, Marie. It is probable that the character of the exiled Dauphin was not unpleasing to him. Having in his time been a rebellious son, Charles saw himself in Louis. But more important, only Louis could calm his angers, his words cast a sort of spell on Charles. The first few days of Louis's reign enlightened Charles as to his character, his ingratitude, his bad habits. And from then on he hated and feared him. Perhaps because he knew he was vulnerable to his words, and because he knew his profound subtlety. So he attributed evil intentions to

him, or at least magnified them. He accused him of wanting to
rule him under the whip, declared himself in a state of legitimate
self-defense, and "seeing how closely he was threatened, and having the courage to prefer trampling, injuring someone else than to
be injured or trampled," he resolved, for reasons of state, to conclude an alliance with Edward IV of York, whose sister Margaret
he married on July 3, 1468. He knew full well that he could not
hope for more heirs—his state of health would not permit it; he
had a fistula in his groin.

PÉRONNE

When pride rides up in front, shame and harm follow closely.

                                                        Louis XI

This marriage plunged Louis into the greatest uncertainty. He
knew that the Duke was at the point of intervening again in the
kingdom at the call of his brother and the Duke of Brittany. Now
Charles had taken to the field to help them and descended on
Picardy. At Péronne he learned that the King had concluded separate peaces with his allies. He could do nothing but leave. He had
come for nothing. Whence his anger. The herald charged with telling him of the affair barely escaped being hanged.

Louis was staying at Compiègne, ears cocked for any news
which might give him ideas or point toward a favorable solution,
when the idea of meeting Charles occurred to him. It didn't take
long until he saw it as the only means of salvation. He would be
able to convince the Duke, to bring him to the peace he desired.
He knew the power he exerted on Charles. He had to see him.
Already messengers were leaving for Péronne. Soon there was an
incessant coming and going between the two cities.

Louis began by sending money to his cousin—120,000 *écus*,
half of which was paid in cash—to help him to maintain this now
useless army he had raised. Louis knew him to be moody, stubborn, he flattered him like a thoroughbred. He would come from
Compiègne to the Somme, it was not far—scarcely a day's journey. No one need know anything about it. He would leave very
early on the pretext of hunting. He would not arrive as a king—

authoritarian, proud, dictating his conditions—but as a friend, as a neighbor. They would negotiate as equals, practically tête-à-tête. He would only bring a few faithful friends with him, the Duke of Bourbon and his brother the Cardinal, Constable St. Pol, Governor Roussillon, Cardinal Ballue, in all scarcely a hundred persons. The guest of the loyal Duke of Burgundy knew he had nothing to fear.

Louis made himself humble before his vassal, Charles. He was reassuring, coaxing. He hadn't set any traps, he had come to put himself in Charles's hands, on his territory. He had put himself under his protection. What more could he want?

On the morning of October 9, 1468, Louis set out across flat fertile land, veined with slow, flowing water, dotted with gray ponds. Winter was near at hand: full barns, stripped vines, hunters lying in wait. Autumn had reddened the trees, yellowed the reeds, brought in its fogs. They were burning off the last grasses, crackling leaves heaped into piles. Here and there in the distance against a pale sky were hamlets colored with red brick and ocher mud. A city, surrounded by bricks, roofs, painted gables, half-timbered façades, rectangles, punctuated by round towers, the old fortified castle—Péronne.

Charles greeted Louis, lodged him in the house of the receiver near the castle where he himself resided but which he didn't judge sufficiently equipped to shelter his sovereign. The conferences were about to begin, when a great tumult arose over the city—the army of Burgundy was making its entrance. The King, surprised, inquired, and learned that this company (all of whom were wearing the Cross of St. Andrew) included Monseigneur Philippe de Bresse, whom he had held in prison for two years, Monseigneur de Bresse, who had recently escaped from his jails, two malcontents who had passed to the other side after having served him: Poncet de la Rivière and Lord Urfé, and lastly the Marshal of Burgundy, from whom Louis had taken the city of Épinal after having given it to him. Such was the parade of enemies.

The King became afraid. What should he do? Flee? There would still be time. Or should he play the card of confidence to the end? He resolved to do the latter. He placed himself under the safeguard of the Duke and asked to stay in the castle for more security. The Duke reassured him: the presence of the troops was

pure coincidence. He was not lying. The King acquiesced. He
wanted nothing better than to believe him: he had come for peace.

Four days passed. They sought ground for understanding, nego-
tiated, proposed, in a rather tense atmosphere. It became clear
that Charles did not want to make concessions on anything. As
soon as the problem of King Louis's brother was raised, Charles
demanded Normandy for him, and Louis refused to grant it.

The outcome was already rather doubtful when messengers arrived on the scene. They came from one of the worst trouble spots
in Charles the Bold's territories: Liège. The entire city had risen
with cries of "Long live the King and his freedoms" at the instigation of exiles wearing the mantle of France, who had returned en
masse to his territory. Two thousand strong, they had gone to
Tongres where the bishop resided and had seized it; they had
brought him to Liège with some of his men, in the midst of the
worst violence. One of them, Robert de Muriamez, his archdeacon
and standard-bearer, had been savagely massacred right before his
eyes, then cut into pieces which the furious people threw about,
just for the fun of it. Without doubt, the killing had continued,
and it was reasonable to believe that at this hour more of their
prisoners were still alive.

While he listened to this tale, Louis, dismayed, remembered
that he had indeed sent two of his agents to Liège charged with
the task of fomenting a rebellion. A mission which had completely
slipped his mind when he made the trip to Péronne.

As was his custom, Duke Charles went into one of his terrible
rages bordering on madness. "It is true then," he cried in his rage,
"that the King only came here to fool me and to keep me off
guard. I was right to be suspicious and to refuse this interview. It
is he who by his ambassadors has stirred up these evil and cruel
people of Liège but, by St. George, they will be rudely punished,
and he will have reason to repent."

In the meantime, he had all the gates of the castle and the city
closed. The King was not let out of sight. The Duke refused to
meet him, forbade all contact with him, and filled Péronne with
the noise of his threats. Anything was possible on the part of this
madman, ready in his fury to listen to the most extreme advice.
He should seize Louis without ceremony, they told Charles. Let
him send in all haste for Monseigneur Charles, and obtain thus a

peace favorable to the princes. He should not let slip this unique occasion furnished by heaven to finish once and for all with this master knave, and he should replace the older brother with the younger. Besides, under the circumstances he had no other choice: "Such a great lord once taken is never delivered, or hardly ever, when one has caused him such offense." Meanwhile the voice of reason tried to make itself heard: "Let us give the King the security he was promised, since he is according the peace that we ask," countered the more sensible and levelheaded.

For two days Louis worked at making these sensible views the majority view. Firm in the tempest, he maintained the calm of great catastrophes and used the innumerable resources of his fertile mind to extricate himself from this difficult situation. Fifteen thousand *écus* were put into circulation to strengthen the hesitant and warm up the cause of loyalty. At the same time he made overtures. They should let him leave for Compiègne from whence he could take care to restore order in the rebellious city. Lords of his entourage would stay in Péronne as hostages and would guarantee his good faith with their lives. No answer. The Duke was anchored in his fury. The third night, he did not go to bed, so completely was he given over to vengeance. In the morning, pale and disheveled, trembling with rage despite his efforts to keep a polite face before his suzerain, his speech halting, he went to the King. He had been warned by a friend—Commynes, who was then Charles the Bold's secretary and who would later pass over to France—to acquiesce without argument to the offers which would be made.

"Do you not wish," asked Charles, "to swear to negotiate as it has been written?"

"Yes," said the King, "and I thank you for your good will."

"And don't you want to come with me to Liège to help me punish the treason that the Liégeois have done me because of you and your journey here? The bishop is your near relative, of the house of Bourbon."

"Yes, dear God," replied the King, "and I was very surprised at their wickedness; but let us start by swearing to the treaty. Then I will leave with as many or as few of my men as you wish."

Thus was it done. The King signed everything Charles wanted. The next day he left for Liège, the Cross of St. Andrew on his hat, to preside over the most bloody repression in which he was ever to take part. It lasted almost three weeks. On November 2, Charles freed him. With a smile on his lips and rage in his heart, Louis returned to Bourges, careful above all to minimize in the eyes of the public the humiliation he had received. The whole of Europe was going to laugh openly at it.

THE UNIVERSAL SPIDER

Henceforth, the ruin of the house of Burgundy became his idée fixe. He would devote almost ten years to a plan to bring it down. By 1473 the era of feudal coalitions had ended. Charles of France, Louis's brother, standard-bearer of the opposition, had died of syphilis. Armagnac was killed; the Count of Alençon, his godfather, was eliminated after a final plot. The county of Foix had fallen to a child; Brittany, isolated, stayed quiet. Only Burgundy was left.

At every turn of a road filled with ambushes, Charles would find Louis waiting. Without tiring, the universal spider spun his web in which his cousin the Duke would eventually be caught. He never attacked head on but worked underground, searching everywhere for possible enemies, organizing leagues, detaching Charles's allies from him, setting traps. There was no place in this world where the Duke could go without bumping into the King.

Louis, through his maneuvers, caused the failure of the Conference of Trèves, where Charles tried to extort from Emperor Frederick III the title of King of the Romans or, barring that, a royal crown for his duchy of Burgundy in exchange for the hand of his daughter Marie. Louis mounted a formidable coalition against him, from which came what history calls the Burgundy Wars. At Charles "the Terrible's" expense, he conciliated two enemies who had been up to then irreconcilable: his old allies the Swiss and the Duke of Austria, Sigismond. He detached Duke René II of Lorraine from Charles's alliance; the following year René united his forces with those of the Rhine cities. He persuaded the Swiss to take to the field. In October 1477 they entered the Franche-Comté; the union of Constance took place in upper Burgundy and in May 1475 he invaded Picardy, the two Burgundies, and Luxemburg.

On July 6 of the same year Edward IV disembarked at Calais with a strong contingent to lend a hand to his brother-in-law, who was held up at the siege of Neuss on the Rhine, proclaiming his rights to the crown of France. Louis decided to do business with Edward. The whole month of July there was constant activity on either side of the Somme, messengers, offers, gifts, the sending of food, fine wines, for the Englishman and his men, who were short of food. They finally met at Picquigny, on a bridge built especially for the interview, separated into two parts by a strong wooden divider. They embraced each other through the holes. The deal was done. For seventy-five thousand *écus* and the promise of an annual pension of fifty thousand *écus,* Edward renounced his rights to the throne of France as well as his allies, abandoned the Duke, his brother-in-law, and returned to his shores, having concluded the agreement in perfect friendship and established a truce of seven years. He would not return. The Hundred Years' War was officially over. Charles the Bold was isolated.

The wars of Burgundy continued. Louis had signed a truce with Charles but, based in Lyon, he secretly lavished money and advice on the Swiss and the Lorrainers, here favored an insurrection, there aided an alliance. On the fifth of January 1477, Charles, having fled the battlefield at Nancy, where the Swiss and the Lorrainers, paid by his cousin, had engaged him in a pitched battle, fell into an ambush not far from there. He was found completely nude, lying in the mud of St. Jean's pool, his face half eaten by the wolves. The King of France had gotten the better of the Great Duke of the West.

THE MOST TERRIBLE KING THERE EVER WAS IN FRANCE

He was a strange one, the man who engineered so well the defeat of the Great Duke of the West. A devil of a man, he was not at all attractive. He was small with thin legs, and a face without grace, featuring long nose, thick lips, and deep-set eyes. He had no style and didn't waste time making up for it by recourse to the artifice of costume. He had the same scorn for jewels that he had for fabrics. Two rings, one set with a diamond, the other enameled, and a gold chain, were all he wore. The King detested ap-

338 WISE AND FOOLISH KINGS

pearances. They were related to the superfluous—a notion he abhorred—as well as to the illusory, a luxury he could not afford.

The King was a simple man, he liked the simple life, simple people, simple amusements, fresh air, hunting, which for him was conquest, good food, women, laughing and joyous talk, and above all, his comfort. When, at the coronation banquet, his crown became annoying, he took it off and placed it on the table amidst the plates and the carafes of wine. A gay companion, bon vivant when he wanted to be, he was not fussy about the choice of his companions, taking more pleasure in the company of burghers than in that of his courtiers. He was not fussy about anything. Although he was descended from Charlemagne and had the genes of a certain number of princely houses of Europe, he was a crude man. He made people think of a country gentleman of the Loire country where he was born. Unlike all the other representatives of his house, he had Latin traits. He probably inherited them from his two grandmothers, Yolande of Aragon and Isabella of Bavaria, whose grandfather was a Visconti. He was a good deal like the Italian princes of his time with whom he got along wonderfully. Was not the Duke of Milan, Francesco Sforza, his hero? "It is as though he had always lived in Italy, and had been raised there," the ambassadors at the court wrote to their masters. The manners of the King were not surprising to them. They were reminded of their own country.

Louis held within him the mark of his childhood. Born in a universe of need, from his earliest childhood used to penury and emergencies, he had no difficulty facing up to things. Not knowing other horizons, Louis did not dream. He was happy with what he had. He was the son of Necessity. She taught him her rules and imposed her limits. She shaped him to her law, the only one he ever recognized. Although he was a believer and a man of piety, he didn't introduce the imperatives of the Most High into his daily conduct. He even showed himself to be totally amoral. Observing his behavior, one would conclude that he believed in neither God nor the Devil. Could it be he liked adversity? He knew so well how to manipulate it! He was in his element there. He revealed himself in it and fulfilled himself there. He had become an expert at it. What was more, he loved it. Far from depressing him, it stirred him up. Never discouraged, never tired, Louis was the man for great catastrophes, for hopeless situations. He always got out. Urgency was always his only master. He learned from it all that he knew. He recognized no other authority but this. For the rest, he recognized only himself, he believed only in what he saw, what he lived through. One could say that he recreated the world. This man belonged to the race of the strong.

One couldn't have found a better leader for the France which he inherited. The kingdom was exhausted by a century and a half of invasions and civil wars and did not need a knight-king. Rather it needed a master who knew how to impose order and peace. Louis XI was, like Charles V, the king the kingdom needed, come at the right moment. Not a long reign—twenty-two years; his grandfather had taken twice as long to destroy and rebuild what they bequeathed him, which was an unfinished work. He made the best of it.

Kingship was the great affair in this man's life. He loved power dearly. He didn't transcend it like Charles V but grabbed it with a keen appetite. He found his meaning and enjoyment in it. Having so long coveted it and waited to possess it, each minute it fulfilled him completely. No woman ever knew how to give him so much pleasure. As long as the crown escaped him, he had no idea of what France was. To love the kingdom, it had to belong to him. He was completely king, he did not tolerate sharing. He required his subjects to be completely his own. He did not compromise. Possessive, demanding, jealous, always searching for new lands— he never had enough—never satisfied, always alert and on the prowl.

Everything in him was subordinate to his action as king. That was his universe, his reason for living. He didn't count for anything. These verbs formed the fabric of life, to be, to have, to give, to know, converged toward this key word: to reign. He existed only for the country, he possessed nothing for himself. All he knew, all he had was for power; he could not love. A king without attachments, he had invested in this passion the totality of his affective forces. Henceforth, he had but one goal, the good of the country.

In the service of this passion, he had talents without equal: intelligence, a profound subtlety which struck his contemporaries, a fertile imagination, a sharp eye which nothing escaped, a capacity to listen. He was supported by a native curiosity which he himself recognized: "I have the nature of a woman; when someone tells me something, I immediately want to know all about it." These traits combined with a faultless memory and the power to work, gave him a kingly character indeed.

In exercising his calling the King relied first on his own experience: "One knows better and can speak more truthfully about those things which are known by experience," as he had Pierre Choisnet explain to his son in the *Rosier des Guerres,* a book of maxims on the act of reigning which he inspired. He worked in the field. He needed direct contact, to ask questions, with that curiosity and attention to detail which reflected both his anxiety and his perfectionism. He spent the first few years of his reign traversing his kingdom under a small escort, in this manner getting to know the problems and trouble spots. For his first destination he chose Guinne, where the English had so many friends. If a conflict was about to break out, he went there immediately, or got as close as he could. There was never a king more ubiquitous than this indefatigable traveler, always on mountains and highways, always ready to take to the road. Often ambassadors from neighboring countries had to seek him for several days before finding him somewhere on the road in a woodcutter's hut. To stay in direct contact with reality—that was his first concern. That was what dictated his decisions. He had no doctrine: he tried things to see what worked. If he committed errors he repaired them. Louis was an empiricist. Only what succeeded was valuable. He had no other theory. That was why about-faces didn't frighten him.

His father had exercised his functions with numerous councilors. Louis worked in a small committee, with his secretaries and his war chiefs. "The King must not commit to others those tasks of his kingdom which are his to carry out," he explained in the *Rosier des Guerres.* "He works by himself without the help of anyone," deplored Chastellain. But Pierre de Brézé admired his talents as a connoisseur. He carried his counsel in his head. "And if he asks for advice, it is more by expounding the problems himself, by thinking out loud that he finds the solution than in listening to the answers he asked for, scarcely giving his entourage time to formulate them. 'Speak briefly,' he ordered, when they had barely opened their mouths."

The King participated in an incredible range of activities. He awakened at dawn and stayed up late into the night. Except for the time allotted for the mass he heard every morning, meals, and a bit of exercise taken at the end of the day, he worked constantly. He read the mail, dictated, even personally wrote—the first French king to write—the letters which he sent by the hundreds to the four corners of Europe (at the end of the reign it was by the thousands).

Louis was by nature in a hurry, impatient. Without news he was lost. "Spare nothing," he said to his men, who were trained listeners. "So many *écus* to him who first brings such and such information," he stimulated them, tossing out the bait. Whatever the hour of the day or night, messengers had access to his bedroom. He had men everywhere. He riddled the courts of Europe with them, agents, spies, familiars, servants, all charged with a limited and precise mission, within which he allowed full liberty. His goal was to act with the maximum number of trumps, to put all the luck on his side, to neglect nothing. And night and day Louis calculated and worked. It is not surprising that the postal system sprang from the fertile brain of this King. It was a necessity to him. He started up a system that had been used in Gaul when Caesar arrived: a service of runners carrying news. He inaugurated it on the nineteenth of June 1464, instituting relays of men and horses charged with carrying his correspondence on the principal arteries of the empire.

But whatever the information furnished might be, to be useful, it must be true. "A king must like crude but true and profitable words better than the sweet words of deceit and flattery.

"And remember to seek the truth of all reports before showing what you intend to do, if you wish to avoid the inconveniences that can happen as a consequence of your actions."

The King liked the truth. He was accustomed since childhood to see truth, naked truth, not beautiful to be sure, but how useful—the essential thing to his eyes.

Another primordial element of his political method was money. Not for himself—the King lived like a monk—but for the country. But money really meant men.

From the bottom to the top of the social ladder, from the humblest valet to the most powerful lord—hearts, minds, consciences, loyalty, the soul and the body—everything could be bought. Persuasion was done with the purse, and one sold himself to the highest bidder. Let us pay what is necessary and without counting. Thus he wanted to have full coffers. The King had great need of money. Too bad if they cried against the stiff tax, tripled during his reign: "And I assure you, Sire, that it is a great sorrow to try to collect the money, for the people have nothing more, and whatever diligence I show, or have others show, I can get nothing." "On my soul, Sire, there is such piteous misery that it is an unbelievable thing to people who don't see it and experience it." "I need the money," responded the King, imperturbable. "Look and find some, even if it is in the magician's box." He contributed to feeding his treasury by taking in the economic domain very daring measures tending to develop commerce.

King Louis, Commynes tells us, showed himself to be a fine connoisseur of men. He was curious about them, and knew their full price. "No king honored good men more." His network of informants functioned: "Truly he knew all people of authority and value who were in England and in Spain, in Portugal, Italy, in the domains of the Duke of Burgundy and in Brittany, as he knew his subjects."

He was also a clever buyer. For what was a man for this blithely disillusioned King? An instrument, a piece of merchandise, with his weight, his price, his label of quality. He was only worth while according to his usefulness. Only one condition governed his choice of those he employed: their usefulness. Each one of them was known, tagged, filed with respect to the use he could be put to.

A collector in his soul, the King spared nothing to acquire more pawns, new specimens. Political action as he saw it required executors in great number as well as accomplices. They were, along with money, its cornerstone. They did not have to show themselves to be great geniuses. It was enough to be a bit lively and especially unwavering.

And he covered his provinces and Europe with a network of agents in his pay, charged with establishing contact, even with bringing back their prize. He played the seducer, used his sweet words, caressed, cajoled, unfolded the fan of his promises, pursued his advantage until, exhausted by the charm, his prey fell into his hands.

Europe was a large chessboard on which it was important to know every large piece as well as every pawn. That was why information was indispensable to him. The King worked man to man. He took on each one in single combat, which he didn't begin until he was informed of his tastes, desires, weaknesses, problems. Every man could be taken. He didn't have one method for getting someone, he had a thousand.

His knowledge of hearts was confined to motives. They were few to his mind—two: interest and fear. If the one did not suffice, Louis had reluctant recourse to the other. He only resorted to it in a hopeless case, once all other methods had been shown to be useless. Unlike his contemporaries, Louis didn't like violence.

He was suspicious of war and feared it. He knew its limits and its horrible consequences. A prudent man, he didn't want to risk expensively acquired advantages on one chance battle. Although he gave over a large part of his liquid assets to constituting a strong army, he only used it as a last resort. The *Rosier des Guerres* abounded in maxims which expose this point of view:

"When a prince comes to reign, if he finds the kingdom in peace, he must take care that in his time he does not begin a war. For there are too many perils, difficulties, labors, tribulations and dangers and destruction of peoples, of lands and of possessions. . . . In war and in lawsuits, there is never one cent of profit.

"A battle is the most perilous thing in the world.

"One must not fight just to fight, but to have peace.

"Subtlety is worth more than force."

Louis was a man of peace. Negotiation was his major weapon.

He whom his numerous detractors called the universal spider worked and spun his vast web across the world of the time, which was reduced to a few kingdoms. Well placed in the center of the work, he held all the strings, lying in wait, a feared hunter. They knew this silent work. They feared his potions and traps. Faced with this vague threat which he let hang over each one, this permanent risk, this hunt which he carried on and had others carry on for him, one felt himself a prey. They knew him to be powerful, they knew him to be pitiless. They saw themselves sooner or later inevitably reduced to doing his will.

From infancy he had carried the image of the absolute monarch, powerful, respected, a dream born of the weakness of his father and of his deteriorated possessions. All great plans come from a lack. "They will obey me," he had doubtless sworn to himself, faced with the disaster of reality.

An urgent need in the juncture of the time, a key problem: "The greatest and most sovereign good that a king can have in his realm is the obedience of his subjects, for God doesn't ask more of his creatures," he had them write in the *Rosier des Guerres*.

The country was dying of anarchy, of disorder; the great did as they pleased, pulling first one way, then another, following their interests. The small got fleeced in any case. He had to re-establish the authority of his house: "I am France," he was used to saying, opposing himself by this to Brittany, Armagnac, Anjou, Orléans, or Burgundy.

And from then on he worked to obtain the obedience of his subjects, to reign as he wanted to. Constantly occupied with the state of his people, "visiting them as the good gardener visits his garden," watching over his subjects like a shepherd; he had received his mission and power from God, and knew better than anyone what his subjects needed.

To traitors he showed himself pitiless. On his order they were decapitated. Powerful people, exemplary recidivists, toward whom he had shown long patience: Constable St. Pol, knight of St. Michel, who had so long played a double game between France and Burgundy, and Jacques d'Armagnac, Duke of Nemours, who never stopped conspiring, had their heads cut off. For Jean Hardy, guilty of treason—attempted poisoning—his justice showed itself to be even more terrible. He was decapitated and his head was displayed in the Place de Grève, planted on the end of a spike, while his limbs were sent to the four great cities at the ends of the kingdom to be exposed in public places.

Was this justice or personal revenge? He himself forestalled the question when he declared: "If it is useful of necessity to punish, one must show that one does it because forced to, and not so as to appear to be for vengeance." But there was in Louis so much passion in the way he fulfilled his office that there is room for question. His enemies, inspired by a virtuous indignation, did not fear to call it perversity, and the authors of the Romantic era, from Casimer Delangue to Walter Scott, finding that this trait fleshed out the character, made of him without the least respect for fact a monster.

It is true that there are some very troubling phrases in his letters. For example, concerning Oudart de Bussy, a parliamentary councilor decapitated by his order for treason: "So that they might all recognize his head, I had it dressed in a pretty furred hood, and placed it in the market of Hesdin, in the place where he presided." Certainly the King allowed himself to be carried away by a bon mot. The King admitted that he was occasionally guilty of intemperance of language. "I know well that my tongue has done me much damage," he stated.

The century was pitiless, and Louis had to be too. He explained his position: "The greatest good a king can do in his kingdom is to remove the bad and reward the good. For if he gives to the miscreants who haven't deserved it, he will remove the impetus to do good from the others. One doesn't punish the criminal for the crime, but as an example."

The authority of a king makes itself felt more by fear than by love. He deplored this, this "cruel King" who commented: "There isn't a worse thing than to be feared. . . ." What an admission from the mouth of a man who was said to have no heart and no attachments!

One could say that he was alone in the world and that he was self-sufficient. Perhaps because in his earliest childhood he felt himself truly alone in the world he constructed the best defense he could. Fearing beyond anything the traps of sensitivity, the links of emotion, he closed himself off from and denied them. He did not attach himself. It seemed better to avoid doing so, as there were too many risks, too many uncertainties. Louis was in essence suspicious. Unlike Charles, he got along well with himself, finding himself in good company. A king is alone by definition. Caesar in his solitude, but in his power. Eventually Louis took things so far as to choose to be buried far from his family, at Cléry, deliberately turning his back on his lineage, which he did not feel a part of.

Yet he was not a misanthrope. People distracted him, amused

him, he was not unhappy in their company. And also he was curious about human nature. However, only the fraction of their personality which was useful to him interested him. He took what he wanted from them; that is, what served him. "What purpose could that man serve?" was the question Charles forced himself to ask. "How can I have him?" added Louis cheerfully. There was in Louis a desire for conquest based at least as much on the pleasure of taking as on that of possessing. Louis was a collector, as we have seen; he was also a great hunter. He liked the game and the capture.

Women did not count for much either. What was a woman for Louis? A dowry and a womb. The love she might have for him left him indifferent. He had no need of it. Out of bed, the feminine sex had no attraction for him. With respect to his own wife, Charlotte, one cannot say that the King showed himself to be attentive or very faithful except after 1472 when he made the vow not to deceive her any longer, having lost a son, François, at birth. The ambassadors were shocked to hear him complain, when Charlotte was giving birth, that her cries kept him from sleeping, and to envision the eventuality that he might marry one of her younger sisters if she died.

As for his daughters, they represented to his eyes no more than one more instrument in the service of his policies. He had the same attitude, by the way, toward the other young girls of the court. Louis was a formidable matchmaker. The three natural daughters he had during his stay in Dauphiné were married off to gentlemen Louis wanted to attach to himself, as was his daughter Anne, whom he loved as tenderly as he was able, and whose husband, Pierre de Beaujeu, was one of his most intimate collaborators. Or else he made them marry gentlemen whose destruction he desired: the representative at the time of the house of Orléans, for example, another Louis, who was forced against his will to marry King Louis's youngest daughter, Jeanne, who was afflicted with congenital malformations incompatible with the state of marriage. "They won't have to worry about feeding the children they will have," he snickered ferociously. A nice throw of the dice, this marriage. The race became extinct by itself. So much gained for the Crown.

Louis was a poor son, a poor husband, and a rather indifferent

father, except as concerned the Dauphin, for whom he took many
pains because he was the successor. Louis had a poorly developed
heart, he knew. He recognized this impotence with the love of
truth which he possessed, even when it worked at his expense.
Whence these phrases from the *Rosier,* pathetic to those who
knew how to read them, and which we have already encountered:
"And who would like to be loved, he must love. . . . The King,
when he knows who loves him, he must hide it well." Louis recognized that he could not love. He preferred his dogs and birds to
people.

Animals are attractive. They live, they move. They are fast,
supple, powerful, with muscles the like of which men do not possess. A heart unlike men's. Faithful. Sure. No possibility of distrust with an animal. No reason to be suspicious. Never betrayed.
Animals console men. And he collected them, as he collected
men, this time for the pleasure of it.

He wasn't quite thirteen when Tanguy du Châtel, knowing his
taste, offered him a young lioness, who strangled herself by falling
from a window, which seemed to affect her young master very
much. Africa first furnished him species little seen in our climate,
but much sought after in an era which loved the exotic: elephants,
camels, lions, and monkeys which he mingled with big animals of
our forests—wolves, bears, and boars.

But his great favorites were the hunting dogs. Hunting was his
favorite sport, which he indulged in to the point of exhaustion.

Except for the smaller hare- and fox-hunting dogs, France
doesn't possess many varied species. Louis, who was a connoisseur, and difficult to please besides, complained: "One doesn't
find any good ones here." He therefore had them sought elsewhere. Every occasion was an excuse to acquire them: a trip, a
debt, an exchange, a service rendered. Here was something which
freed foreign courts from trying to find a gift which would please.
And the different breeds flocked to Plessis: five bulldogs (the
King of England), five greyhounds (the King of Scotland), the
fastest greyhound in France (the Sénéchal de Brégé), a large dog
to guard his room (Lorenzo de Medici). He was not too shy to
ask for them: from the Duke of Milan, little dogs from Chio, from
Jean Bourré, for the price of a concession of houses and gardens,

the annual debt of a blond spaniel, a white greyhound, or two bea-
gles.

He had the same passion for birds: sea birds or birds of prey,
exotic birds, forest or pond birds which filled cages, whistling
birds for the round cages of his bedrooms, sea gulls and white
peacocks, ostriches, eagles, hawks and falcons, quails and par-
tridge, pheasant, herons and egrets, and canaries, linnets, and
goldfinches by the hundreds.

With the years his taste became more refined and he developed
a collector's passion. He always needed more, always rarer specimens. He sent to the four corners of Europe, to Spain for bulldogs,
as far as Naples for his horses, to Sweden and Denmark for elands
and reindeer. He sent as far as Barbary to acquire those small
lions that are the size of a fox.

They had barely arrived when he forgot them and ordered new
acquisitions. Was this the behavior of a collector or a zoophile?
According to Brachet, he showed all the classical symptoms of
zoophilia: the extravagance of his purchases, the indifference of
the buyer, hypersensitivity to his sick animals. The King's love of
animals went so far that he had them kidnaped by armed men to
fill his parks and cages. This happened twice, it is said, the first
time after Péronne. A certain Henri Perdriel was ordered to round
up all the cage birds, magpies, jays, and owls of the capital and to
bring them to Amboise, whereas his colleague Merlin Cordeboeuf
did the same for the stags, does, and cranes.

The second time, during the last months of his life, in January
1483, he posted his men at night along the Loire to intercept birds
being shipped from Turkey to Britanny. And Brachet explains
such behavior: "By an ill-logic which is the mark of this morbid
state, the sick person steals what he covets not because he cannot
buy it, but because to possess it thus is more enjoyable; it is a
conquest."

Louis was a pious man. In this world filled with perils, he
wanted to have heaven on his side, which for him meant the saints
more than God. He worked at it, mounted an assiduous siege, assailing them with requests and promises. There were donations
and innumerable foundations, masses in prodigious quantity,
offerings and alms, and especially objects: ex-votos in wax in
every conceivable form: chalices, lamps, altar cloths, hearts of

precious metal, tabernacles, reliquaries, arms of St. Gilles, St. Charlemagne, and St. Andrew, head of St. Martha at Tarascon, cities of solid silver and a silver grille worth more than two million francs destined to surround the reliquaries of the Basilica of St. Martin of Tours. The saints cost him a veritable fortune. He had the same generosity with respect to the clergy; he gave them exemptions from fees as well as pensions and benefices. As for the poor, guilty of having profaned by crude words the name of God, they were "condemned to give offerings"! "He gave too much to the churches," deplored Commynes, "for he took from the poor to give to those who didn't need it." Could saints be purchased, like men? Was heaven also for sale and, like the rest of creation, not an end for Louis, but a means?

Every good thing that happened to him, every bad situation he got out of, he attributed to the will of his protectors, in the first place the Virgin: Our Lady of Béhuart saved him from drowning, Our Lady of Cléry let him capture Dieppe, she kept Noyon for him, because of her intercession he was able to sign the peace of Picquigny. It was she, helped by St. John the Baptist, who gave him Amiens, and in 1463 Perpignan, this time with the help of St. Martin. She caused the defeat of the Duke of Brittany in 1468. . . . Louis did not hold back his gratitude. He offered her a silver statue five feet high holding a diamond in her hand. He built a church in her honor at Compiègne, Our Lady of Good News. He honored her in all her sanctuaries: at Rouen, Beauvais, Clermont in Auvergne, Boulogne-sur-Mer, Rocamadour, at Cléry finally, which from a modest oratory became a collegiate church with a royal chapel endowed with the same prerogatives as the Sainte Chapelle in Paris, which he chose as his last resting place and where he founded his anniversary mass. He offered her the city of Boulogne in homage, he inscribed her name on his armor, he favored the development of the Angelus in her honor. Louis had a fervent love for the Good Lady.

She didn't hold his exclusive attention, however. Everything that heaven had left in the way of tangible signs of its passage on earth aroused his interest. Louis practiced a veritable cult of relics. He crossed the whole of France to pray before the holy shroud of Cadouin, the holy prepuce of Charroux, the holy tear of Vendôme. He attributed powers to them with an astounding

350 WISE AND FOOLISH KINGS

credibility. As always he was concerned with efficiency, and he wanted to be sure that the relics venerated were appropriate to the saint whose favors he sought. He ordered inquiries. St. Ursinus was venerated both at Bourges and at Evreux. Which bones were his? Did the cross of Monseigneur St. Laud at Angers really possess the powers attributed to it? Thirty-one witnesses confirmed its power. In fact the hair of one of them turned white when he took the oath. A man whose arm was already raised lied when swearing an oath, and he died within the year. Louis was reassured. He used the cross to have his adversaries swear by when he signed a treaty with them.

Louis placed the good of the kingdom above the salvation of his soul. He most likely also thought that he could reach the gates of heaven by observance only, since the era affirmed that man was saved by works.

Faced with the realities of the heart and the requirements of the soul, Louis chose escape. The same attitude was adopted by his father to face the same problems: the flight forward, into work, the lesser evil for Charles, for his son a great good, as we have seen. He lived therefore on the surface, establishing between himself and the irritating parts of his being a divider as watertight as possible, hoping that nothing that might bother him would filter through. Louis was ingenious, he got out of everything, even the worst spots. Heaven at a good price, peace of mind for a small fee, everything can be arranged when one knows how to go about it.

For the universal spider to reign in the world of the time, it was most likely necessary to turn away from himself with determination. King Louis gave his all to his profession, even to the extent of risking his soul.

Louis was full of fear. Fear was at the root of his strange behavior. It was fear which caused him to take four precautions instead of one, to always believe he didn't have enough, to go on ceaseless trips in pursuit of information because he trusted only himself. It was this permanent suspicion which weighed on everyone and which incited him to take astonishing security measures. He never went out unless accompanied by someone dressed as he was. Fear was everywhere. It was at every turn of his thoughts, every fold of his soul. It rendered all defenses superfluous and won every match. Louis carried Charles's anguish within him. He could not deliver himself from him who gave him life. King Louis, whatever he might do, was born of his father and of his childhood. He was not a free man.

They say Heaven helped Louis, since during the twenty years he held the throne, it killed off most of the landed princes who had caused the country so much trouble: his brother Charles of France, the Duke of Burgundy, who engineered his own end, but also the Anjou family, King René, his brother the Count du Maine and his grandson Nicholas, Duke of Lorraine. The Orléans family seemed threatened, since Louis, the only representative of the name, was married through the intervention of the King to his daughter Jeanne, who proved incapable of bearing children. Nonetheless, Louis had to know how to grab up these inheritances. When they were added to his other acquisitions, they gave him the most astonishing record of territorial expansion any French king was ever able to boast of. Who else but a Louis XI could count to his credit the addition of an imposing number of provinces to his patrimony: Artois, Picardy, the Duchy of Burgundy, Maine, Anjou, Provence, Roussillon! And how can we not give an unreserved admiration when this territorial record is matched by the most astonishing of political records: the state of Burgundy dismembered, a great feudal power brought into line, the conflict with England definitively settled, peace re-established across the country, the monarchy restored in its authority and power within the country as well as outside. We have only to quote Commynes: "Spain was at rest with him, and the King and Queen of Spain only wanted friendship. . . . As for the powers of Italy, they only wanted him for a friend and had alliances with him, and often sent their ambassadors. In Germany there were Swiss who obeyed him like subjects. His allies, the kings of Scotland and Portugal and parts of Navarre, did whatever he wished. His subjects trembled before him. What he commanded was immediately done, with no difficulty or excuse. . . . He was so obeyed that it seemed to him that almost all Europe was made only to show him obedience."

This is the work accomplished in twenty years by the successor of King Charles VII.

"Decidedly this man was better made to govern a world than a kingdom," Commynes, who loved him, said elsewhere. Such a judgment does not seem exaggerated.

FOOLING PEOPLE

In the month of March 1479 the King was dining near Chinon and Forges where he had gone to hear mass when suddenly he became pale and agitated, unable to speak. He was taken from the table, and despite his desire for fresh air, which he expressed as well as he could, he was placed near the fire. He lost consciousness. Everyone did his best. The doctor Jean de Vienne had the windows opened immediately. They carried the sick man over to them, the freshness from outside brought back a glimmer of consciousness. With great effort, by signs, he made it known that he wanted to confess and that the official of Tours should be sent for. He also wanted Commynes, his secretary, near him. It didn't take them long to realize that sense as well as speech eluded him. He no longer understood. He spent three days in this semicomatose state. He neither recognized nor spoke nor heard, but he did not seem to suffer. Then life took hold again. Sense and speech came back to him. And from then on, one idea alone obsessed him: to fool people. Fear gripped him—fear of death and of men, all men, friends, strangers, enemies, traitors, children. Whom could he trust? Who was not tired of his yoke in this kingdom which for twenty years he had struggled to bring into submission? They kept silent because they trembled. He determined to make them tremble to the end, to prove that even though he had been stopped for a few days he was still the "most terrible King" and that no one could disobey his orders. And he worked at sowing terror.

He had not yet recovered his speech when he kicked out of his house all those who, thinking they were doing the right things, at the beginning of his illness had kept him near the fire instead of giving him air, as he had told them. He set immediately to work, had the mail read to him, pretended to hear and to understand. They put the dispatches on his knees. He brought them one by one up to his eyes, simulated reading, indicated by a sign the answer to send. He was barely on his feet again when he undertook a voyage from the Loire to Normandy (where his army was) and back again. A second attack, less serious than the first, confined him to his room. He was saved by a vow made to St. Claude by his entourage, who thought him dead. He set out a second time: one month at Argenton at the home of his inseparable Commynes, then at the sanctuary of St. Claude to give thanks and to keep his vow. He could not go on. No one must know that he had been stopped. He knew he was unrecognizable. He would therefore arrange it so no one saw him. And he remained at Plessis, henceforth forbidden to the rest of the world. He denied access to the castle to everyone and especially to the ambassadors. Except for his son-in-law Beaujeu, few nobles were admitted. Half the servants found themselves dismissed. He kept only small, unknown men in his entourage, like his doctor Coictier, who extorted huge sums for his services and treated him so poorly. For the rare people who approached him, as well as for the servants, he worked on his appearance, wearing long red robes trimmed with martin fur which hid his thinness from prying eyes.

In fact, what he feared was a palace revolution, which, on the pretext that his mind had weakened, might take from him his power and give it to his son (he thus had him carefully guarded) or to his daughter Anne, who was nonetheless very devoted and close to him. A handful of resolute men would be enough to infiltrate the château, provided they had made contacts within. He therefore had it fortified and guarded like a border town, iron grilles were built around it, skewers were put in the walls. He ordered his guards to shoot whoever approached at night, and forbade anyone to enter or leave except under heavy guard. The King had foreseen everything, including the possibility that they might say he was dead, since no one ever saw him. He worked at making people talk about him. Within the kingdom there were many changes, executions, pensions cut off or reduced, offices revoked, men-at-arms dismissed. He filled Europe from Naples to Stockholm and from Brussels to Valladolid with envoys charged with diverse missions—friendly words, gifts, purchases of dogs or large animals—to make the people believe that nothing had changed in the kingdom of France.

A delirium of fear possessed the King. It was perhaps motivated by other causes than the fear of losing his authority. Louis XI and his entourage may have taken these attacks for epileptic fits, *grand mal*, St. Jean's disease, the sacred disease, as they called it then, a dishonor, a blot on the sick man's family, and for this reason carefully hidden from the public eye. Especially when the King was the victim.

On this subject the chroniclers remained silent, except one, Gaguin, who categorically named the affliction by its name. This would not be convincing proof (since he was less than impartial with respect to the King) were it not for Brachet, who in his remarkable book, *Mental Pathology of the French Kings,* was able to demonstrate with a rigorous argument that Louis XI had suffered from epilepsy since 1469.

Since it was said that perfumes cured, his apartments were filled with fragrant flowers: tansy, sweet marjoram, violets, thorn flowers, especially roses. Music, according to Barthelemy the Englishman, took away fear and sadness. So they housed at St. Cosmi near Tours a hundred and twenty musicians, as well as shepherds from Poitou who came to play—in a minor key only—before the King's house so that he got pleasure from it and passed the time. This was also to keep him from sleeping, as too much sleep during the day was believed to be a provoking cause of epilepsy according to Hippocrates. The hygiene of the time prescribed strict measures for whoever suffered spasms. The King slept with his head elevated. He must protect his head carefully from the cold as well as the heat, whence his numerous head coverings—a white double cap which he wore at night, a bonnet of scarlet with six threads above, hats of wool or beaver brought by the dozens from Montpellier, or that other famous fur one that the Bishop of Valence brought him from Rome.

Conscientiously he took all the different remedies prescribed for the illness which affected him: hyssop, fumitory, horn of eland, milk of a she-ass, drinkable gold especially, as witness those "one hundred ninety-six *écus* of old gold used to make a certain brew called *aurum potabile* ordered for him as medicine."

Finally the King, in order to be cured, did not hesitate to submit himself to the most painful, even repugnant forms of therapy: cauterizations and cranial incisions to heat and dry his brain; blood treatment—still warm human blood was supposed to be a great remedy for epilepsy. This belief had traveled across the centuries; in 1845 there was the case of a capital execution in Stockholm where an old woman afflicted with epilepsy stood at the foot of the scaffold, ready to plunge into the body of the dead man a piece of bread destined to cure her the minute his head was separated from his body.

It seems reasonable to agree with Brachet's diagnosis of epilepsy. It doesn't exclude the possibility that the King died of what they say he did—three successive heart attacks between 1481 and 1483—but it does explain the behavior of the King at the end of his life, which at first glance appears insane. We can then understand why he holed up at Plessis under the conditions described. None must suspect what went on there. The prejudices of the time forbade anyone to know that he was afflicted with epilepsy.

Little by little his strength left him. His was but the shadow of himself. And yet he wanted to live, for himself, for the kingdom, for peace, which he sought. How did he still manage to work, wondered his constant companion, Commynes. "His great heart carried him," he concluded. He was forced, however, to give up his former activity. He who had been so careful to see to everything himself now took care only of the big affairs. To his credit, the last one was a great one—the marriage of the Dauphin to the heiress of the house of Burgundy, Marguerite, granddaughter of the Bold, who brought as her portion Artois and the Franche-Comté.

If he could only bend the will of heaven and survive. He had never prayed so much or paid so much. The King's gifts reached such exorbitant proportions that Parlement thought it was its duty to oppose several of them. He wanted so much not to die, or at least to know the hour. What anguish to live in fear of each passing instant. Fear of death obsessed him.

They told him that at Doullens there lived a certain Friar Bernardin who held astonishing powers, levitation among others. He sent for the friar, whom he asked to consult God in secret to reveal to him whether the prince would soon recover his health. The friar answered that he would gladly pray for the monarch but that he could not tell anyone the revelations that were made to him. "The Virgin Mary did not dare tell her husband Joseph she was pregnant without the permission of God, revealed to her by an angel." Friar Bernardin was nonetheless sent to the Loire country, where he multiplied his prayers in favor of the prince in the company of a pious woman from Primery in the Nivernais, a holy man from near Orléans, the good hermit of Fleury-sur-Loire, and finally St. Francis de Paule, whom they sought out in Calabria, where he had been living under a rock since the age of eleven. Louis received him as he would have the Pope, bowing down before him, imploring him to lengthen his life. To which the holy man asserted that he did not have the power to do so.

His Holiness, knowing Louis's torments, knowing also how to contribute to easing them, sent him the communion cloth of St. Peter, and divers relics of inestimable value: a fragment of the tunic of the Savior for which the soldiers gambled with dice during the Passion, another fragment of the three tunics St. John the Baptist gave to the three men he raised up, the remains of the body of the Precursor, finally a piece of skin from the head of St. Anthony of Padua. Even the Turk, when told of Louis's illness, sent him holy fragments kept at Constantinople.

Even more precious, he had the holy phial of the coronation brought to Plessis and placed in his bedroom on a sideboard with the Crown of Victory and the rod of Moses and did not take his eyes off it, hoping every minute for a miracle. Death was rapidly approaching. On Monday, August 28, he once more lost the power of speech. He recovered, but he could scarcely bring his hand to his mouth, he was so weak. All his thoughts then turned to the realm. He sent for his son-in-law Beaujeu, consigned the Dauphin to his care, sent to the young prince, still at Amboise, the seals, the captains and archers of his guard, his hunting and falconry staff, asked those leaving him to serve the prince well, and prepared for the worst. He was lucid. The days passed, however, the week drew to a close. Had they forgotten the orders he had given to his servants earlier, that if they saw him in this extremity, they should say only to him "Speak little" and incite him to confess without pronouncing this terrible word, "for it seemed he would never have the courage to hear such a cruel sentence"? His doctor Jacques Coictier, to whom the King's illness was worth a fortune as long as Louis thought him capable of prolonging his life, ignored it completely. Pitiless to the dying man, he didn't mince his words: "Sire . . . have no more hope in this holy man, nor in these other things, for surely you are done for, and thus think of your conscience, for there is no remedy." The King had a strong soul, we know. He withstood the shock: "I have faith in God that He will help me," he answered with great dignity, "for perhaps I am not as sick as you think."

On Saturday the last day of August 1483, Louis XI died, all fear overcome, thinking less of himself than of the destinies of the kingdom.

CHAPTER XI

Charles VIII the Adventurous
(*Born 1470; reigned 1483–98*)

THE SOUL'S SEARCH

Charles VIII was born on June 30, 1470, of the marriage of his father with Charlotte of Savoie. He had a dull childhood at Amboise, shut in between a sweet, pious, quiet mother and tutors of exacting vigilance. His sister was nine years older than he, and an expert traumatizer. She was the picture of the King; and so intelligent, prudent, cunning that it seemed impossible to outshine her. His father was absent and all around the child there was a conspiracy of silence and fear. What good could they tell him about this detested tyrant who was his father? Who dared to talk about him? He had a calm existence, minutely regulated by a suffocating will. Not one word was louder than another, not one day less gray than the previous one. Charles got sick and seemed to be pining away. His father thundered, furious at the idea of seeing the very last bud of the race disappear. He demanded that he be kept informed about the boy. Charles contracted colic and fever. The trembling entourage, fearing the worst, referred the matter to the King, who sent for his doctors. They probed, and bled, and once again Charles got well. They carried the pale child with elaborate precautions onto the terrace to get the benefit of the winter sun, to breathe the soft air on nice days. They worried about the future.

What was to become of the boy? The boy knew that all of this bustle around him wasn't for him but for the inheritor of the name. It
was enough to make him hate the cause for which they feared so
much to lose him. He must have hated the throne early on, because already the King was in his death throes.

They brought him to the bedside of the dying man. The transfer
of power from the unrecognizable old man to the fearful child was
accompanied by such an abundance of advice and imperatives that
they confused and crushed him. If only I don't forget anything,
thought Louis, who ran on endlessly only to withhold the essential, the pleasure which he took in reigning and which he hid, perhaps out of modesty, revealing only the difficulties and burdens of
his office.

Charles promised his father everything he asked. He was just
thirteen years old. At Reims, his soul did not celebrate when they
placed the crown of kings on his head. At the banquet in Tau, his
sister looked askance at him, or at least he thought so. He could
not go on eating. They took him away. Yesterday the father, now
the sister, he never stopped trembling. It was all right to tremble
in front of a father, especially if he was the King, and a Louis XI
in the bargain, but to be afraid of a woman, there was no excuse
for that. It was a question of honor. And he turned his back on
them, on her, on Beaujeu her husband, on everything they represented: duty, statecraft, business. He didn't like obligations. Moreover, on that question, he resembled the deceased. *Le Rosier* he
threw into the fire. As for the kingdom, he left it to them, with a
clear conscience. And he left, in search of . . .

Charles donned his walking hat, a hat in the style of the times,
supple, easy to wear, with a broad brim, tilted up in the back and
on the sides, a decoration on the top. He peered into mirrors, into
Narcissus' pool, and what he saw made him tremble—an enormous
head, large white eyes, flat lips, and the nose, especially the nose,
voluminous, bulbous, so hooked it nearly touched his mouth. This
face was a disaster. The body matched: scanty, short in the waist,
large and fleshy in the behind, perched on endless legs which were
frightfully thin.

A cruel vision rejected with a start: an image, thought Charles.
The power of a king begins with himself. I will be what I want.
This was a shadowy mirror, a mirror which lied about the reality

of bodies. There were others, dream mirrors, word mirrors, another world where another reality was modeled according to his wishes, bent to his desire. The young man pursued his quest therein.

When you go so far out into dreams, you can come back with a laurel-covered head, arms full of roses, dragging along a harvest. It was important to dare to go the whole way. Charles determined to be a knightly king. As for the body, he had recourse to the artifice of clothes. With helmets, breastplates and swords, pourpoints of satin, velvet robes and greatcoats of scarlet he would edify a palace according to his image. Amboise was filled with painters, masons, carpenters that the beauty of olden times might live again. No sooner wished for than achieved. Amboise became a building site. The young nobility came running. The drapers, tailors, embroiderers, hat furriers, peacock hatters, plume makers, gold and silver button makers, the goldsmiths, lapidaries, took over in a great flurry. They carved, cut, built, threaded in and out, embroidered cloths of gold with mottoes and emblems. They attached gold tassels, pounded gold and silver, filed settings, set rubies, pearls, cut diamonds and precious stones. There were hunts, jousts, courtly assemblies. There was friendship and love. Still Charles was not satisfied. He was surprised that this existence left him unfulfilled. Had he chosen the wrong path? Already the jousts in which he fought to exhaustion weren't enough for him. Where was prowess? In books perhaps. He sought out all the romances in the library of his dead father. For whole evenings his knights read him Gawain, Lancelot, Galahad, Eric, Cléomadès. Now he was greatly perplexed. His soul was exalted at these encounters only to fall back immediately. Always the same tribute of emptiness for a few instants of life, sighed Charles. However, reality never provided such moments for him. Was he alone in feeling this cruel lack? Did life take on savor, density, importance only when passed through words? But these were fictions, narrated existences, bottled up in the domain of language. It was only a game. Certainly one could be happy listening to a story about how one would like to live oneself. But that was only living by proxy. Charles hadn't resolved anything.

Then he thought that he might exercise that power which weighed so heavily upon him, providing it was by other means than those used by his father and sister. He would use his own means, even when they opposed those of the Beaujeus.

It turned out that governing for Charles meant becoming conscious of the boredom which encumbered the crown in those times. Amboise was empty, France was empty. The two words resemble each other moreover: *vie* and *vide*. The reality of the kingdom: abuses, taxation, administration, justice, customs, work, the Council, these things didn't make him comfortable. He got that through the family. And the other aspects of this same reality, which were real power, didn't attract him very much either. From what angle could he tackle it in order to get some pleasure out of it? thought Charles, whom nothing and nobody had ever been able to convince to do something that bored him. Was this all there was to living, nothing more, nothing better? For him, living was burning, which he would have found in war. But there were no longer any wars in France for good causes. Nothing happened any more except unimportant things, feudal struggles which no longer interested anyone, except for the participants.

Brittany, arms in hand, persisted in maintaining its independence. He put an end to its dangerous pretensions through a marriage in which he took the part of payee, transforming this procedure from a preventive measure into a curative one. It worked beautifully. The young Duchess of Brittany, Anne, heiress to the late Duke Francis, recently dead (1488), had just married through procuration, without the consent of her sovereign, Maximilian, King of the Romans. Charles would not have it that way. He wanted the hussy for his own. He was already married, it was true, to the very daughter of the Conjoint de la Bretonne, Margaret, who since 1483 had been living with him at court. But he rode roughshod over the sacraments of heaven, the tears of his wife whom he had not touched, and the anger of her outraged father, whose wife, on top of everything, he desired. Let him storm and thunder. It mattered little to Charles. The German states were a long way off, Brittany was at his doorstep. This was no time to hesitate. He assembled his army, marched on Rennes where the Duchess was in hiding: "Your hand, beautiful lady. Here is peace, my heart and my kingdom. You will certainly give me this duchy as part of the bargain. Open up." And young Anne found herself Queen of France *in perpetuum,* the contract stating that if Charles died without descendants she would be expected to dry her tears and wed the successor immediately.

Thus the young monarch quickly settled this litigious question to the sound of the drum and annexed the duchy of Brittany to the kingdom—Brittany which had been the cradle of all rebellions for two hundred years and whose independence had been a thorn in the side of the kingdom. But Heaven may not have been happy about the way he went about it. It rained so much that year that the grapes didn't ripen. The wine turned: "We shouldn't be surprised," sighed the wife sent back to her father, "if the grapes were green and unhealthy this year, since the promises weren't worth anything."

As for the Emperor, his pride hurt to the quick, he threatened and, in order to vindicate his honor, he attacked. He appealed to the sovereigns of Europe, in particular the English and the Spanish.

But Charles wanted peace at any cost, at home as well as with his neighbors. What did the faraway provinces which his father had acquired with so much effort matter? He paid off the recalcitrant kings: Henry VII, who debarked in Calais and left with an exorbitant sum, 745,000 gold crowns; Ferdinand the Catholic, 200,000 gold crowns, plus Roussillon and Cerdagne; Maximilian took over the provinces of Artois, Franche-Comté, and Charolais.

The politicians of the court wailed under their coats. Charles did not want to hear them. What was important had no price. Kings must have great designs, he thought. He decided to leave France, which was stagnating in forms of expression and action long out of date. He sought a wider, more exotic world.

This time, the Pythonesses had spoken. From the depth of their delirium they had pronounced words which had haunted the prince ever since. They spoke of conquest and of empire: Naples, the rights of the Anjou family from which he was descended, of Constantinople, the Turks, of crusades, of chasing away the infidel, reconquering his property, and Jerusalem. They were calling him: Naples had been in the hands of usurpers for two centuries and awaited her savior, as did all of Italy. The Turks were at its gates. They were encircling it with their threats. Ambassadors went back and forth from Milan to Amboise, from Amboise to Rome. Charles was busy and exalted as he left. In order to be sure of having peace at home, he took war elsewhere.

This man had a way of daring to turn his back on obligation, saying no to what bothered him, living for pleasure, with a genial easygoing style. Strength inhabited this scrawny body.

On January 25, 1494, Ferrante, the King of Naples, died. Immediately Charles claimed the crown in the name of the Angevin kings of Sicily, descendants of Louis I of Anjou, by his paternal grandmother, Marie of Anjou. He called together his nobility, he assembled his army, his Gascons, his Picards, his Swiss guards, his mercenaries from Germany, his Albanian cavalry, and left for the conquest of his property.

"Here is peace, my harvest will come to term, I will eat as much as I want this year," thought poor Jack, watching them go by. "Long live the king who comes to deliver me from these plundering men-at-arms. That's governing better than any king ever did. . . ."

In a blazing heat, streaming under the armlets, the thigh pieces, the collar stays, the iron corsets and the tassels, dragging their maces and their halberds, looking for a stream where they could fill their helmets, dog tired, broken, these men crossed the Alps at Mount Genèvre and ended up in Turin, with the King at their head. The date was September 9, 1494.

THE CELEBRATION

On the other side of the mountains it was still summer. Warm golden light, short shadows, like August in the Loire region. In the early morning, on the prairies and the rivers, rose the first mists, which penetrated and stuck to the body like sweat.

Turin, Chieri, Asti, Casale, Pavia, Piacenza, Lucca, Pisa, Florence, Sienna, Rome the thirty-first of December. He arrived in Naples on February 22. It was a long, fruitful, and happy trip, which Charles prolonged.

The towns he saw in the distance coming up out of the dust of the road seemed like mirages, vague masses, red, ocher, or chalky against the deep azure of the evenings, the purples and golds of sunsets smoldering in their glory.

Upon his arrival at one of these cities, banners would be flying, the sharp angle of the ramparts was punctuated with watchtowers, alternating with the powerful square gate towers, each one topped with a flat roof, like the pyxidium with its cover and seigneurial towers.

There were in the hearts of these cities vast spaces surrounded by admirable architecture, high façades which supported arcades where the shade at noon was cool, the evenings perfect, and where the populace assembled.

Suddenly there would be a noise in the distance, which became a commotion louder than the scuffling of horses and people. Entire crowds came from the cities to meet him. They implored him to protect them, greeted him as a liberator.

These were unhoped-for greetings. Were they afraid at the sight of the young king? This was a supreme pleasure when one's childhood had been spent trembling at those bigger than oneself. Who were these French, angels of death, knights of the Apocalypse, hordes of the north, swarming as in olden times across the peninsula, armed with terrifying engines of destruction, diabolic mouths of fire which these barbarians wouldn't hesitate to use? Ancient fears were rekindled. These Gascons, Swiss, and Germans were once the troops of Segovesius and Bellovesius. They were the Insubres, the Boiens, the Franks, the Goths, the Huns, strewing death and desolation after them. Hearing of their arrival, the Italians were very worried, but composed themselves quickly. Optimistic, they opted for the favorable hypothesis that a king of France was a man of honor, that he was only asking for passage. He might decide, once his conquest was finished, to deliver the peninsula from the terrible peril threatening it from the East: the Turks. Why not greet him as a friend? A disarmed man doesn't fight a hunting lion, he nourishes it and tames it and, if possible, uses it. One could hardly act more wisely.

So it was that these people of Turin, Chieri, Asti, Casale, Pisa, and Piacenza donned their most festive clothes, put on cheerful faces, and went out to meet the prince whose singular exploits fascinated them. The image of the conqueror, a new Alexander, rekindled in them that cult of the hero which was celebrated in olden days. They had forgotten their fear. All was joyful. At his approach they got ready in a fever as on great days. The King made his entry into the city which was decorated in his honor.

The church bells rang out at full peal, the little children waved palm fronds, held up placards emblazoned with fleurs-de-lis. "Long live the King of France," they cried out at the top of their voices. "Long live France by land and by sea." The doors and windows were jammed with people. All their colors were displayed, banners of white silk bearing the arms of France crowned and with the mottoes *Voluntas Dei, Missus a Deo*. To the sound of flutes, fifes, and drums the first troops would enter the walls. Sometimes it was necessary to break down several panels of the wall so that they could make their entry. The parade was a spectacle offered to the city.

An army of forty thousand men on parade is a spectacle. Could anything be more beautiful? Enthusiasm triumphed over fears and reticence, and exploded. Amid the hurrahs Charles entered the church where he gave thanks. They acclaimed him once more when he left it to go to the apartments they had provided for him in the castle of Turin or Casale. He no longer knew where to cast his eyes. At every intersection scenes from the Bible or legend were being performed on outdoor stages. This at Turin: Jason in Colchis after the conquest of the Golden Fleece, Hercules and his enormous club, episodes of Lancelot of the Lake. At Chieri they celebrated the victory of King Clovis and the miracle of the fleurs-de-lis, and the miracle of bringing a child into the world, a new mother resting in great finery, while the nurse showed off the child at the front of the stage.

The houses he visited showed a luxury and refinement which he had never known existed; such was the castle of Casale where the Marchesa of Montferrate, a Comnenus, received him with magnificence and put her country, wealth, and person under his protection.

> King in triumph, Charles the chivalrous,
> Chief of the French, savior of the valorous,
> To whom is due the tribute of Prowess . . .
> To crush the proud enemy
> Tyrannizing your fields and your country
> And to rid your subjects of savagery
> You must cross the great perilous mountains. . . .

Thus the poet André de la Vigne sang to him, trying to incite him
to leave. Little poems were sung by three virgins of Chieri perched
on a scaffold decorated with his colors:

> O noble king, O imperial stem,
> O reigning king, sparkling renown,
> By all kingdoms welcomed and sought after,
> Your fame is manifest and well known.
>
> You are the head and the healing arm,
> You are the only lord possessing
> Human hearts, bodies and also souls. . . .

This was what he had always sought. He was finally living. He
no longer had to compensate constantly for what was lacking by
seeking in books what he did not find in living. Reality took on
weight, meaning. Ah, the beautiful country! Would it be the kingdom of his heart? Ought he to recognize himself in its image?
Didn't the hurrahs prove that in his turn he had been recognized?

Completely happy, drunk with joy, Charles tasted every instant
of these warm nights. The noises from the happy city rose toward
him in homage. Why should he leave? he thought. Let us pluck
the rose. . . .

BEAUTY

Charles entered Florence on November 17; he left on the
twenty-fifth. Eight days was a very short time to see the capital of
the arts. A great deal of his time was absorbed by the political situation. The city was in the throes of revolution. They had just
ousted Piero de' Medici in the name of liberty and rigor and were
blindly obeying the exalted harangues of Fratri Girolamo Savo-
narola. The atmosphere was thus scarcely favorable to culture.
Contrary to his tastes and habits, the King did not do much visiting. He stayed at the Medici Palace. He went to hear mass in
Santa Maria dei Fiori in San Lorenzo, in the Annunziata, and in
the monastery of San Marco. That was enough to acquaint him
with the principal masterpieces of the quattrocento.

This was something entirely new for him. Up to now, he had only known Italy by her courts. In the interior of the Duomo, they led him up to the choir so that he could contemplate at leisure the cupola of Brunelleschi, symbol of Florentine power, whose construction had required a special tax. That was his first contact with great architecture. Everywhere were marble friezes of singing children, medallions of terra cotta, polychromatic porcelains. They pronounced the names Donatello, Luca della Robbia . . . and they took him to San Lorenzo. Probably it was there, at San Lorenzo, and through Brunelleschi, that the King had his first encounter with antiquity, about which he must have been curious after the conversations which he heard in the courts where he had been received.

He couldn't have missed the Fra Angelicos of the San Marco monastery, since he went there for mass. How could he not have loved the golds, the pinks, the reds, the perspectives—he whose father and grandfather had patronized Fouquet—when he employed Bourichon as a *valet de chambre* and patronized Jean Perréal of Lyon? The Valois knew how to look. But did such a brief stay leave him the time to go to the Carmine for the Masaccios, to Santa Maria Novella for the Ghirlandaios with their aristocratic women in the supple robes, their veils of mute colors, floating across vast skies of architecture? Did he at least see the Peruginos? His sweet style was causing a sensation at the time, and his friend Lodovico the Moor swore by him. Was he bothered by the masterpieces of Botticelli—*Primavera, The Birth of Venus,* in which the beauty of the female body is visible through the light glistening folds of cloth—accustomed as he was to being shown the human form covered up to the teeth? Would he have seen in them that dazzling world to which he aspired? Would he have found in them the model of the ideal life, of the man he might be, or of cities he might have dreamed of? He must have lingered in front of the frescoes of Benozzo Gozzoli in the Medici Palace, or amused himself by recognizing his hosts.

The Medici Palace didn't resemble anything the prince could have seen in his own country. In the domain of civil architecture it was a novelty and in Florence a success without precedent. From 1450 to 1478 some thirty of these dark stone quadrangles were constructed there. They were austere in appearance, with heavy reliefs which were lightened in the upper stories, and topped with an enormous overhanging cornice. His hosts pointed out as particularly remarkable examples the Pitti Palace, the Strozzi, the Rucella with its diamond-point reliefs. He himself remembered the Palazzo Vecchio where he noticed on the Porte du Lys one of those beautiful wooden marquetry panels representing Dante which were, it seems, so much in favor in Urbino.

Decidedly this city was superb in spite of its insecurity and present difficulties. He would have liked to stay there longer before going on to Rome.

THE CLASSICAL

On the advice of the astrologers, Charles advanced his arrival in the Eternal City by twenty-four hours, the position of the stars being more favorable on the thirty-first of December than the first of January. He entered on the last day of the year, through the People's Gate, at night, by torchlight, with all the houses lit up and bonfires at regular intervals along the streets, in the intersections. The people were shouting, *"Francia, Francia, Colonna, Vincula."* The sight would have been terrifying, if the people hadn't been frightened themselves. A long procession moved through the darkness; the tramp of feet, the faces glimpsed by torchlight inspired respect if not confidence. Rome was nothing more than a thieves' alley in 1494, a great pile of debris, a shambles. The stones were crumbling, empty windows gaped into the dusk. It was cold and muddy.

Charles refused to stay at the Vatican because the Pope did not approve of his plans and chose to be lodged by the Cardinal de Benevento in the Palazzo Venezia. For thirteen days he didn't budge from there. He allowed time for his troops to take up their quarters. That should suffice to give His Holiness the taste for compromise. For the moment the Pope closeted himself in the Castel Sant' Angelo. It wasn't much protection for him, the walls were caving in all by themselves. After the splendors of the cities and courts where he had just stayed, Rome must have seemed to Charles unworthy to be the capital of Christianity. A city was forming however. For half a century the pontiffs had been trying to organize this shapeless city they had found upon their return from Avignon, "so full of destruction that it no longer had the face of a city," into a place worthy of the throne of St. Peter. They still hadn't succeeded. In the forum of the Caesars grass was growing, cattle were grazing tied to the bases of columns, and for centuries, whenever the citizens needed stones for their walls, architraves for their doors, or marble for the lime furnaces, they had taken buildings apart.

The vandalism of ignorance was rivaled by the possessive passion of art lovers, artists, and archaeologists, whose zeal threatened even greater mayhem. Under the impulse of the pontiffs, Rome had become the center of classical archaeology. Everywhere people were making excavations. Everything they found, sculptures, intaglios, medals, money, coins, any vestige whatsoever of those fruitful centuries, was ardently coveted by collectors from all over Italy. In the first rank were the Medicis, the Gonzagas, the Estes, not to mention the late Pope Paul II.

The papacy, confronted with the enthusiasm inspired by this culture, wanted to take up the torch, perhaps to make people forget that the papacy was the cause of the ruin. It possessed circuits and correspondents. Whatever got to it through these channels was piously concentrated on the Capitoline, in the Palace of the Conservators. The most beautiful relics were exposed to public view in the city.

The rest was smuggled away. An important contraband traffic had been constituted over the last few decades. The French put their fair share in their baggage train. Only the archaeologists understood the risk incurred. Fra Giocondo of Verona played Cassandra and tried to temper this excess on the spot.

Fascination with a past open to rediscovery didn't stop Charles, faithful to a religion still entirely medieval, from searching for traces of secular faith in the city of St. Peter.

But he insisted on spacing out his visits. The essential things were happening in the Vatican. Negotiations had produced results, so he left the Palazzo Venezia and set up his quarters there.

It was the only group of buildings worthy of the name which Rome possessed at the end of the quattrocento. Nicholas V, Pope between the years 1447 and 1455, had conceived the grandiose plan of founding a new pontifical city separated from Rome on the spot where St. Peter had been crucified, in the Vatican. He had begun to bring it to life by entrusting the task to Bernardo Rosselino, a follower of Alberti. He had already begun demolishing the old St. Peter's, putting up new chapels, the walls of a palace were rising. He died, but his successors continued his work. Sixtus IV had the chapel, named Sistine in his honor, built and decorated. Innocent VIII had beautiful gardens laid out and the Villa Belvedere built, Alexander VI had the apartments which bear his name enlarged and painted with frescoes.

However, in spite of so much labor, the Vatican where Charles stayed was still only a compromise between Umbrian and Tuscan art. It would not become entirely Roman until Julius II, at this time Cardinal della Rovere, commissioned Michelangelo and Bramante.

Relations between the Holy Father and the King seemed to be centered on the subtleties of precedence, but finally things worked out in the best possible way.

On the twenty-eighth of January Charles took his leave.

He wanted to kiss the Pope's foot; Alexander wouldn't hear of it and they parted good friends, neither having obtained anything from the other.

Charles took to the road again. What memories could he take back from the City of Cities? The written word had great prestige for him; he had the *Mirabilia Urbis Romane,* a medieval book, translated in order to take it back to France.

THE SEA

He was on the road for a month and was involved in skirmishes here and there against small armed bands. He took over a few small fortresses which made attempts at resistance. He took his time. Upon hearing of his arrival, the usurper ran away. The people whom he had freed from their oaths of loyalty came out to meet their new master, crowded in among his bodyguard and possessions, and to prove their devotion to him, offered him the keys to the city. On February 22, Charles entered Naples without striking a blow.

However, resistance was established in two of the fortresses of the city, the Castel Nuovo and the Castel dell'Ovo. Without waiting he besieged them with his well-aimed artillery. He encouraged the men with his regular presence—sometimes in the shade of a pavilion set up under the olive trees not far from the firing, often in the trenches, intrepid amid the crackling powder. He ate his meals and played tarot with the princes. He handed out money to encourage the men to do their duty. He acknowledged and rewarded individual acts of courage: ten gold crowns to his gunner for a marvelously well fired shot, twenty to a sergeant who set off under a hail of stones to swim across to inspect the countermine of the castle. The fire of heaven, the power of falcons, mortars, cannon, and serpentines came down in such a terrible deluge that everything crumbled to earth in pieces and debris. In a thunderous tumult, walls and towers toppled from the cliff into the sea. The sea turned white with thousands of dead fish, bellies up, floating among the pieces of driftwood. The fortresses opened their doors. A haggard, stumbling, exhausted garrison emerged and surrendered to the King in person. It took eight days of labor with men and wagons to empty them of all the goods contained in the fortresses. Gaeta, Taranto, Gallipoli gave up. At the end of March, Charles had conquered his property. After the Normans and Angevins, a Frenchman had again brought his power into the kingdoms of the south. The King of France added the title of King of Naples to his other titles.

For the conqueror there were two possibilities: to make himself feared or to make himself loved. Charles tried the second. According to his command, the French flattered, promised, handed out pardons, gifts, and graces on charters sealed with single and double ribbons. They assured the possessing classes that they could keep certain privileges, among them slavery, which was still going strong in these countries. They would be able to keep their white and black slaves. When the first moments of euphoria had passed they grew bold. They expropriated offices and fiefs. From the great favorite to the lowest domestic, each received his share, even if he had to sell it afterward when necessity imposed itself. They minted money, crowns, ducats, doubles, with the arms of France on one side and the arms of Sicily with the Jerusalem cross on the reverse. In brief, the King had everything arranged according to his wishes and good pleasure.

It only remained for him to enjoy the beautiful sky, the end of winter, and springtime in Naples. He could hardly have chosen a better moment.

Naples was on the edge of a sea which he had never seen. It was filled with palaces and churches—the Naples of the Normans and Angevins. He found a breath of his country in the architecture, the graves, the life-size groups of sculptured wood, like those seen in Burgundy and Languedoc, which represented scenes from the life of Christ. In the mornings he heard mass in the Annunziata, at San Pietro, at San Gennaro, at the Church of the Mount of Olives. He dined at his residence, near San Pietro, or at Monsieur de Clérieux's or Monsieur de Montpensier's, or with the Prince of Taranto in the Sanseverino Palace. The afternoons were for walking, taking the air in the soft sun of spring. He visited the shipyards where galleys were being constructed. He visited the cathedral to see the head of St. Januarius. On the altar stood the venerated bust. In front of it there was a vial full of hardened bloodstone, rock. The King was handed a silver wand. Let him touch this substance with it and state his petition. If it was just, the blood would soften. Miraculously, it was seen to heat up and soften. The prince had come by the will of God, and the saint had given proof of it.

His hosts also took him to the Posillipo grotto. He took his wine in a village on the coast. He went to see Vesuvius smoking. There were sulphur mines and bedrock alum. From one marvelous pit there blew a wind so strong it held up whatever was thrown into it, and from another there came deadly vapors which instantly killed the donkey and the cat they threw into it. There were hot dry chambers next to the great lake of cold water. And the view of the Bay of Naples from the top of the convent of the Carthusians, and the Villa Poggio Reale . . .

It was a very beautiful place, a huge dwelling, open without fear to the outside world, a country palace in the style of the day, avant-garde architecture in the spirit of the Villa Belvedere in Rome, which Guiliano da Majano had designed and constructed just outside of Naples for King Alfonso; it had recently been completed. A large one-story quadrangle surrounded an inner vaulted courtyard. There were four corner towers with three-room apartments, one to a floor, connected by porticos. Everything was designed for amusement. A device set up in one of these rooms permitted the master of the house to douse his visitors, not leaving a hair dry, when it struck his fancy, and with no less promptness to make the water disappear. The house looked over gardens, a park with deer, vegetable gardens, pastures, and a farm which boasted an artificial breeder.

Charles spent half of his days there. In the gardens the roses were in bud, the pinks were opening, gold and garnet wallflowers unfolded their velvet, the fountains gurgled, the water works flowed, and much to the regret of the King time passed.

So he hadn't dreamed in vain. It wasn't a chimera. Those vague aspirations which in France kept him always hungry, that desire for "something else," had found their realization on this Italian soil. That sense of adornment and celebration, that taste for happiness and glory which he carried within him, he had found them in this blessed country, in the hearts of these men who lived in it.

What he had seen during the course of this trip he liked without exception. That was in his nature. Commynes said it in succinct terms: "He joined together all the beautiful things which they bestowed upon him."

He had gone from city to city, from marvel to rapture, transported, fulfilled beyond his hopes. He forced himself to put on an impassive face, to compose an emperor's mask for his entries in the purple of the Caesars. After all, one shouldn't appear to be too easily pleased, too much a country bumpkin toward those people who could sense that they were doing well. Fortunately, in order to get the respect due him, he had taken the trouble to bring along several good cannons and boxes of powder. A few well-placed projectiles, and the haughty walls mounted with battlements were decorated with gaping holes, the proud towers crumbling like card castles. The cannon balls destroyed those impregnable ramparts. Make way for the conqueror, they seemed to say. We have seen how they welcomed him: in terror. He needed this to make himself respected.

Charles was impressed by the beauty of Italian sculpture and painting. He made it his goal to freight as many as possible of these treasures back to France. The marble doors of the Castel Nuovo were unbolted and placed on a wagon, although at the last minute they were left behind. He raided the library of King Alfonso, whose collections were remarkable, and the wagons sagged with booty. Charles took special pains to attach to himself as many of the creators of the new art as possible. Back home, they had everything to learn. And since his soul was gaping wide in amazement, he took into his service whoever had an inclination to come into it. This explained the diversity of those who joined his service, among whom were found decorators, marquetry makers, fine carpenters, gardeners, specialists of the artificial breeder, and some very great humanists, including Joannes Lascaris, the architect Domenico de Cortone, and the archaeologist Fra Giocondo of Verona.

So the time had come to pick the fruits of the quest he had been enjoying since that decisive day when, he had decided to look Elsewhere for the Something Else which was perhaps himself. He had found at the end of the journey a new world, for him, a new man, regenerated in the sun of glory, reborn to the love of Beauty, recognized and rediscovered under these skies. Ah, Beauty, he certainly was taken by her! Happiness, did he finally possess it, at the end of that long adventure which had taken him to the end of this peninsula where he found himself today, contemplating the sea, breathing in the winds, listening to them at night? . . .

Toward what shores moved those great ships, loaded with canvas and fitted out for the unknown? That the earth is round he could see from the charts and world maps he examined in the courts where he had been a guest. He was charmed by the worrisome specter of continents to be discovered, perilous islands, Atlantis rediscovered, the magnificent kingdoms of the Indies, men with jackals' heads or monkeys', monsters, griffons and unicorns.

He was half in love with the agonizing mystery of a world incompletely explored which gave the measure and the limits of human knowledge. An anguish inhabited Charles, to which he didn't give in. Is there anything that man cannot do? he thought. Everything in this country cried out no.

LET'S GO HOME

Charles gave a Last Supper to thirteen paupers. He served them a meal, and to each one he made a gift of thirteen crowns. Twice he touched the scrofula of the sick people who came running in Naples and from the neighboring towns, from Apulia and from the farthest provinces of the boot, Venice and Lombardy. He gave jousts which lasted for eight days. In triumph, attired in imperial robes, with the gold orbicular pommel in his right hand and the great scepter of the Empire of Constantinople in the left, he made an entrance into Naples as the King of France, Sicily, and Jerusalem in the midst of hurrahs. He summoned his subjects to feasts and celebrations. Then he left in haste.

The Pope, the Duke of Milan, the King of the Romans, the people of Venice, and Ferdinand of Aragon had formed a league for defense in order to maintain peace. Rapid return. He didn't dally. He encountered the league in the foothills of the Apennines, at Fornovo di Taro. The *furia francese* did its job. The King on his horse Savoie didn't step out of character; he played the bold knight with great courage up to the end. Each side declared itself the winner. He continued on his way and rested a little near Turin. He understood that Italy praised him more than it loved him. Let us go home, he thought, everything has its end.

France constricted his heart—worse than a mere village. What were Tours, Bourges, Lyon next to Sienna and Pisa—not to mention Florence or Rome? What were Amboise or Plessis-les-Tours compared to the Vatican or Poggio Reale? He contented himself with his kingdom and tried to change it as he himself had changed. He never stopped remembering and telling stories of Italy. Then, having enjoyed his remembrances, he began thinking about his subjects, whom he wanted to see happy, like himself. He thought of getting down to work, of making plans . . . of taking off again to reconquer Naples, which had gone back to its old master practically as soon as he left. But on April 8, 1498, at Amboise, on his way with the Queen to a tennis game, he banged his head violently against the lintel of a door and died on the spot. He was not yet twenty-eight years old. "Be merry if you will, for tomorrow is no certainty . . ." sang Lorenzo the Magnificent in one of his poems.

Charles left no descendants. The two children he had with Anne of Brittany had died at an early age. His closest cousin, Louis of Orléans, took the throne, the name, and (as previously arranged) the widow. No one protested or stirred. The dynasty of the Capetian Valois had died out; that of the Orléans Valois succeeded it. France went on.

CHAPTER TWELVE

Summing Up

Seven men had lived; one hundred and seventy years had passed; the last Capetian Valois had joined the first in the other world. It is 1498, and it's time for us to sum up.

We have tried throughout these pages to evoke the sense of these lives woven into the warp and woof of events. Despite the similarities imposed by their function, none of them resembles the others.

On the political level, the accomplishment is considerable. Peace was restored, the economy was on the way to recovery (with such palpable results that the first successor, Louis XII, would be called Father of the People), the national territory was increased by a considerable number of provinces, the monarchy was strong and well respected—no one spoke of the dukes of Anjou, Burgundy, or Brittany any more. The country was united under the King, unlike the neighboring countries, which were still divided. Under these seven Valois feudal France had become a monarchy. "No country is as united or as easy to govern. That is her strength in my opinion: unity and obedience," a Venetian ambassador would write about France. The kingdom had regained the premier place it occupied in Europe during the best times of the Capetian dynasty.

This was kings' work, no doubt about it. Dearly bought, certainly, at the price of blood. But now the Valois no longer existed; the task had worn them out.

Yet it was a fine line at the beginning. Men of extraordinary vigor; warriors, horsemen, outdoorsmen, wild about violent sports, hunting, and tournaments. But as early as the third in the line it had begun to spoil. Looking at the fourth, it would seem that the weaknesses of his predecessor were fortuitous. Not so. His superb body was undermined by illness, as we know. By the fifth the game was up. He had the physique of a degenerate, the signs of which grow worse with each generation: ugly faces, small eyes, enormous noses, asymmetrical heads, limbs out of proportion to their bodies. The artifice of clothing was no longer sufficient to hide the exhaustion of the blood. It was evident the Valois were at the end of their line.

The inbreeding resulting from centuries of consanguineous marriages explains these facts to some degree, as does the precariousness of living conditions, diet, hygiene, and medical knowledge. But more simply, how to avoid the conclusion that the exhaustion of the blood stems from the exhausting job of kingship?

They worked, it is true, under awful circumstances. But their Capetian predecessors, in a context certainly less tragic but nonetheless difficult, had lasted twice as long, in time as well as in men, three hundred and forty years of reign for fourteen generations of princes. We must therefore look elsewhere for an explanation, probably in a certain fragility of their nervous systems, which we observed in the first and which never ceased to worsen over the years: lack of self-control in Philip VI, rages in John the Good, Charles V's permanent fatigue, Charles VI's psychosis, the neuroses of Charles VII and Louis XI, the exhaustion of Charles VIII. The record is heavy.

From where did the flaw come? Perhaps from the women. Today we know the determining role of the mother in mental disorders. If we don't know much about Philip VI's mother, Margaret of Anjou, who died young, we know what kind of perverse nature his wife Joan of Burgundy manifested. Joan of Bourbon suffered from a psychotic syndrome for a whole year, and Isabella of Bavaria, succumbing to her terrors and outbursts, was carried so far into illness that she seems to have left indelible marks on the psyches of her offspring.

Their private lives showed the signs. The families got along less well together, the sons admired their fathers less, tried to assert themselves against their authority and in the case of one of them went as far as open rebellion. Cousins hated each other to the point of murder. A Queen of France openly displayed her dissolute life in broad daylight and her son set his mistress up at court. As for births out of wedlock, they began with Charles V and continued throughout his descendants. Their Capetian predecessors—where the sons admired and respected the fathers who gave them life, and were pleased to perpetuate them; where a Philip IV punished his adulterous daughters-in-law with terrible rigor—were, if not exemplary, at least endowed with an equilibrium which their successors lacked.

The Valois were neuropaths, that is the conclusion we are obliged to come to. Upon reflection, this is less catastrophic than our prejudices would lead us to believe. Just look at their accomplishments. The last word has not been said about the link between psychic disorders and genius. Shall we add one more example to that discussion by remarking that with the exception of Charles VI it is among the most seriously affected that we must look for true kings?

The first two, Philip VI and John the Good, remained great feudal lords in spite of their titles, and Charles VI and Charles VIII followed them along the same path. They had the look, the manner, the easy affability and, something rarer, that taste for culture and beauty, for books and works of art, first visible in their ancestor, Count Charles, which they carried infinitely farther than their Capetian cousins, who were much less refined.

They were captured in the mirage of royal imagery, like birds caught by mirrors, and never got past the surface of things. It was as if their function was limited to a show of pride and glory, as if rich clothing and luxurious palaces were enough. Knowing neither how to foresee dangers nor how to face them, ill at ease among realities in fact, they sought the pleasures of the moment above all things. The pleasures of money, objects, travel. A prowess confined to the lists. The essential thing for them was not their royalty but themselves, and the unctions of the coronation rite were unable to make them forget. In spite of their piety, which was lively in the manner of their times, the ideal of the Middle

Ages—man entirely in the hand of his Creator—gave way to the heroic ideal. The world grew old. God grew distant.

True royalty among the Valois began with Charles V, passed through Charles VII, and ended with Louis XI. The race engendered two different types of men.

Perhaps even these would not have differed from the others—charming playboys—had it not been for events. Even before they became kings they were overtaken by urgent necessities. It was no longer a question of dazzling your public or of hoping they loved you, but of survival. The future of the country and of the dynasty hung in the balance. For them, to reign meant to fight. They didn't lose out in the bargain, finding in struggle and in victory moments which neither feasting nor their own desires could ever have procured for them. These three understood that their honor no longer depended on chivalry; that their glory would henceforth consist in self-denial; that in order not to lose everything you had to learn to give up everything.

This is not the same as giving oneself to another because you don't know what to do with yourself, but because the gift of self is the precondition for the exercise of power. It didn't take Charles V very long to realize that a prince must embrace the state of royalty as others entered religious orders. And from then on he employed the resources of his lively intelligence to think through the question of his kingly calling. It is doubtless for that reason fitting that history should see in him the greatest of his line. He tried to lay the basis for an ethic of kingship. He brought being and seeming together. He carried out its rituals, but he didn't limit its function to that.

Some fifty years later the Burgundian chronicler Chastellain coined the expression "Man of Sun" to characterize his monarch (an expression which Louis XIV, who styled himself the Sun King took up three centuries later). Charles V had already zeroed in on the beautiful symbol which, in the tradition, makes the star of light the figure of man at the pinnacle of his being; a king, in the image he creates for himself as in the reality of his deeds, owes it to himself to incarnate humanity in the highest meaning of the term. God had chosen him to lead the flock, had raised him above the human condition; he himself tried to be an exemplar.

Kingship nourished by reflection, in which he who exercised it caused the main currents of the human adventure to flow through him and gathered the essential values of human life around the idea which he represented. Kingship of moderation, thought and action dedicated to the public weal. In Charles V the French monarchy reached one of its summits.

Events did not allow his grandchildren, Charles VII and Louis XI, to place their ideals so high. They hardly had the leisure to reflect on the ethics of their office or to recognize any other criteria than those of mere necessity. They had to limit themselves to immediate effectiveness, to base their actions on empiricism: the former, willy-nilly, with great difficulty as we have seen, constantly struggling with his own nature; the latter, obsessed by a devouring passion for a craft which deprived him of all personal merit while paying him back one hundredfold in cares and woes in the process. But they were able to accept reality, to tear away the masks which hid it, to recognize and accept its austere countenance, to open the strait gate and walk the paths of obligation and risk. That was their greatness.

Should we be surprised to learn that they felt more anguish than the others, these workers, these clear-sighted men, tied up to their last breath in events which granted them no respite, while each day provided new fears? Fear of danger, of treason, of failure, fear of being unable to face up, of not knowing how, fear of their own limitations and of the weight of events. They were tough summits they had to climb. The air up there was thin. Stronger men than they would have given out trying to live on it. Moreover—and this has been proven—two of them were afflicted with well-developed neuroses. Can it be denied that these afflictions were aggravated by their circumstances and by daily wear and tear? It's the vicious cycle of nerves frazzled by overwork and of overwork affecting the weakened system even more. Yet it was their love for their calling which kept them alive into respectable old age in an era when the average life span was twenty years. Charles V died prematurely at forty-two. Charles VII and Louis XI lived for nearly sixty years.

The three of them together saved the prize, plugged up the holes, patched up the blunders, built up the credit on which the others lived. The accomplishments, the honor of the name, the line owed to them.

Royalty lived or dreamed, we have seen these seven men oscillate between reality and appearance, necessity and frivolity, desire and need, self-denial and self-indulgence. At grips with the realities of power, some crumbled like saltpeter or sand, the others fulfilled themselves. Perhaps because in the course of this long and difficult game of dice played out between man and himself and which we call a life, the latter were equipped with greater intelligence. What does it matter if history shines the glaring light of failure on the weak ones? In these pages, more than anything I have sought encounters, beyond events which are changing and various, we have met these Valois kings and, despite the five centuries which separate us, found them unchanged, like us. Forever exposed, struggling, always shirking from difficulties, from the hardships which alone develop the soul, always hungry, nowhere sure, nowhere strong, laboring to recognize themselves among earthly realities, dragging along their nostalgia for the impossible, endlessly brought back to their own limitations, seeking after Edens, opaque.

Man perpetually exposed to the anguish of the world.

Paris, April 1968
November 23, 1970

Index

Nuremberg, 290

Offemont, Lord of, 232
Oise River, 11
Order of St. Michel, 330
Order of the Golden Fleece, 275
Order of the Star, 175
Oresme, Nicole, 143, 146
Orgemont, Pierre d', 149
Orléans, 5, 67, 75, 81, 96, 169, 209,
  214, 220–22, 253, 261, 264, 266,
  272, 287, 304, 322, 328, 351, 375.
  See also Armagnacs and
  Burgundians; specific Dukes
Orléans, Evrart d', 42
Orléans, Raoullet d', 142
Ostrevant. *See* William of Ostrevant
Oudart of Renty, 232
Oxford, Count of, 231

Palace of the Conservators, 369
Palais de la Cité, 141
Palamède of the Marquais, 232
Palatinate, 169
Palazzo Vecchio, 368
Palazzo Venezia, 368
Paris, 6, 7, 51, 81–87 ff., 98, 100,
  124, 166, 168–69, 188–89,
  218–19, 222–25, 236, 240–41,
  242, 249, 273, 286 (*See also*
  specific kings, places); Archbishop
  of, 84, 87; and death of Charles
  VII, 300; flagellants approach, 38;
  King of Navarre brought to,
  65–66; and marriage of Henry V
  and Catherine, 251; murder of
  Duke of Orléans in, 210–14; re-
  naming of "Hellsgate" in, 204;
  University of, 6, 88, 219, 223, 251
Parma, 26
Patay, 273
Paul II, Pope, 369
Pavia, 363
Pèlerin of Prussia, 145
Pembroke, Countess of, 102
Pépin of Austrasia, 110
Pépin des Essarts, 93
Perceval of Richebourg, 232
Perdriel, Henri, 348
Périgord, 66, 209
Péronne, 332, 333–35, 348
Perpignan, 349

Perréal, Jean, 367
Perugino, 367
Peter, St., 356
Peter of Bourbon. *See* Pierre de
  Beaujeu
Petit, Jean, 219
Petit-Musc, Hôtel du, 233–35, 237,
  241
Petrarch, 57, 93, 125, 132
Phares, Simon de, 282
Philip. *See also* Philippe
Philip (son of Charles VII), 304
Philip I, 111
Philip III, 6
Philip IV (the Fair), 7, 9, 12, 124,
  275, 378
Philip V, 9, 10
Philip VI (the Fortunate; father of
  John II; grandfather of Charles
  V), 1, 18–41, 37, 42, 51, 52,
  54 ff., 73, 75, 147, 154, 182, 288,
  377, 378
Philip of Charolais. *See* Charolais,
  Count of
Philip of Navarre (cousin of John
  II), 62
Philip of Savoisy, 161
Philip of Vertus. *See* Vertus, Count
  of
Philip the Bold (Duke of Burgundy;
  son of John II; brother of
  Charles V; uncle of Charles VI),
  68, 75, 102, 106, 114, 119, 148,
  158, 163 ff., 175–76, 178, 179,
  185, 187, 193, 195, 196, 205,
  207–8, 209
Philip the Good (Duke of Bur-
  gundy), 250, 251, 275–76, 287,
  296, 315, 317, 320–21 ff., 330
Philippa of Hainault (wife of Ed-
  ward III), 34–35
Philippe. *See also* Philip
Philippe-Auguste, 141
Philippe d'Artois, 187
Philippe de Bar, 187
Philippe du Rouvre, 55, 75, 106
Phoebus, Count Gaston, 184
Piacenza, 363, 364
Picard, Henry, 103
Picardy, 28, 94, 165, 168, 232, 332,
  336, 351
Picquigny, 337, 349; Jean de, 93